ELECTRONIC MEDIA

ELECTRONIC MEDIA

A GUIDE TO TRENDS IN BROADCASTING AND NEWER TECHNOLOGIES 1920–1983

BY
CHRISTOPHER H. STERLING

PRAEGER

PRAEGER SPECIAL STUDIES • PRAEGER SCIENTIFIC

New York • Philadelphia • Eastbourne, UK
Toronto • Hong Kong • Tokyo • Sydney

Library of Congress Cataloging in Publication Data

Sterling, Christopher H., 1943–
    Electronic media.

    Includes bibliographical references.
    1. Broadcasting—United States—Statistics.   I. Title.
HE8689.8.S7295   1984   384.54'0973   83-27019
ISBN 0-03-071468-0 (alk. paper)
ISBN 0-03-054341-X (pbk. : alk. paper)

Published in 1984 by Praeger Publishers
CBS Educational and Professional Publishing,
a Division of CBS Inc.
521 Fifth Avenue, New York, NY 10175 USA

456789 052 9876545321

Printed in the United States of America
on acid-free paper

PREFACE

This volume is a collection of time-series statistics on electronic media in the U.S.—chiefly broadcasting and cable, with some information on newer technologies. It is the second volume in a projected series of reference works, the first of which appeared as *The Mass Media: Aspen Institute Guide to Communication Industry Trends* (Praeger, 1978) by the present author, and Timothy Haight, then of Stanford University. The present work draws heavily on the earlier book, but corrects, greatly updates, and considerably expands the material in it. Of the approximately 150 tables here, virtually all have been revised or updated, and about 30 are totally new to this edition. Material on pay systems (pay cable, STV, and MDS, as well as satellite delivery systems) has been expanded to separate treatment here. An entirely new section on regulation is added. An overall attempt has been made to clarify and improve discussion of sources and their limitations.

This book is intended as a handy single reference source providing the most significant and/or interesting quantitative trend data on electronic media over the longest possible time periods. Its purpose is to create and refine something of a census, or benchmark, of currently available data, allowing researchers of all kinds readier access to what we now know—and suggesting areas where further data generation is still needed. While the book is arranged in eight general subject categories, information is arranged throughout in six "series" number sets to ease (a) comparison within this book for a given medium, and (b) to allow for reader comparisons with the 1978 volume. They are as follows:

    00 general background information, usually on two or more media
    60 broadcasting in general, combining radio and television
    70 radio
    80 television

90 cable television

95 pay television systems (pay cable, STV (subscription, or over the air pay TV), MDS (multipoint distribution service), satellite distribution)

The 10 through 50 series in the parent volume covered the print, recording, and film industries which are not covered here.

Information has been gathered from as many available sources as possible. One intention underlying this series of books is to seek out little-known sources, and indeed, this current volume makes use of several sources which were brought to our attention after publication of the parent volume. The reliability and validity of the data here vary considerably, depending on their source (whether government, industry, academic, etc.), the purpose for which they were gathered (whether they were disseminated to bolster given points of view, even over long periods of time), the method used in gathering them, and many other variables. The discussions in the sections labeled "sources" in each unit of tables are included to make readers aware of the limitations and assumptions inherent in tabular material.

When a project stretches back more than six years, over three different full-time employers, it is impossible to adequately thank all of those who have assisted with it. But special thanks are due to all of the following:

• First and foremost, to a succession of student assistants for essential help. At Temple University, Harvey J. Bondar and Lloyd Komesar did the initial updating in 1979-80, handling correspondence, telephone calls, and legwork necessary to seek out the new or updated information. After my move to Washington, my wife Ellen put in months of almost daily effort to "update the updates." For the final push to publication in 1982-83, Robin G. Berry was invaluable in finding the data, persuading sources to really put out, chasing down permissions, and many other research tasks. Without the cheerful efforts of these people, especially the last two, this book would not be in your hands.

• To several behind-the-scenes supporters of the effort: Robert Smith and Gordon Gray of Temple University's Department of Radio-TV-Film in 1978-80, to then Commissioner Anne P. Jones of the Federal Communications Commission (for whom I served as a special assistant) in 1980-82, and finally to Dean William F. E. Long of the Division of Continuing Education at George Washington University—the cooperation of all of these people was essential to the project.

• And, of course, to the many contributors, personal and institutional, to the data which appears on the pages which follow. Virtually all were forthcoming with data, useful suggestions, corrections when necessary, and finally and not least importantly, ready permission to use and cite their prior work.

• Considerable thanks to my collaborator on the initial 1978 study—Timothy Haight. While he bears no responsibility for the short-comings of this present work, he did provide some of the initial data for many of these tables. His ideas and quest for quality and precision have helped us all.

• And finally, to the Aspen Institute, which supported the initial book in this series. In the summer of 1975, the director of Aspen's Communications and Society Program, journalist Douglass Cater, initiated the idea and planning for what became *The Mass Media*. Cater, and his successor Roland Homet, were crucial to the development and support of that parent volume. While the Aspen Institute was unable to assist in the present (and future planned) continuations of the project, their "pump-priming" support was crucial.

Naturally, as we continue to plan for further elements in this series of statistical reference works, we welcome comment and suggestions. Planned at present is a major volume on telecommunications carriers, and eventually a revision of the entire 1978 volume to reflect new sources and information.

CONTENTS

Preface   v

Introduction   xxi

Section 1
GROWTH OF ELECTRONIC MEDIA

170 Radio Stations   3
    170-A Number of Radio Stations, 1921–1983   5
    170-B Characteristics of AM Radio Stations, 1935–1980   8
    170-C Number of AM and FM Stations in Selected Markets,
        1939–1979   10

171 Network-Affiliate Radio Stations   11
    171-A Number of Network-Affiliate Radio Stations,
        1927–1982   12
    171-B Number of ABC Network Affiliates, by Format,
        1968–1982   15

180 Television Stations and Markets   16
    180-A Number of Television Stations, 1941–1983   18
    180-B Number of Commercial Television Stations, by Market
        Group, 1958, 1968, and 1980   20
    180-C Number of Noncommercial (Public) Television
        Stations, by Market Group, 1958, 1968, and 1980   21
    180-D Reception of Television Broadcast Signals in U.S.
        Communities, 1964–1982   22

181 Network-Affiliate Television Stations   23
   181–A Number of Network-Affiliate Television Stations,
      1947–1982   24
   181–B Number of Network-Affiliate and Independent
      Television Stations in the U.S., by Market Group,
      1958–1975   25

190 Cable Television Systems   26
   190–A Number of Cable Television Systems, 1952–1983   28
   190–B Percentage of Households with Cable Service, by
      County Size, 1968–1982   29
   190–C Number of Cable Television Systems, by System Size,
      1970–1983   30

195 Pay Television Systems   31
   195–A Growth of Pay Television Systems, 1973–1982   33
   195–B Development of U.S. Satellite Distribution Facilities,
      1975–1983   34

Section 2
OWNERSHIP OF ELECTRONIC MEDIA

201 Media Conglomerates   39
   201–A Leading Firms in One or More Media Segments, with
      Other Media Holdings, 1981   40

260 Broadcasting Ownership Patterns   42
   260–A Sales of Broadcast Stations, with Average Price,
      1938–1982   45
   260–B Minority-Owned Broadcast Outlets, 1977 and 1982   46
   260–C Percentage of Broadcast Equipment Sales Controlled
      by Top U.S. Manufacturers, 1954–1977   46
   260–D Selected Leading Broadcasting Firms, 1980   47

261 Newspaper–Broadcasting Cross-Ownership   48
   261–A Newspaper-Broadcasting Cross-Ownership, 1922–1982   50

262 Network Ownership of Broadcast Stations   53
   262–A Network Ownership of Broadcast Stations, 1980   54

270 Group Ownership of Radio Stations   56
   270–A Number of Group-Owned AM Radio Stations,
      1929–1967   57

270–B The Top 15 Group Owners in Radio, 1980   57
270–C AM-FM Combination Holdings, 1968–1980   58

280 Group Ownership of Television Stations   59
  280–A Number of Group-Owned Television Stations,
         1948–1983   60
  280–B Number of Group-Owned Television Stations, by
         Market, 1956, 1966, and 1982   61
  280–C The Top 15 Group Owners in Television, 1980 and
         1959   62

281 Ownership of Public Television Stations   63
  281–A Ownership of Public Television Stations, 1959–1983   64

282 Concentration in Program Production   65
  282–A Concentration in Network Program Production, 1970
         and 1978   66
  282–B Concentration in Syndicated Program Production,
         1968 and 1977   66

290 Ownership of Cable Systems   67
  290–A Cross-Ownership of Cable Systems, 1969–1983   69
  290–B Largest Cable System MSOs, by Number of Subscribers,
         1970–1983   71
  290–C MSO Subscriber Concentration, 1969–1981   72

295 Ownership of Pay Television Systems   73
  295–A Major Pay TV Program Distributors, 1975–1982   74
  295–B Pay TV Service on Affiliated and Unaffiliated MSOs,
         1980   75

Section 3
ELECTRONIC MEDIA ECONOMICS

302 Consumer vs. Advertiser Investment in Broadcasting   79
  302–A Consumer vs. Advertiser Expenditures in Broadcasting,
         1935–1978   80

303 Advertising Rates and Expenditures in Broadcasting   81
  303–A Advertiser Expenditure in Broadcasting, 1935–1982   83
  303–B Index of Media Advertising Rates, 1965–1982   86
  303–C Cost-Per-Thousand Rates of Selected Media, 1970–1982   87

360 Public Broadcasting Station Finances   88
   360–A   Income and Expenditures of Public Television Stations,
         1970–1980   90
   360–B   Income Sources for Public Television Stations,
         1966–1982   91
   360–C   Direct Operating Expenditures of Public Television
         Stations, 1970–1982   92
   360–D   Income and Expenditures of CPB-Qualified Public
         Radio Stations, 1970–1980   93

361 Public Broadcasting National Finances   94
   361–A   Federal Government Appropriations for Public
         Broadcasting, 1967–1983   96
   361–B   Revenues and Expenses of the Corporation for Public
         Broadcasting, 1969–1980   97
   361–C   Revenues and Expenses of the Corporation for Public
         Broadcasting, 1980–1983   99
   361–D   Income Sources of the Children's Television Workshop,
         1968–1982   100
   361–E   Ford Foundation Grants for Public Broadcasting,
         1951–1983   102

370 Commercial Radio Station Finances   103
   370–A   Revenues and Expenses of the Typical Commercial Radio
         Station, 1960, 1970, and 1980   106
   370–B   Revenues, Expenses, and Earnings of Commercial Radio
         Networks and Stations, 1937–1980   107
   370–C   Profit Ratios of Commercial Radio Networks and
         Stations, 1937–1980   109
   370–D   Revenues, Expenses, and Earnings of Commercial FM
         Stations, 1948–1980   111
   370–E   Number of AM and FM Radio Stations Reporting
         Profits or Losses, 1962–1980   113

380 Commercial Television Station Finances   114
   380–A   Revenues and Expenses of the Typical Commercial
         Television Station, 1960, 1970, and 1980   115
   380–B   Revenues, Expenses, Earnings, and Profit Ratios of
         Commercial Television Stations, 1948–1980   116
   380–C   Revenues, Expenses, and Earnings of Commercial VHF
         and UHF Stations 1953–1980   118

381 Network Television Finances 121
    381-A Revenues, Expenses, Earnings, and Profit Ratios of
        Television Networks and Their Owned-and-Operated
        Stations, 1948–1980 123
    381-B Measures of Network Television Commercials,
        1965–1981 125
    381-C Index of Network Television and Affiliate Station
        Incomes, 1964–1977 126

382 Network Television Programming Expenses 127
    382-A Prime-Time Network Program Costs, 1949–1973 128
    382-B Production Costs for Selected Network Television Drama
        Programs, 1950–1974 130

390 Cable Television System Finances 133
    390-A Revenues, Expenses, and Income of Cable Systems,
        1975–1981 134

Section 4
ELECTRONIC MEDIA EMPLOYMENT AND TRAINING

403 Educational Programs in Electronic Media 139
    403-A Educational Programs, Enrollments, and Faculty in
        Broadcasting, 1956–1980 140
    403-B Number of Broadcasting Theses and Dissertations,
        1920–1972 141

460 Employment in the Broadcasting Industry 142
    460-A Number of Radio and Television Network and Station
        Employees, 1930–1980 144
    460-B Average Weekly Salary of Non-Supervisory Broadcast
        Employees, 1940–1981 146
    460-C Number of Members and Earnings of Selected
        Television Unions, 1961–1981 147
    460-D Minority and Female Employment in Commercial and
        Public Television Stations, 1971–1981 149
    460-E Broadcast-Related Employment in Manufacturing,
        Retail, and Repair Firms, 1933–1981 150

490 Employment in Cable Television 151
    490-A Employees and Minority Employment in Cable
        Systems, 1974, 1980, and 1982 152

Section 5
ELECTRONIC MEDIA CONTENT TRENDS

500 Public Uses and Views of the News Media   155
     500–A Surveys Measuring Most Frequent Source of News for
            the Public, 1959–1982   158
     500–B Surveys Measuring Public Trust in Credibity of News
            Media, 1939–1982   159
     500–C Surveys Measuring the Public's Daily Use of News
            Media, 1957–1977   160
     500–D Surveys Measuring Public Confidence in the Leadership
            of Television and the Press, 1974–1982   16]

501 Media Costs and Coverage of Political Campaigns   16ᴣ
     501–A Surveys Measuring Media as Sources of Information on
            Local, State, and National Elections, 1952–1982   165
     501–B Broadcast Political Advertising Costs for General
            Elections, 1952–1972   166
     501–C Presidential Campaign Advertising Expenditures,
            1968–1980   167
     501–D Air Time and Viewing Time of Paid Network Television
            Political Advertising, 1960–1980   168
     501–E Air Time and Viewing Time of National Convention and
            Election Night Coverage, 1952–1980   169
     501–F Free Network Time Given to Presidential Campaigns,
            1956–1972   170

560 Broadcast News Programming   170
     560–A Total Weekly Hours of Regularly Scheduled Network
            Radio and Television News Programs, 1930–1978   172
     560–B Number and Type of Documentary News Programs
            Produced by Network Television, 1948–1982   173
     560–C Amount of Television Network News Programming,
            1970–1976   175
     560–D Prime-Time and Total Hours of Non-Entertainment
            Programming by Commercial Television Stations,
            1973–1979   176
     560–E Presidential Appearances on Network Television,
            1960–1982   177
     560–F Broadcast Station Editorials, 1959–1975   177

570 Commercial Radio Station Programming   178

570–A Program Formats of AM and FM Radio Stations,
        1964–1982   180
570–B Ethnic and Foreign Language Radio Programming, 1979   182

580 Commercial Television Station Programming   183
580–A Program Content of Selected Major Market Television
        Stations for Selected Years, 1951–1970   185
580–B Sources of Television Station Programming, 1954–1972   185
580–C Number of Available Syndicated Television Series,
        1951–1975   186
580–D Number of Available Syndicated Television Series, by
        Content Type, 1965–1982   187
580–E Top 15 Syndicated Television Series, 1981   187

581 Public Television Programming   189
581–A Hours, Format, and Sources of Public Television Station
        Programming, 1954–1980   190
581–B Content Trends in Public Television Station
        Programming, 1956–1982   191
581–C Content of Public Broadcasting Service (PBS)
        Programming, 1973–1979   192

582 Network Television Programming   193
582–A Content of Prime-Time Network Television
        Programming, 1949–1973   195
582–B Content of Daytime Network Television Programming,
        1949–1973   197
582–C Content of Prime-Time and Daytime Network Television
        Programming, 1973–1982   198
582–D Content Trends in Prime-Time Network Television
        Specials, 1950–1981   199
582–E Format, Source, and Length of Network Television
        Programs, 1956–1972   200

583 Violence in Network Television Programming   201
583–A Gerbner Violence Profile of Network Television
        Programming, 1967–1980   203

590 Cable Television Programming   204
590–A Channel Capacity and Program Content of Cable
        Systems, 1966–1983   206
590–B Basic Satellite Distributed Cable Television Networks
        Programming Services, 1980–1983   207–208

Section 6
THE AUDIENCE FOR ELECTRONIC MEDIA

660 Production and Sales of Broadcast Receivers   211
     660-A Number of Radio and Television Receivers Produced in the U.S., 1922–1982   212
     660-B Factory Value of Radio and Television Receivers Produced in the U.S., 1922–1982   214
     660-C Number of Radio and Television Receivers in Use, 1922–1982   216
     660-D Number of Radio-Television Stores and Repair Services, 1929–1977   218

661 Hours of Broadcast Listening/Viewing   219
     661-A Average Daily Hours of Radio and Television Use, 1931–1981   220

670 Distribution of Radio Receivers   221
     670-A Number and Percentage of U.S. Households and Automobiles with AM Receivers, 1922–1981   222
     670-B Factory Production of Household and Automobile FM Receivers, 1960–1982   225

671 Characteristics/Preferences of Radio Audiences   227
     671-A Characteristics of the Radio Audience, by Hours of Daily Listening, 1947, 1968, and 1982   228
     671-B Radio Audience Attitudes and Preferences, 1947 and 1968   229
     671-C Format Preferences of Radio Audiences, 1972–1980   230
     671-D Format Preference of Male, Female, and Teenaged Radio Listeners, 1972, 1976, and 1980   231
     671-E Format Preference of Radio Listeners, by Age and Sex, 1977 and 1982   232
     671-F Ranking and Average Weekly Cumulative Audience of Radio Networks, 1978 and 1982   233

680 Distribution of Television Receivers   235
     680-A Households with Television Receivers, and Average Receiver Cost, 1946–1982   236
     680-B Percentage of Homes with Television Receivers, by Region and County Size, 1950–1980   239

681 Characteristics/Preferences of Television Audiences   240

681-A Average Weekly Hours of Television Use, by Household
Size, and Other Characteristics, 1960–1980 241
681-B Average Daily Television Use, by Sex and Age of
Viewers, and Time of Day, 1955–1980 242
681-C Surveys Measuring Selected Viewer Attitudes on
Television, 1960, 1970, and 1980 243

682 Preferences of Network Television Audiences 244
682-A Ranking of the Top-20 Network Television Entertainment
Episodes, 1960–1983 246
682-B Ranking of the Top-12 Network Television Entertainment
Series, 1960–1976 246
682-C Ranking of the Top 50 Motion Pictures Shown on
Network Television, 1956–1982 247
682-D Selected Major Televised News Event Audiences,
1960–1980 248

683 Characteristics/Preferences of Public Television Audiences 249
683-A Households Viewing Public Television, and Cumulative
Ratings by Program Type, 1970–1983 251
683-B Households Viewing Public Television by Income,
Education, and Occupation by Head of Household,
1973–1981 252

684 Development of the Home Video Market 253
684-A Sales and Use of Home Video Equipment, 1978–1982 254

695 Pay Television System Audiences 254
695-A Growth of the Pay Television System Audience,
1973–1982 255

Section 7
INTERNATIONAL ASPECTS OF ELECTRONIC MEDIA

700 Foreign News Coverage by Network Television 259
700-A Network Television Evening News Coverage of Events in
50 Countries, 1972–1981 261
700-B Foreign News as a Percentage of Total Evening Network
Newscast Time, 1972–1981 267
700-C Subject Matter of Foreign News on Evening Network
Newscasts, 1972–1981 268

701 International Broadcasting Activities 269

701-A Weekly Broadcast Hours of U.S. and other Government
      Radio Services, 1945–1980   270

701-B Weekly Broadcast Hours of Voice of America, by
      Language of Broadcast, 1950–1980   271

701-C Sources of Financial Support for Radio Liberty and
      Radio Free Europe, 1950–1980   271

701-D Subject Matter of Broadcasts by Radio Free Europe and
      Radio Liberty, 1982   272

750 U.S. Trade in Consumer Electronics   272

750-A Value of U.S. Imports/Exports of Electronics Industry
      Products, 1965–1980   274

750-B Value of U.S. Imports/Exports of Consumer
      Electronics Products, 1958–1982   275

750-C Penetration of U.S. Consumer Electronic Products
      Market by Foreign Imports, 1966–1973   276

760 U.S. Trade in Radio/Television Receivers   277

760-A U.S. Imports/Exports of Radio Receivers, by Units
      and Value, 1950–1982   278

760-B U.S. Imports/Exports of Television Receivers, by
      Units and Value, 1960–1982   280

760-C Producers of U.S. Television Receivers, 1968–1980   282

Section 8
REGULATION OF ELECTRONIC MEDIA

860 Growth of Federal Telecommunication Regulation   289

860-A Budget and Personnel of the Federal Telecommunication
      Regulatory Agencies, 1915–1982   291

860-B Statistical Profile of FCC Commissioners, 1952–1983   292

860-C Communications Industry Affiliations of FCC
      Commissioners and Other High-Level Staff Officials,
      1945–1970   294

861 State Regulation of Broadcasting   294

861-A State Regulation of Broadcasting, by Subjects of
      Statutes, 1972   295

862 FCC Administrative/Legal Sanctions Against Broadcast
    Licensees   296

862–A Number of Broadcast License Denials and License/
      Permit Revocations by the FCC, 1934–1982   298
862–B Reasons Cited for FCC Deletion of Licenses, 1934–1978   299
862–C Number, Frequency, and Reasons for Broadcast License
      Forfeitures (Fines) by the FCC, 1961–1978   300
862–D Number and Reasons for Broadcast License Short-Term
      Renewals by the FCC, 1960–1981   302

863 Public Participation in the Broadcast Regulatory Process   302
863–A Categorization of Public Correspondence with the FCC
      on Broadcast Matters, 1966–1980   304
863–B Public Complaints to the FCC Regarding the Fairness
      Doctrine and Equal-Time Provisions, 1960–1981   304
863–C Public Participation in the Broadcast License Renewal
      Process, 1967–1981   306

890 State Regulation of Cable Television   307
890–A State Statutes on Cable Television, 1972–1982   308

Sources and References   311

INTRODUCTION

While this volume is intended primarily for reference, one aim in creating it was to pinpoint subject areas for which data either do not exist, or for one reason or another are impossible to locate. This brief introduction speaks to that point, though as a kind of conclusion to this research effort, it might just as well appear at the end. It provides a highlighting of some of that "missing" information in the hope that some may well turn out to exist in usable form after all, or that researchers will give serious consideration to developing it.

The initial book in this series (Sterling and Haight, 1978)*, provided a detailed opening essay on the general state of media statistics, as well as a discussion of what was and is still needed to turn the available information into viable, policy-relevant communication *indicators*. That essay compared our judgment on the availability and quality of media data with the information contained in a pioneering book along similar lines issued two decades earlier (Chapin, 1957). This short discussion builds on that more general review, focusing here on specific electronic media research yet to be done. To set the stage, however, here is a tabular comparison of Chapin's 1957 assessment of electronic media data availability and reliability with an assessment a quarter of a century later. Naturally, because cable and newer services were not included in the earlier book, only a 1983 assessment appears here. Overall, a good deal of work is still needed—even in the broadcast services now many decades old. Indeed, economics and politics are diminishing the governmental role in gathering data just as some degree of reliability of some of those measures was being achieved! The comparative table, and the paragraphs which follow, are both arranged into the eight sections in which this book is divided.

---

*All sources are listed by author in the bibliography.

Table 1 Status of Electronic Media Statistics, 1957 and 1983

Subject Category	Radio 1957	Radio 1983	Television 1957	Television 1983	Cable[a] 1983	Pay TV[a] 1983
Growth and Scope (Number of producers)	4	4	4	4	3	1
Ownership	3	3	3	4	2	1
Economics						
Revenues	3	4	3	4	2	0
Expenses	3	3	3	3	1	0
Income	3	4	3	4	2	0
Investment	3	3	3	3	1	0
Employment	2	3	2	3	1	0
Content[a]	N/A	2	N/A	3	1	0
Audience						
Numbers	3	3	3	3	1	1
Consumption	3	2	1	3	0	0
Expenditures	2	3	2	3	0	1
U.S. Media Overseas[a]	N/A	2	N/A	2	0	0
Regulation[a]	N/A	1	N/A	1	1	N/A

Sources: 1957 data: Chapin (1957), p. 141; 1983 data: developed by the author based on information in this volume.

Notes: The ratings key was established by Chapin (1957): 4 = plentiful and reliable statistical data; 3 = available and acceptably reliable statistical data; 2 = available statistical data which are too limited for general use; 1 = unacceptable statistical data; 0 = unavailable statistical data; N/A indicates data not available. [a]Indicates a medium or subject not included in Chapin's 1957 study.

The Growth of Electronic Media

Growth of electronic media information, as the table suggests, are generally plentiful and reliable. There are, however, important problem areas. Data on cable and the newer pay television systems are far less reliable than statistics for broadcasting. This is partially due to the greater degree of regulation of the older services, said regulation calling for gathering of official statistics on a regular basis. But as deregulation expands in the 1980s, and as economic/political constraints on government activity continue to cut into government data-gathering, the government is becoming much less active as a data gatherer and compiler. Unofficial sources, usually lacking the clout of official information-gathering, will and already are taking over. So, ironically, data on broadcasting may become as statistically unreliable as that for the newer services. But one older service is deficient in broadly comparable data, and that is noncommercial radio. What little information on such service does exist is included here, but refers only to "CPB (the Corporation for Public Broadcastings)-qualified" stations (see Unit 360 for a definition of this factor), which comprise no more than a quarter of all noncommercial stations on the air. The otherwise uncounted 75 percent (several hundred stations) must be pulled into the data mainstream if we are to understand the full picture of this service.

Other data areas are troublesome. Data for FM stations is not as good as that for AM, despite the fact that FM has for the last several years achieved virtual audience parity with its older sister service. Data on the number of FM stations per community, the number of signals receivable, the number of stations by various Federal Communications Commission (FCC) classifications, and the use of subcarrier facilities (which date back to 1955, though greatly expanded in value by the FCC decisions of 1983) appears unavailable over any kind of time-series. Information on the recently developed pay television systems are understandably spotty—for example, there is no good estimate of the number of receive-only earth stations in service at any point over the past five years. The data available, and included here, is mere guesswork. Deregulation of such facilities by the FCC in the late 1970s took away the need for licensing statistics. We have no consistent data on the new satellite-based networks that is anywhere near comparable to the time-series information on the traditional broadcasting networks. It will be a loss to researchers and policymakers alike if such information is not captured in these early developing years.

Media Ownership

Ownership is, of course, one of the touchiest subject areas covered in this volume. Considerable controversy has long surrounded measures of concentration and diversity of control. Debates over general policy, and more specific legal proceedings, suggest the following areas are deficient, or missing entirely.

Interlocking directorates of major conglomerate corporations have received increasing policy attention in recent years, and some snapshot data has resulted (see especially U.S. Senate Committee on Governmental Affairs, 1980) which includes a number of media-involved firms). But some means of quantifying overall cross-media trends in electronic and other media would be of great value as researchers attempt to trace changing ownership patterns as limiting regulation is lifted.

Remarkably little consistent information on minority and female ownership of various media exists, despite the public attention such ownership has enjoyed in recent years. Part of the problem is that the proportions of media so owned are so miniscule—but this is unlikely to change unless data clearly illustrating that state of affairs is made readily and regularly available.

Much data on "ownership" merely indicates some element of ownership participation—though real control may not be exercised. Distinguishing between minority financial ownership, ownership versus managerial participation, and other such matters need to be more clearly traced to support policy analyses of existing rules and regulation. This becomes more important as large financial institutions (banks, retirement funds, and investment firms) purchase equity in one or more media.

While some national aggregate data exist on cross-ownership of various kinds (see, for example, Unit 261), lacking is much data on colocated (same market) cross-ownership, surely of more concern to critics that media under one ownership entity, but spread across many different markets. On the other hand, given the generalizability of the data available, too many researchers compare entities by number of media units controlled, rather than a truer comparison of the size of markets in which the unit operates. The old complaint about equating 20 stations in small markets with 20 stations divided across the top 10 cities is a case in point. We need more trend data on ownership patterns which take market size and colocation factors into account.

Badly needed are hard data on the control which older media exercise over newer systems. While this situation may be difficult to conceptualize in some cases, examples would be broadcaster or newspaper investment in cable systems—or teletext or telephone company purchase of cable systems or activity in videotex. In broadcasting, the pattern was that established AM owners helped to get FM and television started. Is that pattern being repeated today?

Media Economic Data

Economic data makes up the largest section of this book, thanks to advertiser demands and interests, and (up through 1980) government data collection. There are more data on revenue, expenses, and income of electronic media than on most other aspects of these services. But even here, some data needs are evident.

Some means of effectively comparing expenditures by consumers, media owners, and advertisers must be developed if we are accurately to judge who is supporting what and to what degree. This problem is partly a matter of definition, but more a matter of consistent and comparable primary data.

Information on comparative network economics would be of value, first for the traditional three broadcast services, then across both those and the newer satellite-delivered networks. Aggregation of network financial data into that of parent firms (such as NBC into RCA, and HBO into Time, Inc.) makes it very difficult to judge network performance.

There appears no available information of such traditional measures as revenue, expenses, and income for the newer services: pay cable, over-the-air subscription television, MDS, and the like. And there will be no more government data on the older broadcast and cable services after the 1980 figures reported here, for such collection efforts have been stopped as an economy move by the FCC. We will have to depend on trade association or investment analyst data from now on—data based on estimates and often on quite small samples or averages.

Little public information on comparable program costs, including those reported by medium or by specific market size, appears available over time. The varied impacts of inflation and expanding distribution opportunities would be interesting to study.

Nonbroadcast income by broadcasters, such as that from facility rental, or the growing use of subcarriers, is little understood. Auxiliary services by various electronic media need to be more clearly analyzed, and likely will be, as they grow to even minimal importance, given the demands of the stock market.

Cable appears to be taking off as a viable advertising medium in the mid-1980s. Thus far, precious little data on advertising income is available for cable television where in a few years, advertiser and subscriber income may vie for primacy. The other side of this matter is the lack of any data on subscriber payment for the various pay television options, from pay cable "tiers," to STV, MDS, the forthcoming DBS, and others. How many pay how much for which services will be important information, surely gathered on a proprietary basis, which needs to be made at least generally available for research.

Media Employment

Employment information, heretofore plentiful for broadcasting and cable services, will become harder to find with the post-1980 cessation of information gathering by the FCC. Among other data concerns:

1. There is no information on employment levels or patterns in any of the newer (post-cable) technologies. Whether there are differences between older and newer electronic media in this regard is simply not known. In the future, shifts from older to newer media will be harder to trace unless some of this data is generated.
2. Very little trend, let alone comparative, information is available on the many unions serving the electronic media—technical, trade, and business-

related. We report what we could find (see Table 460-C), but a much fuller picture is needed of the changes in unionization as the media themselves change. Is unionization in this field in decline? Also, union information on a market by market basis would allow useful conclusions as to unionization and urbanization levels.

3. We know very little, statistically speaking, about training and education for the electronic media fields. There is some outline information on college-level programs (see Table 403-A), but very little on what is actually being taught (even the names of courses over time). There appears to be no record of noncollege training programs, and little or no information of the increasingly important retraining process so many workers now go through as they move from fields with little opportunity to fields (such as electronic media) with more.

Media Content Considerations

Content trends, while of almost daily interest to viewers on one level, are, perhaps ironically, one of the hardest topics on which to find any kind of reliable and consistent information. Here are but a few examples:

1. A change in government organization responsibilities brought an end to the collection of most information on political campaign broadcasting. The last published data are for 1972 (see Tables 501-B and 501-F). During general elections in presidential years, at least, questions on the costs of broadcast advertising, and the impact of media on overall campaign costs arise—yet the data is more, not less, scattered and incomplete.

2. Much information once collected by survey or even educated estimate is no longer collected. Some kind of occasional spot survey of such things as broadcast station editorializing (both quantity and perhaps even a subject matter survey), program sources for local television stations (see Table 580-B), and radio network programming would be useful informal indicators of change.

3. A very useful research project would be individual market surveys of local television and cable programming (see Table 560-A for examples up to 1970). Such data for markets of different size categories would be a useful supplement to the widely available network information. Interestingly, in recent years, considerable individual market data on radio formats has surfaced (see Table 570-A for discussion).

4. There is, as yet, still no statistical information available to the public on content trends in pay television. A comparison of HBO, Showtime, and other pay services would be of value—and could well be supplemented by data on the basic services. For other than the names of some specialized services, there is no consistent information on the often discussed, but as yet undocumented, expansion in viewer choice delivered by these "new technologies," including developing MDS and the soon to arrive DBS operations.

Media Audiences

Audience information is, on the one hand, abundant to the point of being overpowering (ratings data on network programs, local market TV ratings and rankings, trends in top-ranked programs, etc.), or, at the opposite extreme, either much too narrow for practical public understanding and application, or not available at all. Here again, there are many areas in need of investigation.

Research is only beginning on the ways that new delivery technologies, including home video recording, which is not included in this volume, are dividing up the audience at any given time, as well as over time, from what had been either radio listeners and over-the-air TV watchers. The extent, let alone the impact, of this audience diversion is, as yet, little understood. Needless to say, there is little time-series information of any value presently.

The impact of "traditional" broadcasting, let alone newer media, on children is widely and deeply researched—but there is little time-series information that we can find. For example, we nearly included the findings of Schramm et al (1961) on use of various media by children up to age 12—but could find no directly comparable information for even one recent year to allow some sense of trends. This is an example of a lot of research rather narrowly focused with too few broader examinations.

International Aspects

International aspects of electronic media are covered here only in the most summary fashion, for there is a wealth of information, especially on domestic systems, in other countries. The intent of Section 7 is to demonstrate some of the international broadcasting activities, coverage of foreign affairs on American television, and trade aspects of electronic media. Here, depending on your point of view, unanswered questions abound:

1. Import and export of receivers and other equipment for electronic media would benefit from more recent information on country of origin. Table 750-C, for example, is a useful demonstration of trends in a period of important transition—but more recent information has not been located. Scattered spot information appears in the press when treaties (or complaints) with other countries are reported, but consistent information, by country, over time, has not been found.
2. Likewise, the data does not appear to exist to either support or deny the allegation of American media dominance of the world, especially developing countries. There are but scattered data on TV program imports and exports as to content and producing country, and virtually no information on radio or other electronic media trends in import/export.

3. Much of the data on American international broadcasting (Unit 701) is aggregate or reported in terms of language used. There is no available content trend information over time for any of the American radio services—nor, for that matter, for the services received here. Indeed, there is precious little information on the number of Americans with shortwave reception capability.

Media Regulation

Regulation is difficult to quantify. The material in Section 8 covers primarily broadcasting and cable, while Unit 860 includes all of telecommunications. Among the research problems here are:

1. Some means of quantifying Congressional interest in electronic media issues would be of value—even a mere count of published hearings and reports on related matters would go a long way toward filling the gap.
2. Thus far, only spot data on state regulation of broadcasting (Unit 861) and cable (Unit 890) exist—some summarizing and trend study is needed to assess the direction and impact of this least known aspect of electronic media regulation.
3. Numerous other measures of interest and possible value might be developed: what is the number of communications lawyers specializing in electronic media issues, the number of court cases at varied levels (especially the Appeals Court for the D.C. Circuit, and the Supreme Court), their impact on FCC decisions, and others.

Comment

The research suggestions and problems noted above are but a nick at the surface of the areas involved. They are mere indications that, despite the wealth of material we do have, much of it at least summarized herein, there is a great deal we either do not know at all, or do not have sufficient quantifiable data on. If this book and the suggestions above provoke some immediate replies (either that we have missed something which does exist, or that research is now underway to fill a specified gap), then it will have achieved part of its goal.

In the meantime, it remains useful to re-read a short list of general suggestions to guide researchers (and their funders) in gathering statistical information on communications media. Appearing originally at the conclusion of our introduction to *The Mass Media* (1978), these suggestions still appear warranted five years later:

1. *Define the universe of American mass media firms and their foreign subsidiaries.* We need to go beyond the approximations developed by counting lists.
2. *Develop uniform definitions of terms and data-collection categories.* These definitions should be decided among government agencies and with private industry statisticians.
3. *Provide full technical information or references.* This information should accompany each major presentation of industry statistics, public or private.
4. *Collect adequate information for all of the mass media, regardless of size.* For example, data for recordings and cable systems should not be aggregated with larger industrial classifications.
5. *Support national, industry-wide studies of content and audiences on a continuing basis.*
6. *Compile information now supplied to government but not analyzed.* This compilation could include such sources of information as reports to the Federal Elections Commission and the annual publishers' statements to the United States Postal Service.
7. *Use sampling techniques to estimate sales below the minimum amount for which government reports are required.* This is especially important in the foreign trade area.
8. *Expand the information available for data analysis on a company-by-company basis.*
9. *Create new measures to be incorporated into government data collection.* A good start would be a continuing measure of the impact of new technologies on production.
10. *Protect companies' legitimate rights to confidentiality, while providing the best possible overall analysis.*

SECTION ONE
GROWTH
OF
ELECTRONIC MEDIA

170
RADIO STATIONS

Interpretation of the Tables

Prior to World War I, AM broadcasting stations appeared on the air experimentally both in the United States and abroad. However, regularly scheduled and continuing AM broadcasting began with station KDKA in Pittsburgh in November, 1920. FM experimental stations did not appear until the late 1930s and were not subject to regular licensing until January 1, 1941. Since few radio stations sold much advertising time in these early years, the "commercial" designation is a misnomer for AM radio up to 1930, and for FM well into the 1960s. Perhaps the designation is best viewed as a declaration of intent.

The numerical supremacy of AM over FM radio is clearly evident in Table 170-A. This dominance by AM has been due to a number of factors, including: (1) AM's well-developed network structure, which predated FM's inception; (2) the lack of separate programming on most FM stations until the late 1960s; and (3) the greater expense of FM receivers. These conditions and others led to AM's larger audiences and, thus, to greater advertiser interest. Only in the 1970s did the gap between AM and FM radio begin to close.

The early growth of AM radio was sudden and unregulated. The combination of a government allocation policy and the Great Depression finally checked this growth and led to a decline in the number of radio stations from 1928 through 1935. A construction freeze during World War II also held down any notable increase in stations, but the number of AM stations rose dramatically after 1945—a result of increasing demand for local radio service in suburban and rural communities. Indeed, so many new stations were established that, by the 1970s, the FCC was imposing power limitations and daytime-only operations on about half the stations in order to reduce interference. Twice since 1962, the FCC has placed freezes on the processing of applications for AM stations, and the Commission now encourages, as much as possible, the expansion of FM stations.

The last column on Table 170–A represents the proportion of broadcast stations—both AM and FM—to 10,000 population. Though this proportion increased regularly through the late 1960s, the declining rate of new stations going on the air led to a slowing of that growth in the 1970s. Now, with the end in sight not only for AM growth but also for FM expansion (as FM's allocations are gradually filled), the number of stations per 10,000 population will level off. And it is reasonable to expect that in the 1980s, this figure will begin to decline as population growth outstrips any increase in the number of stations.

Regulatory changes in the 1980s, including a general trend toward deregulation in the program and other "behavioral" aspects of broadcasting, and the opening of such new opportunities as non-broadcast uses of subcarriers on both AM and FM stations, may provide a new impetus to growth. While the FCC in 1981 rejected a plan to reduce AM channel spacing from the long-standard 10 kHz to 9 kHz (to allow many new stations to take to the air) after substantial industry pressure, the Commission did make progress on a parallel plan to "drop in" perhaps several hundred new FM stations. Even without these changes, however, it appears that by the mid-1980s the combined number of commercial and educational FM stations will finally surpass the number of AM stations on the air.

Table 170–B traces changes in: (1) the number of AM radio stations per U.S. community; (2) the number of AM stations by station class designation; and (3) the percentage of AM stations with daytime-only operations. The reader will note that for educational AM stations, no separate category exists under "number of stations by station class." The reason for this omission is that no specific AM educational allocation was ever created, and only sporadic information is available on educational AM broadcasting. The bits and pieces of information on this subject indicate that the number of nonprofit AM licensees reached a peak in the early and mid-1920s, then declined in the late 1920s and throughout the 1930s, and finally leveled off to a plateau of approximately 30 stations by 1940. About the same number are operating today.

Prior to 1960, FM radio also had a checkered career. Some of FM's difficulties have already been mentioned. Another difficulty—perhaps the most damaging—was that, in 1945, FM had to cope with the problem of having to begin anew on a higher frequency allocation which was in competition with both expanding AM stations and the newly developing television stations (see Unit 180). Congress and the FCC did their best to encourage FM

Table 170-A   Number of Radio Stations, 1921–1983

Year	AM Stations	FM Stations Commercial	FM Stations Educational	FM Stations Total	Total Radio Stations	Average Number of Stations: Per 5 year Period	Average Number of Stations: Per 10,000 Population
1921	5	—	—	—	5	—	—
1922	30	—	—	—	30		
1923	556	—	—	—	556		
1924	530	—	—	—	530		
1925	571	—	—	—	571		
1926	528	—	—	—	528		
1927	681	—	—	—	681	613	.005
1928	677	—	—	—	677		
1929	606	—	—	—	606		
1930	618	—	—	—	618		
1931	612	—	—	—	612		
1932	604	—	—	—	604	603	.004
1933	599	—	—	—	599		
1934	583	—	—	—	583		
1935	585	—	—	—	585		
1936	616	—	—	—	616		
1937	646	—	—	—	646	652	.005
1938	689	—	—	—	689		
1939	722	—	—	—	722		
1940	765	—	—	—	765		
1941	831	18	2	20	851		

Table 170–A   Number of Radio Stations, 1921–1983 (cont.)

Year	AM Stations	FM Stations			Total Radio Stations	Average Number of Stations:	
		Commercial	Educational	Total		Per 5 year Period	Per 10,000 Population
1942	887	36	7	43	930	893	.006
1943	910	41	8	49	959		
1944	910	44	8	52	962		
1945	919	46	8	54	973		
1946	948	48	9	57	1,005	1,585	.011
1947	1,062	140	10	150	1,212		
1948	1,621	458	15	473	2,094		
1949	1,912	700	27	727	2,639		
1950	2,086	733	48	781	2,867		
1951	2,232	676	73	749	2,981	3,033	.019
1952	2,331	637	85	722	3,053		
1953	2,391	580	98	678	3,069		
1954	2,521	560	112	672	3,193		
1955	2,669	552	122	674	3,343		
1956	2,824	540	123	663	3,487	3,684	.022
1957	3,008	530	125	655	3,663		
1958	3,196	537	141	678	3,874		
1959	3,326	578	151	729	4,055		
1960	3,456	688	162	850	4,306		
1961	3,547	815	175	990	4,537		

1962	3,618	960	194	1,154	4,772	4,780	.026
1963	3,760	1,081	209	1,290	5,050		
1964	3,854	1,146	237	1,383	5,237		
1965	4,044	1,270	255	1,525	5,569		
1966	4,065	1,446	268	1,714	5,779		
1967	4,121	1,643	296	1,939	6,060		
1968	4,190	1,753	326	2,079	6,269	6,048	.030
1969	4,265	1,938	362	2,300	6,565		
1970	4,292	2,184	413	2,597	6,889		
1971	4,343	2,196	472	2,668	7,011		
1972	4,374	2,304	511	2,815	7,189	7,206	.035
1973	4,395	2,411	573	2,984	7,379		
1974	4,407	2,502	652	3,154	7,561		
1975	4,432	2,636	717	3,353	7,785		
1976	4,463	2,767	804	3,571	8,034	8,209	.038
1977	4,497	2,837	839	3,676	8,173		
1978	4,513	3,001	926	3,927	8,440		
1979	4,526	3,107	982	4,089	8,615		
1980	4,559	3,155	1,038	4,193	8,752	—	—
1981	4,589	3,282	1,092	4,374	8,963	—	—
1982	4,634	3,349	1,118	4,467	9,101	—	—
1983	4,708	3,421	1,090	4,511	9,219		

Sources: 1921–1926 data: U.S. Department of Commerce. 1927–1934 data: Federal Radio Commission. 1935–1977 data: Federal Communications Commission, as reprinted in Sterling and Kittross (1978), p. 511, which details the secondary sources used for the official data. 1978 data from *Broadcasting* (January 23, 1978), p. 66. 1979 data from *Television Digest* to author. 1980–1983 data from the FCC, as reprinted in various issues of *Broadcasting* (with 1983 data as of March 30).

Table 170–B   Characteristics of AM Radio Stations, 1935–1980

	1935	1945	1950	1960	1970	1980
Number of Stations per Community						
4 or more	N/A	43	113	143	202	N/A
3	N/A	31	68	120	106	N/A
2	N/A	57	174	319	321	N/A
1	N/A	435	897	1,660	1,611	N/A
Total Number of Radio Communities	N/A	566	1,252	2,242	2,240	N/A
Number of Stations, by Station Classification[a] and Percentage of Total Number						
Dominant Clear Channels (I–A and I–B Stations)	44	68	N/A	63	56	59
Percent of Total	7	7	N/A	2	1	1
Secondary Clear Channels (II Stations)	50	74	N/A	754	1,151	1,413
Percent of Total	8	8	N/A	21	27	31
Regional (III Stations)	280	345	N/A	1,748	2,088	2,139
Percent of Total	44	36	N/A	50	49	46
Local (IV Stations)	260	474	N/A	944	1,005	1,025
Percent of Total	41	49	N/A	27	23	22
Total Number of Stations	634	961	N/A	3,509	4,300	4,636
Daytime-Only AM Stations						
Percent of Total	12	8	29	47	49	51[b]

Source: Compilations by L. W. Lichty of the University of Maryland, based on figures in *Broadcasting Yearbook* (1936, 1945, 1960, 1971), with 1980 data supplied to the author by the FCC Mass Media Bureau. Notes: [a]For background on AM and FM station classifications, see Head and Sterling (1982), pp. 59–64. [b]Indicates 1979 figure.

expansion during these post-war years, but as Table 170–A shows, FM experienced a sharp decline throughout the 1950s until 1958, when AM reached urban saturation and the first spurt of television expansion was complete.

The subsequent growth of FM radio was aided by the development of (1) the federal government's program of Subsidiary Communications Authorizations (1955), which allowed nonbroadcast services to be transmitted by FM stations, thus increasing their income potential; (2) the achievement of a technology for stereo broadcasting in 1961; and (3) the FCC's nonduplication programming requirements after 1965, which separated FM station content from the content of co-owned AM stations, thereby providing for more FM diversity. As a result of these developments, FM has firmly estab-lished its own identity since the early 1960s and has won sufficient audience acceptance to become the fastest growing broadcast medium in the United States. Even educational FM stations have steadily increased in number, though many operate with merely 10 watts and cover an area of only three to five miles. (There has been a special educational FM allocation—the lowest 20 channels on the FM band—since 1945.) Recognizing the demand for edu-cational licenses, in the early 1980s the FCC began to force low power sta-tions (the 10 watt operations) to increase power (to at least 100 watts) or to move to commercial channels in a nonprotected status (if a full-power appli-cant came along, it would have precedence as a more efficient user of spec-trum).

Table 170–C provides another way of looking at the increase in number of radio stations over a half-century period. Shown here are the number of AM (1939) and AM and FM stations (for other years) in several random mar-kets of different populations. Only stations actually licensed to the commu-nity listed (or immediate suburbs) are shown—in fact, of course, most of these towns could actually receive many more signals than those listed. Most post-1959 expansion has been on the FM band.

Sources

All information given in Table 170–A was drawn from various FCC reports. The 1978 through 1983 data are from tables in *Broadcasting* and *Television Digest*. With the exception of 1927–1947, figures in this table refer to stations actually on the air, regardless of license status. Information for the earlier years includes stations listed as "authorized" and/or "licensed" some of which may not actually have been on the air. All data is as of Janu-ary 1, with the following exceptions: 1923 (March 1), 1924 (October 1), 1925 (June 20), and the years 1926–1932 (June 30). The last column of Table 170–A is based upon the population figures given in Sterling and Haight (1978) Table 100–B. The figures in this column are subject to slight variation due to averaging and rounding of both station and population informa-tion.

Table 170–B information was hand-counted from *Broadcasting Year-book* listings, with the exception of 1980 data which was supplied directly to the author by the FCC.

Table 170–C was developed by FCC Broadcast (later Mass Media) Bu-reau staff researchers during the long radio deregulation (1979–1981) pro-ceedings. The markets were chosen by a method that assured an even distri-bution of market size, but within each market size category, the particular market included was randomly selected. Markets were ranked according to

Table 170-C Number of AM and FM Stations in Selected Markets, 1939–1979

Market	Number of Stations on the Air As of:				
	1939[a]	1949	1959	1969	1979
Pittsburgh, Pennsylvania	6	19	22	31	35
Cincinnati, Ohio	5	8	13	21	25
Birmingham, Alabama	3	10	13	17	20
Greensboro, North Carolina	2	6	9	13	17
Las Vegas, Nevada	—	3	6	11	13
Austin, Texas	2	4	7	11	13
Roanoke, Virginia	1	5	7	10	12
Lincoln, Nebraska	1	3	4	8	11
Sarasota, Florida	1	3	4	9	10
Canton, Ohio	1	4	6	9	9
Eau Claire, Wisconsin	1	4	5	7	8
Erie, Pennsylvania	1	4	5	6	8
Tyler, Texas	1	2	4	6	7
Wichita Falls, Texas	1	3	3	5	6
Gastonia, North Carolina	1	3	4	5	5
Bay City, Michigan	1	1	2	4	4

Source: FCC, *Inquiry and Proposed Rulemaking in Docket, 79-219, Deregulation of Radio. 44 Federal Register 57672* (October 5, 1979), Table 2. *Notes:* The years that stations began operation, which underlie this table, come from Standard Rate & Data Service, Inc., *Spot Radio Rates and Data,* Vol. 61, No. 3, March 1, 1979, Skokie, Illinois; *Broadcasting Yearbook 1979;* and FCC license records. [a] AM only.

the number of stations. The number of stations was based on those licensed in those communities in the year indicated.

Further Information

Official statistics and some background discussion appear in the annual reports of the Federal Radio Commission (1927–1934) and FCC (since 1935), with summary data appearing regularly in such trade sources as *Broadcasting Yearbook*, *Television Factbook*, and the weeklies on which both annuals are based. Useful historical discussions can be found in Lichty and Topping (1975), Sterling and Kittross (1978), and Head and Sterling (1982). A good analysis of the rise and decline of educational AM radio, and subsequent changes in public radio, is found in Wood and Wylie (1977).

171
NETWORK-AFFILIATE
RADIO STATIONS

Interpretation of the Tables

Table 171–A offers a statistical profile of the number and percentage of affiliates held by each of America's four radio networks: NBC, CBS, ABC, and Mutual. The National Broadcasting Company (NBC), a subsidiary of Radio Corporation of America (RCA) throughout its history, was the first to broadcast in September 1926. In January 1927, NBC added a second parallel network, and the two systems became known as NBC Red (not only the first, but financially the more important) and NBC Blue.

The Columbia Broadcasting System (CBS) went through 18 months of name changes and uncertainty before the Paley family took control in 1928. At that point, however, the network quickly became a strong competitor for NBC. The competition was ensured when, in 1941, an FCC ruling, upheld by a landmark 1943 Supreme Court case (*National Broadcasting Co., Inc., et al v. United States et al* 319 U.S. 190—May 10, 1943), forced RCA to divest itself of one of its two networks. RCA therefore sold off the Blue Network, and it became the American Broadcasting Company (ABC) in 1945.

Unlike NBC, CBS, and ABC, Mutual began as a program cooperative rather than a centralized network operation. For many years—until ABC's

Table 171–A   Number of Network-Affiliate Radio Stations, 1927–1982

Year	NBC Affiliates No.	%	CBS Affiliates No.	%	Mutual Affiliates No.	%	ABC Affiliates No.	%	Total AM Stations	Total Network Stations No.	%
1927	28	4.1	16	2.3	—	—	—	—	681	44	6
1928	52	7.7	17	2.5	—	—	—	—	677	69	10
1929	58	8.3	49	7.0	—	—	—	—	696	107	15
1930	71	11.5	60	9.7	—	—	—	—	618	131	21
1931	75	12.3	76	12.4	—	—	—	—	612	151	25
1932	86	14.2	84	13.9	—	—	—	—	604	170	28
1933	88	14.7	91	15.2	—	—	—	—	599	179	30
1934	88	15.1	92	15.8	4	0.7	—	—	583	184	32
1935	88	15.0	97	16.6	3	0.5	—	—	585	188	32
1936	89	14.4	98	15.9	39	6.3	—	—	616	226	37
1937	111	17.2	105	16.3	80	12.4	—	—	646	296	46
1938	142	20.6	110	16.0	107	15.5	—	—	689	359	52
1939	167	23.1	113	15.7	116	16.1	—	—	722	396	55
1940	182	23.8	112	14.6	160	20.9	—	—	765	454	59
1941	225	27.1	118	14.2	166	20.0	—	—	831	509	61
1942	136	15.3	115	13.0	191	21.5	116	13.1	887	558	63
1943	142	15.6	116	12.7	219	24.1	143	15.7	910	620	68
1944	143	15.7	133	14.6	245	26.9	173	19.0	910	694	76
1945	150	16.3	145	15.8	384	41.8	195	21.2	919	874	95
1946	155	16.4	147	15.5	384	40.5	195	20.6	948	881	93
1947	162	15.3	157	14.8	488	46.0	222	20.9	1,062	1,029	97
1948	167	10.3	162	10.0	519	32.0	256	15.8	1,621	1,104	68
1949	170	8.9	167	8.7	526	27.5	269	14.1	1,912	1,132	59
1950	172	8.2	173	8.3	543	26.0	282	13.5	2,086	1,170	56
1951	180	8.1	183	8.2	552	24.7	295	13.2	2,232	1,210	54
1952	191	8.2	194	8.3	560	24.0	302	13.0	2,331	1,247	53
1953	207	8.7	203	8.5	560	23.4	348	14.6	2,391	1,318	55

Year											
1954	212	8.4	205	8.1	560	22.2	360	14.3	2,521	1,337	53
1955	208	7.8	207	7.8	563	21.1	357	13.4	2,669	1,335	50
1956	205	7.3	204	7.2	558	19.8	342	12.1	2,824	1,309	46
1957	199	6.6	201	6.7	525	17.5	334	12.1	3,008	1,259	42
1958	203	6.4	200	6.3	431	13.5	299	9.4	3,195	1,133	35
1959	209	6.3	198	6.0	441	13.3	286	8.6	3,326	1,134	34
1960	202	5.8	198	5.7	443	12.8	310	9.0	3,456	1,153	33
1961	201	5.7	195	5.5	428	12.1	339	9.6	3,547	1,163	33
1962	200	5.5	206	5.7	510	14.1	342	9.5	3,618	1,258	35
1963	200	5.4	207	5.5	510	13.6	366	9.7	3,760	1,283	34
1964	202	5.2	227	5.9	500	13.0	353	9.2	3,854	1,282	33
1965	209	5.2	237	5.9	501	12.5	355	8.9	4,044	1,302	32
1966	215	5.3	239	5.9	520	12.8	361	8.9	4,065	1,335	33
1967	216	5.2	240	5.8	N/A	N/A	337	8.2	4,121	N/A	N/A
1968	217	5.2	243	5.8	515	12.4	500	12.0	4,170	1,475	35
1969	222	5.2	245	5.7	492	11.5	1,013	23.8	4,265	1,972	46
1970	220	5.1	247	5.8	523	12.2	1,175	27.4	4,292	2,165	50
1971	230	5.3	249	5.7	538	12.4	1,074	24.7	4,343	2,091	48
1972	231	5.3	242	5.5	545	12.5	1,169	26.7	4,374	2,187	50
1973	233	5.3	243	5.5	568	12.9	1,246	28.4	4,395	2,290	52
1974	230	5.2	248	5.6	632	14.3	1,293	29.3	4,407	2,403	55
1975	232	5.2	247	5.6	657	14.8	1,322	29.8	4,432	2,458	55
1976	223	5.0	257	5.8	684	15.3	1,353	30.3	4,463	2,517	56
1977	236	5.2	266	5.9	755	16.8	1,546	34.4	4,497	2,803	62
1978	245	5.4	270	6.0	800a	17.7	1,554	34.4	4,513	2,869	64
1979	268	5.9	278	6.1	950a	21.0	1,561	34.5	4,526	3,057	67
1980	281	6.2	321	7.0	934	20.5	1,574	34.5	4,559	3,110	68
1981	315	6.7	400	8.8	902	19.7	1,591	34.7	4,589	3,208	70
1982	370	8.0	425	9.2	876	19.0	1,631	35.1	4,634	3,302	71

Sources: Individual networks, as reported in Sterling and Kittross (1978), pp. 512–513, through 1977; and directly from networks to the author for years since. Total AM stations from Table 170–A. Note: aEstimates by Mutual.

ascendency in the early 1970s—Mutual was numerically the largest radio network. However, its affiliates have always held less broadcast power and drawn smaller audiences than any of the three networks.

After a network-affiliation peak during the years immediately following World War II, the radio networks declined in importance as hundreds of new nonaffiliated stations went on the air and the competition from television began. The radio networks today are little more than general news services with a few features added for seasoning.

In recent years, there have been a few attempts to revive radio networking. In 1968, for example, the ABC network split into the four specialized-format networks shown in Table 171–B. At this point, ABC became the biggest of the radio "webs." The recent increase in ABC affiliate stations is also due to this four-way split. NBC experimented with a network-level, all-news service in 1975–77, but that experiment failed due to a lack of affiliates.

Under increasing competitive pressure (from radio satellite-delivered program services, after 1981), both ABC and NBC announced further network splits, with ABC adding a Rock Radio and "Direction" networks, with yet a seventh announced, and NBC announcing two services to supplement its main feed. Clearly, radio networking as a support service for diversified format radio stations was, by the 1980s, playing an increasingly important role in the business, as attested to by the rise in the radio affiliation proportion shown in Table 171–A.

Until the 1960s, virtually all radio network affiliations were AM stations. By the 1970s, however, each of the networks had some FM affiliates as well (as shown in Table 171–B, ABC has devoted one of its network services solely to FM). Thus, the figures for the networks in Table 171–A include some FM stations, especially in the past decade or so. The inclusion of FM stations makes the final two columns somewhat misleading and a bit high, since the base column ("total AM stations") does not include the FM network affiliates.

Sources

The affiliation figures in Tables 171–A and 171–B were obtained by the author in correspondence with the networks and supplemented by data in *Broadcasting Yearbook*. The figures vary because radio stations sometimes hold affiliations with more than one network. Also, the number of affiliates in each network will vary according to how many stations an advertiser wants and is willing to pay for. Thus, the statistics for any given network might change dramatically in a single day. The data given here are basically

Table 171–B Number of ABC Network Affiliates, by Format, 1968–1982

Year	Entertainment	Contemporary	Information	FM Network	Total
1968	132	76	200	92	500
1969	251	224	362	176	1,013
1970	298	262	425	190	1,175
1971	275	242	348	209	1,074
1972	306	276	387	200	1,169
1973	322	300	414	210	1,246
1974	347	319	412	215	1,293
1975	365	329	419	209	1,322
1976	382	334	442	195	1,353
1977	423	372	557	194	1,546
1978	467	385	497	205	1,554
1979	477	397	491	196	1,561
1980	479	404	495	196	1,574
1981	476	400	522	193	1,591
1982	491	377	567	196	1,631

Source: ABC, Inc.

averages of the number of affiliates as of January 1 of each year. The percentage breakdowns were calculated by the author. The Mutual network data for the late 1970s should be used with caution, since they are no more than "approximations" provided by Mutual when the network was in a continuing struggle with an expanding ABC for affiliate stations.

Further Information

Additional historical information on radio networks appears in the FCC's *Chain Broadcasting* (1941), and Chapter 13 of the FCC's *Network Broadcasting* (1958). Lists of radio network affiliates, along with details on their officers, appear in the annual editions of *Broadcasting Yearbook*. For a very useful narrative history, see the early chapters of Bergreen (1980). Not shown on the tables are the affiliates of the National Public Radio network which began in 1971 with 107 "affiliates," and grew to 174 member stations by 1974, some 215 in late 1978, and 280 by 1983. To be affiliated, noncommercial stations must meet minimum qualifications set by the Corporation for Public Broadcasting (CPB). In all, NPR serves about 20 percent of all AM and FM noncommercial stations.

180
TELEVISION STATIONS
AND MARKETS

Interpretation of the Tables

After many years of experimental operation with both mechanical and electronic systems of television, the FCC finally approved regular television station operation on July 1, 1941. A handful of stations got on the air before the war, but manpower and equipment shortages closed down most of them for the duration of the conflict.

As Table 180–A reveals, television did not experience an immediate spurt of growth after the war. Several factors held television back during these early years, including the high cost of station construction and operation (as compared with radio); the limited number of VHF-only channels available in major cities, and some serious allocation problems in 1947–1948. Finally, in the fall of 1948, the FCC placed a six-month freeze on the processing of station applications while it dealt with such problems as limited channels, educational allocation, and color TV standards. However, as it turned out, the freeze did not end until 1952—which explains the flat rate of growth for those four years. It was in April 1952 that the FCC's *Sixth Report and Order* added the UHF channels 14–83 to its system of allocations.

The following six years saw substantial growth on the more desirable VHF channels, which had greater range (and thus larger audiences) and simpler tuning mechanisms. After that period, commercial television growth slowed down. Less than 80 new commercial VHF stations have appeared in the past 15 years due to both a lack of available frequencies (see Table 180–B), and a lack of economic viability for the unused channel assignments.

Like FM radio, commercial UHF television enjoyed an initial burst, but then declined for several years. UHF's problems were even more complex than those of VHF. The relatively limited range of UHF, combined with the problem of getting television sets equipped for UHF reception, resulted in small audiences and, thus, in limited advertiser interest in the UHF stations. Finally, the scarcity of VHF channels forced TV expansion to the UHF channels.

Even so, UHF stations clearly could not compete with VHF network affiliates. Only in the late 1960s, after the passage of an all-channel receiver law (see Unit 680) did the number of UHF commercial allocations increase. Table 180–B sketches UHF's varied pattern of development, with statistics showing the number of stations on the air for selected years and the number of pending and unassigned channels as of 1980.

Noncommercial television began in 1952, when the FCC ended its freeze and promulgated an allocation for nonprofit educational television stations. As with commercial television, the growth in educational television stations was slow at first—the result of high operating costs—and came first to VHF channels. Table 180–C provides an outline of educational/public station increases for 1958, 1968, and 1980, and shows how few VHF channels now remain, compared with the substantial number of UHF channels still awaiting assignment to public broadcasting.

Major federal funding for educational and public stations was introduced during the 1960s (see Unit 360). Amounts were then increased at the end of that decade, after the creation of the Corporation for Public Broadcasting (CPB). The substantial growth of public television in the 1970s, evident in Table 180–A, was made possible by even greater federal government funding and by a national policy of encouraging public television alternatives to commercial television. Since about 1970, public television stations, operating under many different kinds of financial constraints, have outstripped the growth in the number of commercial television stations, though the differences in growth rate are small.

Table 180–D lists the expanding numbers of TV stations "receivable per community," which is another type of measure of the increasing number of television stations on the air. Back in 1952, before the end of the television "freeze," 69 percent of U.S. households could receive only one-to-three television stations (fully one-third could receive but one station). Only 30 percent of households had access to four or more stations. By 1958, only 3 percent of American households were limited to one station, 18 percent received two or three stations, and 80 percent received four or more. However, the spread of cable television (see Unit 190), with its multiple channels for subscribers, is responsible for this upward trend in the number of stations receivable in a community. Nevertheless, according to the data presented here, most homes in the United States have access to the three main network signals, plus one or more educational/public independent stations.

Sources

FCC figures for Table 180–A are for January 1 of each year and refer only to stations on the air, regardless of license status. The A. D. Little Co., which arranged the FCC figures for 1958 and 1968 in Tables 180–B and

Table 180–A   Number of Television Stations, 1941–1983

Year	VHF Stations			UHF Stations			Total		Total Number of Stations
	Commercial	Educational	Total	Commercial	Educational	Total	Commercial	Educational	
1941	2	—	2	—	—	—	2	—	2
1942	4	—	4	—	—	—	4	—	4
1943	8	—	8	—	—	—	8	—	8
1944	8	—	8	—	—	—	8	—	8
1945	8	—	8	—	—	—	8	—	8
1946	6	—	6	—	—	—	6	—	6
1947	12	—	12	—	—	—	12	—	12
1948	16	—	16	—	—	—	16	—	16
1949	51	—	51	—	—	—	51	—	51
1950	98	—	98	—	—	—	98	—	98
1951	107	—	107	—	—	—	107	—	107
1952	108	—	108	—	—	—	108	—	108
1953	120	—	120	6	—	6	126	—	126
1954	233	1	234	121	1	122	354	2	356
1955	297	8	305	114	3	117	411	11	422
1956	344	13	357	97	5	102	441	18	459
1957	381	17	398	90	6	96	471	23	494
1958	411	22	433	84	6	90	495	28	523
1959	433	28	461	77	7	84	510	35	545

1960	440	34	474	75	10	85	515	44	559
1961	451	37	488	76	15	91	527	52	579
1962	458	43	501	83	19	102	541	62	603
1963	466	46	512	91	22	113	557	68	625
1964	476	53	529	88	32	120	564	85	649
1965	481	58	539	88	41	129	569	99	668
1966	486	65	551	99	49	148	585	114	699
1967	492	71	563	118	56	174	610	127	737
1968	499	75	574	136	75	211	635	150	785
1969	499	78	577	163	97	260	662	175	837
1970	501	80	581	176	105	281	677	185	862
1971	503	86	589	179	113	292	682	199	881
1972	508	90	598	185	123	308	693	213	906
1973	510	93	603	187	137	324	697	230	927
1974	513	92	605	184	149	333	697	241	938
1975	514	95	609	192	152	344	706	247	953
1976	511	97	608	190	162	352	701	259	960
1977	515	101	616	196	160	356	711	261	972
1978	515	102	617	201	164	365	716	266	982
1979	515	107	622	209	167	376	724	274	998
1980	516	109	625	218	168	386	734	277	1,011
1981	519	111	630	237	171	408	756	282	1,038
1982	517	112	629	260	176	436	777	288	1,065
1983	519	114	633	294	179	473	813	293	1,106

Sources: FCC data (as of January 1 each year) as reprinted in *Television Factbook*. Data for 1982 and 1983 supplied directly to the author from the *Television Factbook* staff.

Table 180-B Number of Commercial Television Stations, by Market Group, 1958, 1968, and 1980

Market Group	UHF Stations					VHF Stations				
	1958	1968	1980 Licensed	1980 Pending	1980 Vacant	1958	1968	1980 Licensed	1980 Pending	1980 Vacant
Markets 1–10	1	23	⎱ 81	87	25	40	41	⎱ 157	—	—
Markets 11–50	11	31	⎰	35	51	114	126	⎰	1	—
Markets 51–100	37	42	58	40	83	102	112	107	7	3
Markets 101–200	18	37	50	33	84	131	160	167	10	56
Markets 201 and up	10	21	25			15	23	71		
Total Stations, All Markets	77	154	214	195	243	402	462	502	18	59

Sources: 1958 and 1968 data: A. D. Little Co. (1969), p. 143, Table 57. 1980 data: FCC, *Television Channel Utilization* (1980), Table 1, showing data as of June 30th.

Table 180-C Number of Noncommercial (Public) Television Stations, by Market Group, 1958, 1968, and 1980

Market Group	UHF Stations					VHF Stations				
			1980					1980		
	1958	1968	Licensed	Pending	Vacant	1958	1968	Licensed	Pending	Vacant
Markets 1–10	2	10	} 54	3	40	4	5	} 28	2	1
Markets 11–50	3	24		4	37	11	19		—	—
Markets 51–100	2	14	35	4	37	4	16	17	—	8
Markets 101–200	—	10	32	7	62	1	10	28	1	8
Markets 201 and up	—	39	47	11	235	3	26	34	4	13
Total Stations, All Markets	7	97	168	25	374	23	76	107	7	22

Sources: 1958 and 1968 data: A. D. Little Co. (1969), p. 148, Table 62, 1980 data: FCC, *Television Channel Utilization* (1980), Table 1, showing data as of June 30th.

Table 180-D Reception of Television Broadcast Signals in U.S. Communities, 1964-1982

Number of Signals Receivable in a Community	Percentage of all Communities					
	1964	*1968*	*1972*	*1976*	*1980*	*1982*
1 to 3 signals	22	7	6 ⎫	12	9	6
4 signals	19	11	11 ⎭			
5 signals	14	13	12	11	10	7
6 signals	19	9	10	12	10	10
7 signals	12	20	18	18	10	9
8 signals	6	11	12	9	7	10
9 signals	4	9	11	11	11	11
10 or more signals	4	17	20	27	43	47

Sources: Nielsen Television Index information as found in *Television Audience 1980*, p. 9, except 1968, for which see *Broadcasting* (August 19, 1971), p. 31. 1982 data from *Television Audience 1982*, p. 9.

180-C, based the market rankings on the number of prime-time television households as of December 1968. However, the reader should note that only the 1968 data are for December; the 1958 figures were compiled in February. The 1980 data, which were taken directly from the FCC's *Television Channel Utilization* (1980), represent the period ending June 30. Thus, there are slight differences among the rankings for the three years represented on the tables. Still, the basic comparisons remain valid.

The television stations counted for the 1958 and 1968 data in Tables 180-B and 180-C were all licensed and on the air. The 1980 figures represent three categories: (1) licensed stations (whether on the air or not—most are); (2) pending stations, which are either awaiting approval of applications or seeking construction permits (a few of the latter may be on the air with tests); and (3) vacant channels for which no applications have been made. For 1980, all commercial allocations then current are accounted for in the tables.

The statistics offered in Table 180-D are based on A. C. Nielsen's ratings research and are therefore estimates by sample, not actual counts for all markets.

Further Information

Useful historical information is found in Barnouw (1975), Sterling and Kittross (1978), FCC, *Network Broadcasting* (1958), *New Television Networks* (1980), Head and Sterling (1982), and for the earliest years, Udelson (1982). Updated information appears in *Broadcasting* and *Television Digest*, or contact the FCC's Mass Media Bureau, the National Association of Broadcasters, and/or the Corporation for Public Broadcasting.

181
NETWORK-AFFILIATE
TELEVISION STATIONS

Interpretation of the Tables

Whereas radio network systems developed over two decades, declined and have only recently come back as news services (see Unit 171), television began as and remains a network-dominated medium. As Table 181–A reveals, however, the press of independent stations and cable competition, however, has begun to cut into that hegemony.

From the beginning, NBC has been the largest television network, though CBS is also able to reach the entire country. ABC, because it began acquiring affiliates much later, and because it operated so long under severe financial constraints, was always the third network in both size and importance. However, ABC's ratings strength since 1976 shows that it appears to be improving its ability to gather more and better station affiliates.

Not represented in Table 181–A are the two attempts to create a permanent fourth television network. The more recent and least successful was the United (formerly Overmyer) Network, which broadcast an evening program to 106 stations in early 1967. The system continued for a month before it ran out of funds. The earlier attempt, the DuMont Network, lasted for six years during the 1950s. Because there were only a few market areas at the time with four allocated channels, the DuMont Network was never able to attract a sufficient number of primary affiliates. *Broadcasting Yearbook* reports that DuMont had contracts—usually secondary or even tertiary affiliations—with 45 stations in 1949, 52 in 1950, 62 in 1951–1952, and 133 in 1953. Its affiliation figures reached a peak of 195 stations in 1954, then dipped to 158 during the next year. The DuMont network ceased operations in September 1955. Also not shown on the table is the Public Broadcasting Service (PBS), which increased its affiliations from 182 at the end of 1969, to 300 by 1983.

Table 181–A includes primary affiliates only. However, many of the nonaffiliated independent stations represented in the totals in Table 181–B have secondary network affiliations, which permit them to carry network programs that are not picked up by the local primary affiliate. In some smaller markets, these independent stations may even have contracts with two or three networks, giving them the freedom to choose programs from all of the companies. This phenomenon was especially common in the early

Table 181-A   Number of Network-Affiliate Television Stations, 1947-1982

Year	NBC Affiliates Number	Percent	CBS Affiliates Number	Percent	ABC Affiliates Number	Percent	Total Commercial Stations	Total Network Affiliates Number	Percent
1947	2	16.7	1	8.3	1	8.3	12	4	33
1948	9	56.3	3	18.8	6	37.5	16	16	100
1949	25	49.0	15	29.4	11	21.6	51	50	98
1950	56	57.1	27	27.6	13	13.3	98	96	98
1951	63	58.9	30	28.0	14	13.1	107	107	100
1952	64	59.3	31	28.7	15	13.9	108	108	100
1953	71	56.3	33	26.2	24	19.0	126	125	99
1954	164	46.3	113	31.9	40	11.3	354	317	90
1955	189	46.0	139	33.8	46	11.2	411	374	91
1956	200	45.4	168	38.1	53	12.0	441	421	95
1957	205	43.5	180	38.2	60	12.7	471	445	94
1958	209	42.2	191	38.8	69	13.9	495	469	95
1959	213	41.8	193	37.8	79	15.5	510	485	95
1960	214	41.6	195	37.9	87	16.9	515	496	96
1961	201	38.1	198	37.6	104	19.7	527	503	95
1962	201	37.2	194	35.9	113	20.9	541	508	94
1963	203	36.4	194	34.8	117	21.0	557	514	92
1964	212	37.6	191	33.9	123	21.8	564	526	93
1965	198	34.8	190	33.4	128	22.5	569	516	91
1966	202	34.5	193	33.0	137	23.4	585	532	91
1967	205	33.6	191	31.3	141	23.1	610	537	88
1968	207	32.6	192	30.2	148	23.3	635	547	86
1969	211	31.9	190	28.7	156	23.6	662	557	84
1970	215	31.8	193	28.5	160	23.6	677	568	84
1971	218	32.0	207	30.4	168	24.6	682	593	87
1972	218	31.5	209	30.2	172	24.8	693	599	86
1973	218	31.3	210	30.1	176	25.3	697	604	87
1974	218	31.3	212	30.4	181	26.0	697	611	88
1975	219	30.8	213	30.0	185	26.0	706	617	87
1976	218	30.7	213	30.0	182	25.6	701	613	87
1977	212	29.1	210	28.8	190	26.1	711	612	86
1978	213	29.3	208	28.6	195	26.8	716	616	86
1979	213	29.3	208	28.6	202	27.5	724	623	86
1980	213	28.6	200	26.8	202	27.1	734	615	84
1981	213	28.3	200	26.6	207	27.5	756	620	82
1982	215	27.8	200	25.8	206	26.6	777	621	80

Sources: Number of network affiliates: Sterling and Kittross (1978), p. 515 for data through 1977, and directly from networks to the author for years since. Column on total stations from Table 180-A.

Table 181–B   Number of Network-Affiliate and Independent Television Stations in the U.S., by Market Group, 1958–1975

Market Group	Network Affiliates				Non-Affiliated Independents				Total Commercial Stations			
	1958	1965	1968	1975	1958	1965	1968	1975	1958	1965	1968	1975
Markets 1–10:												
Number of Stations	29	30	30	31	12	17	34	36	41	47	64	67
Percent of All												
Commercial Stations	71	64	47	46	29	36	53	54	100	100	100	100
Markets 11–50:												
Number of Stations	113	118	119	126	12	17	38	37	125	135	157	163
Percent of All												
Commercial Stations	90	87	76	77	10	13	24	23	100	100	100	100
Subtotal (Markets 1–50):												
Percent of All												
Commercial Stations	86	81	67	68	14	19	33	32	100	100	100	100
Markets 51–100:												
Number of Stations	136	144	148	170	3	4	6	6	139	148	154	176
Percent of All												
Commercial Stations	98	97	96	97	2	3	4	3	100	100	100	100
Markets 101 and up:												
Number of Stations	169	196	214	216	5	6	27	7	174	202	241	223
Percent of All												
Commercial Stations	97	97	89	97	3	3	11	3	100	100	100	100
Total, All Market Groups:												
Number of Stations	447	488	511	543	32	44	105	86	479	532	616	629
Percent of All												
Commercial Stations	93	92	83	86	7	8	17	14	100	100	100	100

Sources: Data for 1958–1968: A. D. Little Co. (1969), pp. 142, 193, citing information from *Television Factbook* (February 1958, February 1965, December 1968). 1975 data for "top-100 markets": *Broadcasting Yearbook 1976*. 1975 data for "market groups 101 and up": provided to the author by the Association of Independent Television Stations, Inc.

days of television, when there were limited numbers of stations in a market area (see Unit 180). Today, such a situation is more unusual, since most markets have access to the three network signals.

Sources

The information in Table 181–A was reported by the television networks themselves. The 1978–1979 figures for CBS were taken from the Television Information Office. The 1978 CBS figure actually represents the number of affiliates as of November 10, 1977; the 1979 figure is for November 10, 1978. The 1980–1982 data from CBS appears to be an estimate. Part of this data has also been published in Lichty and Topping (1975), p. 193, and in Sterling and Kittross (1978), p. 515.

The A. D. Little Company supplied information for the years 1958, 1965, and 1968 in Table 181–B. The Little Company's source was the February 1958, February 1965, and December 1968 editions of *Television Factbook*. Little ranked the markets by "number of prime-time TV households in 1968," which is apparently a reference to the Arbitron Company's "Areas of Dominant Influence" (ADIs). The data for 1975 regarding the top 100 markets were figured by the authors from information supplied by *Broadcasting Yearbook 1976*. For markets 101 and up, the authors relied on research done by the Association of Independent Television Stations, Inc., which supplied information as of April 1, 1975.

The reader should note in Table 181–B that the total number of network affiliates for 1975 includes 65 satellite-affiliate stations not listed in the market-breakdown columns. The reader should also be aware that the authors defined a "network affiliate" as a station with a contractual right of first refusal on network programs. Clearly, the data presented in this table are subject to wide variations in reliability, since they were drawn from several different sources. The authors believe, however, that the resulting overall percentage trends represent actual conditions.

Further Information

The sources listed in Units 170 and 180 are of value to the reader seeking further information on television network affiliates. The FCC's *Network Broadcasting* (1958) is especially useful. For a narrative history, see Bergreen (1980), while current policy problems are highlighted with useful statistical information in the FCC volume, *New Television Networks* (1980), including discussion of the options for various kinds of "fourth" networks. For cable networks, see Table 590–B.

190
CABLE TELEVISION SYSTEMS

Interpretation of the Tables

Cable television originated in 1949, when communities in poor reception areas began erecting "community" antennas on nearby hills. Cables were run from these antennas to the homes of subscribers, who would underwrite costs by paying an installation charge and a monthly maintenance fee. By the mid–1960s, cable systems had expanded into areas already served by one or more TV signals, in order to pull in a diversity of distant signals. By the late 1960s, an increasing number of cable systems were originating their own programming as well (see Unit 590).

From 1965 to early 1972, the FCC limited expansion of cable systems into the top 100 markets, until a detailed and definitive set of rules could be issued for the regulation of cable systems. Throughout this period, a combination of economic uncertainty and ever more complicated layers of local, state, and federal regulations severely limited the potential of cable television to become a dominant new communications industry. After 1977, cable system expansion had begun again as a result of improving economic conditions and several court decisions in 1977 which struck down the FCC's restrictive pay-cable regulations.

Tables 190–A and 190–B illustrate the relatively slow growth of cable systems throughout the United States during the past two decades. Table 190–B reveals the more rapid expansion of cable in low-population suburban counties, where reception is sometimes less reliable and where the FCC regulatory policies have been less restrictive. Cable growth in major urban areas (the "A" counties in Table 190–B) has generally been limited by: (1) the high cost of building cable systems in cities, (2) the difficulty of supplying innovative programming to residents already well-served by broadcast television and other media; (3) the confusion over the complex cable regulations, especially prevalent in the major market areas, and (4) the difficulties of obtaining investment capital for the less affluent core-city areas.

Cable system expansion has also been limited in the rural areas (the "D" counties), where the costs involved in connecting widely dispersed populations are prohibitive. In view of these facts, it seems likely that most cable system growth will continue to be found in the suburban areas (the "B" and "C" counties). However, the lifting of the FCC's pay-cable restrictions in 1977 promoted cable growth generally, since pay-cable operations offer a good potential for highly profitable returns on an investment (see Unit 195).

Table 190–C, in combination with the data of Table 190–A, suggests that cable television did not begin to serve a significant proportion of the country's population (perhaps 5 percent) until after 1968. The service then tripled in another eight years. It is important to be aware, however, that statistics concerning cable growth can be misleading. Cable systems with fewer than 1,000 subscribers outnumber all other size categories. Yet the largest cable systems, with 10,000 or more subscribers, have grown substantially since 1970, while the smaller systems have remained essentially static in number. If data on the mean and median number of subscribers per system were available, the real effect of additional large systems (see Unit 290) would be more apparent than the simple growth trend indicated by the "average" column of Table 190–A.

Table 190-A   Number of Cable Television Systems, 1952-1983

Year	Number of Systems	Number of Subscribers (In Thousands)	Percent of TV Homes with Cable	Average Number of Subscribers per System
1952	70	14	0.1	200
1953	150	30	0.2	200
1954	300	65	0.3	217
1955	400	150	0.5	375
1956	450	300	0.9	667
1957	500	350	0.9	700
1958	525	450	1.1	857
1959	560	550	1.3	982
1960	640	650	1.4	1,016
1961	700	725	1.5	1,036
1962	800	850	1.7	1,063
1963	1,000	950	1.9	950
1964	1,200	1,085	2.1	904
1965	1,325	1,275	2.4	962
1966	1,570	1,575	2.9	1,003
1967	1,770	2,100	3.8	1,186
1968	2,000	2,800	4.4	1,400
1969	2,260	3,600	6.1	1,593
1970	2,490	4,500	7.6	1,807
1971	2,639	5,300	8.8	2,008
1972	2,841	6,000	9.6	2,112
1973	2,991	7,300	11.1	2,441
1974	3,158	8,700	13.0	2,755
1975	3,506	9,800	14.3	2,795
1976	3,651	10,800	15.3	2,958
1977	3,832	11,900	16.6	3,105
1978	3,875	13,000	17.4	3,355
1979	4,150	14,100	18.5	3,398
1980	4,225	16,000	20.0	3,787
1981	4,375	18,300	25.3	4,183
1982	4,825	21,000	28.3	4,352
1983	5,748	26,400	35.0[a]	4,513

Source: Television Factbook, annual issues; all figures are estimates as of January 1, except 1983 which is as of March 1st. Note: [a]estimate.

Table 190-B Percentage of Households with Cable Service, by County Size, 1968-1982

	County Size				
Year	A	B	C	D	All Counties
1968	1	4	15	9	4
1969	2	5	17	10	6
1970	2	5	17	11	8
1971	2	6	20	12	9
1972	3	8	23	14	10
1973	4	9	25	15	11
1974	4	10	26	15	13
1975	5	11	27	17	14
1976	6	14	30	18	16
1977	7	16	32	20	17
1978	8	17	33	21	17
1979	8	19	35	22	18
1980	10	22	38	24	21
1981	15	31	43	29	26
1982	23	39	48	35	33

Source: A. C. Nielsen Co. data as printed in annual issues of *Television Factbook*. All data as of May except 1969 (November), 1970 (March), and 1982 (July). Note: County-size definitions as used by Nielsen: "A"—All counties in the 25 largest metropolitan areas according to the 1970 census. "B"—All counties not in "A" with populations of over 150,000 or in metropolitan areas over 150,000. "C"—All counties not in "A" or "B" with populations over 35,000 or in metropolitan areas over 35,000. "D"—All other counties.

Sources

Data for all three tables in this unit were taken from *Television Factbook*, which takes an annual survey of the cable industry. Table 190-B is A. C. Nielsen Co. data, gathered as a part of its larger television ratings business. Data for all tables should be considered fairly close estimates. But as different systems supply data on different measures, totals will often vary (as with tables 190-A and 190-C).

Further Information

For an introduction to what cable is and how it operates, see Hollowell (1977, 1980, and 1983), and Baldwin-McVoy (1983). The National Cable Television Association can supply recent statistical information and other data. *Television Factbook* and *Broadcasting Yearbook* annual provide detailed directories of all systems. For basic cable networks, see Table 590-B.

Table 190-C   Number of Cable Television Systems, by System Size, 1970–1983

Size of Systems (Number of Homes)	1970	1971	1972	1973	1974	1975	1976	1977	1978	1979	1980	1981	1982	1983
20,000+ Homes	8	12	22	31	42	53	68	85	101	122	N/A	205	N/A	296
10,000–19,999 Homes	50	60	83	119	142	171	181	197	227	244	N/A	301	N/A	369
5,000–9,999 Homes	144	176	215	252	289	328	345	368	390	391	N/A	469	N/A	554
2,000–4,999 Homes	402	458	566	593	644	685 ⎫	1,407	1,460	1,471	1,548	N/A	1,715	N/A	1,977
1,000–1,999 Homes	423	462	500	545	605	639 ⎭								
500–999 Homes	427	476	514	587	577	602 ⎫	1,688	732	725	730	N/A	816	N/A	990
Below 500 Homes	776	765	843	852	851	862 ⎭		1,047	1,058	1,071	N/A	1,073	N/A	1,454
Systems of Unspecified Size	260	169	96	53	40	65	26	22	25	74	N/A	58	N/A	108
Total Number of Systems	2,490	2,578	2,839	3,032	3,190	3,405	3,715	3,911	3,997	4,180	N/A	4,637	N/A	5,748

Source: Television Factbook, annual issues. Data is for various months: March (1970–72), June (1973), September (1974–1979), June (1981), and March (1983). *Note:* Total number of systems varies from Table 190-A. See text.

195
PAY TELEVISION
SYSTEMS

Interpretation of the Tables

Regular pay cable operation began in November 1972, when Home Box Office, a subsidiary of Time, Inc., began service in Wilkes-Barre, Pennsylvania. Other similar services were initiated soon after, all providing a combination of new feature films and live sporting events. Typically, the service was provided to homes already receiving basic cable service. The cable household paid an additional charge for the pay channel, in a flat monthly fee or on a per-program basis.

Most pay cable programming was "bicycled" (i.e., mailed or shipped) from system to system, as there was no adequate means of interconnection. There were some attempts at transmission by microwave, but the costs were such that regional, let alone national service, remained out of the question. Even with this limited potential, the pay cable enterprises were further limited by FCC regulation in the early 1970s, when the commission, under pressure from broadcasters, restricted the categories of films or sporting events that could be carried on pay cable.

The real expansion of pay cable began in September 1975, when Home Box Office became the first pay cable operator to distribute programming by means of communications satellite—thus allowing wide coverage (to subscribing systems with receiving dishes) at a far lower cost. Evidence of this rapid expansion can be seen in Table 195–A, in the figures after 1975. A second system began use of satellite transmission early in 1978.

The most important factor in the growth of pay cable was the lifting of the FCC restrictive policies by an Appeals Court decision in 1977. This decision effectively removed all limitations on pay cable content, and as a result, many local cable systems began their own pay channels. Some local systems began to carry a local or regional pay service as well as one of the national distributors, such as Home Box Office. By the late 1970s, many observers in cable television were crediting the income potential of pay systems as a key factor behind the growth of overall cable penetration (see Unit 190).

Table 195-A details the expansion in number of cable systems carrying at least one channel of pay programming. By the early 1980s, the important pay cable trend was termed "tiering," where two, three, and more pay channels were offered to subscribers on a sliding scale of monthly fees.

Although older in concept, subscription television, or STV, developed later due to long regulatory delay and fears of the movie and television industry over pay-TV competition. Only in 1977 did the first (other than experimental) STV station take to the air. Into the early 1980s, STV expansion was limited by FCC limits such as the "complement of four" rule which called for at least four commercial stations in a market before permission would be given for a (fifth) to undertake STV. While pay cable options appeared even on rural cable systems, the economics of STV restricted the medium to the largest markets. By the early 1980s, while restrictive FCC rules had largely been lifted, competition from multi-channel cable systems was severely cutting into potential STV markets. Indeed, by mid-1983, it was evident that STV had already "peaked" and was in actual decline. By September of 1983, for example, eight fewer stations than a year earlier were broadcasting pay programming, the operations having converted to full-time indepenent "free" TV status. The basic problem cited widely by firms cutting back—or getting totally out of STV—was that cable penetration increases combined with the poor general economy of the early 1980s was cutting off the ability of STV to obtain even break-even audience penetration. Specifically, STV operating expenses, when added to a rising rate of subscriber disconnects to the single-channel offerings, made many STV operations marginal—so much so that cable and the economy provided the final push to close down.

In light of the decline in STV's fortunes, confusion about DBS, direct broadcast satellite operations projected for 1986 and beyond, was expressed, though DBS offered three to five channels per service. The problem in this case was the start-up, including design and launch, costs—again, in the face of powerful cable expansion.

Likewise with the multipoint distribution systems, or MDS. This common carrier (not broadcast) service has long existed, but only became economically viable when, in 1974, the FCC allowed television channel bandwidth (6 MHz) MDS channels. MDS had, by the early 1980s, spread to many of the top 50 markets, and in some cities more than one MDS service operated. Using the 2 GHz spectrum range, MDS suffered from severely limited coverage (up to 10 miles and seldom more) and the requirement that apartment buildings or homes use expensive converter equipment to translate the video signal from the 2 GHz range down to broadcast frequencies for reception on a normal home receiver. Like STV stations, the MDS licensee controls the facilities and licenses out the programming to a separate entity (this being required in the common carrier MD field).

Of the three pay video options, pay cable is by far the most widespread (see also Unit 695) and best known. For one thing, a single cable system can provide several different pay signals, while both STV and MDS are limited to one channel per service at a time.

But what has made pay cable especially valuable is the advent of satellite networks (see Table 590–B, and Unit 695). Table 195–B details the growth in the capacity of communications satellites (domestic satellites only), the number of transponders carried (devices which can receive and then re-transmit TV signals, one transponder equaling one television channel), the number of video services provided (HBO being the first in 1975), and the number of earth stations able to receive the signals.

The earth station market shows explosive growth around 1980 both because of FCC deregulation of technical and licensing requirements for receive-only earth stations, and because of economies of scale bringing down the per-unit earth station cost from something over $100,000 in the mid-1970s to often under a tenth of that five years later. Cable systems were the first, and remain the largest, user of satellite transponders because of the number of "basic" or free, and pay video signals directed to cable systems by programmers using satellite delivery. While used by commercial networks for news specials, regular full-time use of satellites in place of terrestrial land-line and microwave network interconnection was first accomplished by the noncommercial PBS television, and later by the NPR radio networks.

Table 195–A Growth of Pay Television Systems, 1973–1982

Year	Pay Cable Systems		STV Stations	MDS
	Systems	As a Percent of Basic Cable Systems		
1973	10	—	—	—
1974	45	1	—	4
1975	170	24	—	11
1976	364	22	—	17
1977	604	25	2	27
1978	1,029	35	3	29
1979	1,822	41	6	44
1980	3,072	51	14	54
1981	1,975	69	24	73
1982	4,826	76	29	99

Source: Pay Cable, National Cable Television Association, Cable Television Developments (Jan. 1983), citing Paul Kagan Associates; STV and MDS Paul Kagan Associates publications. Note: Figures as of December 31 each year; MDS figures as of June 30 each year for 1974–1976.

Table 195-B   Development of U.S. Satellite Distribution Facilities, 1975–1983

Year	Number of Available Domestic Satellites	Total Transponders Carried	Video Services:			Earth Stations		
			Basic	Pay	Total	Radio	TV	Cable
1975	3	48	—	1	1	N/A	N/A	N/A
1977	6	120	3	1	4	N/A	N/A	161
1979	8	156	14	4	18	N/A	150	1,579
1981	8	156	19	8	27	1,200	300	3,100
1983	19	420	30	11	41	4,856	970	8,000

Sources: See text for details. Data through 1981 from Sterling, in Compaine (1982), p. 416. Data for 1983 is from a variety of sources as reported to the author from the National Association of Broadcasters and the National Cable Television Association. For further information on video services, see Units 690 and 695.

Note: [a]Many of these are for business service and carry no audio or video broadcast services.

Table 195-A data are all drawn from publications of Paul Kagan Associates, and provide data as of June 30th in each case except 1973, which is for April. Pay cable information is from the Kagan's *Pay TV Census* of December 1980. STV data from Kagan's *Pay TV Newsletter* (July 31, 1981), p. 5. MDS information from "Statistical Progress of MDS," from the Kagan's *MDS Databook 1981,* p. 56. Because of different methods of counting and varied sources within each industry, the figures given here should not be taken as strictly comparable, and should be considered as close estimates. Pay cable data for 1981 includes some 800 systems carrying more than one pay cable service, or tier. There is no official government gathering of data for these businesses.

Table 195-B information comes from a variety of sources, chiefly trade magazine reports. The trade-weekly *Cablevision* is the source for data on the number of domestic communication satellites and transponders in service, with satellite and transponder information for 1983 from *Satellite Digest,* direct to the author. It should be noted, however, that in 1981, only about a third of the transponders shown were used for video transmission (the others were for voice and data communication), and many of those were used part-time for network news feeds and other applications not directly aimed at viewers. Data on earth stations is highly suspect as so many are now in service and no adequate records have been kept. The estimates here, supplied to the author by HBO, are from the following sources:

1. Radio figures through 1981 from *TV/Radio Age* (May 18, 1981), p. 37; 1983 data direct to the author from the National Association of Broadcasters.

2. Television data from *Broadcasting* (August 10, 1981) for data through 1981 (the 1979 figures reflect primarily Public Broadcasting Service, or noncommercial, TV stations while by 1981, some 150 commercial stations were estimated to have TV receive-only dishes); 1983 data direct to the author from the National Association of Broadcasters.
3. Cable data through 1979 to the author from HBO researchers, citing Kagan Associates information for late 1977; *Satellite Communications* (May 1, 1979) projecting data for October of that year; and *TV Digest* direct to the author for October 1981 estimates; 1983 data from National Cable Television Association, citing Kagan.

Further Information

Useful background information on these "new technologies" can be had in Gross (1983), Hollowell (1977, 1980, and 1983), Mahoney et al. (1980), and (for STV) in Howard and Carroll (1980). *Cablevision* had developed by 1980 into the single most important trade-weekly in cable and related media, with a wealth of statistical information. Paul Kagan Associates *The Pay TV Newsletter,* along with its various spinoff annuals and other newer newsletters, is the key source for trends in STV and MDS. Developments in this field are so rapid that the few books available are chiefly for background—periodicals are crucial to keep up. A useful exception is the annual *Home Video and Cable Yearbook*.

SECTION TWO
OWNERSHIP
OF
ELECTRONIC MEDIA

201
MEDIA CONGLOMERATES

Interpretation of the Table

While a good deal of attention has been given to broadcast, cable, and newspaper chains, and to cross-ownership of media outlets (see Units 261, 262, 270, 280, and 290), there has not been as much research on the relatively recent phenomenon of multimedia firms in mass communications. Table 201-A provides a very approximate measure for a single year of firms which have acquired holdings in several different media across all markets.

Table 201-A names firms considered leaders (in some measure of size) in four media, three, two, and leaders in but one medium while often holding other media as well. Radio and television are combined into a single medium for this list, as otherwise it would have been much longer with a disproportionate number of small companies. Companies are listed alphabetically within sections designating the different types of media they own. Measures of "leading" vary by medium:

- Newspapers and magazines are determined by total circulation,
- Books are measured by revenue of the publisher,
- Theatrical film is determined by the number of theaters owned,
- Broadcasting is measured by its potential audience, and
- Cable is determined by the number of subscribers to the multiple system operator (MSO) controlled by each entity.

Thus, there is considerable variance in determination of "leading" by various media, making any direct comparison of figures misleading. So this table offers merely two very approximate measures: a "leading" firm is one of the largest (typically the top 10–15 in a given medium) in terms of the measure noted above, while "other holdings" less than "leading" are also indicated with no real sense of major or minor investment or audience penetration. The result is that Table 201–A simply provides a somewhat fuzzy snapshot of multimedia activity for some 65 different companies. This data is current to the end of 1981.

Two other limitations are noteworthy. For one thing, company holdings change rapidly so that any such snapshot, even a fuzzily-defined one, goes out of date quickly. Secondly, the table likely underestimates the degree of cross-media ownership due to the confused nature of such information. Subsidiaries of a company will often be listed by different names than the corporate parent. Some companies are privately held with but limited public information available.

Table 201–A Leading Firms in One or More Media Segments, with Other Media Holdings, 1981

Company	News-papers	Broad-casting	Cable TV	Magazines	Books	Theatrical Film[a]
Leader in Four Media:						
Newhouse	+		+	+	+	
Leader in Three Media:						
CBS Inc.		+	0	+	+	0
Cox[b]	+	+	+			
Time Inc.	0	0	+	+	+	
Times Mirror Co.	+	0	+	0	+	
Leader in Two Media:						
Gannett	+	+				
Hearst	+	0		+	0	
McGraw-Hill				+	+	
New York Times Co.	+	0	0	+	0	
Reader's Digest Assn.				+	+	
E. W. Scripps[c]	+	+				
Storer Broadcasting		+	+			
Tribune Co.	+	+	0			
Warner Communications			+		0	+
Washington Post Co.	0	+		+	0	
Westinghouse		+	+			
Leader in One Medium:						
Allied Artists						+
American Broadcasting Cos.		+		0	0	
American Multi Cinema						+
Avco-Embassy Pictures[e]						+
Bonneville		+				
Capital Cities Communications	0	+		0		
Charter Co.				+		
Columbia Pictures Industries	0					+
Continental Cablevision			+			
Doubleday		0	0		+	

Table 201–A Leading Firms in One or More Media Segments, with Other Media Holdings, 1981 (cont.)

Company	News-papers	Broad-casting	Cable TV	Magazines	Books	Theatrical Film[a]
Dow Jones Co.	+		0	0	0	
Encyclopaedia Britannica					+	
Field Enterprises	0	+				
Gaylord Broadcasting Co.	0	+				
General Cinema			0			+
General Electric		+				
Grolier					+	
Gulf + Western					0	+
Harcourt Brace Jovanovich				0	+	
Inner City		+				
Knight-Ridder	+	0	0		0	
Macmillan					+	
MCA Inc.				0	0	+
Meredith	0			+	0	
Metro-Goldwyn-Mayer						+
Metromedia		+				
Playboy Enterprises				+	0	
Plough		+				
Plitt Theatres						+
Prentice-Hall					+	
RCA		+				
RKO General[d]		+	0			
Rogers UA Cablesystems			+			
Sammons Communications			+			
San Juan Racing		+				
Scholastic Magazines				+	0	
Scott & Fetzer[f]					+	
SFN Cos.					+	
Taft Broadcasting		+				
Tele-Communications, Inc.	0		+			
Thomson Newspapers[g]	+					
Triangle Publishing				+		
Twentieth Century-Fox		0				+
United Artists Theatre Circuit						+
United Cable			+			
Viacom International		0	+			
Walt Disney Productions						+
Ziff Davis		0		+		

Source: Compaine et al. (1982) pp. 452–453 copyright © 1982 Knowledge Industry Publications, Inc.

Notes: + = Leading firm. 0 = Area of other holdings. [a]Production, distribution or exhibition. [b]Includes interests of Cox family, including Cox Enterprises and 40% interest in Cox Communications. [c]Includes Scripps-Howard Newspapers and Scripps Broadcasting. [d]Parent is General Tire Co. In 1982 RKO lost the license for WNAC-TV in Boston. [e]Avco-Embassy Pictures was sold in December 1981 to Embassy Communications, jointly owned by Norman Lear and Jerry Perenchio. [f]Parent of World Book-Childcraft International. [g]Controlling interest held by International Thomson Organisation, Ltd., which has other media interests.

Source

This table is taken from Compaine (1982), pp. 452–453. It is, in turn, a summary of many other tables of data in that study, including the data for broadcasting reproduced in the present volume in Tables 270–B and 280–C, the main input data for the column in Table 201–A on broadcasting, and the main input for the column in Table 290–B on cable TV. All of those original tables are based on a variety of industry trade directories and government sources. The lack of specificity in this table is due in part to this multiplicity of sources, for the details would be misleading. Users should thus consider Table 201–A as an approximation, at one point in time, of the pattern of media conglomerates.

Further Information

For a far more detailed and exact portrayal of media conglomerates as of 1977, see Sterling and Haight (1978), pp. 65–72. Useful background studies on media concentration issues include Rucker (1968), Baer et al. (1974), Seiden (1975), Phillips (1977), Federal Trade Commission (1979), U.S. House of Representatives, Committee on Energy and Commerce (1981), Compaine et al. (1982), and *The Knowledge Industry 200* (1983). For studies more specifically dealing with electronic media, see the suggested readings for other Units in this section.

260
BROADCASTING
OWNERSHIP PATTERNS

Interpretation of the Tables

This is the first of several units which analyze the ownership of both commercial and public broadcast stations in the United States. Table 260–A provides summary information on the number and prices of commercial radio and television stations sold over the 40–year period from 1938 to 1982. The recent marked decline in the sales of combination radio-television operations is due to a 1971 FCC ruling which requires divestiture of such combinations by the new owner within a specified period of time after purchase.

As Table 260–A indicates, the prices of broadcast stations rose rather sharply in the late 1960s and early 1970s. Clearly, the inflation rate during those years was largely responsible for these increases. But another important factor in this trend has been the scarcity of new broadcast channels. The lack of opportunities to place new stations on the air makes existing stations all the more valuable and expensive. The result is a narrowing of the number of potential buyers with sufficient capital to purchase a station—which means that more and more stations are being absorbed by the larger and wealthier group owners (see Units 270 and 280).

Table 260–B offers a comparison of the number of minority-owned outlets in television and radio with the number of outlets for those entire industries. Only in commercial television does minority ownership exceed 1 percent of the total. While still a very small proportion of broadcast outlets, minority ownership of broadcast stations has increased over the five'year period shown, largely thanks to the combined efforts of both the FCC (distress sale and tax certificate programs, and a merit for minority ownership in comparative proceedings), and the broadcast industry (fund raising and advice and assistance to minority interests). Of the stations shown in Table 260–B, 128 (11 television and 117 radio) are controlled by blacks, 31 (3 television and 28 radio) by Hispanics, 3 (radio) by native-Americans, and two (also radio) by Asian-Americans. Needless to say, however, given the proportion of these groups in society (especially if regional concentrations are taken into account), equality of ownership along racial lines has a long way to go (see Unit 290 for minority control of cable systems).

Table 260–C provides information on ownership concentration among companies which manufacture broadcast-related equipment. From 1954 to 1972, the concentration of control in the manufacture of radio and television receivers decreased slightly. However, this decline is due more to massive imports (see Units 750 and 760) than to the increasing number of manufacturing firms. (The 1954 data on radio/TV receivers is also not strictly comparable to later information.) Ownership concentrations in the production of cathode-ray picture tubes have also declined slightly, but it is noteworthy that more than half of the companies which were operating in 1963 no longer report any manufacturing activity. (Competition from imports and the increased complexity of color tubes are probably the major factors in the decreasing numbers of companies in this field.) The "radio-television equipment" category is a very broad one which includes all broadcast and studio equipment.

Table 260–D provides a glimpse at a number of interesting relationships. Listed here are 16 of the largest communications-electronics firms, in descending order of overall corporate revenue for 1980. Only firms actually owning broadcast stations were included. The table provides data on the role of broadcasting's contribution to corporate revenues as well as two different trade magazine rankings of firm size. The *Broadcasting* "Top 100" list includes electronic firms with manufacturing or cable interests, while the older *Fortune* "500" list includes a more diversified list of companies. Note the 1970–1980 comparison of rankings for the companies listed—comparatively speaking, most of the companies are smaller in 1980 than in 1970, when the earnings and growth of many non-broadcast firms are taken into account. But the data provided here, while perhaps indicative, are too scattered to clearly provide any trends one way or another.

Sources

Table 260–A is based on FCC data from *Broadcasting Yearbook 1981*. The source provides information for the odd-numbered years omitted on the table, but apparently there is no consistent information available for the years 1947–1953. The authors computed averages by dividing dollar totals by the number of stations sold in each category. Only those sales approved by the FCC are included. However, since any license transfer must be approved by the FCC, these figures are probably quite accurate. The averages for any one year may be skewed by unusually large or small sales. As of 1978, AM and FM station sales are counted as separate transactions.

Table 260–B is developed from two different sources for the two years shown—and neither provides any detail on how the stations were counted up (the total outlets figure comes from Units 170 and 180). So the data must be considered an approximation. It is assumed (but no more than that) that all stations listed are, in fact, under the control (over 50% of stock) of one or more minorities.

Table 260–C is from the *Census of Manufacturers*, now done in years ending in "2" and "7." It indirectly suggests the impact of foreign imports in that concentration has changed little over the period covered—and in some cases has even decreased, a trend generally opposite that of industry in general.

Table 260–D is based on the listing of "The Top 100 Companies in Electronic Communications," *Broadcasting* (January 5, 1981), pp. 39–72, plus the *Fortune* "500" Directory issues of May 1970, May 4, 1981, and June 15, 1981. Missing information (usually 1980 corporate revenues, and some data on stations owned or the contribution of broadcasting to corporate reve-

Table 260-A Sales of Broadcast Stations, with Average Price, 1938–1982

Year	Number of Transactions				Average Price per Each FCC-Approved Transaction (In Dollars)			Inflation Index (1972 = 100)
	Radio Only	TV Only	Radio/ TV	Total	Radio Only	TV Only	Radio/ TV	
1938	20	—	—	20	46,039	—	—	28.3
1940	12	—	—	12	98,708	—	—	28.8
1942	21	—	—	21	92,404	—	—	32.5
1944	58	—	—	58	226,871	—	—	36.6
1946	52	—	—	52	441,589	—	—	43.9
1954	187	27	18	232	54,674	885,435	1,456,295	59.7
1956	316	21	24	361	103,049	849,066	2,717,169	62.9
1958	407	23	17	447	122,526	730,273	3,580,742	66.0
1960	345	21	10	376	150,039	1,091,915	2,464,840	68.7
1962	306	16	8	330	195,793	1,437,977	2,352,843	70.6
1964	430	36	20	486	121,620	2,396,513	3,359,288	72.7
1966	367	31	11	409	208,811	986,259	2,591,864	76.8
1968	316	20	9	345	225,667	1,679,403	5,284,070	82.6
1970	268	19	3	290	321,988	4,602,846	346,155	91.4
1972	239	37	—	276	478,764	4,240,699	—	100.0
1974	369	24	5	398	457,989	4,957,644	3,960,000	116.4
1976	413	32	3	448	437,442	3,389,364	600,000	132.3
1978	586	51	5	642	565,797	5,680,804	6,090,000	150.4
1980	424	35	3	462	801,024	15,261,428	9,000,000	178.4
1982	597	30	—	627	788,480	17,589,180	—	206.8

Source: 1938–46 data from the FCC (1947), p. 87, while the remainder is from *Broadcasting* (January 10, 1983) p. 46. Average prices computed by the author from dollar volume figures in sources. Inflation index is the Gross National Product (GNP) deflator.

Table 260–B   Minority-Owned Broadcast Outlets, 1977 and 1982

	1977		1982	
Type of Outlet	total outlets	minority	total outlets	minority
Television:				
Commercial VHF	514	1	524	9
Commercial UHF	208	7	250	5
Noncommercial	243	—	271	4
Total	965	8	1045	18
Radio:				
Commercial AM	4469	32	4634	100
Commercial FM	2845	9	3349	50
Noncommercial	861	2	1118	28
Total	8175	43	9101	178

Sources: Communications Resource Center (1977); National Association of Broadcasters (1982).

Table 260–C   Percentage of Broadcast Equipment Sales Controlled by Top U.S. Manufacturers, 1954–1977

Company Type and Year	Number of Companies Reporting	Percent of Sales Controlled by:			
		Top 4	Top 8	Top 20	Top 50
Radio-TV Receiving Sets[a]					
1954[b]	N/A	42	62	87	N/A
1963	322	41	62	82	94
1967	303	49	69	85	95
1972	343	49	71	86	96
1977	546	51	65	81	92
Cathode-Ray TV Picture Tubes					
1963	148	91	95	97	99
1967	95	84	98	99+	99+
1972	69	83	97	99+	99+
1977[c]	125	58	78	95	99
Radio-Television Equipment[d]					
1963	1,001	29	45	69	84
1967	1,111	22	37	61	81
1972	1,524	19	33	58	77
1977	1,873	20	33	57	73

Source: 1977 *Census of Manufacturers.* Notes: [a]Includes phonographs and public address systems. [b]1954 information is not directly comparable to later years as the means of computing companies in the category changed. [c]In the 1977 Census, due to the overall decline in tube manufacture, the Cathode-Ray TV Picture Tube category was collapsed into a single category of all electronic tubes, including receiving and transmitting devices. Thus, 1977 data is not directly comparable to earlier information. [d]Includes electronic communications equipment and parts (except for telephone and telegraph facilities), high energy particle accelerator systems and parts, and other related equipment.

Table 260-D   Selected Leading Broadcasting Firms, 1980

Firm	Corporate Revenues 1980 (In Millions of Dollars)	Fortune "500" Ranking 1980	Fortune "500" Ranking 1970	Broadcasting Top "100" Rank 1980	Role of Broadcasting: Contribution to Corporate Revenues	Role of Broadcasting: Stations Held Radio	Role of Broadcasting: Stations Held TV
General Electric	24,959	10	4	1	N/A	8	3
Westinghouse	8,514	34	17	4	4	12	6
RCA	8,011	41	21	5	19	8	5
CBS	3,963	94	99[a]	13	41	14	5
ABC	2,256	168	159[a]	18	87	13	5
General Tire	2,215	171	106	19	N/A	14	4
Times-Mirror	1,857	194	256	21	7	—	7
Schering-Plough	1,740	209	406/563[b]	22	N/A	12	—
Gannett	1,215	270	532	26	10	13	7
McGraw-Hill	1,000	300	251	30	5	—	4
Capital Cities	472	485	—	45	35	13	6
Metromedia	454	497	—	46	44	13	7
Cox	309	601	—	57	50	12	5
Taft	236	723	—	62	43	12	7
Storer	197	788	—	68	N/A	1	7
Scripps-Howard	77	—	—	84	93	6	6

Source: Sterling, in Compaine et al. (1982), p. 326. Notes: [a]This is a simulated ranking assigned by *Fortune* as the firm did not definitionally qualify for top 500 ranking. [b]Existed as two separate firms in 1970.

nues) came from Standard & Poor's *Standard Corporate Records.* As the rankings and financial information are based on widely reported and publicly verifiable and standardized financial reports, the rankings can be assumed to be accurate at least as to order, if not specific figures. Not all companies report the role of broadcast income on corporate revenues. Of stations owned, the maximum figure which can be listed would be 14 for radio (7 AM and 7 FM) and 7 for television.

Further Information

The most concise overview of both trends in and regulation of broadcast ownership is Sterling, in Compaine et al. (1982), Chapter 6. See also FTC (1979), Levin (1980), Bunce (1976), Howard (1976), and Cherington et al. (1971). Very policy-oriented discussions dealing mainly with video are found in U.S. House of Representatives, Committee on Energy and Commerce (1981). The best overview of studies and data on impact of concentration is in Baer et al. (1974), while a useful legal analysis is in Branscomb (1975). Statistics and directories appear in the many annual yearbooks of the trade already discussed, especially those of *Broadcasting*, *TV Digest*, and *Cablevision*, the first two of which regularly report station sales statistics (including news stories of especially high prices).

NEWSPAPER–BROADCASTING CROSS-OWNERSHIP

Interpretation of the Table

Table 261–A reveals national trends in cross-ownership of newspapers and broadcast stations, whether in a single Standard Metropolitan Statistical Area (SMSA) market or in different markets. Historically, most cross-ownership of media outlets has been within single markets. In 1955, for example, 82 percent of newspaper-owned television stations occupied the same market as their owners. But by 1974, only 46 percent of such stations occupied their owners' market areas (Bunce, 1976, p. 45). Apparently, a new pattern has developed.

To some extent, this shift may be due to increasing regulatory attempts to discourage common ownership of multiple means of advertising and news communication within a single market area. Critics first expressed this concern in the late 1930s, when newspaper owners began to buy up AM radio stations as a means of protecting themselves from radio's potential competition in news coverage and advertising. From 1941 to 1944, the FCC investigated this phenomenon and heard arguments from both sides regarding newspaper-broadcasting cross-ownership. However, no specific conclusions were reached.

In the years following World War II, the press became a prominent owner of both FM radio and television stations. At the same time, its control of AM radio began a slight, and then an absolute, decline. Newspaper control of both AM and FM radio continued to drop throughout the 1950s, as more stations controlled by non-newspaper owners went on the air. The press-owned portion of television stations also decreased, though very slowly and less dramatically, from initial levels of over one-third of all television operations on the air to approximately one-fourth of these outlets in the 1960s. Since 1974, newspaper ownership of television stations has increased slightly.

The declines in newspaper ownership in the 1960s and 1970s relieved regulatory concern to such an extent that, when the FCC finally did issue new rules in 1975, media cross-owners escaped forced divestiture in all but eight small cities, where the *only* newspaper controlled the one radio or television station in town. However, the data accumulated by the FCC during its 1970–1975 investigation soon became the basis of new litigation. In the spring of 1977, the Court of Appeals for the District of Columbia ordered the FCC to reconsider the issue; and this time, the end result was a complete prohibition of same-market cross-ownership combinations. The Supreme Court in mid-1978 upheld the original FCC decision.

Unlike national trends in common ownership, regional patterns of concentration still have not been adequately documented. Many critics suggest that cross-ownership problems are most serious among the small, one-paper, one-station markets. Other critics are more concerned about the major, top-20 markets, where newspaper-television combinations are centered. And so the arguments continue—with the newspapers stating that they have as much right as anybody to control stations, while their opponents stress the dangers (not only for news and entertainment communication, but for advertising as well) that could result from such concentrations of ownership among different media in the same market.

Sources

The Table 261–A figures through 1960 are based on information in Sterling (1969), which in turn was drawn from Willey and Rice (1933), for 1922–1930 data is as of June 30; from Wagner (1976), for 1931–1941 data is as of January 1; and from Levin (1960), for 1945–1960 data is as of January 1. Data after 1960 were initially gathered and published by *Broadcasting Yearbook*. The author employed these data as they were aggregated in the *Statistical Abstract*.

Figures for total stations on the air (commercial only, except for AM, which includes about 30 educational stations) were taken from the sources listed in Units 170 and 180. All percentages were calculated by the author. With so many different sources and means of data-gathering, the reader is cautioned to avoid a strict comparison of all the information in Table 261–A, and to focus instead on the overall trends.

Further Information

Newspaper-owned or -controlled radio and television stations are listed annually in *Broadcasting Yearbook*. *Television Factbook* also provides information on press-television station ties. The most important historical analysis of newspaper-broadcasting cross-ownership is Levin (1960), updated by Levin (1971). The reader will find the newspaper industry's views and studies in "Comments of American Newspaper Publishers Association in Opposition" (1971). Baer et al. (1974) present a useful policy option review.

Table 261-A Newspaper-Broadcasting Cross-Ownership, 1922–1982

Year	AM Stations			FM Stations			Television Stations		
	Total Stations	Newspaper-owned		Total Stations	Newspaper-owned		Total Stations	Newspaper-owned	
		Number	Percent of Total		Number	Percent of Total		Number	Percent of Total
1922	382	48	12.6	—	—	—	—	—	—
1923	556	60	10.8	—	—	—	—	—	—
1924	530	38	7.2	—	—	—	—	—	—
1925	571	33	5.8	—	—	—	—	—	—
1926	528	38	7.2	—	—	—	—	—	—
1927	681	38	5.6	—	—	—	—	—	—
1928	677	41	6.1	—	—	—	—	—	—
1929	606	34	5.6	—	—	—	—	—	—
1930	618	36	5.8	—	—	—	—	—	—
1931	612	68	11.1	—	—	—	—	—	—
1932	604	78	12.9	—	—	—	—	—	—
1933	599	80	13.4	—	—	—	—	—	—
1934	583	90	15.4	—	—	—	—	—	—
1935	585	122	20.9	—	—	—	—	—	—
1936	616	159	25.8	—	—	—	—	—	—
1937	646	180	27.9	—	—	—	—	—	—
1938	689	203	29.5	—	—	—	—	—	—
1939	722	226	31.3	—	—	—	—	—	—
1940	765	250	32.7	—	—	—	—	—	—
1941	831	249	30.0	—	—	—	—	—	—

Year									
1942–44	N/A	N/A	N/A	N/A	N/A	N/A	N/A	N/A	N/A
1945	12.5	1	8	37.0	17	46	28.3	260	919
1946	N/A	N/A	6	N/A	N/A	48	28.6	271	948
1947	N/A	N/A	12	N/A	N/A	140	30.0	319	1,062
1948	N/A	N/A	16	72.3	331	458	27.4	444	1,621
1949	25.5	13	51	40.0	280	700	24.2	463	1,912
1950	41.8	41	98	37.2	273	733	22.6	472	2,086
1951	42.1	45	107	34.2	231	676	21.8	487	2,232
1952	45.4	49	108	33.3	212	637	20.8	485	2,331
1953	69.0	87	126	34.3	199	580	20.0	478	2,391
1954	36.7	130	354	32.7	183	560	18.6	469	2,521
1955	36.3	149	411	30.8	170	552	17.4	465	2,669
1956	36.3	160	441	28.9	156	540	16.4	463	2,824
1957	33.1	156	471	26.8	142	530	14.7	441	3,008
1958	33.9	168	495	27.0	145	537	13.8	440	3,196
1959	35.5	181	510	24.7	143	578	13.0	431	3,326
1960	34.0	175	515	21.1	145	688	12.4	429	3,456
1961	N/A	N/A	527	N/A	N/A	815	N/A	N/A	3,547
1962	29.8	161	541	15.3	147	960	11.4	412	3,618
1963	N/A	N/A	557	N/A	N/A	1,081	N/A	N/A	3,760
1964	30.9	174	564	12.8	147	1,146	9.9	381	3,854
1965	31.8	181	569	12.5	159	1,270	9.5	383	4,044
1966	29.7	174	585	11.8	170	1,446	9.6	391	4,065
1967	28.2	172	610	10.8	177	1,643	9.4	387	4,121
1968	27.9	177	635	10.3	181	1,753	9.1	383	4,190
1969	27.6	183	662	9.9	191	1,938	8.9	381	4,265

Table 261-A (cont.)

	AM Stations			FM Stations			Television Stations		
	Total Stations	Newspaper-owned		Total Stations	Newspaper-owned		Total Stations	Newspaper-owned	
Year		Number	Percent of Total		Number	Percent of Total		Number	Percent of Total
1970	4,292	394	9.2	2,184	245	11.2	677	189	27.9
1971	4,343	402	9.3	2,196	248	11.3	682	191	28.0
1972	4,374	318	7.3	2,304	209	9.1	693	176	25.4
1973	4,395	325	7.4	2,411	171	7.1	697	178	25.5
1974	4,407	304	6.9	2,502	211	8.4	697	179	25.7
1975	4,432	321	7.2	2,636	236	9.0	706	193	27.3
1976	4,463	320	7.2	2,767	238	8.6	701	197	28.1
1977	4,497	322	7.2	2,837	238	8.4	711	209	29.4
1978	4,513	314	7.0	3,001	238	8.0	716	211	29.5
1979	4,526	319	7.0	3,107	252	8.1	724	221	30.5
1980	4,559	318	7.0	3,155	257	8.1	734	226	30.8
1981	4,589	315	6.9	3,282	264	8.0	756	230	30.4
1982	4,634	311	6.7	3,349	277	8.3	777	246	31.7

Sources: 1922–1960 data: Sterling (1969), pp. 227–236, 254, tables 1 and 2. Sterling drew his material from Willey and Rice (1933), p. 196 (for 1922–1930 data is as of June 30); Wagner (1976), p. 189 (for 1931–1941 data is as of January 1); and Levin (1960), p. 53 (for 1945–1960 data is as of January 1). 1961–1982 data: *1982 Statistical Abstract*, p. 560, using material initially gathered and published by *Broadcasting Yearbook*. Notes: All data are for "on-air" stations as of January 1, except: 1962—September 1, 1961; 1964—September 30, 1963; 1965—October 31, 1964; 1966—October 31, 1965; 1967—November 10, 1966; 1968—November 1, 1967; 1969—December 4, 1968; 1970—December 1, 1969; 1971—February 1, 1971; and December 1 of *previous* year for 1972–1982. "Total" column for AM radio includes educational stations which, after 1940, maintained a fairly steady figure of about 30. For FM and television, however, "total" means commercial stations only.

262
NETWORK OWNERSHIP
OF BROADCAST STATIONS

Interpretation of the Table

Table 262–A provides current (1980) information on network-owned and operated (O&O) television and radio stations in the United States, with an emphasis on television as the more important medium. Under each of the three networks—ABC, CBS, and NBC—the table lists all of the network's O&O television stations, in the order of their SMSA-market ranking. A station's call letters and channel number are identified on the first line; the second line notes the year the station was constructed (C) or purchased (P). The letter R is added if there is also a network radio O&O station in that city. Entries in italics indicate an O&O station which is no longer owned by the network. The *second* date in these italicized entries is the year when the network sold the station.

A fundamental goal of the networks has been to locate all of their O&O stations in the largest markets in the country. To a remarkable degree they have succeeded. In terms of the potential number of households reached, the networks hold the top three positions among group owners of television stations in this country (see Unit 280). ABC, the newest network, has always had the fewest affiliate stations. However, the network's phenomenal programming successes in recent years have considerably strengthened its financial position vis-à-vis the other two networks.

Both CBS and NBC have bought and sold several stations over the years; and in the late 1950s, both experimented briefly with two UHF stations before concluding that the financial prospects of UHF were dim (see Table 380–C). Regarding the previous CBS ownership of television stations in Los Angeles (KTTV), Washington, and Minneapolis-St. Paul, the reader should note that the network held only minority shares (45 to 49 percent in each case) of these stations.

NBC and the independent Group W (Westinghouse) stations were involved in a bizarre decade-long struggle involving affiliate stations in Cleveland (where NBC was based) and the larger market of Philadelphia (where Group W had a station which NBC coveted). In 1955, NBC forced a trade, providing Westinghouse with $3 million and the Cleveland station (WKYC) in exchange for Group W's KYW in Philadelphia. Investigations by the Department of Justice, Congress, and the FCC eventually led to an undoing of this deal in 1965, when NBC agreed to return to its Cleveland base. The Cleveland station is thus the only O&O station which has been controlled by a network at two separate times.

Most network O&O station operations are radio-television combinations, but an FCC ruling in 1971 requires radio-television station combinations within the same market to be divested once they are sold (see Unit 260 for a more complete discussion of this ruling). Thus, this pattern of ownership may gradually change if the networks sell some stations (most likely their radio affiliates) in order to buy others. Early in 1979, NBC announced plans to increase its holdings to the ownership limit in both AM and FM stations.

Table 262–A   Network Ownership of Broadcast Stations, 1980[a] (cont.)

ADI Market Ranking and Number of TV Households[b]	*Percent of All U.S. TV Households*	*ABC-Owned Stations*	*CBS-Owned Stations*	*NBC-Owned Stations*
1. New York 6,432,000	8.3	WABC/7 (1948,C,R)	WCBS/2 (1941,C,R)	WNBC/4 (1941,C,R)
2. Los Angeles 4,181,600	5.4	KABC/7 (1949,C,R)	KNXT/2 (1951,P,R) *KTTV/11 (1948–51,P)*	KNBC/4 (1947,P)
3. Chicago 2,847,200	3.7	WLS/7 (1948,C,R)	WBBM/2 (1953,P,R)	WMAQ/5 (1948,C,R)
4. Philadelphia 2,358,400	3.1	—	WCAU/10 (1958,P,R)	*WRCV/3 (1955–65,P)*
5. San Francisco 1,917,800	2.5	KGO/7 (1949,C,R)	(R only)	(R only)
6. Boston 1,859,900	2.4	—	(R only)	—
7. Detroit 1,606,200	2.1	WXYZ/7 (1948,C,R)	—	—
8. Washington 1,400,400	1.8	(R only)	*WTOP/9 (1950–54,P)*	WRC/4 (1947,C,R)
9. Cleveland 1,328,800	1.7	—	—	WKYC/3 *(1948–55,C)* (1965,P)
12. Houston 1,151,400	1.5	(R only)	—	—
13. Minneapolis-St. Paul 1,009,500	1.3	—	*WCCO/4 (1952–54,P)*	—
14. St. Louis 1,000,800	1.3	—	KMOX/4 (1957,P,R)	—

Table 262–A   Network Ownership of Broadcast Stations, 1980[a] (cont.)

ADI Market Ranking and Number of TV Households[b]	Percent of All U.S. TV Households	ABC-Owned Stations	CBS-Owned Stations	NBC-Owned Stations
22. Hartford-New Haven 676,100	.9	—	WHCT/18 (1956–58,P)	WNBC/30 (1956–58,P)
28. Milwaukee 660,700	.9	—	WXIX/18 (1954–59,P)	—
29. Buffalo 629,900	.8	—	—	WBUF/17 (1955–58,P)

Sources: Sterling, in Compaine et al. (1982), p. 335. Market and rank data from Arbitron *Population Book 1980–81*, p. 52; station data taken from Sterling and Kittross (1978), p. 266. Notes: [a]Listings show the television station call letters and channel number on the first line, and, in parentheses below, the year the station began operations for that network. The symbol C indicates the station was constructed by the network; P indicates purchased by the network from a previous owner, R indicates a combination AM-FM radio station owned by the network in that market. Those stations in italics are no longer network-owned. The end date, if any, indicates the year the network relinquished control of the station. [b]ADI means "Area of Dominant Influence," an Arbitron term indicating counties which are served from a nearby large city.

Sources

Due to the public nature of station ownership, and the small number of stations involved, the information in Table 262–A is very accurate. Market rankings and the figures for number and percentage of television households are drawn from Arbitron Television's *ADI Book, 1976–77*. The other information in the table comes primarily from Sterling and Kittross (1978), with some input from Lichty and Topping (1975).

Further Information

For historical information on network radio stations, see the FCC's *Report on Chain Broadcasting* (1941). Background on the network television stations can be found in the FCC's *Network Broadcasting* (1958) and FCC, *New Television Networks* (1980). Financial information on the television networks is found in Unit 380; programming information is in Unit 582. The reader will also find useful discussions of network O&O stations in Rucker (1968), in an ownership report by Baer et al. (1974), and in Owen (1975) and Bunce (1976). Lists of network-owned and operated television and radio stations appear annually in *Broadcasting Yearbook*. *Television*

Factbook details all current information regarding television O&O stations. See also the comments in the Further Information sections of Units 181 and 260.

270
GROUP OWNERSHIP
OF RADIO STATIONS

Interpretation of the Tables

Until the 1941 inception of commercial FM service, it was rare for a single owner to control more than two AM stations with overlapping coverage (indeed, such practice was banned by the FCC's duopoly rules). The development of FM, however, especially after 1945, was closely related to investment by AM broadcasters. The three tables in this Unit provide measures of group (stations held in several markets) and combined (AM-FM in one market) ownership.

Table 270-A provides scattered information on radio group owners over a 40-year period. As in the broadcasting community generally, the trend evident (and likely increasing, though radio group ownership statistics since 1967 have not been located) is toward more groups and a larger proportion of radio stations so controlled.

Table 270-B lists the top 15 radio group owners, ranked not by revenue but rather by total listeners reached in an average rating week. Most of the firms listed are also group owners of television stations (see Table 260-D), and most own both AM and FM stations. Naturally, much of the total audience listed for each group will overlap with other groups—the networks, for example, overlap ownership in the largest three markets (see Unit 262).

Table 270-C traces trends in AM-FM ownership units, nearly all of which are in the same or nearby markets. Note that the overall trend is the slowly growing concentration of radio ownership, with more than half of all stations held in such combinations. But note also the trend-within-the-trend: the proportion of AM stations so held is rising fairly rapidly, while the proportion of FM stations held in combinations is dropping—indication, perhaps, of the changing economic role the two radio services play. While the

FCC has often considered the policy questions raised by combined control of AM and FM stations, it has just as consistently (with a brief exception in 1970) turned down attempts to force divestiture—most recently early in 1982.

Table 270–A   Number of Group-Owned AM Radio Stations, 1929–1967

Year	Total Number of Stations	Number of Group Owners	Number of Group-Owned Stations	Percent of AM Stations under Group-Ownership
1929	600	12	20	3.3
1939	764	39	109	14.3
1951	2,232	63	253	11.3
1960	3,398	185	765	22.5
1967	4,130	373	1,297	31.4

Sources: 1929 data: Agee (1949), p. 414, table 2. All other data: Rucker (1968), p. 189, table 14.

Table 270–B   The Top 15 Group Owners in Radio, 1980

Rank	Ownership Unit	Number of Stations Owned	Total Weekly Listeners
1.	CBS	14	7,208,000
2.	ABC	13	6,932,000
3.	Group W	12	5,843,000
4.	Metromedia	13	5,239,000
5.	Capital Cities	12	4,760,000
6.	RCA (NBC)	8	4,657,000
7.	RKO	11	4,258,000
8.	SJR	9	3,749,000
9.	Bonneville	11	3,326,000
10.	Cox	12	3,307,000
11.	Taft	12	2,786,000
12.	Gannett	11	2,636,000
13.	Inner City	6	2,514,000
14.	Plough	12	2,120,000
15.	GE	8	1,742,000
	Total	164	—

Source: Sterling, in Compaine et al. (1982), p. 330, citing information in Duncan (1981). See text for discussion. Notes: Total audience measures are misleading in that repeat listeners are not accounted for, but the figures provide at least a sense of magnitude difference. Data includes AM and FM stations. Source counts simulcast AM-FM stations as single stations, and includes only those groups with five or more stations showing up in market rating books (which does not substantially impact the above list).

Table 270–C   AM-FM Combination Holdings, 1968–1980

Year	Number of AM-FM Combinations[a]	Combination Holdings as Percentage of:		
		All AM	All FM[b]	All Radio
1968	1,455	35	83	49
1970	1,641	38	75	51
1972	1,745	40	76	52
1974	1,879	43	75	54
1976	2,059	46	74	57
1978	2,167	48	72	58
1980	2,341	51	74	61

Source: FCC Mass Media Bureau. Notes: [a]Each combination represents two stations. [b]Does not include educational FM stations.

Sources

Table 270–A is from Rucker (1968) except for the 1929 figures which come from Agee (1949). Figures include all types of group owners, as well as those with newspaper interests. Because data were originally derived from several different sources, each of which developed its own definitions and counting procedures, the figures should be (a) viewed as approximations, and (b) not directly compared.

Table 270–B is from Sterling, in Compaine et al. (1982), p. 330. The original data is from Duncan (1981), p. A–28. Total audience measures are misleading in that repeat listeners are not controlled for—but the figures provide at least a sense of magnitude difference. Data includes both AM and FM stations. The source counts simulcast AM-FM stations as single stations, and includes only those groups with five or more stations showing up in recent Arbitron rating books. The latter fact likely does not substantially affect the list given.

Table 270–C is based on FCC tabulations done by economists of the Broadcast (now Mass Media) Bureau, but never formally published or released. The counts are based on ownership information annually filed with the Commission. Each of the ownership units, of course, counts for two stations, one AM and one FM. The percentages, figured by the author, are based on total AM and total FM data also figured by the Bureau, which may differ slightly (due to difference in date of measure) from those shown in Unit 170.

Further Information

See discussions under Units 260 and 261.

280
GROUP OWNERSHIP OF TELEVISION STATIONS

Interpretation of the Tables

Group ownership has always been a way of life for commercial television in the United States, and the concentration of station ownership increases annually. Table 280–A provides an overall picture of this trend, showing a rise both in the number of group owners in this country and in the proportion of commercial television stations controlled by group owners (defined as a single owner holding at least two stations).

The peculiar percentage drop in group ownership in the 1950s was due to the large number of new stations going on the air at that time. As fewer new stations were established and more channels changed hands through sales, the proportion of group-owned television stations resumed its steady rise. Besides the FCC restrictions on same-market ownership (see Units 260 and 262), the only apparent limiting factor on further group-ownership in the industry is the number of UHF stations now operating. Note in Table 280–B the substantially lower group holdings among UHF stations.

Table 280–B illustrates the higher concentrations of group ownership in the largest SMSA markets, although this trend is also evident in nearly all other market categories over the past two decades. Among the top 15 group owners of television stations (ranked in Table 280–C according to their net weekly audience), the networks and RKO occupy four of the five top slots in each sample year. The network and RKO stations also occupy the largest markets in the nation. Likewise, Group W, WGN–Continental, Storer, and Triangle (sold to Capital Cities in the early 1970s)—all companies controlling stations in the larger market areas—have maintained a steady position among the top 10 audience-ranked companies.

Thus, Table 280–C demonstrates that the *number* of stations controlled by an ownership group is not as important as the markets in which the group stations operate. For example, in 1959, WGN–Continental's *two* stations ranked sixth among all group owners, whereas owners with five and six stations appear much lower in the listings. The "percentage of households" columns in Table 280–C represent the proportion of national households included in the markets in which each group owner operates.

Table 280-A   Number of Group-Owned Television Stations, 1948–1983

Year	Number of Groups	Number of Group-Owned Stations	Total Commercial Stations	Percent of Group Control
1948	3	6	16	37.5
1949	10	24	51	47.1
1950	17	52	98	53.1
1951	19	53	107	49.5
1952	19	53	108	49.1
1953	38	104	126	82.5
1954	48	126	354	35.6
1955	62	165	411	40.1
1956	60	173	441	39.2
1957	65	192	471	40.8
1958	82	241	495	48.7
1959	85	249	510	48.8
1960	84	252	515	48.9
1961	87	260	527	49.3
1962	89	268	541	49.5
1963	97	280	557	50.3
1964	106	299	564	53.0
1965	109	310	569	54.5
1966	111	324	585	55.4
(Data for 1967–1974 not available.)				
1975	115	405	706	57.4
1976	119	415	701	59.2
(Data for 1977–1979 not available.)				
1980	144	506	734	68.9
1981	N/A	N/A	756	N/A
1982	158	563	777	72.5
1983	174	596	813	73.3

Sources: The first two columns (through 1966) are from Kroeger (1966), pp. 30–31; the third column is taken from figures in Table 180-A. Data for 1975–76 is from Howard (1976), 1980 from Howard (1980), 1982 from Howard (1982), and 1983 from Howard (1983).

Table 280-B Number of Group-Owned Television Stations, by Market, 1956, 1966, and 1982

Year/Type of Station	Markets 1-10	Markets 1-50	Markets 51-100	Markets 1-100	Markets 101 and up[c]	Total Stations
1956[a]						
All TV stations	—	163	134	297	159	456
Group-owned stations	—	92	48	140	65	205
Percent group-owned	—	56	36	47	41	45
1966[a]						
All TV stations	—	193	164	357	235	592
Group-owned stations	—	134	112	246	150	396
Percent group-owned	—	69	68	69	64	67
1982[b]						
VHF: All TV stations	41	160	103	263	N/A	524
Group-owned stations	40	144	82	226	N/A	N/A
Percent group-Owned	98	90	80	86	N/A	N/A
UHF: All TV stations	36	90	67	157	N/A	250
Group-owned stations	25	64	42	106	N/A	N/A
Percent group-owned	69	71	63	68	N/A	N/A
Total: All TV stations	77	250	170	420	N/A	774
Group-owned stations	65	208	124	332	N/A	N/A
Percent group-owned	84	83	73	79	N/A	N/A

Source: Sterling, in Compaine et al. (1982), p. 325. Notes: [a]Data as of early Spring. [b]Data as of January 1st. [c]Data for 1982 limited to top 100 markets only.

Table 280-C   The Top 15 Group Owners in Television, 1980 and 1959

	Rank		Stations		Net Weekly Circulation		Percent of US Households	
Ownership Unit	1980	1959	1980	1959	1980	1959	1980	1959
CBS	1	1	5	5	16.0	11.3	22	22
ABC	2	3	5	5	15.8	9.6	22	19
RCA (NBC)	3	2	5	5	15.2	10.8	21	21
Metromedia	4	7[a]	7	4	13.9	3.9	20	8
RKO General	5	4	4	4	9.5	5.4	17	11
Westinghouse	6	5	6	5	9.0	4.7	11	9
WGN/Continental	6	6	3	2	8.6	4.5	13	9
Storer	8	8	7	5	7.0	3.3	10	6
Field	9	—	5	—	6.1	—	14	—
Capital Cities	10	9[b]	6	6	5.8	2.8	7	5
Taft	11	—	7	—	5.6	—	9	—
Gaylord	12	—	7	—	5.6	—	9	—
Cox	13	—	5	—	5.2	—	6	—
Scripps-Howard	14	11	6	3	4.1	1.9	5	4
Post-Newsweek	15	—	4	—	4.1	—	5	—

Source: Sterling, in Compaine et al. (1982), p. 329. Notes: [a]Known as Metropolitan stations in 1959. [b]Known as Triangle stations in 1959.

Sources

In Table 280–A, the information through 1966 comes from Kroeger (1966), pp. 30–31, which does not supply details on method of counting, exact date for each year, etc., but appears to be both consistent and accurate as to trends. The period since has not been researched consistently—the scattered information for the 1970s and early 1980s is reported briefly by Howard (1976, 1980, and 1982), which also does not specify methods of counting, though the data appears to be for the first of the year in each case.

Table 280–B is from Sterling, in Compaine et al. (1982), p. 325. It is drawn from Cherington et al. (1971), p. 40, exhibit 2 which details the methods used by United Research in developing the statistics. The time period is not made clear for Cherington et al.'s 1956 and 1966 data, but appears to be spring in each case. The information was gathered as a part of an industry group docket filing with the FCC concerned about television station ownership concentration. The 1982 information is from Howard (1982), done under contract for the National Association of Broadcasters. Data for 1982 is as of January first—but covers only the top 100 markets.

Table 280–C is also from Sterling, in Compaine et al. (1982), p. 329. The 1959 data is from Larson (1977) while the 1980 information is from Howard (1980). While the base study for 1980 was restricted to only the top 100 markets, that does not appear to change the relative comparison with the 1959 study which covered all markets. The market ranking is based on net weekly circulation which indicates how many millions of households are served by each group, taking all the markets they serve (in which they have a station) collectively. Percent of U.S. (television) households for 1980 added by the author using the Arbitron *1980–81 Population Book* (1981).

Further Information

See Units 260, 261 and 262 for general sources. The weekly trade journal *Broadcasting* includes a statistical summary of broadcast station sales in a late January or early February issue annually, reprinted in *Broadcast Yearbook*.

281
OWNERSHIP OF PUBLIC TELEVISION STATIONS

Interpretation of the Table

Ownership of public television (PTV) stations is reported in Table 281–A in the four ownership categories commonly recognized in the industry: (1) colleges and universities, (2) public school systems, (3) state and/or municipal agencies, and (4) community organizations. The table shows the number of stations (not licensees) in each ownership category; and the percentage of all PTV stations within each category.

Colleges and universities, already experienced with educational radio, were the first in the field of educational television. Iowa State University put WOI-TV on the air in 1950, two years before the FCC's allocation of frequencies for educational stations had been established. Public school systems have always been the smallest ownership category, and their position has declined even further in recent years, due mainly to the serious budgetary problems in most school districts.

State/municipal agencies include not only several state-run networks and a few local operations (such as the City of New York's WNYC-TV), but also four nondomestic licensees in American Samoa, Guam, Puerto Rico, and the Virgin Islands. Since 1970, state/municipal authorities have operated the largest bloc of PTV stations. The state authorities, and the number of transmitters controlled by them, are: Alabama (9), Connecticut (3), Georgia (9), Kentucky (14), Maine (3), Mississippi (8), Nebraska (8), New Jersey (4), and South Carolina (7). The Alabama system has earned the dubious distinction of being the first educational licensee to lose its license at renewal, due to charges of discrimination in employment and programming. The eventual status of the Alabama Educational Television Commission's nine stations took several years to resolve (all were eventually renewed).

Community organizations are privately created nonprofit corporations and foundations, usually consisting of some combination of community cultural organizations. Some of the most important program-producing public stations in the country fall into this category, including WGBH in Boston, WNET in New York, KCET in Los Angeles, WETA in Washington, WQED in Pittsburgh, and KQED in San Francisco.

Table 281-A Ownership of Public Television Stations, 1959–1983

Year	Colleges and Universities		Public School Systems		State and Municipal Authorities		Community Organizations		Total Stations
	Number	Percent	Number	Percent	Number	Percent	Number	Percent	
1959	9	26	3	9	10	29	13	37	35
1962	12	19	19	31	13	21	18	29	62
1964	24	27	19	22	20	23	25	28	88
1966	29	26	19	17	24	21	41	36	113
1967	27	23	21	18	34	29	37	31	119
1968	31	21	22	15	52	36	41	28	146
1969	58	31	22	12	57	30	52	28	189
1970	59	30	24	12	60	31	52	27	195
1971	61	29	23	11	67	32	56	27	207
1972	67	30	21	9	74	33	61	27	223
1973	72	31	20	8	81	34	63	27	236
1974	74	30	20	8	84	35	65	27	243
1975	76	30	19	8	87	35	69	27	251
1976	78	29	19	7	97	36	73	27	267
1977	76	28	19	7	101	37	74	27	270
1978	79	28	19	7	110	39	74	26	282
1980	77	27	18	6	112	39	83	29	290
1981	77	26	18	6	117	40	82	28	294
1982	73	24	16	5	121	40	89	30	299
1983	73	24	15	5	123	41	89	30	300

Sources: 1959 data from the Joint Council on Educational Television (1959); 1962–1970 data from *One Week of Educational Television* series; 1971–1981 from the Corporation for Public Broadcasting (no data available for 1979).

Sources

Table 281-A figures for 1959 come from the Joint Council on Educational Television (1959). The 1962–1970 information is from the *One Week of Educational Television* series; the 1971–1981 data is from Corporation for Public Broadcasting. Although all of the information is for various dates in the spring of each year, the variation in dates creates a few very slight numerical discrepancies among the different sources. However, due to the public nature of station ownership, the figures in Table 281-A can be considered generally accurate. In recent years there has been some confusion over categories, according to CPB.

Further Information

The CPB and the Public Broadcasting Service (PBS), will supply current and historical information on the PTV systems. Other useful statistical information on public television ownership appears in the CPB's annual *Public Television Licensees*. Background reading on the development, operation, and future of public broadcasting appears in Cater and Nyhan (1976) and Wood and Wylie (1977).

282
CONCENTRATION IN
PROGRAM PRODUCTION

Interpretation of the Tables

Discussions of ownership in broadcast-related businesses typically examine only control of actual transmission facilities, as indeed Section Two of this book does. This is due primarily to the fact that more statistics are available on facility control than production of programs. The two tables here, however, shed some light on different aspects of national television programming.

Table 280-A measures, for 1970 and 1978, the market share of the leading firm as well as the top 4, top 8 and top 20 companies providing prime-time and daytime series to network television. Evident in the eight years covered is a slight trend to increasing concentration–largely due to marginal companies pulling out of an increasingly expensive business. The number of program series included in each case is given as "N" right after the "series" category, the first number indicating 1970, and the second 1978.

Table 280–B provides parallel measures for nationally syndicated (non-network) programming for 1968 and 1977. Here the break-out is for all program series in syndication (many of those former network programs, and shows long in syndication), while the second part of the table refers only to the much smaller number of original productions, never shown on networks, made expressly for syndication. In syndication, an independent (non-network) firm, often the very firm which produced the series, contracts with individual television stations (usually but one to a market) for one to three showings of the series.

Table 282–A Concentration in Network Program Production, 1970 and 1978

| | \multicolumn{8}{c|}{Market Share of Leading Firms (In Percent)} | | | | | | | |
| | Leading Firm | | Leading 4 | | Leading 8 | | Leading 20 | |
Category	1970	1978	1970	1978	1970	1978	1970	1978
A. Network Prime-Time Shows:								
Series (N = 93 and 113)	8	18	27	35	41	49	59	74
Hours	13	18	33	37	46	53	68	81
Audience Share	13	17	30	36	44	53	68	81
B. Network Daytime Shows:								
Series (N = 39 and 36)	15	17	39	53	56	72	88	100
Hours	16	22	41	62	60	82	94	100
Audience Share	20	25	49	67	67	85	97	100

Source: FCC, *New Television Networks*, Volume II (1980), pp. 571 and 574. Figures here are rounded off from those in the source.

Table 282–B Concentration in Syndicated Program Production, 1968 and 1977

| | \multicolumn{8}{c|}{Market Share of Firms (In Percent)} | | | | | | | |
| | Leading Firm | | Leading 4 | | Leading 8 | | Leading 20 | |
Category	1968	1977	1968	1977	1968	1977	1968	1977
A. All Series:								
Series (N = 165 and 196)	5	5	15	16	23	28	38	48
Hours	13	7	36	23	48	39	69	67
Audience Share	17	6	42	21	58	38	78	70
B. First-Run Series:								
Series (N = 47 and 73)	6	8	19	25	30	34	55	51
Hours	31	11	68	38	78	57	91	83
Audience Share	39	10	73	37	82	62	95	88

Source: FCC, *New Television Networks*, Volume II (1980), pp. 580 and 583. Figures here are rounded off from those in the source.

Sources

The information here was developed by researchers for the Network Inquiry Special Staff of the FCC, who worked in 1978–1980. The data is based on returns from network and program production companies, verified by various kinds of cross-checking. Unfortunately, such information is not regularly gathered and/or analyzed. Indeed, the data here is based partially on earlier studies for earlier FCC investigations. Figures here are rounded off from those in the original source, and the data is arranged somewhat differently to allow a clearer comparison.

Further Information

There is a good deal of information on the economics of programming, especially for network television. See especially A. D. Little Co. (1969), Owen et al. (1974), McAlpine (1975), and Levin (1980). A great deal of data flowed into the FCC during its reconsideration of the network "financial interest" rules—see especially, ICF, Inc. (1983), Bolter (1983), and CBS, Inc. (1983). See also citations for Units 580 and 582.

290
OWNERSHIP OF
CABLE SYSTEMS

Interpretation of the Tables

As with most other media, the trend in cable system ownership in recent years has been toward greater concentration. The three tables in this Unit provide different ways of assessing that concentration.

Table 290–A provides limited data on cross-ownership of cable systems and other media. As discussed in more detail below, however, "ownership" is very loosely described here, and the categories overlap—so the overall trends are evident but little more. With that caveat, it appears that radio and television broadcasters control by far the largest proportion of the cable business. Due to FCC rules, a television station can not control a cable system within its coverage area—and national broadcasting networks can not control cable systems at all. Established in 1970, these rules led to some divestiture at the time. By 1982, there was considerable pressure to eliminate the network-cable system ban, and an initial waiver had already been granted to CBS. 1970 also saw a ban on telephone company ownership of cable systems within the telephone franchise area. In 1981, that rule was loosened a bit to allow rural telephone companies to build and/or operate cable systems in areas so sparsely populated that independent cable existence was and is unlikely.

Table 290–B traces, in round figures, the subscriber counts for selected large multiple system operators, or MSOs. Ranked in their order of size as of early 1983, the figures for a 14 year period suggest the rapid growth spurts common to MSOs as systems are purchased or built. Not shown on the table (but see Unit 201) is the fact that many of these MSOs are, in turn, controlled by larger conglomerates. Examples: number one ranked ATC is a subsidiary of Time, Inc., Teleprompter is now owned by Westinghouse, Times-Mirror is part of a multi-media conglomerate, and UA-Columbia is now owned by the Canadian-based Rogers firm. There has never been any FCC ownership limitation on number of systems controlled by any one owner, though the issue has been considered several times.

Table 290–C provides a more formal economic analysis of the concentration of subscribers served by MSOs. Note that for the 15 year period covered, concentration has increased steadily as the costs of gaining franchises and then building them has increased. To a considerable degree, the large-scale (100 channel and more) systems proposed in the late 1970s and early 1980s were paced by increasing pay cable income potential (see Units 195 and 295). Even by 1970, cable's days of "mom and pop" companies were fast fading as concentration was forced by costs of operation and the need to rebuild older 12 (and fewer) channel systems.

Sources

Table 290–A is taken from annual listings published in *Television Factbook*, which gathers its data through annual surveys of the industry. Because some lesser ownership categories are omitted in this table, and because the figures include multiple listings of owners falling into more than one ownership category, the subtotals of cable systems do not always equal the total number of systems surveyed. Users are cautioned, however, that systems with *any* degree of cross-ownership are counted, thus inflating the proportion of cable systems held by any of the categories, as many minor holdings are thus included. Further, comparisons are made more difficult by the fact that systems with ownership in more than one category are counted in each, thus leading to an undetermined amount of double and multiple listing of the same systems. The apparent anomalies in some categories for 1978 and 1981, where numbers of systems controlled appear to drop sharply, are as reported

Table 290–A Cross-Ownership of Cable Systems, 1969–1983

| | Number of Systems and Percent of Systems Surveyed for | | | | | | | | | |
| | 1969 (February) | | 1970 (March) | | 1971 (March) | | 1972 (March) | | 1973 (June) | |
	Number of Systems	Percent of Systems Surveyed	Number of Systems	Percent of Systems Surveyed	Number of Systems	Percent of Systems Surveyed	Number of Systems	Percent of Systems Surveyed	Number of Systems	Percent of Systems Surveyed
Number of CATV Systems Surveyed	2,300	—	2,490	—	2,578	—	2,839	—	3,032	—
Category of Ownership:										
Broadcasters	741	32	910	37[a]	766	30	1,077	38	1,048	35
Newspapers	220 }	10 }	207	8	175	7	180	6	308	10
Publishers	}	}					75	3	221	7
TV Programming Producers/Distributors	N/A	N/A	N/A	N/A	N/A	N/A	217	8	604	20
Theater Owners	N/A	N/A	N/A	N/A	N/A	N/A	97	3	130	4
Telephone Companies	150	7	146	6[a]	132	5	57	2	50	2
Community or Subscriber Ownership	N/A	N/A	N/A	N/A	N/A	N/A	81	3	75	2
TV Manufacturers	N/A	N/A	N/A	N/A	N/A	N/A	N/A	N/A	320	11

Table 290–A   Cross-Ownership of Cable Systems, 1969–1983 (Cont.)

	1974 (June)		1975 (September)		1976 (September)		1977 (September)		1978 (September)		1979 (October)		1981 (June)		1983 (March)	
	Number of Systems	Percent of Systems Surveyed	Number of Systems	Percent of Systems Surveyed	Number of Systems	Percent of Systems Surveyed	Number of Systems	Percent of Systems Surveyed	Number of Systems	Percent of Systems Surveyed	Number of Systems	Percent of Systems Surveyed	Number of Systems	Percent of Systems Surveyed	Number of Systems	Percent of Systems Surveyed
	3,190	—	3,405	—	3,715	—	3,911	—	3,997	—	4,180	—	4,637	—	5,748	—
	1,178	37	1,090	32	1,183	32	1,179	30	1,216	30	1,371	33	1,776	38	1,608	28.0
	463	15	486	14	476	13	474	12	506	13	547	13	729	16	943	16.4
	230	7	247	7	492	13	501	13	431	11	463	11	545	12	548	9.5
	744	23	772	23	729	20	772	20	701	18	736	18	967	21	1,540	26.8
	146	5	296	9	313	8	301	8	162	4	166	4	144	3	142	2.5
	143	4	61	2	69	2	73	2	74	2	104	2	149	3	222	3.9
	83	3	88	3	96	3	106	3	101	3	99	2	96	2	76	1.3
	606	19	630	19	455	12	422	11	213	5	282	7	97	2	141	2.5

Sources: Perry (1974) for data through 1973; *Television Factbook* for data since. See text for important limitations. Not shown for 1983 are the following "other" categories: 758 (13.1) for common-carrier microwave firms, 113 (1.9) for MDS systems, and 9 cable systems cross-owned by TV translator systems. Note: No 1980 or 1982 data is available. [a]In 1970, the FCC issued new rules banning co-located tv station-cable system on local telephone company-cable system cross-ownership of any cable systems. [b]See text under Sources.

Table 290-B Largest Cable System MSOs, by Number of Subscribers, 1970–1983

Top 10 Ranked as of Early 1981	In Thousands of Subscribers													
	1970	1971	1972	1973	1974	1975	1976	1977	1978	1979	1980	1981	1982	1983
1. American Television and Communications Corp.	112	180	264	350	443	474	513	585	690	905	1220	1424	1900	2198
2. Teleprompter Corp.	243	535	658	800	1034	1074	1094	1050	1112	1183	1338	1337	1700	1904[a]
3. Tele-Communications, Inc.	142	142	249	387	497	526	550	557	576	673	1034	1277	2000	2197
4. Cox Cable Communications	190	197	242	275	335	345	394	437	504	610	884	959	1666	1348
5. Warner-Amex	N/A	N/A	342	450	503	513	532	554	570	630	725	760	907	1260
6. Storer Cable Communications	N/A	N/A	90	100	125	135	146	179	199	285	534	628	922	1229
7. Times-Mirror Cable TV	N/A	N/A	N/A	49	64	56	71	82	88	412	545	606	675	817
8. Viacom Communications	150	150	183	254	295	306	324	324	363	400	467	495	522	640
9. UA-Columbia Cablevision	N/A	N/A	65	150	173	182	198	214	238	280	380	429	520	618
10. Sammons Communication	N/A	N/A	200	221	234	253	278	286	309	340	398	418	451	538

Sources: Television Digest, especially spring NCTA special issues, citing figures as of (generally) March or April of year indicated. 1970–1973 data from Perry (1974), pp. 5–7 citing data from *Moody's Industrial Manual* and *TV Factbook* as of January 1 for each year. Note: [a]In June 1982 Teleprompter Corp. merged with Group W Cable, Inc. and the name was changed to Group W Cable, Inc.

Table 290–C   MSO Subscriber Concentration, 1969–1981

Year	Percent of all cable subscribers served by the largest:			
	4 firms	8 firms	25 firms	50 firms
1969	16.3	26.7	47.9	61.1
1970	17.2	28.0	50.3	64.0
1971	21.7	31.6	53.7	67.3
1972	25.7	37.6	58.6	70.2
1973	27.2	40.3	61.7	73.4
1974	26.2	38.6	58.6	69.3
1975	26.4	38.1	58.5	69.8
1976	24.9	36.6	56.8	68.7
1977	23.1	34.2	54.1	66.7
1978	22.7	33.9	54.1	67.3
1979	24.0	36.5	58.4	71.5
1980	25.8	·38.6	62.1	74.5
1981	27.3	40.9	63.9	77.8

Sources: Braunstein (1980), p. 14 for data through 1979; and *Television Digest* for 1980 and 1981 (as cited in Table 290–B).

in (but not explained by) the original source. See the theater owner category for 1978, and television manufacturer category for both 1978 and 1981. This is likely due to problems in the survey returns on which the data is based.

Table 290–B data is from Perry (1974) for 1970–1973, who in turn cited a variety of sources including *Moody's Industrial Manual* and *Television Factbook*. All of these data are as of January 1. The 1974 data (actually September 1973) were provided to the author by the National Cable Television Association. The data for 1975–1981 come from *Television Digest*'s spring special supplement issues. All of the data in this table is based on responses to annual *Digest* surveys of cable owners.

Table 290–C is taken from Braunstein (1980), p. 14. This was data assembled by an outside consultant for the FCC's special study of networks in 1978–1980. Data for 1980–1981 was figured by the author from *Television Digest*'s spring listings of the top 50 MSOs.

Further Information

For further information, see Sterling, in Compaine et al. (1982), chapter 7, and FCC Office of Plans and Policy (1981). Braunstein (1980) is a detailed examination of trends in policy during the 1970s. Specific MSO information appears regularly in *Television Digest*, *Cablevision*, and *Broadcasting*—and can be obtained from the National Cable Television Association. See also "Top 50 Companies in Cable," *Cablevision* (June 20, 1983), pp. 137–221 and the sources noted under Unit 190.

295
OWNERSHIP OF PAY TELEVISION SYSTEMS

Interpretation of the Tables

It is difficult to show much of a trend in the pay television businesses (pay cable, MDS, STV, etc.) because they are so new. Both tables here, therefore, concentrate on national pay programming distributors rather than local market facilities.

Table 295–A shows the audience share or proportion of the largest three pay program distributors, most of the audience being on pay cable systems. The benefits of being in on the ground floor of a new medium are evident in the lasting dominance of pay subscribers by Time Inc.'s subsidiary, Home Box Office (HBO). As noted in Unit 195, HBO began pay service in 1972 but, more importantly, was the first pay program distributor to provide communications satellite interconnection in the fall of 1975. Time Inc. for many years operated Telemation Program Services, (TPS, now HBO Program Services) as a non-satellite-distributed supplement or alternative to HBO, and more recently has provided Cinemax as an alternative, mainly movies, "tier" for larger cable systems wishing to carry more than one cable pay service. Main pay cable competitor Showtime began satellite service in 1978, and is now owned by Viacom and Westinghouse-Teleprompter. The Warner service shown on the table is actually two totally different services operated by the same parent at different times. Not shown are some 10 other services for pay, and perhaps 35 basic or "free" services all available by satellite delivery in the early 1980s, most less than two years old.

Table 295–B provides an important aspect of pay programming concentration which is fast disappearing in the early 1980s. Until 1982, cable systems able to carry a pay service typically carried but one. In the early 1980s, it became slowly more common to carry a main service (HBO or Showtime) plus one or more supplementary or specialized "tier" services. But only the largest systems in the early 1980s carried more than one of the main services, due partially to contract limitations, and partially to channel capacity. The result is evident in Table 295–B which shows the very high correlation between pay service and the percentage of pay TV customers provided with that service by the three MSOs with ownership of the pay distributor. In other words, ATC, which along with HBO, is controlled by Time Inc.,

Table 295–A Major Pay TV Program Distributors, 1975–1982

Year	Total Pay Subscribers (In Thousands)	HBO Subs	HBO Share (In Percent)	Showtime Subs	Showtime Share (In Percent)	Warner[a] Subs	Warner[a] Share (In Percent)	TPS[b] Subs	TPS[b] Share (In Percent)	Others Subs	Others Share (In Percent)
1975	189	90	48	—	—	8	4	33	17	58	31
1976	794	475	60	—	—	34	4	176	22	109	14
1977	1,244	718	58	50	4	N/A	N/A	226	18	250	20
1978	2,502	1,545	62	154	6	N/A	N/A	281	11	522	21
1979	4,801	2,889	60	720	15	143	3	303	6	746	16
1980	8,103	5,000	62	1,175	15	401	5	253	3	1,274	16
1981	12,881	7,000	54	2,000	16	1,025	8	—	—	N/A[c]	N/A
1982	19,922	9,800	49	3,050	15	2,300	12	—	—	N/A	N/A

Source: Paul Kagan Associates. All data as of June 30, except 1975, which is as of March 30. The "Total Subscribers" column includes pay cable, MDS, and STV services, the latter two adding about a half million subscribers in 1979, a million in 1980, 1.5 million in 1981, and 2.3 million in 1982. Notes: [a]Was Warner *Star Channel* until 1979, and was then renamed *The Movie Channel*. [b]Television Program Services was a subsidiary of HBO (Time Inc.) which did not use satellite delivery, but filled in HBO service to systems lacking ground stations—and thus its dramatic drop in importance as TVROs (see Table 195–B) became available. It was renamed HBO Program Services in 1980. [c]Data cannot be figured due to tiering of services.

Table 295–B   Pay TV Service on Affiliated and Unaffiliated MSOs, 1980

	Percentage of Pay TV Customers on:		
Pay Service	*ATC*	*Teleprompter*	*Warner-Amex*
Home Box Office	87[a]	3	5
Showtime	3	75[a]	—
The Movie Channel	1	2	79[a]

Source: Figured by CBS Inc. researchers based on data in Paul Kagan Associates, *The Pay TV Census*, December 31, 1980. [a]Indicates MSO-Pay Service are owned by same parent.

provided only HBO (of these three main services) to its subscribers, while Teleprompter, half owner of Showtime, provided only its co-owned service to subscribers on its cable systems. The development of "tiering" of multiple pay service options should see this aspect of concentration reduced sharply by the mid-1980s.

Sources

Table 295–A is based on self-reported (and often rounded or estimated) subscriber figures supplied by the pay TV distributors to Paul Kagan Associates, and summarized by Kagan in the *Pay TV Newsletter*. The number of subscribers listed includes STV and MDS systems after 1979, though pay cable systems were, and remain, the mainstay of this business. But users are cautioned that this data is estimated and only larger trends are at all reliable.

Table 295–B was developed by CBS researchers, using basic data from the Kagan *Pay TV Newsletter* and related annual *Pay TV Census* (now issued with data as of December each year).

Further Information

See Units 195 and 695, and, for "basic" cable networks, Table 590–B.

SECTION THREE
ELECTRONIC MEDIA
ECONOMICS

302
CONSUMER VS. ADVERTISER INVESTMENT IN BROADCASTING

Interpretation of the Table

Figuring out who really pays for the broadcast media has to take into account at least three groups: broadcasters and their investment in plant personnel and programming, advertisers and their purchase of time on the air, and the consumer's purchase and repair of receivers. It is generally assumed that advertising is the primary source of support for most media in the U.S. Table 302-A attempts to temper this assumption with data on consumer expenditure on receiver purchase and upkeep. A fuller picture would have to include broadcaster investment, but sufficient comparable information on that subject is apparently not available.

Examination of average annual consumer expenditure in Table 302-A shows two sharp increases, the first in 1950-1954, and the second in 1965-1969. Both were due to the initial wave of television receiver purchases—black and white sets in the earlier period, and color receivers in the 1960s. Likewise, the very slow rate of growth in the early 1940s was due to a ban on the manufacture of consumer products, including receivers, during the years of World War II.

The percentage columns are slightly misleading, in that "total" in this case refers only to advertising and consumer expenditures, ignoring substantial broadcaster investment.

Sources

Table 302-A data on consumer expenditures for radio/television receivers were calculated by the author from the figures on sales of broadcast receivers in Tables 660-A and 660-B. These figures, in turn, were taken from

Table 302-A Consumer vs. Advertiser Expenditures in Broadcasting, 1935–1978

Five Year Period	Average Annual Consumer Expenditures		Average Annual Advertiser Expenditures	
	Receiver Purchase/ Repair (In Millions of Dollars)	Percent of Total Expenditures	Radio-Television Advertising (In Millions of Dollars)	Percent of Total Expenditures
1935–39	383	72	150	28
1940–44	404	59	286	41
1945–49	838	62	517	38
1950–54	1,932	64	1,079	36
1955–59	1,945	51	1,869	49
1960–64	2,278	46	2,628	54
1965–69	4,256	51	4,095	49
1970–74	5,204	48	5,685	52
1975–78	6,057	39	9,586	61

Source: Sterling, in Compaine et al. (1979), p. 76.

Broadcasting Yearbook 1977. Because there was no available information on *radio* retail sales for the years 1950–57, the author estimated an average sales figure of $2.1 billion for both the 1950–54 and 1955–59 periods. (The averaged total for radio sales for 1945–49 was $2.6 billion; for 1960–64, $1.9 billion.) The reader should refer to the "Sources" section in Unit 660 for a discussion of some other serious reliability problems with the figures in Tables 660-A and 660-B. However, the trend indicated by these data remains valid.

Radio–TV repair figures, which were added by the author to the consumer-expenditures totals, were taken from *Historical Statistics* (1975), for the years 1935–1970, and from *Statistical Abstract* for 1970–1978. The author averaged the totals for each five year period.

The advertiser-expenditures totals were calculated by the author from the revenue figures in Units 370 (radio) and 380 (television). See those units for the government and industry sources of the base data.

Due to the averaging and the wide variety of sources for Table 302-A, the figures must be regarded as little more than approximate estimates, which are intended only to indicate trends.

Further Information

For a very interesting attempt to arrive, by a different route, at answers to the question of advertiser versus consumer support of the mass media, see McCombs (1972).

303
ADVERTISING RATES
AND EXPENDITURES IN
BROADCASTING

Interpretation of the Tables

This Unit provides some aggregate national data on trends in advertiser expenditures and advertising rates in the broadcast media in the United States. In Table 303-A, the term "spot" refers to commercials which are placed by an advertiser or agency on a regional or national basis, without using the services of networks. (In other words, the commercials are "spotted" by advertisers among the specific stations or areas they wish to reach.) The term "local" indicates advertising sold by local stations only. A network-affiliated broadcast station would carry all three types of advertising, while an independent (nonnetwork) station must subsist on spot and local sales.

As Table 303-A indicates, local radio advertiser expenditures first began to exceed network expenditures during the post-World War II period. The high proportion of radio advertising compared to *all* media advertising in the 1940–1946 period is due to (1) a lack of paper supplies, which limited advertising in newspapers and magazines; and (2) a wartime excess-profits tax, which allowed advertising expenditures to be exempted from taxation— thus creating a huge advertising market despite the limited manufacture of consumer goods.

Television rose very rapidly as an advertising medium of importance— surpassing all radio advertising by 1954. Network television surpassed network radio advertising three years earlier. However, until 1978, local radio advertiser expenditures remained consistently higher than those for local television. This dominance by local radio is due to both the greater importance of network and spot advertising in television, and the far greater number of local radio stations (see Units 170 and 180).

Although network radio revenues have clearly withered in the face of television's competition (the rise of radio network income in the 1970s is more a feature of inflation than a real increase in time sales), the general assumption of an overall decline in the advertising role of radio is somewhat of a myth. Only in the 1954–1956 period did overall radio income decline. In subsequent years, local and spot radio sales have expanded to fill the gap created by declining network advertising.

Daily newspapers are by far the single largest advertising medium, taking about 30 percent of all advertiser expenditures. With the exception of daily newspapers, radio and television combined have, since the early 1970s, earned more advertising dollars than *all* of the other media.

Table 303–B provides a 17-year time-series on changes in the advertising rates of the various media. The table is in the form of a cost-per-thousand (CPM) index, with the base figure of 100 for the year 1970. The CPM rate index is the common denominator that allows comparison between media advertising priced in different ways—that is, by lines or column inches in the print media or by airtime in broadcasting. The index enables the advertiser to determine which medium is the most economical means of reaching 1,000 households with a given advertising message. The figures in Table 303–B are aggregate national CPMs, but advertisers also develop specialized CPMs for particular characteristics of the audience, such as sex, location, age, and interests.

Table 303–C provides an indication of actual cost-per-thousand rates for selected media, including several types of broadcasting time. Note that the CPM-advertising rates remained fairly steady in the early 1970s (actually declining in the case of daytime television), but rose sharply with inflation after 1973. Note also that while network prime-time television is often blamed for the high prices charged to advertisers, the CPM of prime-time television is actually lower than that of any of the print media listed in the table. However, much of this difference in rates can be explained by the fact that CPM-advertising rates are directly affected by the size of the audience—and the audience for network prime-time television is far larger than that of any daily newspaper or top consumer magazine.

Sources

Table 303–A is based on information supplied directly to the author by Robert J. Coen of McCann-Erickson, Inc., who has been developing these statistics since 1950. The statistical foundations for Mr. Coen's work were established by his two predecessors in the Marketing Services Research department of McCann-Erickson.

All of the figures in Table 303–A are estimates; the percentages were calculated by the author. The broadcast data shown here are based on the annual FCC financial reports on the industry. The more recent data are generally more reliable, although data for the past two or three years are often revised on receipt of more refined information (the 1978 data are definitely preliminary). Because the radio-television figures are *current* dollars, and the "All advertising media" column is *constant* dollars (1972 = 100), the data in this table are not directly comparable.

Table 303-A   Advertiser Expenditure in Broadcasting, 1935–1982

Note: All Dollar Figures are in Millions.

Year	Radio Advertising					Television Advertising					All Advertising Media	
	Network	Spot	Local	Total	Percent of All Advertising	Network	Spot	Local	Total	Percent of All Advertising	Total	Percent of Annual Change
1935	63	15	35	113	7	—	—	—	—	—	6,255	(4)[a]
1936	75	23	24	122	7	—	—	—	—	—	6,993	12
1937	89	28	48	165	8	—	—	—	—	—	7,241	4
1938	89	34	44	167	9	—	—	—	—	—	6,820	(6)
1939	99	35	50	184	9	—	—	—	—	—	7,128	5
1940	113	42	60	215	10	—	—	—	—	—	7,326	3
1941	125	52	70	247	11	—	—	—	—	—	7,401	10
1942	129	59	72	260	12	—	—	—	—	—	6,646	(10)
1943	157	71	86	314	13	—	—	—	—	—	7,074	6
1944	192	87	114	393	14	—	—	—	—	—	7,377	4
1945	198	92	134	424	15	—	—	—	—	—	7,553	2
1946	200	98	157	455	14	—	—	—	—	—	7,608	1
1947	201	106	199	506	12	—	—	—	—	—	8,571	13
1948	211	121	230	562	12	—	—	—	—	—	9,171	7
1949	203	123	245	571	11	30	9	19	58	1	9,905	8
1950	196	136	273	605	11	85	31	55	171	3	10,634	7
1951	180	138	288	606	10	181	70	81	332	5	11,204	5
1952	162	141	321	624	9	256	94	104	454	6	12,310	10
1953	141	146	324	611	8	320	145	141	606	8	13,141	7
1954	114	135	310	559	7	422	207	180	809	10	13,652	4
1955	84	134	327	545	6	550	260	225	1,035	11	15,000	10

Advertising Rates and Expenditures   83

Table 303-A Advertiser Expenditure in Broadcasting, 1935–1982 (cont.)

Note: All Dollar Figures are in Millions.

	Radio Advertising					Television Advertising					All Advertising Media	
Year	Network	Spot	Local	Total	Percent of All Advertising	Network	Spot	Local	Total	Percent of All Advertising	Total	Percent of Annual Change
1956	60	161	346	567	6	643	329	253	1,225	12	15,755	5
1957	63	187	368	618	6	690	352	244	1,286	12	15,800	—
1958	58	190	372	620	6	742	397	248	1,387	13	15,621	(1)
1959	44	206	406	656	6	776	486	267	1,529	13	16,696	7
1960	43	222	428	693	6	820	527	280	1,627	13	17,409	4
1961	43	220	420	683	6	887	548	256	1,691	14	17,114	(2)
1962	46	233	457	736	6	976	629	292	1,897	15	17,606	3
1963	56	243	490	789	6	1,025	698	309	2,032	16	18,296	4
1964	59	256	531	846	6	1,132	806	351	2,289	16	19,464	6
1965	60	275	582	917	6	1,237	892	386	2,515	17	20,525	5
1966	63	308	639	1,010	6	1,393	988	422	2,823	17	21,654	6
1967	64	314	670	1,048	6	1,455	988	466	2,909	17	21,354	(1)

Year											
1968	63	360	767	1,190	7	1,523	1,131	577	3,231	18	21,900	3
1969	59	368	837	1,264	7	1,678	1,253	654	3,585	19	22,399	2
1970	56	371	881	1,308	7	1,658	1,234	704	3,596	18	21,389	(5)
1971	63	395	987	1,445	7	1,593	1,145	796	3,534	17	21,568	1
1972	74	402	1,136	1,612	7	1,804	1,318	969	4,091	18	23,210	8
1973	68	400	1,255	1,723	7	1,968	1,377	1,115	4,460	18	23,611	2
1974	69	405	1,363	1,837	7	2,145	1,497	1,212	4,854	18	23,126	(2)
1975	83	436	1,461	1,980	7	2,306	1,623	1,334	5,263	19	22,176	(4)
1976	105	518	1,707	2,330	7	2,857	2,154	1,710	6,721	20	25,160	13
1977	137	546	1,951	2,634	7	3,460	2,204	1,948	7,612	20	26,737	6
1978	147	620	2,285	3,052	7	3,975	2,607	2,373	8,955	20	28,811	8
1979	161	665	2,484	3,310	7	4,599	2,873	2,682	10,154	20	29,866	4
1980	183	779	2,740	3,702	7	5,130	3,269	2,967	11,366	21	29,997	—
1981	230	879	3,121	4,230	7	5,575	3,730	3,345	12,650	21	30,942	3
1982	255	923	3,492	4,670	7	6,210	4,360	3,759	14,329	21	32,161	4

Source: All information supplied to the author by Robert J. Coen, Senior Vice President, McCann-Erickson, Inc. This table is an updating and condensation of Tables 303–A, 303–B and 303–C in Sterling and Haight (1978). Notes: The radio-television figures are in *current* dollars; the "all advertising media" column is in *constant* dollars (1972 = 100). The figures are therefore not directly comparable. [a]Percentage figures in parentheses represent declines. [b]Data for 1982 are preliminary.

Table 303-B   Index of Media Advertising Rates, 1965–1982

		General-Interest	Radio		Television Network,	Network,	
Year	Newspapers	Magazines	Network	Spot	Prime-Time	Daytime	Spot
1965	82	94	107	92	91	80	96
1966	87	95	106	97	95	91	99
1967	87	95	104	98	95	91	102
1968	90	95	100	98	99	93	105
1969	94	98	100	100	102	98	107
1970	100	100	100	100	100	100	100
1971	104	97	99	102	93	87	98
1972	107	102	89	108	100	84	92
1973	112	104	89	108	112	95	91
1974	130	110	89	109	121	105	93
1975	147	118	90	115	123	110	93
1976	161	120	99	129	133	137	116
1977	175	122	108	140	167	177	122
1978	190	124	116	148	182	191	122
1979	205	134	123	155	205	200	133
1980	224	N/A	129	166	232	222	144
1981	244	N/A	139	178	248	239	150
1982[a]	266	N/A	151	190	267	250	158

Sources: 1965–1970 data from *Encyclomedia, 1977 Newspaper Edition*, p. 32; 1971–1981 data from *Broadcasting* (March 2, 1981), p. 76; and 1982 from *Marketing and Media Decisions* (Fall 1982), p. 36. Note: [a]Estimated. See text for details and limitations.

Table 303-B is taken from two sources. Data through the base year (for this table only) of 1970 was taken from *Encyclomedia, 1977 Newspaper Edition*, citing the following sources:

- For newspapers—Newspaper Advertising Bureau and J. Walter Thompson Co. (Estimates are based on the cost of 1,000 lines in black-and-white.)
- For consumer magazines—Magazine Advertising Bureau and J. Walter Thompson Co. (Estimates are based on the cost of a one-page, four-color advertisement.)
- For network radio—the radio networks, RADAR® research reports, and J. Walter Thompson Co. (Estimates are based on the cost of 60-second announcements.)
- For radio spots—Pulse, Inc., and J. Walter Thompson Co. (Estimates are based on the cost of 60-second announcements.)
- For network television, prime-time, daytime, and spots—A. C. Nielsen Co. and J. Walter Thompson Co. (Estimates are based on the cost of 30-second announcements.)

Table 303-C Cost-Per-Thousand Rates of Selected Media, 1970–1982

Year	Television (CPM Homes per 30 seconds)			Radio (People, 12 + per 60 seconds)		Magazines (Top 50 Consumer Magazines) (Per Page)		Newspapers (Per 1,000 Lines)	
	Network Prime-Time	Network Daytime	Fringe Spot	Network	Spot	Black and White	4-Color	Sunday	Daily
1970	2.10	.88	1.38	1.04	1.45	4.33	5.98	3.47	4.26
1972	1.98	.88	1.45	1.04	1.45	4.36	6.00	3.77	4.63
1974	2.40	.98	1.60	1.02	1.51	4.49	6.14	4.24	5.21
1976	2.98	1.23	1.98	1.20	1.74	4.94	6.77	5.50	6.92
1978	3.75	1.62	2.26	1.58	2.02	5.86	8.05	6.40	8.06
1980	4.60	1.95	2.71	1.92	2.32	7.10	9.70	8.40	10.10
1982	5.60	2.30	3.38	2.38	2.80	8.63	11.80	10.65	13.21

Source: McCann-Erickson, Inc. Note: Figures are in dollar amounts.

For the years since 1970, data is that developed by the Ted Bates advertising agency, as reported in *Marketing and Media Decisions* (Fall 1982, Vol. 17, No. 11), p. 36. The means of measuring individual media is as for the pre-1970 data, except that radio network CPM is based on 30- rather than 60-second announcements.

Table 303–C was supplied directly to the author by Robert Coen of McCann-Erickson, Inc., based on research done in his office. For the various measures shown in the Table itself, the data is a median for national data. The data are in current, not constant, dollars.

Further Information

Sources of information on advertising are considerable—see especially such trade periodicals as *Advertising Age* (weekly) and *Marketing & Media Decisions* (monthly). The standard rate card directory is issued by Standard Rate and Data Service in volumes for each medium, usually monthly. The business section of any good library can supply several bibliographic guides to the literature in this field. Good current textbooks in advertising for all of the media abound.

360
PUBLIC BROADCASTING
STATION FINANCES

Interpretation of the Tables

The four tables in this Unit illustrate recent trends in public television station income and expenses, as well as a limited view of public radio economics. Table 360–A provides both national and average per-station figures for fiscal-year income and direct operating expenditures (the latter does *not* include capital expenses and in-kind expenditures). These figures indicate that average per-station income has increased nearly 300 percent during the eight-year period from 1970 to 1978. However, this figure does not account for inflation. If inflation is considered in the calculations, the real growth in station income is less than 175 percent. Direct operating expenditures have increased about 252 percent in the same period (163 percent in constant dollars).

Table 360–B lists the sources of public television station income in terms of the proportional contribution of each source. The percentages are calculated on the basis of aggregate national data. These figures indicate that federal government support for public television stations more than doubled, from 12 percent in 1966 to 29 percent in 1978, before the sharp decline of the 1980s. In contrast, support from local governments and school boards has declined by half (see Unit 281 for the ownership ramifications of this decline). There has been a like decline in foundation support, due at least partially to the Ford Foundation's withdrawal from a portion of its major role in supporting public television over the years (see Unit 361). Somewhat as a result of these declines, the support of individuals (by direct payment, subscriptions, or auctions) has tripled.

Table 360–C provides an aggregate percentage breakdown of the direct operating costs of public television stations. The figures illustrate a predictable trend—the increase in the funds that are expended directly by the stations for development and fund-raising. This trend is, of course, parallel to the increases in direct public support noted in Table 360–B.

The financial information on public radio in Table 360–D is subject to some significant limitations which are discussed below. Still, the table provides a very rough approximation of the overall and per-station finances of public radio.

Sources

The data for all of the tables in this unit come from the Corporation for Public Broadcasting (CPB). Some of the data are published in the CPB's *Public Television Licensees* and *CPB-Qualified Public Radio Stations*. These CPB annuals, issued under various titles since 1970, provide accurate fiscal-year information based on surveys of all public television stations and the limited number of "qualified" public radio stations. The 1966–1968 data in Table 360–C precede the establishment of the CPB and are therefore found in annual publications of the National Association of Educational Broadcasters (NAEB).

The information on public radio in Table 360–D is severely limited in its completeness and accuracy, mainly because the CPB-qualified stations analyzed in the CPB annual are but a small fraction (20 percent) of all public radio stations on the air. In an attempt to compensate for these omissions, the author combined the number of CPB-qualified educational FM radio stations with the roughly 30 public AM stations which are not listed in CPB publications. These stations are omitted by the CPB because they do not

Table 360-A Income and Expenditures of Public Television Stations, 1970–1980

	1970	1971	1972	1973	1974	1975	1976	1977	1978	1979	1980
National Totals (In Millions of Dollars)											
Income	105.5	149.2	168.3	191.6	221.5	263.3	320.4	379.2	432.8	499.5	549.8
Direct Operating Expenditure	83.7	113.4	122.9	137.2	161.2	199.6	246.5	281.0	325.5	377.1	420.5
Number of PTV Licensees	123	129	134	150	154	158	159	161	164	160	170
Number of PTV Stations[a]	195	211	228	239	247	260	266	274	280	281	288
Per-Station Averages[b] (In Thousands of Dollars)											
Income	541.0	707.1	738.5	801.6	896.7	1,062.6	1,204.5	1,383.9	1,545.7	1,777.5	1,909.0
Direct Operating Expenditure	429.2	537.4	539.0	574.0	652.6	767.6	926.6	1,025.5	1,162.5	1,341.9	1,460.0

Source: All data supplied to the author from the Corporation for Public Broadcasting. Dollar figures refer only to broadcasting, not ancillary activities. Notes: [a]Number of stations shown above sometimes disagrees with Table 180–A due to variance in reporting date. [b]Data is based on the number of stations, not licensees (latter is truer indication of actual programming, as many "stations" are merely repeater transmitters controlled by same licensee).

Table 360–B Income Sources for Public Television Stations, 1966–1982 (In Percent)

Income Source	1966	1967	1968	1969	1970	1971	1972	1973	1974	1975	1976	1977	1978	1979	1980	1981	1982
Public Broadcast Agencies[a]	—	5	7	5	8	11	11	10	12	14 ⎫							
Federal Government	12	10	6	7	5	6	9	7	7	8 ⎭	27	27	29	26	26	24	22
State Governments and Boards of Education	27	16	24	29	28	33	24	30	31	29	25	23	21	25	25	22	22
Local Governments and School Boards	19	23	23	24	21	14	13	13	12	9	8	7	8	8	6	6	5
Universities and Colleges	11	10	11	6	9	7	12	8	8	7	9	10	12	8	9	10	9
Foundations	14	15	9	8	9	11	12	10	7	7	6	5	3	4	3	2	3
Subscribers and Auctions	6	8	10	9	10	9	10	14	15	16	14	13	14	15	15	18	21
Business/Industry, Other	11	13	9	11	10	9	9	8	8	10	11	14	13	14	15	19	19

Sources: 1966–1976 data supplied directly to the author by CPB. 1977 data from the Carnegie Commission (1979), p. 341; 1978 from CPB, *Summary Statistical Report of Public Television Licensees* (1980), p. 92; 1979 from CPB, *Status Report . . . 1980*, p. 19; 1980 from CPB, *Summary Statistical Report of Public Television Licensees* (1981), p. 58; 1981–82 from CPB to author; citing *Public Broadcasting Income. FY 1982* (CPB, December 1983) Table 2, p. 5. Note: [a]Primarily CPB, but also includes such agencies as CTW (Children's Television Workshop), and National Educational Radio, etc.

Table 360-C Direct Operating Expenditures of Public Television Stations, 1970–1982 (In Percent)

Direct Operating Expenses	1970	1971	1972	1973	1974	1975	1976	1977	1978	1979	1980	1981	1982
Technical	26	23	22	24	24	22	21	19	23	23	21	21	20
Programming	16	15	14	14	11	14							
Production	22	29	27	26	29	29	47	47	49	50	50	47	47
Instruction and School Services	8	8	7	6	6	5							
Development and Fund Raising	4	4	4	6	6	7	10	10	11	12	12	8	10
Promotion	3	3	3	3	3	3						6	6
Training and Personnel Development		—	1	1	1	2							
General and Administrative	15	14	17	16	16	14	15	15	17	15	17	17	17
Other	6	5	6	5	5	4							

Sources: Data supplied directly to the author by CPB through 1977; 1978 from CPB, *Summary Statistical Report of Public TV Licensees* (1980), p. 43; 1979 from CPB, *Status Report on Public Broadcasting* (1980), p. 23; and 1980 from CPB, *Summary Statistical Report of Public Television Licensees* (1981), p. 32, 1981–82 direct to author from Policy Development and Planning Office, CPB.

Table 360-D Income and Expenditures of CPB-Qualified Public Radio Stations, 1970–1980

	1970	1971	1972	1973	1974	1975	1976	1977	1978	1979	1980
National Totals (In Millions of Dollars)											
Income	11.2	14.1	17.7	21.8	26.1	32.4	40.8	52.0	64.6	77.5	101.8
Direct Operating Expenditure	8.6	10.6	12.9	15.9	19.2	24.7	30.3	36.5	44.4	51.9	64.9
Number of Stations											
Total	445	495	565	659	733	804	860	926	982	1038	1076
CPB-Qualified	96	109	132	144	153	165	179	189	199	218	244
Per-Station Averages (In Thousands of Dollars)											
Income	116.6	129.3	134.0	151.3	170.5	196.3	227.9	275.1	324.6	355.5	417.2
Direct Operating Expenditure	89.5	97.2	97.7	110.4	124.8	149.6	168.7	192.5	223.1	238.0	265.9

Source: All data supplied to the author from Corporation for Public Broadcasting. Dollar figures refer only to broadcasting, not ancillary activities. All dollar figures based *only* on CPB-qualified stations.

meet the minimal staff and budget levels which qualify a station for CPB support and survey inclusion. Thus, the CPB-qualified stations are nearly always the bigger and better-financed operations—another reason why the figures in Table 360–D must be considered rough and even misleading.

The reader should also keep in mind that despite the care of the CPB's survey procedures and analysis, all of the data in these four tables are gathered and reported for a purpose: to back up the CPB's annual requests for funding from Congress. Thus, there is likely to be a touch of advocacy in the development and arrangement of these figures.

Further Information

The Corporation for Public Broadcasting is the current repository and reporter of economic information for public television and CPB-qualified public radio stations, at least back to 1970. For what little consistent information is available for earlier years, see publications of the National Association of Educational Broadcasters, the report of the Carnegie Commission (1967), and Schramm and Nelson (1972). For more recent data on the growing plight of station funding see, among other sources, the second Carnegie Commission report (1979) and the summary report of the Temporary Commission on Alternate Funding for Public Telecommunications (1982). Further national financial information is in the following Unit 361.

361
PUBLIC BROADCASTING
NATIONAL FINANCES

Interpretation of the Tables

The four tables in this Unit provide detailed information on the important role played by the federal government in public broadcasting over the past decade. The tables also present a retrospective look at the even longer involvement of the Ford Foundation in subsidizing public broadcasting activities.

Most federal money for public broadcasting enters the system along one of the three main routes shown in Table 361–A: (1) through the Educational Broadcasting Facilities Program, which in 1979 was renamed the Public Telecommunications Facilities Program, and which was approved in 1962 but not actually funded until 1967; (2) through grants to the Children's Television Workshop (CTW); and (3), most recent and sizable, through grants to the Corporation for Public Broadcasting (CPB). Naturally, CPB grants go to CTW as well, and these grants are also federal money (see Table 361-C for details). In addition, the CPB issues grants to broadcasting facilities (see Table 361-B). The categories in Table 361-A represent the basic levels of support, ignoring subsequent "cross-fertilization" between programs.

Not shown in Table 361-A are grants from the National Endowment for the Arts and the National Endowment for the Humanities, both of which provide program funding. Additional funding will also dribble down through other sources, such as research grants from the National Science Foundation; but the channels listed in Table 361-A represent the lion's share of the support for public broadcasting.

Tables 361-B and 361-C provide a detailed look at the fiscal-year budgets of the CPB since 1969. Among the eight expenses categories listed in the budget, the following might be clarified with some additional commentary:

1. Expenditures for *PTV Program Production* primarily involve the major annual grants to PBS, CTW, and the producing PTV stations for programming. CPB has been increasingly criticized in recent years for spending relatively little of its funds directly for programming—about 15 percent in 1976.
2. *Program Distribution* is nearly always a single grant to PBS for running the network of public TV stations, now connected by domestic satellite.
3. *Public Radio Programs* refers to both production and distribution expenditures, with most of these funds going to National Public Radio.
4. *Engineering and Development* expenditures are generally research-oriented and do not include grants to stations for technical improvements.
5. *Development of Program Quality* refers to special support for experimentation and for the support of talent outside of public broadcasting.
6. Expenditures for *Support of Station Operations* are mainly grants to stations for general operating expenses.

In 1981, the Corporation radically changed their method of reporting both income and expenditures, thus making it impossible to compare data from the 1970s with that for the 1980s. The reason given for this change was that there was need to bring the budget reporting process into line with actual CPB practice. Thus, Table 361-C provides data for CPB's 1980–83 budgets using the current reporting structure. Data for 1980 is provided for both Table 361-B and 361-C. Otherwise, it is nearly impossible to directly compare information for the 1980s with data for the 1970s.

That *Sesame Street* and its offshoots have been successful (as well as expensive) is demonstrated by the increasing levels of CTW fundings shown in Table 361–D. Most of this funding has come from direct federal government grants, but the reader might also note that CTW-program "spin-offs" (magazine sales and product royalties) have also been providing revenues to CTW since 1972. In 1977, this spin-off income represented the biggest single source of support for CTW.

Table 361–E details the support of public broadcasting (especially television) by the Ford Foundation. Beginning in the early 1950s, Ford money, totaling more than 300 million dollars, has been crucial to the establishment of national public broadcasting, as well as of many of the earliest educational television stations.

Table 361–A   Federal Government Appropriations for Public Broadcasting, 1967–1983

	(1) Educational Broadcasting Facilities	(2) Children's Television	(3) Corporation for Public	(4) Total Federal Government	(5) Federal Support in Constant
Year	Program	Workshop	Broadcasting	Support[d]	(1972) Dollars
1967	32.0[a]	—	—	32.0	40.5
1968	—	1.4	—	1.4	1.7
1969	4.4	1.6	5.0	11.0	12.7
1970	5.1	1.0	15.0	21.1	23.1
1971	11.0	2.9	23.0	36.9	38.4
1972	13.0	7.0	35.0	55.0	55.0
1973	13.0	6.0	35.0	54.0	51.0
1974	15.7	4.0	47.5	67.2	57.7
1975	12.0	5.9	62.0	79.9	63.5
1976	12.9	6.2	96.0[b]	115.1	86.9
1977	15.0	5.0	103.0	123.0	88.0
1978	19.0	2.5	119.2	140.7	93.5
1979	18.4[c]	2.2	120.2	140.8	86.2
1980	26.0	4.0	152.0	182.0	102.0
1981	22.0	2.0	162.0	186.0	95.3
1982	18.0	3.0	172.0	193.0	93.3
1983	15.0	N/A	137.0	N/A	N/A

Note: All Figures in Millions of Dollars.

Sources: Data through 1978 for columns (1) and (2) from the U.S. Office of Education; data after that from NTIA for column (1) and CTW for column (2). Data on federal funds for CPB in column (3) was supplied to the author from CPB. Column (4) was added by the author, and column (5) was figured by the author based on GNP deflator (1972 = 100). Notes: [a]Single authorization covers the 1963–67 period, inclusive. [b]Includes 17.5 million dollars for the transition quarter to allow for change in the federal fiscal year. [c]This funding changed its title to Public Telecommunications Facilities Program, and moved to NTIA administration. [d]Does not include some lesser grants from National Endowments for the Arts and Humanities, given chiefly for programming to both stations and national agencies of public broadcasting.

Table 361-B Revenues and Expenses of the Corporation for Public Broadcasting, 1969–1980

Budget Item	1969[a]	1970[a]	1971	1972	1973	1974	1975	1976	1977[b]	1978	1979	1980
	Revenues (In Thousands of Dollars)											
Federal Appropriations	5,000	15,000	23,000	35,000	35,000	47,750	62,000	78,500	120,500	119,200	120,200	152,000
Federal Grants and Contracts	—	12	711	225	36	113	90	106	116	223	168	117
Nonfederal Contributions[c]	2,753	1,173	5,113	5,601	4,025	5,597	9,334	5,577	897	382	388	968
Earned Interest	206	251	235	694	353	853	1,330	952	4,079[d]	4,636	5,829	4,121
Carry-over of Year-end Net Assets from Previous Year	—	1,045	1,128	2,210	3,634	1,647	3,771	4,538	5,252	23,536	32,253	26,132
Unliquidated Budget Commitments from Previous Year	—	940	1,368	1,296	597	966	1,411	5,017	9,305	—	—	—
Total	7,959	18,421	31,555	45,026	43,645	56,925	77,936	94,690	140,150	147,977	158,838	183,338
	Expenses (In Thousands of Dollars)											
Grants and Awards[e]	3,986	10,252	24,587	37,165	37,273	48,056	63,883	74,948	109,074	108,722	122,878	142,653
PTV Program Production	—	4,897	9,902	15,308	16,131	17,124	17,444	14,849	14,351	19,405	15,934	21,569
Program Distribution	—	957	6,775	9,818	9,100	8,146	9,948	11,459	15,142	12,621	11,718	8,822
Public Radio Programs	—	151	1,085	2,291	3,501	3,931	5,383	5,541	8,349	9,170	12,225	15,772
Communication Research	—	—	—	—	92	75	239	439	462	761	653	471
Engineering and Development	—	—	—	53	151	109	372	1,290	684	2,490[f]	734	631
Development of Program Quality	—	498	222	767	367	105	133	326	285	276	387	236
Support for Station Operations	—	4,244	4,374	7,002	6,960	18,211	30,012	40,666	68,731	63,167	79,854	93,799
Program Promotion and Advertising	—	—	2,054	1,142	1,062	355	352	378	1,069	832	1,373	1,353

Table 361-B Revenues and Expenses of the Corporation for Public Broadcasting, 1969–1980 (cont.)

Budget Item		Expenses (In Thousands of Dollars)										
	1969[a]	1970[a]	1971	1972	1973	1974	1975	1976	1977[b]	1978	1979	1980
Programs Administered by CPB	1,197	3,857	1,224	987	693	787	1,002	792	4,161[g]	4,011	3,691	4,438
Administrative Support	791	1,816	2,237	2,643	3,065	2,900	3,496	4,393	3,611	2,991	2,800	3,116
Amortization of Satellite Systems	—	—	—	—	—	—	—	—	—	—	3,337	5,084
Current Unliquidated Budget Commitments	940	1,368	1,296	597	966	1,411	5,017	9,305	23,304[h]	32,253	26,132	28,047
Carry-over of Year-end Net Assets to Next Year	1,045	1,128	2,210	3,634	1,647	3,771	4,538	5,252				
Total	7,959	18,421	31,555	45,026	43,645	56,925	77,936	94,690	140,150	147,977	158,838	183,338

Source: Corporation for Public Broadcasting, *Annual Report*. Some figures do not add up due to rounding. Notes: [a]1969–1970 figures are unchecked and unverifiable. [b]Data for 1977 is for a 15 month year as the CPB converted to the federal budget year schedule (October 1 to September 30). [c]Nonfederal contributions are almost entirely from foundations and businesses. [d]Earned interest rose sharply at this point as the federal appropriation was given to the CPB in a lump sum rather than quarterly, allowing the CPB to take advantage of the rising bank interest rates. [e]See the text for definitions of the various "grants and awards" categories. [f]The substantial jump is due to the costs of satellite distribution system (PBS, then NPR) installation. [g]Includes "project-administration costs" and "other project related costs" from this year forward. [h]At this point, the CPB began to depreciate equipment purchases.

Table 361–C   Revenues and Expenses of the Corporation for Public Broadcasting, 1980–1983

Budget Item	1980	1981	1982	1983
Support and Revenue (in thousands)				
Federal Appropriation	$152,000	$162,000	$172,000	$137,000
Interest Income	4,121	5,101	13,932	7,150
Grant Refunds	915	229	712	700
Grants and Contracts	170	581	300	700
Total	157,206	167,911	186,944	144,850
Expenses (in thousands)				
Program Services:				
1) Direct TV Support CSG's[a]	75,659	81,407	85,645	68,500
Program Distribution	8,409	5,570	5,500	5,000
Program Production	21,569	24,670	23,732	18,390
2) Direct Radio Support CSG's[a]	12,680	14,707	18,843	16,800
Expansion/Improvement Grants	3,483	2,359	1,743	525
Program Distribution	2,675	2,956	800	325[b]
Program Production	13,097	14,102	14,800	12,100
3) Other Direct Support[c]	5,425	8,044	9,170	6,350
4) Research, Education, Training, and Other[d]	4,778	6,398	5,134	5,666
Support: CPB Administration	7,517	8,946	8,477	6,046

Source: Corporation for Public Broadcasting, *Annual Report* for 1981 and 1982; 1983 data direct to author from CPB. Notes: (a) Community Service Grants; (b) cited by source as "temporary interconnection"; (c) includes music royalty, satellite amortization, interest and loan commitment fees; and (d) includes minority and women's training grants, engineering research and development, communications research, grants to enhance use of public broadcast materials in education, and other assistance to stations and others.

Table 361–D Income Sources of the Children's Television Workshop, 1968–1982 (In Thousands of Dollars)

	1968	1969	1970	1971	1972	1973	1974	1975	1976	1977	1978	1979	1980	1981	1982
Federal Funding															
Office of Education	1,340	1,330	655	2,600	7,000	6,000	4,000	5,500	5,231	5,000	2,500	2,200[a]	4,000[a]	2,000[a]	1,000
Office of Economic Opportunity and Office of Child Development	50	300	300	300	—	—	—	—	—	—	—	—	—	—	—
National Institute for Alcohol Abuse and Alcoholism	—	—	—	—	—	—	—	250	—	—	—	—	—	—	—
National Endowment for the Humanities	—	—	—	—	—	—	—	48	1,000	—	1,617[b]	183[b]	—	65	—
National Cancer Institute	—	—	—	—	—	—	—	197	—	—	—	—	—	—	—
Others	25	—	—	—	—	—	—	—	—	—	—	—	—	—	138[c]
Corporation for Public Broadcasting	—	—	750	500	2,000	5,000	5,000	2,200	25	—	1,150	375	373	—	—
Public Broadcasting Service	—	—	—	—	—	—	—	4,255	4,165	3,601	2,199	2,310	2,423	2,779	2,995
Commercial Stations	—	—	—	115	241	303	188	178	123	136	56	48	70	72	62
Foundations															
Carnegie Corporation of New York	100	1,400	—	600	1,000	500	—	—	—	—	—	—	—	—	—
The Ford Foundation	250	1,288	—	1,000	1,000	2,000	—	2,025	500	525	1,000[b]	—	—	—	—
The John & Mary Markle Foundation	—	—	250	—	—	38	—	—	—	—	25	—	—	—	—
The Robert Wood Johnson Foundation	—	—	—	—	—	50	292	1,396	—	—	—	—	—	—	—
The Commonwealth Fund	—	—	—	—	—	100	—	100	—	—	—	—	—	—	—
Edna McConnell Clark Foundation	—	—	—	—	—	—	250	25	—	—	—	—	—	—	—

The Surdna Foundation	—	—	—	—	—	100	—	—	—	—	—	—	—	—
Revson Foundation	—	—	—	—	—	—	—	—	—	—	—	—	—	300
Others	—	160	10	119	88	—	66	54	65	20	—	30	—	72
Commercial Firms														
Mobil Oil Corporations	—	—	250	250	100	25	—	—	—	—	—	—	—	—
General Telephone & Electronics Corporation	—	—	—	—	—	—	—	—	—	—	750[b]	—	—	—
Xerox Corporation	—	—	—	260	740	50	—	—	—	—	—	1,800	—	—
Exxon Corporation	—	—	—	—	38	—	—	—	—	—	1,154	—	—	—
Aetna Life Insurance Company	—	—	—	—	—	450	650	—	—	—	—	—	—	—
Others	11	26	48	—	—	2	—	—	—	628	—	1,532	78	94
Non-Broadcasting Activities														
Magazine Sales	—	104	639	1,439	1,051	1,330	2,093	2,793	4,013	4,954	6,110	8,006	9,894	12,344
Royalties on Products	—	—	642	897	944	2,050	1,702	4,217	6,238	6,743	7,265	7,030	8,507	9,570
International Programming	—	—	15	363	851	2,936	1,510	2,946	1,568	4,473	4,642	4,782	3,002	2,766
Other	1	16	176	113	242	263	314	9	41	714	980	2,240	2,493	1,020
Total	1,415	1,992	4,964	7,195	15,218	20,030	15,483	25,194	20,525	21,176	26,399	25,371	35,237	28,957

Source: Children's Television Workshop. All figures are for fiscal years ending in June. Notes for 1978–82 period: [a]Office of Education funding includes 2 million dollars in 1979 and 1980 for "Sesame Street," and 200,000 dollars in 1979 plus 2 million dollars in 1980 for CTW's science program. [b]Matching grants from NEH for history series. [c]Consists principally of interest earned on temporary working capital investments. [d]Expense exceeded related income. [e]Most coming from National Science Foundation.

Table 361-E   Ford Foundation Grants for Public Broadcasting, 1951–1983
(In Dollars)

Fiscal Year	TV and Radio	Radio Only[a]
1951	1,439,091	492,800
1952	2,646,106	—
1953	4,490,021	150,905
1954	4,776,068	—
1955	3,139,195	—
1956	9,979,675	—
1957	4,749,720	74,750
1958	3,965,932	200,000
1959	11,126,112	12,600
1960	7,708,701	1,500
1961	8,140,359	15,000
1962	19,580,006	—
1963	7,423,652	—
1964	7,560,522	—
1965	7,171,903	—
1966	16,288,700	—
1967	23,000,544	38,000
1968	10,998,411	36,500
1969	25,301,843	185,572
1970	17,098,172	75,000
1971	18,155,198	—
1972	19,103,000	—
1973	10,683,699	—
1974	28,974,773	—
1975	3,680,000	—
1976	15,063,034	—
1977	2,212,457	—
1978	4,772,150	—
1979	1,092,000	—
1980	910,504	28,200
1981	329,840	79,840
1982	20,000	—
1983[b]	—	405,978
Totals	301,581,388	1,796,645

Sources: "Ford Foundation Activities in Noncommercial Broadcasting, 1951–76" (1976), p. 23. 1977–1983 data direct to the author from the Ford Foundation. Notes: [a]"Radio only" figures refer only to monies specifically for radio. These figures are included in the first column. Combined radio-TV grants are listed only in first column. [b]First six months only.

Sources

Though much of the information in this Unit is self-reported, it can be considered accurate because it is part of the public record and annually audited. Table 361–A was compiled by the U.S. Office of Education, the CPB, and the author. Tables 361–B and 361–C were done by the CPB.

Table 361–D information was supplied to the author by the CTW. Table 361–E is adapted from Ford Foundation data, which were based, in turn, on the foundation's own audited annual reports. The 1977–1978 grant figures were for television production only.

Further Information

For more information on government funding of public broadcasting, see the annual congressional hearings and committee reports regarding CPB and other related appropriations. The Office of Education was in charge of the Facilities program from its inception through 1978 when it was transferred to the National Telecommunications and Information Administration (NTIA), Department of Commerce, which keeps current records. For information on CPB, CTW, and the Ford Foundation, the reader might consult the published annual reports of each, as well as the material cited in Unit 360 of this book. For further information on the role of various foundations in public broadcasting, see Lashner (1976 and 1977). Interesting financial information can be found in reports of the two Carnegie Commissions (1967, 1979)—especially the latter, which compares public and commercial funding levels both in the United States and abroad. For narrative background on the government's role, see Gibson (1977).

370
COMMERCIAL RADIO
STATION FINANCES

Interpretation of the Tables

As the tables in this Unit illustrate, there are a number of different ways to approach the economics of commercial radio stations. Table 370–A offers a breakdown of national data into the median revenues and expenses of the "typical" local radio station. In addition, the 1980 figures on this table provide a further breakdown for the comparison of full-time AM station and FM station finances. Since less than half of all AM stations in existence today are full-time (see Unit 170), the financial variance between the two types of services (full-time and part-time) is worth noting.

Of course, like all statistical averages, the data in Table 370–A can be misleading. In 1980, for example, the National Association of Broadcasters (NAB) reported some large market stations with profit ratios of 26 percent, or more than 3 million dollars. Yet, that same year a small station in a minor market of under 10,000 persons might clear but 7,000 dollars.

This data summarizes information from a substantial annual report long issued by the NAB—and now the only regular economic information on the radio industry to be made available. For, after the information for 1980 was published, the Federal Communications Commission stopped collecting and publishing a financial profile of the radio business.

Thus, Table 370–B provides a "closed" statistical measure of just over four decades of radio networks and individual stations. While radio networks can be seen to be approaching their high income levels of the 1940s, this is more an artifact of inflation in the 1970s than a revival of the network role.

Table 370–C, based on the raw financial figures in Table 370–B, lists the profit ratios for the radio networks, their owned-and-operated (O&O) stations, and all other AM and AM-FM stations. The ratios were derived by the author by dividing earnings by revenues in each category. The results are profit ratios before taxes. The proportion of total radio industry profits (last two columns) was derived by dividing network and O&O station earnings by total earnings (these figures were then checked by dividing other station earnings by total earnings).

The table illustrates the decline in network radio as a strong financial element in the industry after the rise of television. Note that nearly all of the profit after about 1955 comes from the stations. Compare these results with those for the television industry (Table 380–B), in which network domination is the rule, following the old radio pattern.

Table 370–D provides what little aggregate data is available on commercial FM radio after 1948. While most of these statistics concern independent stations (stations not owned by an AM-station company), fuller information on AM-owned FM stations has been made available since 1969. These figures indicate that only just recently has the FM radio industry become profitable—first among the AM-owned FM stations, and then, in 1976, among the independent FM stations as well. Only in 1977 did a *majority* of the independent FM stations report a profit (the average was 77,000 dollars). But these data are limited severely by the fact that some 1,500 other FM stations (nearly all AM-owned) do not report their FM finances separately. (The figures in Tables 370–A, 370–B, and 370–C all include FM-station revenues which are not reported separately.) With the FCC having withdrawn from the collection of financial data, it will be extremely difficult to follow the continuing changes between AM and FM station economics.

Overall, the radio industry is very profitable—though a few large AM stations take the lion's share of the profits, and a fairly steady proportion of stations lose money each year. Moreover, two large groups of stations—daytime AM operations, and independent FM stations—have long faced a "soft" income situation. Table 370-E provides summary data on the profit-loss situation for three classes of stations:

1. AM stations, along with AM-owned FM stations not reporting separately;
2. AM-owned FM stations for which separate financial data are reported to the FCC; and
3. Independent (i.e., *not* AM-owned) FM stations.

Note that for the 15 year period covered in the table, there is no clear pattern of profit or loss among the AM and AM-FM outlets. Of course, this table provides only a national summary, thus glossing over such differences as station class, market size, etc.—all of which are clearly related to station profitability.

As with other advertising media, including newspapers and television, the income of the radio industry is somewhat cyclical, depending on both the overall state of the economy and the state of the advertising business. In "good" years, radio industry income has increased by 50–60 percent over the previous year, but lack of growth, or even decline (when inflation is taken into effect), is also an expected occurrence in the industry.

Sources

Data for Table 370-A, drawn from the NAB's annual *Radio Financial Report* (1961, 1971, and 1981), were gathered by a survey of all stations. Although not all stations responded to this survey, the NAB research department reports that its results generally parallel those of the FCC's more definitive research. With the demise of the FCC data-gathering function, the NAB series becomes the only annual measure which attempts to economically define the whole industry. But as with the FCC information, reports are based only on those stations which respond, and as a voluntary effort, the NAB series has generally been based on far fewer stations than the once-required FCC filings.

The remaining tables are all FCC figures, or are based on those surveys—and thus are closed with the 1980 information included here. It will be impossible to update these data runs in the future unless the Commission returns to this function—and even then a number of years' data will be lost.

Table 370–A   Revenues and Expenses of the Typical Commercial Radio Station, 1960, 1970, and 1980 (In Thousands of Dollars)

Budget Category	1960 Amount (N = 1,118)	1960 Percent	1970 Amount (N = 1,374)	1970 Percent	1980 Full-Time AM Amount	1980 Full-Time AM Percent (N = 1,672)	1980 Full-Time FM Amount	1980 Full-Time FM Percent
Revenue:								
Total Time Sales	110.3	100	162.3	100	483.7	100	421.9	100
Network Compensation	—	—	—	—	—	—	—	—
Spot Sales	15.9	14	20.2	13	60.9	13	62.0	15
Local Sales	94.4	86	142.0	88	422.8	87	359.9	85
Expenses:	101.8	100	151.7	100	488.8	100	385.8	100
Total Salaries	(60.7)[a]	*	(84.0)	*	(213.5)	*	(174.6)	*
Technical Costs	10.9	11	12.6	8	24.7	6	23.9	6
Programming Costs	33.5	33	46.7	31	124.3	28	99.9	26
Sales and Promotional Costs	18.7	18	28.1	19	104.1	23	96.5	25
General and Administrative Costs	38.7	38	64.3	42	195.7	44	165.5	43
Outside News Service Fees	N/A	N/A	N/A	N/A	(7.0)	*	(4.6)	*
Music License Fees	N/A	N/A	(4.6)	*	(11.7)	*	(9.4)	*
Depreciation/Amortization	(5.6)	*	(7.4)	*	(22.7)	*	(21.2)	*
Interest	N/A	N/A	N/A	N/A	(2.3)	*	(12.7)	*
Income (Before Tax)	8.4	8	10.5	7	25.7	5	12.7	3

Source: National Association of Broadcasters, *Radio Financial Report,* Annual, issues for 1961, 1971, and 1981. Note: [a]Figures shown in parentheses with percentages entered as an asterisk are included in other budget items, being broken out here for illustration.

Table 370-B Revenues, Expenses, and Earnings of Commercial Radio Networks and Stations, 1937–1980

Note: All Dollar Figures are in Millions. Figures in Parentheses Indicate Losses.

Year	Total Number of Stations	Number of Networks	Networks and Network O & O Stations				Other Stations [a]				Total, All Stations		
			Number of Stations	Total Revenues	Total Expenses	Pre-Tax Earnings	Number of Stations Reporting	Total Revenues	Total Expenses	Pre-Tax Earnings	Total Revenues	Total Expenses	Pre-Tax Earnings
1937	629	3	N/A	N/A	N/A	N/A	N/A	N/A	N/A	N/A	114.2	91.6	22.6
1938	660	3	23	54.8	35.5	9.2	637	65.5	56.9	9.5	111.4	92.5	18.9
1939	705	3	23	48.4	37.6	11.0	682	75.3	62.6	12.8	123.9	100.1	23.8
1940	765	3	31	56.4	42.2	14.1	734	90.6	71.5	19.1	147.1	118.8	33.3
1941	817	3	33	62.0	44.2	18.0	784	106.6	79.6	27.1	168.8	124.0	44.8
1942	851	4	32	63.7	46.8	16.9	819	115.1	87.4	27.7	178.8	134.2	44.6
1943	841	4	31	76.6	53.0	23.6	810	138.6	95.8	42.8	215.3	148.8	66.5
1944	875	4	32	94.6	68.4	26.2	843	180.7	116.6	64.1	275.3	185.0	90.3
1945	911	4	28	100.9	77.9	23.1	873	198.3	137.8	60.5	299.3	215.7	83.6
1946	1,025	4	29	102.0	82.6	19.4	996	220.6	168.5	57.1	322.6	246.1	76.5
1947	1,464	4	27	104.4	84.8	19.6	1,437	259.3	207.1	52.2	368.7	291.9	71.8
1948	1,824	4	27	109.1	91.0	18.1	1,797	298.0	252.0	46.1	407.0	342.9	64.1
1949	2,021	4	27	108.1	90.6	17.5	1,994	305.7	266.9	38.8	413.8	357.5	56.3
1950	2,229	4	26	110.5	91.5	19.0	2,208	334.0	284.8	49.2	444.5	376.3	68.2
1951	2,266	4	25	104.0	93.9	10.1	2,241	346.4	299.0	47.4	450.4	392.9	57.5
1952	2,380	4	25	100.6	89.4	11.2	2,355	369.1	320.2	48.9	469.7	409.6	60.1
1953	2,479	4	22	97.3	86.9	10.4	2,457	378.0	333.4	44.6	475.3	420.3	55.0
1954	2,598	4	21	88.6	80.4	8.2	2,577	361.0	327.3	33.7	410.5	407.7	41.8
1955	2,742	4	19	78.3	72.4	5.9	2,724	375.0	335.0	40.0	453.4	407.4	46.0
1956	2,966	4	19	70.2	69.8	0.4	2,947	410.4	361.6	48.8	480.6	431.4	49.2
1957	3,164	4	21	73.5	73.5	0.0	3,143	444.4	389.8	54.6	517.9	463.3	54.6
1958	3,290	4	23	69.4	73.0	(3.7)	3,267	453.7	412.8	40.9	523.1	485.8	37.3
1959	3,528	4	19	60.4	64.9	(4.5)	3,529	499.6	452.7	46.9	560.0	517.6	42.4
1960	3,688	4	19	63.0	66.0	(3.0)	3,669	534.7	485.8	48.9	597.7	551.8	45.9
1961	3,610	4	19	61.5	61.3	0.2	3,591	522.1	490.2	31.8	583.6	511.6	32.0

Table 370–B Revenues, Expenses, and Earnings of Commercial Radio Networks and Stations, 1937–1980 (cont.)

Note: All Dollar Figures are in Millions. Figures in Parentheses Indicate Losses.

Year	Total Number of Stations	Networks and Network O & O Stations					Other Stations[a]				Total, All Stations		
		Number of Networks	Number of Stations	Total Revenues	Total Expenses	Pre-Tax Earnings	Number of Stations Reporting	Total Revenues	Total Expenses	Pre-Tax Earnings	Total Revenues	Total Expenses	Pre-Tax Earnings
1962	3,698	4	19	64.1	61.9	2.2	3,679	562.7	518.2	44.5	626.8	580.1	46.7
1963	3,832	4	19	68.9	63.0	5.0	3,813	600.7	548.6	52.1	669.7	611.6	53.1
1964	3,896	4	19	71.1	66.8	4.3	3,877	648.0	578.5	69.3	719.2	645.4	73.8
1965	3,941	4	19	74.4	71.3	3.0	3,922	702.4	624.4	78.0	776.8	695.7	81.1
1966	4,019	4	19	79.4	75.8	3.6	4,000	773.2	676.2	97.0	852.7	752.1	100.6
1967	4,068	4	19	77.1	79.1	(2.0)	4,057	807.6	720.5	87.0	884.7	799.6	85.0
1968	4,161	4	20	81.3	86.5	(5.2)	4,141	913.4	790.9	122.5	994.7	877.4	117.3
1969	4,194	4	20	84.5	85.0	(0.5)	4,174	955.8	844.1	111.7	1,040.3	929.2	111.2
1970	4,209	4	20	86.1	84.4	1.7	4,189	991.2	888.9	102.2	1,077.4	973.4	104.0
1971	4,252	4	20	97.0	89.4	7.5	4,232	1,079.4	969.2	110.2	1,176.3	1,058.6	117.8
1972	4,271	4	20	106.3	93.4	12.9	4,251	1,185.7	1,051.7	134.1	1,292.1	1,145.0	147.0
1973	4,267	4	18	102.3	96.3	6.0	4,269	1,254.5	1,137.3	117.3	1,356.9	1,233.6	123.3
1974	4,267	4	18	104.4	102.1	2.3	4,343	1,305.3	1,212.8	92.5	1,409.7	1,314.9	94.8
1975	4,355	7	17	118.4	109.5	9.0	4,338	1,361.3	1,274.7	86.5	1,479.7	1,384.3	95.4
1976	4,363	7	17	143.8	133.4	10.3[b]	4,346	1,543.1	1,396.0	147.2	1,686.9	1,529.4	157.5
1977	4,292	8	18	182.9	138.6	44.3	4,274	1,663.0	1,502.8	160.2	1,846.0	1,641.5	204.4
1978	4,316	8	36[c]	236.4	192.6	43.7	4,280	1,828.4	1,634.8	193.6	2,064.8	1,827.4	237.4
1979	4,253	8	35	252.0	214.8	37.2	4,218	2,621.6	2,427.3	194.3	2,873.6	2,642.2	231.4
1980	4,259	8	35	292.8	265.3	27.5	4,224	2,913.2	2,782.0	131.6	3,206.0	3,047.3	159.1

Source: Federal Communications Commission, annual financial reports on the radio business, as partially reprinted in the *Annual Report.* Notes: [a]Independent FM stations are not included in the totals after 1968. [b]This sharp rise is primarily due to network earnings of over 25 million dollars compared to a 5 million dollar loss the year before. [c]This sharp rise in station count is because the FCC began to include FM stations.

Table 370–C   Profit Ratios of Commercial Radio Networks and Stations, 1937–1980

Note: All Figures are in Percent. Figures in Parentheses Indicate Loss. Dashes Indicate Less than 1 Percent Either Way.

	Profit Ratios			Proportion of Total Profits	
Year	Networks and O&O Stations	Other Stations	Total Radio	Networks and O&O Stations	Other Stations
1937	N/A	N/A	20	N/A	N/A
1938	17	15	17	49	51
1939	23	17	19	46	54
1940	25	21	23	42	58
1941	29	25	27	40	60
1942	27	24	25	38	62
1943	31	31	31	35	65
1944	28	35	33	29	71
1945	23	31	28	28	78
1946	19	26	24	25	75
1947	19	20	20	27	73
1948	17	15	16	28	72
1949	16	13	14	31	69
1950	17	15	15	28	72
1951	10	14	13	18	82
1952	11	13	13	19	81
1053	11	12	12	19	81
1954	9	9	9	20	80
1955	8	11	10	13	87
1956	—	12	10	—	100
1957	—	12	11	—	100
1958	—	9	7	(1)	100
1959	(1)	9	8	(11)	100
1960	(1)	9	8	(7)	100
1961	—	6	5	—	100
1962	3	8	7	5	95
1963	9	9	9	10	90
1964	6	11	10	6	94
1965	4	11	10	4	96
1966	5	13	12	4	96
1967	—	11	10	(2)	100
1968	(1)	13	12	(4)	100
1969	—	12	11	—	100
1970	1	10	10	2	98

Table 370–C   Profit Ratios of Commercial Radio Network Stations, 1937–1980 (cont.)

Note: All Figures are in Percent. Figures in Parentheses Indicate Loss. Dashes Indicate Less than 1 Percent Either Way.

| | Profit Ratios | | | Proportion of Total Profits | |
Year	Networks and O&O Stations	Other Stations	Total Radio	Networks and O&O Stations	Other Stations
1971	8	10	10	6	94
1972	12	11	11	9	91
1973	6	9	9	5	95
1974	2	7	7	2	98
1975	8	6	6	9	91
1976	7	10	9	6	93
1977	24	10	11	22	78
1978	19	11	11	18	82
1979	24	7	8	16	84
1980	9	5	5	17	82

Source: Based on FCC data in Table 370–B.

The Commission financial data included (but did not separately report) independent FM stations until 1961, and AM-owned FM stations (the majority—see Table 270–C) until 1969, when, respectively, both categories were reported separately. In Tables 370–B and 370–D, only the column of Total Revenues (under Total, All Stations) includes all income to all FM stations, regardless of control. The total columns for expenses and earnings include only the combined totals of the independent FM and AM-owned FM stations. Figures may not add up due to rounding.

Specific definitions, methods of gathering the information, and limitations to the FCC research is found in the annual mimeograph versions of the reports, which are largely summarized in both the FCC's *Annual Report* and the issue of *Broadcasting* published closest to the date of the report's initial release.

Further Information

Financial information on radio is more difficult to obtain than that for television. With the end of the FCC's statistical role, researchers must approach a trade organization such as the National Association of Broadcasters, or the Radio Advertising Bureau. See also sources listed under Unit 170.

Table 370-D   Revenues, Expenses, and Earnings of Commercial FM Stations, 1948–1980

Note: All Dollar Figures are in Millions. Figures in Parentheses Indicate Losses.

Year	Number of Stations	Independent FM Stations				FM Stations Owned by AM Stations				Total, All Stations		
		Number of Stations	Total Revenues	Total Expenses	Pre-Tax Earnings	Number of Stations	Total Revenues	Total Expenses	Pre-Tax Earnings	Total Revenues	Total Expenses	Pre-Tax Earnings
1948	682	87	1.1	4.2	(3.1)	—	—	—	—	1.7	—	—
1949	723	104	1.6	5.1	(3.5)	—	—	—	—	3.6	—	—
1950	699	86	1.4	4.0	(2.6)	—	—	—	—	2.8	—	—
1951	626	66	1.2	3.0	(1.8)	—	—	—	—	3.0	—	—
1952	611	56	1.1	2.1	(1.0)	—	—	—	—	2.6	—	—
1953	594	45	.8	1.6	(.8)	—	—	—	—	2.1	—	—
1954	528	43	.8	1.4	(.6)	—	—	—	—	1.9	—	—
1955	493	38	1.0	1.4	(.4)	—	—	—	—	1.9	—	—
1956	472	51	1.4	1.8	(.4)	—	—	—	—	2.4	—	—
1957	499	67	2.0	2.5	(.5)	—	—	—	—	3.1	—	—
1958	533	93	2.5	3.2	(.7)	—	—	—	—	4.0	—	—
1959	662	148	4.3	5.9	(1.6)	—	—	—	—	5.7	—	—
1960	789	218	5.8	8.2	(2.4)	—	—	—	—	9.4	—	—
1961	938	249	7.1	9.7	(2.6)	—	—	—	—	10.0	—	—
1962	993	279	9.3	12.5	(3.2)	—	—	—	—	13.9	—	—
1963	1,071	294	11.4	14.6	(3.2)	—	—	—	—	16.3	—	—
1964	1,175	306	12.8	15.8	(3.0)	—	—	—	—	19.7	—	—
1965	1,381	338	15.7	19.0	(3.3)	—	—	—	—	24.7	—	—
1966	1,575	381	19.4	22.7	(3.3)	—	—	—	—	32.3	—	—
1967	1,706	405	22.6	26.8	(4.2)	—	—	—	—	39.8	—	—
1968	1,888	433	28.3	32.2	(3.9)	—	—	—	—	53.2	—	—
1969	1,961	442	33.4	38.9	(5.5)	179	12.1	16.9	(4.8)	67.4	55.8	(10.3)
1970	2,105	464	40.6	46.8	(6.2)	225	18.9	23.8	(4.9)	84.9	70.6	(11.1)

Commercial Radio Station Finances   111

Table 370-D Revenues, Expenses, and Earnings of Commercial FM Stations, 1948–1980 (cont.)

Note: All Dollar Figures are in Millions. Figures in Parentheses Indicate Losses.

Year	Number of Stations	Independent FM Stations				FM Stations Owned by AM Stations				Total, All Stations		
		Number of Stations	Total Revenues	Total Expenses	Pre-Tax Earnings	Number of Stations	Total Revenues	Total Expenses	Pre-Tax Earnings	Total Revenues	Total Expenses	Pre-Tax Earnings
1971	2,235	527	55.3	64.4	(9.0)	241	26.3	32.3	(6.0)	115.0	96.7	(15.0)
1972	2,328	590	77.4	86.2	(8.8)	275	37.5	41.4	(3.9)	151.9	127.6	(12.7)
1973	2,390	616	96.1	106.1	(10.0)	361	57.5	58.3	(.8)	198.3	164.4	(10.8)
1974	2,552	678	128.0	141.1	(13.1)	397	65.4	63.0	2.9	248.2	204.1	(10.2)
1975	2,669	703	142.9	152.4	(9.4)	477	102.4	97.7	4.7	245.3	250.1	(4.7)
1976	2,756	713	180.0	115.7	4.3	562	152.5	135.7	16.9	332.5	251.4	21.2
1977	2,844	741	225.3	215.8	9.4	586	203.4	171.1	32.2	428.7	386.9	41.6
1978	3,085	777	285.3	261.8	23.5	655	285.2	235.0	50.2	570.5	496.8	73.7
1979	3,161	835	361.5	348.1	13.5	631	335.5	290.5	45.0	697.0	638.6	58.4
1980	3,377	904	441.1	437.0	4.0	715	422.2	369.6	52.8	863.3	806.6	56.7

Source: FCC annual financial reports on AM-FM broadcasting.

Table 370–E Number of AM and FM Radio Stations Reporting Profits or Losses, 1962–1980

Year	AM and AM-FM Stations				AM-Owned FM Stations Reporting				Independent FM Stations			
	Total Stations	Number with Profit	Percent with Profit	Number with Loss	Total Stations	Number with Profit	Percent with Profit	Number with Loss	Total Stations	Number with Profit	Percent with Profit	Number with Loss
1962	3,533	2,318	66	1,215	N/A	N/A	N/A	N/A	279	71	25	208
1963	3,685	2,451	67	1,234	N/A	N/A	N/A	N/A	294	86	29	208
1964	3,739	2,660	71	1,079	N/A	N/A	N/A	N/A	306	93	30	213
1965	3,858	2,708	70	1,150	N/A	N/A	N/A	N/A	338	102	30	236
1966	3,912	2,810	72	1,102	N/A	N/A	N/A	N/A	381	111	29	270
1967	3,976	2,654	67	1,322	N/A	N/A	N/A	N/A	405	115	28	290
1968	4,061	2,912	72	1,149	N/A	N/A	N/A	N/A	433	148	34	285
1969	4,118	2,790	68	1,328	179	45	25	134	442	136	31	306
1970	4,131	2,743	66	1,388	225	71	32	154	464	144	31	320
1971	4,176	2,838	68	1,338	241	80	33	161	527	182	35	345
1972	4,221	3,054	72	1,167	275	106	39	169	590	224	38	366
1973	4,213	2,907	69	1,306	361	167	46	194	616	239	39	377
1974	4,294	2,809	65	1,485	397	215	54	182	678	273	40	405
1975	4,295	2,618	61	1,677	477	259	54	218	703	284	40	419
1976	4,275	2,875	67	1,400	562	349	62	213	713	351	49	362
1977	4,216	2,783	66	1,433	586	371	63	215	741	385	52	356
1978	4,214	2,823	67	1,391	640	429	67	211	722	412	57	310
1979	4,079	2,447	60	1,632	658	421	64	237	753	392	52	361
1980	5,539	3,268	59	2,271	682	416	61	266	813	407	50	407

Source: FCC annual financial reports on AM-FM broadcasting.

Commercial Radio Station Finances   113

380
COMMERCIAL TELEVISION
STATION FINANCES

Interpretation of the Tables

The three tables presented in this Unit provide an overview of the revenues, expenses, earnings, and profit ratios of commercial television stations in the United States. The reader will note in Tables 380–A and 380–B that television profit ratios are a good deal higher than those of *radio* stations (see Tables 370–A and 370–B, and Unit 382). However, averages of television statistics, such as the figures in Tables 380–A can be misleading. For example, a major-market, VHF, network-affiliate station may have a profit of over 17 million dollars (and a profit ratio of 38 percent or better), while a small-market, VHF, independent station might realize only 100,000 dollars before taxes (about a 9 percent profit ratio). Moreover, UHF stations, almost without exception, do not do nearly as well as their VHF competitors.

Another key factor in the financial performance of both VHF and UHF stations is the matter of network affiliation. According to the FCC, in 1975, 87 percent of VHF network-affiliate stations, but only 73 percent of VHF independents, made a profit. In that same year, only 52 percent of UHF stations—affiliated and independent—drew a profit (see Table 380–C). Similar annual performance statistics over the past two decades form a fairly consistent pattern.

Tables 380–B and 380–C are based on the now-discontinued FCC financial reports (see comment in the Unit 370 text). Table 380–B provides an overall summary, while Table 380–C compares the financial record of VHF and UHF stations.

Table 380–B presents the official FCC data on television station economics for the years 1948 through 1980 (the information on profit ratios is supplied by the author). The "commercial stations" columns include all VHF and UHF, network-affiliate and independent stations, but exclude the 15 network owned-and-operated (O&O) stations. The "industry total" columns include data on the O&O stations, to give the reader a broader view of television economics. However, for the full picture, the reader should use this table in conjunction with the tables in Unit 382 to compare the television networks and their O&O stations with all other commercial stations.

Table 380–A Revenues and Expenses of the Typical Commercial Television Station, 1960, 1970, and 1980 (In Thousands of Dollars)

Budget Category	1960 Amount (N = 277)	1960 Percent	1970: all Stations Amount (N = 677)	1970: all Stations Percent	1970: UHF only Amount (N = N/A)	1970: UHF only Percent	1980: all Stations Amount (N = 462)	1980: all Stations Percent	1980: UHF only Amount (N = N/A)	1980: UHF only Percent
Revenue:										
Total Time Sales	962.8	100	1,792.7	100	978.0	100	4,962.5	100	3,028.6	100
Network Compensation	251.3	26	324.4	19	75.3	8	456.6	9	157.5	5
Spot Sales	413.0	43	735.0	41	340.3	35	2,218.2	45	1,299.3	43
Local Sales	298.5	31	715.3	40	562.4	58	2,287.7	46	1,571.8	52
Expenses:	756.3	100	1,340.3	100	989.8	100	3,397.3	100	2,598.0	100
(Total Salaries)	(318.7)[a]	*	(573.0)	*	(360.5)	*	(1,287.2)	*	(741.7)	*
Technical Costs	124.0	16	206.4	15	155.4	16	383.9	11	335.2	13
Programming Costs	280.9	37	475.8	36	357.3	36	1,209.4	36	891.1	34
Sales and Promotional Costs	97.9	13	171.6	13	122.7	12	496.0	15	361.1	14
General and Administrative Costs	265.5	34	486.5	36	354.4	36	1,308.0	39	1,010.6	39
Outside News Service Fees	N/A	—	N/A	—	N/A	—	(27.9)	*	10.8	*
Music License Fees	N/A	—	N/A	—	N/A	—	(72.4)	*	(42.9)	*
Depreciation/Amortization	(78.9)	*	(142.5)	*	(110.4)	*	(309.0)	*	(240.1)	*
Interest	N/A	—	N/A	—	N/A	—	(14.7)	*	(72.9)	*
Film/Tape Costs	(85.4)	*	(110.9)	*	(74.0)	*	(311.9)	*	(215.8)	*
Income (before Tax)	139.2	15	284.9	18	-54.8	-6	945.9	22	219.8	8

Sources: National Association of Broadcasters, *Television Financial Report*, Annual, issues for 1961, 1971, and 1981; and "Typical UHF can see Break-Even Point," *Broadcasting* (August 23, 1971), p. 49, reporting a special NAB survey. Note: [a]Figures in parentheses with percentages entered as an asterisk are included in other budget items, being broken out here for illustration.

Table 380-B Revenues, Expenses, Earnings, and Profit Ratios of Commercial Television Stations, 1948–1980

Note: All Dollar Figures are in Millions. Figures in Parentheses Indicate Losses.

	All Non-O&O Stations[a]						All Commercial Stations[b]				
Year	Number of Stations	Revenue	Expenses	Earnings before Taxes	Profit Ratio (In Percent)	Percent of Total TV Industry Profits	Number of Stations	Revenue	Expenses	Earnings before Taxes	Profit Ratio (In Percent)
1948	40	3.9	12.4	(8.5)	(218)	—	50	8.7	23.6	(14.9)	(171)
1949	84	15.0	29.0	(13.5)	(90)	—	98	34.3	59.6	(25.3)	(74)
1950	93	50.4	49.6	.8	2	—	107	105.9	115.1	(9.2)	(9)
1951	98	107.3	76.7	30.6	29	74	108	235.7	194.1	41.6	18
1952	107	144.0	98.4	45.6	32	82	122	324.2	268.7	55.5	17
1953	318	201.0	151.0	50.0	25	74	334	432.7	364.7	68.0	16
1954	394	286.3	232.5	53.8	19	60	410	593.0	502.7	90.3	15
1955	421	370.0	288.5	81.5	22	55	437	744.7	594.5	150.2	20
1956	459	454.6	350.4	104.2	23	55	475	896.9	707.3	189.6	21
1957	485	475.3	386.0	89.3	19	56	501	943.2	783.2	160.0	17
1958	495	513.3	418.4	94.8	18	55	514	1,030.0	858.1	171.9	17
1959	504	587.8	453.4	134.4	23	60	521	1,163.9	941.6	222.3	19
1960	515	627.9	479.0	148.9	24	61	530	1,268.6	1,024.5	244.1	19
1961	525	643.0	493.0	150.0	23	63	540	1,318.3	1,081.3	237.0	18

1962	539	732.0	531.8	200.2	27	64	554	1,486.2	1,174.6	311.6	21
1963	550	776.9	569.9	207.0	27	60	565	1,597.2	1,254.0	343.2	21
1964	560	864.6	605.5	259.1	30	62	575	1,793.3	1,377.7	415.6	23
1965	573	941.0	654.7	286.3	30	64	588	1,964.8	1,516.9	447.9	23
1966	593	1,036.7	730.6	306.1	30	62	608	2,203.0	1,710.1	492.9	22
1967	604	1,058.8	804.3	254.5	24	61	619	2,275.4	1,860.8	414.6	18
1968	627	1,212.9	897.0	316.0	26	64	642	2,520.9	2,026.1	494.8	20
1969	658	1,328.9	1,001.3	327.5	25	59	673	2,796.2	2,242.6	553.6	20
1970	671	1,351.1	1,064.6	286.4	21	63	686	2,808.2	2,354.4	453.8	16
1971	673	1,371.4	1,127.2	244.3	18	63	688	2,750.3	2,361.2	389.2	14
1972	648	1,581.1	1,242.3	338.8	21	61	663	3,179.4	2,627.3	552.2	17
1973	651	1,706.8	1,341.4	365.4	21	56	666	3,464.8	2,811.7	653.1	19
1974	659	1,855.2	1,448.9	406.3	22	55	669	3,776.3	3,039.2	737.1	20
1975	654	2,024.7	1,558.8	465.9	23	60	669	4,094.1	3,314.1	780.0	19
1976	687	2,594.1	1,798.5	795.6	31	64	702	5,198.5	3,945.3	1,250.2	24
1977	682	2,804.1	1,958.5	845.6	30	60	697	5,889.0	4,488.0	1,401.1	24
1978	699	3,400.7	2,307.2	1,093.5	32	66	714	6,949.8	5,296.5	1,653.3	24
1979	708	3,782.6	2,667.7	1,114.9	29	66	723	7,875.0	6,184.8	1,690.2	21
1980	710	4,242.2	3,122.9	1,119.4	26	68	725	8,807.7	7,154.2	1,653.5	19

Source: FCC annual financial reports on the television business, partially reprinted in the FCC's *Annual Report*. Notes: Figures may not add up due to rounding. [a]Includes all commercial stations (VHF and UHF, independent and affiliate) except the 15 network-owned and operated stations. [b]Includes network-owned and operated stations.

Table 380–C   Revenues, Expenses, and Earnings of Commercial VHF and UHF Stations, 1953–1980

Note: All Dollar Figures are in Millions. Figures in Parentheses Indicate Losses.

Year	Number of Stations Reporting	Revenue	Expenses	Earnings before Taxes	Percent of Stations Reporting Profits
1953					
VHF	206	190.6	134.3	56.3	N/A
UHF	*112*	*10.4*	*16.7*	*(6.3)*	*N/A*
1954					
VHF	269	260.9	197.1	63.8	N/A
UHF	*125*	*25.4*	*35.4*	*(10.0)*	*N/A*
1955					
VHF	318	342.2	255.5	86.7	63
UHF	*103*	*28.5*	*33.0*	*(4.5)*	*27*
1956					
VHF	364	422.1	316.0	106.1	73
UHF	*95*	*32.5*	*34.4*	*(1.9)*	*39*
1957					
VHF	397	448.6	355.8	92.8	81
UHF	*88*	*26.7*	*30.2*	*(3.5)*	*32*
1958					
VHF	416	487.2	390.1	97.1	71
UHF	*76*	*26.1*	*28.3*	*(2.2)*	*37*
1959					
VHF	427	559.8	424.9	134.9	78
UHF	*77*	*28.0*	*28.5*	*(.5)*	*51*
1960					
VHF	439	597.1	448.5	148.6	81
UHF	*76*	*30.8*	*30.5*	*.3*	*50*
1961					
VHF	444	611.6	461.0	150.6	79
UHF	*81*	*31.4*	*32.0*	*(.6)*	*39*
1962					
VHF	456	697.6	498.3	199.3	81
UHF	*83*	*34.4*	*33.5*	*.9*	*57*
1963					
VHF	464	737.8	531.0	206.8	83
UHF	*86*	*39.1*	*38.9*	*.2*	*58*
1964					
VHF	468	820.3	563.9	256.4	85
UHF	*92*	*44.3*	*41.6*	*2.7*	*68*
1965					
VHF	473	891.3	604.8	286.5	87
UHF	*100*	*49.7*	*49.9*	*(.2)*	*66*

Table 380–C   Revenues, Expenses, and Earnings of Commercial VHF and UHF Stations, 1953–1980 (cont.)

Note: All Dollar Figures are in Millions. Figures in Parentheses Indicate Losses.

Year	Number of Stations Reporting	Revenue	Expenses	Earnings before Taxes	Percent of Stations Reporting Profits
1966					
VHF	479	976.9	663.5	313.5	87
UHF	*114*	*59.8*	*67.1*	*(7.4)*	*59*
1967					
VHF	471	989.9	717.7	272.2	83
UHF	*133*	*68.9*	*86.6*	*(17.7)*	*42*
1968					
VHF	473	1,122.1	776.5	345.6	86
UHF	*154*	*90.9*	*120.4*	*(29.5)*	*45*
1969					
VHF	489	1,214.9	844.2	370.7	83
UHF	*169*	*114.0*	*157.2*	*(43.2)*	*35*
1970					
VHF	491	1,226.6	894.7	331.9	82
UHF	*180*	*124.5*	*170.0*	*(45.5)*	*32*
1971					
VHF	491	1,223.3	946.3	277.0	81
UHF	*182*	*148.2*	*180.8*	*(32.7)*	*32*
1972					
VHF	490	1,395.6	1,040.9	354.7	86
UHF	*173*	*185.4*	*201.4*	*(15.9)*	*44*
1973					
VHF	489	1,497.4	1,124.3	373.1	86
UHF	*177*	*209.4*	*217.0*	*(7.7)*	*47*
1974					
VHF	494	1,626.9	1,215.9	411.1	86
UHF	*175*	*228.2*	*233.1*	*(4.9)*	*47*
1975					
VHF	477	1,762.2	1,305.8	456.2	86
UHF	*177*	*262.6*	*252.7*	*9.9*	*52*
1976					
VHF	460	2,231.1	1,500.4	730.7	91
UHF	*178*	*363.0*	*298.2*	*64.8*	*67*
1977					
VHF	489	2,403.2	1,628.7	774.7	92
UHF	*181*	*400.9*	*329.8*	*71.0*	*73*
1978					
VHF	513	2,886.3	1,887.1	999.1	92
UHF	*201*	*514.4*	*420.1*	*94.3*	*73*

Table 380–C   Revenues, Expenses, and Earnings of Commercial VHF and UHF Stations, 1953–1980 (cont.)

Note: All Dollar Figures are in Millions. Figures in Parentheses Indicate Losses.

Year	Number of Stations Reporting	Revenue	Expenses	Earnings before Taxes	Percent of Stations Reporting Profits
1979					
VHF	512	3,196.6	2,150.9	1,045.7	92
UHF	211	586.0	516.8	69.2	73
1980					
VHF	507	3,552.0	2,472.3	1,079.8	89
UHF	218	690.2	650.5	39.7	58

Source: FCC annual financial reports on the television business, partially reprinted in the FCC's *Annual Report.* Note: The VHF figures *exclude* network O&O stations (all of which are VHF); the final column of percentages is supplied by the FCC and *does* include network O&Os, though it is often based on fewer stations than shown in column one.

Table 380–C compares VHF and UHF commercial stations from the end of the FCC freeze on channel capacity in 1953 (see Unit 180) through 1980. The differences between UHF and VHF profitability are evident. A decline in UHF station profits after 1967 was undoubtedly due to the many new stations going on the air at that time (nearly all stations tend to lose money in the start-up process). By the mid-1970s, however, UHF stations were breaking into the black once again.

Sources

For a discussion of source validity for the tables in this unit, the reader should refer to the "Sources" section in Unit 370; for the tables in this unit were constructed from parallel sources and are subject to the same general limitations. While Table 380–B does not include all stations on the air (see Unit 180), it is the most complete listing available. The accuracy of the data through 1957 in Tables 380–B and 380–C is somewhat limited, because many of the television stations listed for those early years were actually on the air during only part of a year, and many UHF stations went dark each year. Also, there is an apparent lack of consistency in the FCC's reporting of profitable stations in those years.

Finally, the VHF data in Table 380–C purposely does not include network O&O stations, in order to permit a more equitable comparison of stations. However, the percentage column in the table does include network

O&Os. These percentage figures are often based on fewer stations than shown in column one.

Further Information

With the demise of FCC reporting of financial data, users must rely on the annual radio and television reports on the National Association of Broadcasters, which are reprinted in summary fashion in *Broadcasting*. This includes comparisons by type of station, as well as market and revenue size categories. It does *not* include individual markets. Industry reporting activities are being developed, as this book goes to press, to at least partially fill the gap left by the end of the FCC's role. Summary financial data appears in the annual *Television Factbook* and *Broadcasting Yearbook*. For deeper analyses, consult Owen et al. (1974), Owen (1975), and Bunce (1976).

381
NETWORK
TELEVISION FINANCES

Interpretation of the Tables

Television network earnings come from two sources: the networks themselves and their owned-and-operated (O&O) stations (five in each network, for a total of 15). Because the network stations are in the largest broadcast markets (see Unit 262), these stations typically achieve annual profits of 15 to 30 million dollars (a 35 percent or more margin of profit). Thus, the network O&O stations contribute substantially to overall network earnings.

The networks themselves were money-losers in the early years of television, due to the costs of interconnection and programming. In the mid-1950s, they began to achieve limited profits, but the O&O stations remained the major sources of overall network earnings. (The DuMont network is the fourth network counted in the 1948–1955 period.) By 1971, however, the demand for network time exceeded supply and drove up the network charges for advertising time. As a result, the networks surged ahead of the O&O stations in total earnings.

The dramatic changes in 1971 also resulted partially from outside regulations. Cigarette advertising was banned on January 2, 1971, and the FCC's prime-time access rule was invoked in September of that year. Table 381–A shows that network profit margins more than doubled in the 1970s, while the O&O station margins, although still substantial, had slipped from the high levels of a decade before. The old argument that the networks could not survive without O&O station income is clearly no longer applicable.

Table 381–B documents several important changes in network television advertising patterns between 1965 and 1981. During this period, for example, the total number of minutes for television advertising increased about 22 percent, while the number of television commercials grew by more than 100 percent. The latter development occurred as the 30-second commercial unit became the industry norm—a change forced in large part by the sharply rising charges for network time.

Those cost increases also led to substantial changes in the ways that programming was supported. Most television programs in the early 1950s were entirely supported by a single advertiser which had a strong identity with a given show. This had been the pattern for radio network programming. By the mid-1950s, however, sponsored television shows had declined to 39 percent of all prime-time programs, while "participating-advertiser" programs were clearly on the rise. The participating-advertiser program is produced by the network, which then sells advertising time at a set rate to any advertiser willing to pay the charges. The advertiser has no influence over the program other than selecting the time at which the commercial will appear. The advertiser merely "participates" in covering the production and broadcast costs of the show.

By the early 1970s, the regularly sponsored weekly show had disappeared from prime-time television, and few such sponsors were left in the daytime hours. The participating-advertiser format, combined with the predominance of 30-second commercials, has greatly contributed to viewer (and advertiser) complaints of "clutter" on the air.

Table 381–C provides a comparative series of index figures illustrating one point of view (see below under sources) concerning the economic interrelationships of networks and their affiliate stations. Using 1964 as a base year, the table shows how the network's financial picture has markedly improved, especially in the past five years, while the affiliate "share" of this network revenue has not improved nearly as much. The rise in network fortunes is supported in Table 381–A (see column on profit margin under "Networks Only"), though as Table 381–B (profit ratio column under "all non-O&O stations) shows, commercial stations in general are doing well. The point is that individual station income increases are coming more from spot and local sales rather than participation in network income. This is one reason why an increasing number of stations in the late 1970s were willing to drop some

Table 381–A Revenues, Expenses, Earnings, and Profit Ratios of Television Networks and Their Owned-and-Operated Stations, 1948–1980

Note: All Dollar Figures are in Millions. Figures in Parentheses Indicate Losses.

Year	Number of Networks	Number of Network-Owned Stations	Combined Network/Station Revenues and Earnings					Networks Only			Network-Owned Stations		
			Revenues	Expenses	Pre-Tax Earnings	Profit Ratio (In Percent)	Percent of Total TV Industry Profits	Pre-Tax Earnings	Percent Change	Profit Ratio (In Percent)	Pre-Tax Earnings	Percent Change	Profit Ratio (In Percent)
1948	4	10	4.8	11.2	(6.4)	(133)	—	N/A	N/A	N/A	N/A	N/A	N/A
1949	4	14	19.3	31.4	(12.1)	(63)	—	N/A	N/A	N/A	N/A	N/A	N/A
1950	4	14	55.5	65.5	(10.0)	(18)	—	N/A	N/A	N/A	N/A	N/A	N/A
1951	4	15	128.4	117.4	11.0	9	26	N/A	N/A	N/A	N/A	N/A	N/A
1952	4	15	180.2	170.3	9.9	5	18	N/A	N/A	N/A	N/A	N/A	N/A
1953	4	16	231.7	213.7	18.0	8	26	N/A	N/A	N/A	N/A	N/A	N/A
1954	4	16	306.7	270.2	36.5	12	40	N/A	N/A	N/A	N/A	N/A	N/A
1955	4	16	374.0	306.0	68.0	18	45	N/A	N/A	N/A	N/A	N/A	N/A
1956	3	16	442.3	356.9	85.4	19	45	N/A	N/A	N/A	N/A	N/A	N/A
1957	3	16	467.9	397.2	70.7	15	44	N/A	N/A	N/A	N/A	N/A	N/A
1958	3	19	516.7	439.7	77.0	15	45	N/A	N/A	N/A	N/A	N/A	N/A
1959	3	17	576.1	488.2	87.9	15	40	32.0	—	7.3	55.9	—	40.6
1960	3	15	640.7	545.5	95.2	15	39	33.6	5.0	6.8	61.6	10.2	42.2
1961	3	15	675.3	588.3	87.0	13	37	24.7	(26.5)	4.7	62.3	1.1	41.9
1962	3	15	754.2	642.8	111.4	15	36	36.7	48.6	6.3	74.7	19.9	44.1
1963	3	15	820.3	684.1	136.2	17	40	56.4	53.7	8.9	79.8	6.8	43.3
1964	3	15	928.7	772.2	156.5	17	38	60.2	6.7	8.4	96.3	20.7	44.5

Table 381-A Revenues, Expenses, Earnings, and Profit Ratios of Television Networks and Their Owned-and-Operated Stations, 1948–1980 (cont.)

Note: All Dollar Figures are in Millions. Figures in Parentheses Indicate Losses.

Year	Number of Networks	Number of Network-Owned Stations	Combined Network/Station Revenues and Earnings					Networks Only			Network-Owned Stations		
			Revenues	Expenses	Pre-Tax Earnings	Profit Ratio (In Percent)	Percent of Total TV Industry Profits	Pre-Tax Earnings	Percent Change	Profit Ratio (In Percent)	Pre-Tax Earnings	Percent Change	Profit Ratio (In Percent)
1965	3	15	1,023.8	862.2	161.6	16	36	59.4	(1.3)	7.5	102.2	6.1	43.5
1966	3	15	1,166.3	979.5	186.8	16	38	78.7	32.5	8.7	108.1	5.8	41.2
1967	3	15	1,216.6	1,056.5	160.1	13	39	55.8	(29.1)	5.9	104.3	(3.5)	39.6
1968	3	15	1,307.9	1,129.2	178.8	14	36	56.4	1.1	5.5	122.4	17.4	42.0
1969	3	15	1,467.3	1,241.3	226.1	15	41	92.7	64.4	8.1	133.4	9.0	41.3
1970	3	15	1,457.1	1,289.6	167.5	11	37	50.1	(46.0)	4.4	117.3	(12.1)	37.5
1971	3	15	1,378.9	1,234.0	144.9	11	37	53.7	7.2	4.9	91.2	(22.3)	32.0
1972	3	15	1,598.4	1,385.0	213.4	13	39	110.9	106.5	8.7	102.5	12.4	31.3
1973	3	15	1,758.0	1,470.3	287.7	16	44	184.9	66.7	13.2	102.8	0.3	29.1
1974	3	15	1,921.1	1,590.3	330.8	17	45	225.1	21.7	14.6	105.7	2.8	28.2
1975	3	15	2,069.4	1,755.3	314.2	15	40	208.5	(7.4)	12.5	105.7	0.0	26.7
1976	3	15	2,604.4	2,149.8	454.6	17	36	295.6	41.8	14.0	159.0	50.4	34.9
1977	3	15	3,084.9	2,529.5	555.4	18	30	406.1	37.4	15.7	149.3	(6.1)	29.7
1978	3	15	3,549.1	2,989.3	559.8	16	34	373.5	(8.0)	12.6	186.3	24.8	31.9
1979	3	15	4,092.4	3,517.1	575.3	14	34	370.2	(0.9)	10.7	205.1	10.1	32.2
1980	3	15	4,565.5	4,031.4	534.1	12	32	325.6	(12.0)	8.4	208.5	1.7	29.8

Sources: FCC figures as released annually (see Unit 380), with profit margins and percentage change figures added by the author (some data from *Broadcasting Monthly* [May–June 1977], p. 25).

Table 381-B Measures of Network Television Commercials, 1965–1981

Year	Total Number of Commercial Minutes (3 Networks)	Commercials by Length (In Percent)			Number of Commercials		Number of Prime-Time Programs by Type of Sponsorship	
		30 second	60 second	P/B's[a]	Number	Index	Sponsor	Participating
1965	N/A	0	77	23	N/A	N/A	32	51
1967	100,000	6	49	43	103,000	100	20	60
1969	100,424	14	34	51	108,600	105	6	67
1971	99,867	53	16	30	132,300	128	3	63
1973	101,955	72	9	19	158,000	153	0	70
1975	109,135	79	6	15	180,400	175	N/A	N/A
1977	116,420	82	5	13	194,342	189	N/A	N/A
1979	121,184	83	3	12	234,330	N/A	N/A	N/A
1981	122,297	87	2	11	238,256	N/A	N/A	N/A

Sources: Total number of commercial minutes and number of commercials, both through 1977, originally from Broadcast Advertising Research (BAR) as reported by Westinghouse Broadcasting Company, Inc., "*Reply Comments*" (1978), Chart 4, as reprinted in UCLA School of Law (1979), p. 76. Number of prime-time programs by type sponsorship from L. W. Lichty, University of Maryland. Commercials by length and all material for 1979 and 1981 from BAR direct to the author. Note: Data in first six columns are for the indicated calendar year, while the last two columns represent the season (which in 1965, for example, ran from September 1964 through August 1965). [a]Indicates "piggyback" commercials.

Table 381–C   Index of Network Television and Affiliate Station Incomes, 1964–1977

				Payments by Networks to Stations:			
Year	Consumer Price Index[a]	Network Sales	Network Income	Index	As Percent of Network Income	As Percent of Station Income	Station Income
1964	100	100	100	100	23.1	19.8	100
1965	102	109	99	107	24.0	19.6	109
1966	105	125	131	114	21.2	18.8	117
1967	108	130	93	115	20.6	18.7	101
1968	112	136	94	115	19.5	16.3	123
1969	118	150	154	118	18.6	15.4	130
1970	125	148	83	112	17.3	14.4	114
1971	131	143	89	107	17.4	13.9	94
1972	135	161	184	105	15.0	12.0	124
1973	143	180	307	109	14.2	11.3	132
1974	159	191	374	116	13.8	11.1	144
1975	174	206	346	120	13.4	10.7	161
1976	184	256	491	124	11.3	8.8	269
1977	196	310	675	134	10.0	8.7	280

Sources: 1964–1973 data from "Petition for Inquiry, Rule Making and Immediate Temporary Relief," filed before the Federal Communications Commission on September 3, 1976 by Westinghouse Broadcasting Company, Inc., charts 11 and (for two columns on income percentages) 7. 1974–1977 data from Westinghouse "Reply Comments" (1978), charts 6 and 11 as reprinted in UCLA School of Law (1979), pp. 82–83. Based on official FCC financial figures. Note: [a]1964 = 100.

network programs for local or "mini-network" presentations which allowed a greater financial return to the local outlet.

Sources

The data in Table 381–A derived from FCC figures, which were first printed in mimeo releases and then reprinted in the FCC's *Annual Report* and in *Television Factbook* (see Unit 380). The profit margin and percentage-change figures were calculated by the author (some of these figures were also found in *Broadcasting Monthly* [May–June 1977]). Because all financial figures are rounded to the nearest hundred-thousand, totals may not add up exactly. Specific network and O&O station data are not broken out in FCC reports prior to 1959.

The figures in Table 381–B, which are aggregates for all three networks, come mainly from Broadcast Advertising Research, a trade group which keeps track of network and major station advertising activity, reporting regularly to major advertising agencies and advertisers. Data through 1977 was assembled by Westinghouse Broadcasting in a proceeding before the FCC claiming networks were being unfair to their affiliates. Data since is from BAR. Material on the type of program sponsorship is direct to the author from L. W. Lichty of the University of Maryland, gathered as a part of his longitudinal research on network program trends. These last two columns refer only to prime-time programs, while the other data refers to the entire day.

Likewise, all of the data in Table 381-C came from the Westinghouse petition referred to above—and thus was all gathered and reported in support of a specific argument before the FCC. Because the source material does not make clear the exact data and approach used to construct the indexes, it has not been possible to bring the table down to date. The underlying data used to build the indexes comes from the FCC annual financial data reports (see Table 318–A).

Further Information

The end of FCC financial reporting for the television business will sharply reduce what is known of network television finances. Annual reports of the network companies themselves are of less value due to variance in accounting practices and grouping of networks with their O&Os and sometimes other activities (especially for NBC, a part of RCA). Useful information on the 1970s is found in FCC, *New Television Networks* (1980), as well as some of the limited-circulation staff research reports leading up to that final report. Scattered statistical information appears from time to time in major trade weeklies, including *TV/Radio Age*, *Broadcasting*, and *Television Digest*.

382
NETWORK TELEVISION PROGRAMMING EXPENSES

Interpretation of the Tables

The chief "risk" investment of television networks is in programming—a risk becoming more evident in the late 1970s as costs of programming went up sharply, and as the increasingly tight ratings war between the three national commercial networks forced some network decisions to "buy out" new series even before all episodes shot had been shown. Network entertainment programs are produced by firms on the West Coast (some connected with the motion picture industry, others are "independents") which assemble, produce, and complete programs for showings by specific networks on a contract basis.

Table 382–A Prime-Time Network Program Costs, 1949–1973

Year	Number of Prime-Time Programs	Average Episode Cost: 60-Minute Programs			Average Episode Cost: 30-Minute Programs		
		Number of Programs	Current Dollars	Constant (1972) Dollars	Number of Programs	Current Dollars	Constant (1972) Dollars
1949	33	6	7,000	13,233	27	3,100	5,860
1950	52	12	13,500	25,187	40	7,200	13,433
1951	102	24	23,600	41,187	78	10,500	18,325
1952	94	19	30,100	51,897	75	13,100	22,586
1953	87	13	36,000	61,121	76	16,200	27,504
1954	100	13	39,800	66,667	87	17,100	28,643
1955	105	17	48,000	78,689	88	22,300	36,557
1956	98	17	62,200	98,887	81	30,600	48,649
1957	97	23	57,200	88,000	74	33,100	50,923
1958	111	20	75,200	113,939	91	36,100	54,697
1959	99	23	75,000	111,111	76	36,300	53,778

Year							
1960	103	29	90,000	131,004	74	37,500	54,585
1961	98	33	91,200	131,601	65	41,300	59,596
1962	92	44	94,000	133,144	48	45,000	63,739
1963	82	44	111,600	155,866	38	55,000	76,816
1964	76	45	119,300	164,099	31	56,500	77,717
1965	83	40	131,200	176,581	43	59,400	79,946
1966	88	35	145,000	188,802	53	65,400	85,156
1967	80	39	159,000	201,266	41	76,900	97,342
1968	72[a]	39	179,000	216,707	32	87,500	105,932
1969	73	39	185,000	213,379	34	88,000	101,499
1970	74[a]	39	198,400	217,068	33	N/A	N/A
1971	68[a]	35	200,000	208,333	31	98,700	102,813
1972	68[a]	25	N/A	N/A	30	N/A	N/A
1973	64[a]	21	208,461	197,033	31	104,194	98,482

Source: Copyrighted and unpublished data from L. W. Lichty.
Note: [a] total number of prime-time programs includes longer shows (90 and 120 minute) not broken out in other columns.

Table 382–B Production Costs for Selected Network Television Drama Programs, 1950–1974

Cost Item	Typical Live Drama—1950 (Half Hour)	Typical Film Mystery—1952 (Half Hour)	"Defenders" 1961 (Hour)	"Bonanza" 1969 (Hour)	Typical Film Drama—1974 (Half Hour)
"Above the Line" Costs					
Script	500	1,000	8,000	7,750	7,500
Producer, Director	450	750	15,706	22,990	18,000
Miscellaneous	—	—	2,400	11,380	5,000
Cast	1,100	2,750	17,500	55,885	27,000
Total, Above the Line Costs	**2,050**	**4,500**	**43,606**	**98,005**	**57,500**
Percent of Total Costs	*29*	*35*	*40*	*46*	*49*
"Below the Line" Costs					
Production Staff	—	540	2,152	3,053	2,000
Cameraman, Camera	—	800	3,704	5,379	2,500
Grips, Set Operations	—	250	3,300	6,869	2,000

Electrical	—	889	3,360	6,276	2,500
Scenery	—	—	6,000	4,479	3,500
Sound Recording	—	654	2,023	6,310	3,000
Makeup, Hair Dressing	—	238	815	4,199	500
Set Dressing, Props	750	550	3,537	5,722	2,500
Location	—	50	1,805	6,463	—
Transportation	—	200	925	1,511	1,000
Stage, Studio	—	850	4,525	13,550	15,000
Film Editing	—	875	2,590	8,704	4,000
All Other Costs:					
Rerecord, Stock, Titles, Royalties, Wardrobe, Misc.	4,120	2,421	30,009	41,015	21,000
Total, Below the Line Costs	**4,870**	**8,317**	**64,745**	**113,530**	**59,500**
Total Costs for One Episode	**6,920**	**12,817**	**108,351**	**211,535**	**117,000**
Total in Constant (1972) Dollars	*12,910*	*22,098*	*156,351*	*243,985*	*100,515*

Source: Lichty and Topping (1975), p. 444, table 40.

Table 382–A shows the rising curve of prime-time entertainment program per-episode costs over a 25-year period. Naturally, daytime productions (serial "soap-operas," most of which are produced in New York by the networks themselves), news, and documentary programs cost considerably less to produce per "episode." While average data on prime-time programs is not available after 1973, costs have risen sharply. In the Fall of 1974, for example, per-episode costs were running well over 100,000 dollars per half-hour, with specials and movies going at appreciably higher costs. By the Fall of 1977, inflation had pushed those per-episode costs to 175,000–200,000 dollars per half-hour program in prime-time, and upwards of 350,000–400,000 dollars and more per one-hour program. Programs with special expenses for special effects or cast often had costs considerably higher, while the two-hour movie slots by the late 1970s were pushing a million dollars in per-episode costs. As always, variety formats cost considerably less to produce than drama (game shows are perhaps the least expensive format in production, one reason such programs dominate many daytime hours, and the so-called Prime-Time Access period of 7:30-8:00 p.m. ET).

Table 382–B provides a breakdown of production costs for sample television shows over the 1950–1974 period. "Above-the-line" costs (salaries and fees for the creative staff, writers, and actors) have increased steadily as actors' unions and directors' and writers' guilds have been able to demand higher-paying contracts earlier in the life of a television series. "Below-the-line" costs (wages of production personnel and costs of materials, facilities, and services) have also increased steadily and markedly over the years, partly because of the greater sophistication—and, therefore, higher costs—of both television programming and television and film equipment. However, the primary sources of these cost increases are union-contract wages for production personnel and the general effects of inflation on materials and services.

By the 1960s, program-production costs were typically met by an independent packaging agency, which capitalized the project and hired the creative personnel, then sold the completed program to the network for a lump-sum payment. Very often, this payment does not cover program costs, which are fully recouped only when the program or series is sold to stations in syndication for rebroadcast.

Sources

All the data in Table 382–A are from the copyrighted and soon-to-be published data of L.W Lichty (in progress), based on averages of published information for different types of prime-time programs. A. D. Little Co. (1969) is the source of the information on costs of pilot programs (television shows produced as a sample of a proposed series). These figures on pilot programs costs are aggregates of all three national networks. All cost data in

Table 382-A are for programs on the air in the third week in January of each season.

The production cost figures in Table 382-B were gathered by Lichty and Topping (1975), who used several trade periodical articles as sources. Two of the sample programs—"Defenders" and "Bonanza"—were above average in cost for those years. A script for "Defenders" cost about twice the 1961 norm. The 1974 drama sample, which is based on a real production budget rounded to the nearest 500 dollars for each cost item, did not involve superstars or special settings. Since information of this type is not commonly published, these random examples of series costs provide the most accurate picture the author was able to obtain.

Further Information

Details on program costs are hard to come by over long periods of time. Scattered current data often appear in *Variety*, *Broadcasting*, and other trade periodicals. McAlpine (1975) provides a useful assessment of background factors in the television programming industry, though the rate of inflation since then will have made the financial data obsolete. An interesting collection of facsimile reprints of related trade data and articles appears in the annual revisions of Clift and Greer's *Broadcast Programming*. For background in network programming decisions—and the role economics plays in those decisions (see Eastman et al. 1980).

390
CABLE TELEVISION SYSTEM FINANCES

Interpretation of the Table

Only relatively late in its development, and for but a very short time, were official government figures gathered on cable television system finances. In June 1977, the FCC issued a first attempt at such an economic census, which was based on returns from about 80 percent of the "cable entities" then operating. The FCC defined a cable entity as one or more cable systems which report to the Commission on its Form 326 as a single business entity, no matter how many different cable systems may be controlled. While

Table 390–A Revenues, Expenses, and Income of Cable Systems, 1975–1981

	1975	1976	1977	1978	1979	1980	1981
Number of Cable Entities	2,443	2,349	2,557	2,865	2,992	2,868	3,600
Average Monthly Subscriber Rate (In Dollars)	6.21	6.49	6.85	7.03	7.37	7.69	7.94
Industry Annual Totals (In Millions of Dollars)							
Operating Revenues	894.9	998.8	1,205.9	1,511.0	1,817.1	2,238.0	3,589.0
Pay-Cable Revenue[a]	N/A	41.1	85.9	191.9	355.4	574.8	1,170.0
Proportion of Revenue from Pay-Cable (In Percent)	N/A	4	7	13	20	26	33
Operating Expense	567.4	615.9	716.9	918.0	1,126.6	1,438.9	1,387.4
Income (Before Tax)	26.9	57.7	133.7	137.1	199.3	168.1	40.1
Profit Margin[b] (In Percent)	3	6	11	9	11	8	1
Assets	2,131.5	2,515.7	2,450.5	2,870.7	3,211.6	4,443.0	7,914.8

Source: FCC, "Cable TV Industry Revenues", annual. Data for the first two years from FCC, "CATV Industry Financial Data for the Period November 1975–October 1976," FCC Mimeo 85210 (June 10,1977). Notes: [a]This is included in operating revenue figure immediately above. [b]Figured as income before taxes divided by operating revenue.

the first survey was announced as covering the 1975–1976 period, subsequent reports indicated that the data was more properly credited to calendar 1975 alone.

Surveys were taken in 1977–1981, inclusive, using computer-aided analysis, and reaching the vast majority of systems each time—around 90 percent. The figures in Table 390-A provide the highlights of all the surveys taken, for the 1981 data will be the last issued by the Commission, the FCC having paralleled its broadcast data action (see Units 370 and 380) a year later with cable. The results show an industry in growth—with profit margins dropping as construction (and interest) charges soared as cable began to build the major-market franchises given out late in the 1970s and early 1980s. Note also the rising importance of pay cable revenues' contribution to cable's bottom line.

Sources

Data for all survey years is for the calendar year. Data for the first column in Table 390-A was not computer-generated, and was later reported by the FCC to have been essentially 1975 data, given the financial reporting practices of the cable systems (see *Broadcasting*, June 26, 1978, p. 25). Data for 1976 and 1977 is for the calendar year. The figures used here are for FCC estimates of all cable entities (defined as one or more cable systems which report to the FCC on Form 326 as a single business entity, no matter how many separate cable systems are controlled) based on actual returns from 80 percent, 84 percent, and 90 percent of those entities, respectively.

Further Information

See the sources noted under Units 190 and 290. In addition, *Cablevision* regularly provides data on cable, both statistical and narrative. The National Cable Television Association trade group was considering some kind of financial data-gathering process as this book went to press.

SECTION FOUR
ELECTRONIC MEDIA
EMPLOYMENT
AND TRAINING

403
EDUCATIONAL PROGRAMS
IN ELECTRONIC MEDIA

Interpretation of the Tables

As researchers speak more and more of an information economy, attention turns to education and training programs for the media and the other elements of such an economy. One indication of media growth is the expansion of education in broadcasting and the newer technologies in recent years.

Table 403-A provides statistics on educational programs, student enrollments, and the number of faculty in American colleges and universities over a quarter century period. While radio courses appeared as early as the 1920s, structured degree programs were not created until the 1930s. These degree programs were established first in the land-grant colleges of the Middle West and, in most cases, evolved within departments of speech. Major developments in broadcasting programs accompanied increasing student enrollments after about 1950, and the number of broadcasting programs rose dramatically during the 1960s as such programs became separate communications or broadcasting departments. As is typical of many "new" academic fields, the field of broadcast education is identified in a wide variety of ways—sometimes closely allied with journalism and/or film, and sometimes as part of broader telecommunications concerns with common carrier policy which increasingly overlaps media regulation.

Table 403-B indicates the expansion of graduate education in broadcasting as revealed by the number of masters theses and doctoral dissertations produced during five year periods from 1920 through 1969 and the three year period of 1970 through 1972. The steadily growing numbers of degrees completed over this half-century can be seen to have accelerated significantly after 1950. Details on graduate education expansion over the past decade are unfortunately not available—other than the summary data in Table 403-A.

Sources

Table 403-A, taken from Sterling (1977) was based on biennial reports by Harold Niven (1956, 1961, and 1965) as updated by Niven (1970, 1975, and 1981). Undergraduate information applies to juniors and seniors only. No information on the number of degrees granted each year was available. Niven's data are gathered by mail surveys of departments known to offer courses or a degree program in broadcasting or a closely related field. Faculty statistics include instructors—and in some schools, graduate assistants, and thus the totals are inflated by perhaps 5 percent from "true" faculty measures.

Table 403-B was taken from Kittross (1978) and is based on an extensive 1973 survey of college and university broadcasting departments, as well as on earlier secondary sources. The data were computerized to eliminate

Table 403-A   Educational Programs, Enrollments, and Faculty in Broadcasting, 1956–1980

	1956	1960	1965	1970	1975	1980
Number of Colleges/Universities with Broadcast-Emphasis Programs:						
two-year	N/A	N/A	N/A	52	62	126
undergrad	86	97	126	173	205	278
masters	} 58 {	50	60	87	99	104
doctoral		15	17	23	27	24
Number of Students in These Programs						
two-year	N/A	N/A	N/A	2,415	3,641	8,000
undergrad[a]	3,149	3,009	3,527	9,017	17,251	34,245
masters	} 566 {	489	773	1,524	1,852	3,054
doctoral		121	180	291	253	298
total	3,715	3,619	4,480	13,247	22,997	45,597
Number of Faculty in Broadcasting Programs						
Full-Time Instructors	N/A	272	345	631	983	1,333
Part-Time Instructors	N/A	245	392	572	707	902
Total	N/A	517	737	1,203	1,690	2,235

Sources: Sterling (1977) citing Niven data through 1965, and Niven (1970, 1975, and 1981) for data since. Note: (a) includes only Juniors and Seniors as declared majors.

Table 403-B   Number of Broadcasting Theses and Dissertations, 1920-1972

Years	Masters Theses	Doctoral Dissertations
1920–1924	1	1
1925–1929	6	2
1930–1934	45	4
1935–1939	113	20
1940–1944	136	25
1945–1949	279	31
1950–1954	439	105
1955–1959	390	152
1960–1964	466	256
1965–1969	622	435
1970–1972	386	285

Source: Kittross (1978), table VII.

duplications and to provide for other summary data found in the original source. It is unlikely, however, that this table includes all broadcast-related theses and dissertations completed during the indicated time period, since the 1973 survey focused mainly on departments which offered degrees either in broadcasting or with a specialty in broadcasting. The many broadcasting studies in political science, law, economics, and related fields are, in most cases, not represented here. In that sense, Table 403–B underestimates the number of graduate students granted degrees after detailed study of the broadcast industry.

Further Information

Background on education programs for broadcasting is available in Sterling (1977), which cites many earlier articles on the field. The most reliable statistics for this area are those prepared by John M. Kittross for articles appearing in *Journal of Broadcasting* and based on Niven's periodic surveys. Current guides to further broadcast education are identified in the *Aspen Handbook on the Media* and in the section on education which is included at the end of recent *Broadcast Yearbooks*. Detailed information and statistics on television education appear in the biennial *American Film Institute Guide to College Courses in Film and Television*. Data on doctoral programs in both broadcasting and instructional media can be found in Brown's *Educational Media Yearbook*. *Hope Reports* is the standard source for information concerning the entire educational media and audiovisual field. For a broad overview of higher education for the media (print journalism, film, and broadcasting) in the United States and abroad, see Katzen (1975), a documented discussion providing useful tabular summaries and an extensive bibliography.

460
EMPLOYMENT IN THE BROADCASTING INDUSTRY

Interpretation of the Tables

Tables 460–A through 460–E provide most of what is known of national employment patterns in the broadcasting industry, and in broadcast-related manufacturing and retail and service industries. Table 460–A presents a count of employed personnel in radio and television stations and networks in the United States. Even though television networks and stations are far larger financial operations than their radio counterparts, there are many more radio stations in this country (see Units 170 and 180) and, therefore, far greater numbers of radio employees.

The reader will note the relatively slow growth of total broadcasting employment until the post-World War II years, when the burgeoning numbers of radio and television stations doubled industry employment by 1954. At that point, the industry's growth rate slowed down to evolutionary rather than revolutionary expansion, and it was 20 more years before the total doubled again. The reader should also note that the television network employment figures in Table 460–A do not include film-industry personnel working on television series in Hollywood (see Table 460–C). In addition, the total television-employment data for the 1970s include public television station employees, who represent about 15 percent of the totals.

Table 460–B provides average weekly salary figures for nonsupervisory personnel in the broadcasting industry, while Table 460–C lists the number of members and total annual member earnings for the major unions involved in network television production. In Table 460–C, the American Federation of Television and Radio Artists (AFTRA) includes most on-air personnel of the networks and large radio and TV stations.

The Screen Actor's Guild (SAG) is comprised of actors and actresses working in theatrical films, television films and series, and radio and television commercials. Detailed data reveal that member earnings from television commercial work outpaced both film and television series income. Some figures cannot be readily explained. The near-doubling of television production income in 1971–1972, for example, is more likely due to differing ways of counting income than to an actual income increase of that magnitude. On the other hand, it is clear that television series production income among SAG members has increased rapidly in the inflationary 1970s, while theatrical film income has remained constant or, taking inflation into account, has dropped considerably.

The figures from the Writer's Guild of America West are difficult to assess, since each year's total represents a combination of all television, film, and commercials income. If these figures were broken down into income sources, the greatest percentage would undoubtedly be for television production work. The Hollywood craft unions represent the aggregate earnings of several unions, and the method of data gathering is not known.

Table 460–D traces the gradual change in the employment of minorities and women by both commercial and noncommercial television stations. The reader will note that the "best" employment record is for women at public television stations. It is also worth noting that much of the employment of women and minorities in all categories is part-time work. Not shown here is a breakdown of job levels for these groups (see "Sources" section below).

Table 460–E provides limited information on employment levels in selected broadcast-related industries—three categories of manufacturing firms and two retail and service categories. Clearly, these data do not present a complete picture of broadcast-related employment, since they do not include advertising, public relations, or miscellaneous other manufacturing and retail or service industries. This table is simply an indication of the size of the broadcasting industry's "support" groups.

The manufacturing figures in Table 460–E provide stark evidence of the increasing importation of broadcast equipment into the United States (see Units 750 and 760), and the resultant decrease of employment opportunities within the American economy. The steady declines in the electronic receiving-tubes industry are evidence of technological changes in the industry. Transistors and solid-state devices are increasingly used in place of tubes for most radio and television receivers. The retail radio-television store data in Table 460–E are incomplete, in that today's buyers can find this equipment in many other kinds of stores—for example, most department stores and general discount stores. The repair-shop employment figures suggest the growing complexity of servicing color television and transistor products.

Table 460–A   Number of Radio and Television Network and Station Employees, 1930–1980

		Radio				Television		
Year	Networks	AM/AM-FM Stations	FM Stations Only	Total Radio Employees	Networks	All Stations	Total Television Employees	Total Number of Broadcast Employees
1930	N/A	N/A	—	6,000	—	—	—	6,000
1935	N/A	N/A	—	14,600	—	—	—	14,600
1938	N/A	N/A	—	22,500	—	—	—	22,500
1939	N/A	N/A	—	23,900	—	—	—	23,900
1940	N/A	N/A	—	25,700	—	—	—	25,700
1941	N/A	N/A	N/A	27,600	—	—	a	27,600
1942	N/A	N/A	N/A	29,600	—	—	a	29,600
1943	N/A	N/A	N/A	31,800	—	—	a	31,800
1944	N/A	N/A	N/A	34,300	—	—	a	34,300
1945	N/A	N/A	N/A	37,800	—	—	a	37,800
1946	N/A	N/A	N/A	40,000	—	—	a	40,000
1947	N/A	N/A	N/A	N/A	—	—	a	N/A
1948	N/A	N/A	N/A	48,300	—	—	a	48,300
1949	N/A	N/A	N/A	52,000	N/A	N/A	3,800	55,800
1950	N/A	N/A	N/A	N/A	N/A	N/A	9,000	N/A
1951	N/A	N/A	N/A	N/A	N/A	N/A	N/A	N/A
1952	N/A	N/A	N/A	51,000	N/A	N/A	14,000	65,000
1953	N/A	N/A	N/A	51,800	N/A	N/A	18,200	70,000
1954	N/A	N/A	N/A	42,600	N/A	N/A	29,400	72,000
1955	N/A	N/A	N/A	45,300	N/A	N/A	32,300	77,600
1956	N/A	N/A	N/A	47,600	N/A	N/A	35,700	83,300
1957	N/A	N/A	N/A	48,900	N/A	N/A	37,800	86,700
1958	N/A	N/A	N/A	48,800	N/A	N/A	39,400	88,200
1959	N/A	N/A	N/A	50,400	N/A	N/A	40,300	90,700
1960	1,200	50,500	1,300	53,000	9,600	31,000	40,600	93,600
1961	1,000	51,500	1,700	54,200	8,800	31,300	40,100	95,300
1962	1,100	53,000	2,000	56,100	9,100	32,800	41,900	98,000
1963	1,100	54,500	2,300	57,900	9,700	34,000	43,700	101,600
1964	1,200	56,600	2,400	60,200	10,700	35,000	45,700	105,900
1965	1,200	58,300	2,700	60,200	11,000	36,700	47,700	109,900
1966	1,100	60,500	3,200	64,800	11,200	39,100	50,300	115,100
1967	1,100	62,400	3,700	67,200	11,500	40,200	51,700	118,900
1968	1,100	65,600	4,000	70,700	12,200	43,100	55,300	126,000
1969	1,100	63,500	5,400	70,000	12,900	44,900	57,800	127,800
1970	1,100	63,800	6,100	71,000	13,200	45,200	58,400	129,400
1971	900	65,000	7,500	73,400	12,000	46,100	58,100	131,500
1972	900	66,600	8,700	76,200	12,400	46,900	59,300	135,500
1973	900	66,500	10,100	77,500	12,400	47,800	60,200	137,700
1974	900	67,900	11,300	80,100	13,200	48,800	61,900	142,000

Table 460-A   Number of Radio and Television Network and Station Employees, 1930-1980 (cont.)

	Radio				Television			
Year	Networks	AM/AM-FM Stations	FM Stations Only	Total Radio Employees	Networks	All Stations	Total Television Employees	Total Number of Broadcast Employees
1975	1,000	67,900	12,900	81,800	13,300	49,000	62,300	144,100
1976	900	70,800	14,600	86,300	13,800	51,000	64,800	151,100
1977	800	69,700	15,900	86,400	14,200	53,000	67,200	153,600
1978	900	N/A	N/A	91,700	14,500	56,300	70,800	162,500
1979	1,000	N/A	N/A	94,400	16,000	59,500	75,500	169,900
1980	1,000	N/A	N/A	98,000	16,600	61,700	78,300	176,300

Sources: 1930 figure: U.S. Department of Commerce estimate; 1935-1965 data: FCC, as printed in annual mimeographed financial reports for the radio and television industries; 1965-1980 data: FCC, as reprinted in the FCC's *Annual Report.* Notes: All figures are rounded to the nearest hundred. ªTelevision data for 1941-1948 are included in the radio totals.

Sources

Except for the 1930 figure, which is a U.S. Department of Commerce estimate, Table 460-A data were provided by the FCC. The figures are current as of the last day of each year and were rounded to the nearest 100 by the author. Both full- and part-time employment are included in the totals. The FM radio data are for independent FM stations only; data on AM-FM combination stations appear in the AM/AM-FM column. The total broadcast-employees figures are provided by the author and probably overstate the actual employment situation, since many radio or television station employees work in both media and would therefore be counted twice in the total figures. The author had to recalculate the totals for radio, which were incorrectly reported in *Broadcasting.*

Due to changes in FCC data-gathering procedures (see Units 370 and 380), there will be no further FCC reports on overall industry employment as are given here. The only official source of data will now be the U.S. Bureau of Labor Statistics, Department of Commerce.

The salary data in Table 460-B are from *Broadcasting* for 1940-1941; UNESCO's *Press Film Radio, Volume IV* (1950) for 1942-1949; and the U.S. Department of Labor (1976) for 1958-1974. All constant dollar conversions (1972 = 100, using the Consumer Price Index) were done by the author. Table 460-C data to 1971 were reported by the Office of Telecommunications Policy (OTP) (1973). The 1972-1981 figures were obtained directly from unions by the author. These figures are thus unverified by any official or separate agency.

Table 460–B   Average Weekly Salary of Non-Supervisory Broadcast Employees, 1940–1981

	Average Weekly Salary	
Year	Current Dollars	Constant (1972) Dollars
1940	43.51	129.88
1941	45.15	128.27
1942	49.79	127.99
1943	52.26	126.54
1944	57.18	135.82
1945	60.05	139.65
1946	65.40	140.04
1947	69.14	129.48
1948	71.77	124.82
1949	77.41	135.81
1958	100.70	145.73
1959	104.88	150.47
1960	110.40	155.93
1961	109.06	152.53
1962	113.84	157.45
1963	118.84	161.99
1964	122.29	165.03
1965	125.84	169.14
1966	126.49	163.00
1967	130.72	163.81
1968	135.74	163.15
1969	142.11	162.23
1970	147.45	158.89
1971	159.22	164.48
1972	172.73	172.73
1973	178.42	168.00
1974	186.80	158.44
1975	193.80	150.58
1976	206.66	151.56
1977	224.58	158.46
1978	250.80	N/A
1979	264.27	N/A
1980	283.46	N/A
1981	310.34	N/A

Sources: 1940–1941 data from *Broadcasting* (May 11, 1942); 1942–1949 data from UNESCO (1950), p. 487; 1958–1971 data from Bureau of Labor Statistics (1976a); 1972–1981 data supplied direct to the author from Bureau of Labor Statistics, Philadelphia Office, citing SIC Code 483 information.

Table 460-C Number of Members and Earnings of Selected Television Unions, 1961–1981

Note: All Dollar Figures are in Millions

| | AFTRA[a] | | Screen Actors Guild (SAG) | | | | | | Writers Guild of America West | |
| | | | | Member Earnings from: | | | | | | |
Year	Number of Members	Total Member Earnings	Number of Members	Television Production	Television Residuals	Television Commercials	Theatrical Films	Total Member Earnings	Number of Members	Total Member Earnings[c]
1961	—	—	—	—	—	—	—	—	—	26.0
1962	15,506	—	14,365	21.6	6.4	—	—	73.7	—	27.0
1963	16,351	—	14,650	19.7	7.7	—	—	76.9	—	27.0
1964	16,780	—	15,290	23.2	7.7	—	—	83.9	—	32.0
1965	17,073	—	16,117	26.6	7.3	38.6	25.7	97.8	2,336	32.0
1966	17,565	—	16,791	32.2	8.3	40.6	23.7	104.7	2,448	34.0
1967	18,184	—	18,471	24.8	11.1	46.3	26.6	108.9	2,596	37.0
1968	18,897	—	21,571	23.9	12.1	51.6	25.0	112.8	2,723	42.0
1969	21,076	—	21,600	25.4	10.5	57.1	27.6	121.2	2,740	45.0

Table 460-C Number of Members and Earnings of Selected Television Unions, 1961–1981 (cont.)

Note: All Dollar Figures are in Millions

| | AFTRA [a] | | Screen Actors Guild (SAG) | | | | | | Writers Guild of America West | |
| | | | Member Earnings from: | | | | | | | |
Year	Number of Members	Total Member Earnings	Number of Members	Television Production	Television Residuals	Television Commercials	Theatrical Films	Total Member Earnings	Number of Members	Total Member Earnings [c]
1970	24,000	107.3	22,446	23.4	11.0	61.4	17.9	114.3	2,909	39.0
1971	22,752	132.1	24,996	20.5	13.5	59.2	20.6	114.4	2,948	37.0
1972	23,714	131.6	26,610	38.6	13.1	62.3	22.2	136.2	2,865	39.2
1973	24,576	140.9	27,904	37.4	11.0	73.5	25.3	147.2	2,998	42.6
1974	26,220	156.3	29,797	47.9	12.8	78.7	24.8	164.3	3,172	56.1
1975	25,490	166.0	31,522	53.0	18.9	86.3	24.4	182.8	3,550	72.6
1976	29,672	214.4	32,434	63.6	—[b]	110.7	33.7	208.0	3,961	76.0
1977	34,049	245.3	35,118	84.2	—	125.2	42.0	251.4	4,380	92.0
1978	38,610	279.9	38,981	111.5	—	147.6	44.9	304.0	4,780	109.3
1979	44,083	307.6	43,241	113.7	—	166.3	57.9	357.9	5,252	135.7
1980	40,083	341.4	47,132	126.8	—	192.6	65.9	385.3	5,717	142.7
1981	52,233	395.6	50,424	161.3	—	211.2	66.8	439.3	6,003	113.5

Sources: AFTRA: 1961–1969, Office of Telecommunications Policy (1973); 1970–1977, MATHTEX–Number of Members, III 10, Number of Earnings, III 28; 1978–1981, Direct to the author from AFTRA Office of National Secretary. SAG: data to 1971 from Office of Telecommunications Policy (1973); 1972–1981 (all categories), Direct to the author from SAG Office of National Executive Secretary. Writers Guild of America West: Number of Members, 1965–1978, MATHTEX, III 33; 1979–1981, Direct to the author from Office of Director; Total Member Earnings, 1961–1971, Office of Telecommunications Policy (1973); 1972–1981, Direct to the author from Writers Guild of America West Office of the Director. Notes: [a] American Federation of Television and Radio Artists. [b] Amount now split between TV Production and Theatrical Films. [c] Includes earnings from television commercials and theatrical films.

Table 460–D   Minority and Female Employment in Commercial and Public Television Stations, 1971–1981 (In Percent)

	1971	1972	1973	1974	1975	1976	1977	1978	1979	1980	1981
Commercial Television Stations											
Minority Employees											
Full-Time Employees	8	10	11	12	13	14	14				
Part-Time Employees	15	18	20	20	21	22	22	16ᵃ	17	16	17
Total, All Minority Employees	9	11	12	13	13	15	15				
Female Employees											
Full-Time Employees	22	22	23	24	25	26	28				
Part-Time Employees	24	26	27	30	31	33	35	29	31	32	32
Total, All Female Employees	22	23	23	25	26	27	29				
Public Television Stations											
Minority Employees											
Full-Time Employees	8	10	11	11	12	12	13				
Part-Time Employees	10	9	9	10	11	12	12	17	15	17	17
Total, All Minority Employees	9	10	10	11	12	12	13				
Female Employees											
Full-Time Employees	28	29	30	31	32	33	34				
Part-Time Employees	25	25	31	32	34	38	39	35	37	37	39
Total, All Female Employees	27	28	30	31	32	34	35				

Sources: Data through 1976 taken from United Church of Christ, Office of Communication, *Television Station Employment Practices*, appropriate annual issues; data for 1977–1981 from FCC, *EEO Trend Report* (1981), pp. 2 and 8. Note: ᵃData from latter source does not include part-time personnel.

Table 460–D is based on FCC-gathered statistics which are reanalyzed each year by the Office of Communication of the United Church of Christ in its annual publication, *Television Station Employment Practices*. The category of "minorities" includes blacks, orientals, native Americans, and Hispanic Americans. The United Church of Christ warns that station-reported data may overestimate minority employment, especially in higher-ranking jobs (one reason that such information has not been included here). Part of the problem is also due to the fact that the categories used in FCC forms are standard government categories which do not particularly fit the broadcasting industry.

In Table 460–E, the manufacturing data through 1972 were taken from the *Census of Manufactures*, and the more recent data came from the *Annual Survey of Manufactures*. The employment figures for radio and television receivers also include the manufacture of phonographs, tape recorders, and other home music/entertainment equipment. The *Census of Retail Trade* provided figures for retail radio-television stores, and the *Census of Selected Service Industries* is the source of data on radio-television repair shops. Employment figures for stores and repair shops do not include proprietors of these establishments, since these data were not consistently reported in the sources.

Table 460-E Broadcast–Related Employment in Manufacturing, Retail, and Repair Firms, 1933–1981

Year	Manufacturing Firms			Retail Radio-TV Stores	Radio-TV Repair Shops
	Radio and TV Receivers[a]	Cathode-ray TV Picture Tubes	Electronic Receiving Tubes		
1933	N/A	N/A	N/A	N/A	6,123
1948	N/A	N/A	N/A	14,676	10,262
1954	N/A	N/A	N/A	19,941	18,281
1958	66,500	8,600	37,000	35,804	23,532
1959	74,900	7,600	37,400	N/A	N/A
1960	71,700	8,000	36,200	N/A	N/A
1961	76,800	7,500	27,200	N/A	N/A
1962	83,000	6,800	26,600	N/A	N/A
1963	81,300	10,900	25,800	30,611	25,012
1964	86,500	11,300	21,900	N/A	N/A
1965	100,100	14,300	22,300	N/A	N/A
1966	130,200	24,700	24,300	N/A	N/A
1967	116,700	27,600	21,000	46,376	29,415
1968	112,500	27,200	18,700	N/A	N/A
1969	105,500	23,400	17,100	N/A	N/A
1970	89,700	19,200	14,300	N/A	N/A
1971	89,900	17,200	12,200	N/A	N/A
1972	86,500	15,800	11,400	99,673	38,015
1973	92,100	16,900	9,300	N/A	N/A
1974	87,700	15,500	8,100	N/A	N/A
1975	68,800	13,300	5,700	N/A	N/A
1976	71,500	13,900	4,200	N/A	N/A
1977	74,600	36,700[b]		72,949	40,275
1978	76,700	36,200		84,014	38,849
1979	68,400	37,900		89,058	38,084
1980	65,000	30,500		87,507	36,754
1981	60,600	36,200		N/A	N/A

Sources: Manufacturing data through 1977 from *Census of Manufactures* (1977); data for 1978–1981 from *Annual Survey of Manufactures*, appropriate years. Retail store data through 1977 from *Census of Retail Trade*; data for 1978–1980 from *County Business Patterns*, appropriate years. Repair shop data through 1977 from *Census of Selected Service Industries*; 1978–1980 data from *County Business Patterns*, appropriate years. Notes: [a]Includes auto radios and tape players, public address systems, and music distribution apparatus; [b]Definition of the two tube categories expanded in 1977 to cover all electronic tubes.

Further Information

Given their importance, there is remarkably little information available on unions in electronic media. Indeed, with the end of annual FCC reporting, it will be harder than ever to keep track of overall employment patterns in this field, now undergoing substantial transition. The best, though now dated, overview is found in Keonig (1970), but see also the more recent and critical analyses in Mosco and Wasko (1983). A useful critique of employment statistics as a means of tracing minority employment is found in U.S. Commission on Civil Rights (1977). Trade reports on employment and union activity appear in *Broadcasting* and *Television Digest*. For overall broadcast employment statistics, see U.S. Bureau of Labor Statistics, *Employment and Earnings*.

490
EMPLOYMENT IN
CABLE TELEVISION

Interpretation of the Table

For only a few years in the late 1970s and early 1980s did the FCC collect employment information on cable television—and even then it only covered cable systems with more than five full-time employees, thus eliminating most small systems. Table 490–A summarizes what little is known of cable system and headquarters employment, and minority/female employment. The scattered data provides another indication of the rapid development and expansion of cable television in the period covered. Yet cable employment is but a fraction of that in the older and larger broadcasting business.

Source

Table 490–A was tabulated from several different FCC surveys, based, in turn, on cable entity filings of Form 395 forms (employment) by all entities with more than five employees. From those filings, the FCC estimated for the whole industry—both the survey and larger estimate figures show on

Table 490-A   Employees and Minority Employment in Cable Systems, 1974, 1980, and 1982

	1974	1980	1982
Total Number of Cable Systems (estimated)	3,200	4,106	4,399
Total Number of Cable System and Headquarters Employees (estimated)	24,300	39,300	71,493
Reporting Cable Systems	1,040	1,541	1,992
Employees of Reporting Systems	17,300	30,630	52,484
Percentage of Minority Employees	9	13	15
Percentage of Female Employees	26	32	38

Sources: 1974 data from the FCC, "Cable Industry EEO Study, 1975;" 1980 data from the FCC, "Cable Television Employment Statistics" and 1982 from FCC data as reported in Communication Daily (July 19, 1983), p. 2.

the table. The basis for making the estimate is not made clear in the FCC documents. With the end of FCC financial data gathering for broadcasting and cable, there will presumably be no more FCC information on cable employment after the 1982 data included here.

Further Information

From time to time both the National Association of Broadcasters, and the National Cable Television Association issue collections of statistical data, including employment patterns.

SECTION FIVE
ELECTRONIC MEDIA
CONTENT TRENDS

500
PUBLIC USES AND VIEWS
OF THE NEWS MEDIA

Interpretation of the Tables

For a number of years, national opinion polls have been used to measure the American public's attitudes about and uses of the different mass media. This method of measurement has a number of limitations, the most important being the fact that the wording of questions and the categories for responses have an effect on the answers of the survey respondents. Consequently, a time-series of poll responses can be misleading or unuseable if the wording of the questions or the categories for responses differ significantly among the surveys being compiled.

During the late 1950s, the Television Information Office (TIO) began employing the Roper Organization to regularly measure public attitudes about the media and about television in particular. For this reason, some comparable annual survey information is available. Yet the figures collected for this survey must be somewhat suspect, in that they were sponsored by an organization dedicated to promoting the interests of television. The Gallup organization has conducted similar studies for the American Newspaper Publishers Association (ANPA), using different questions and coming up with different results. A third survey, performed by the National Opinion Research Center, also produced different, though related, results with a completely different set of questions. The tables in this unit present the results of these three public opinion polls.

Table 500–A features the results of several of the Roper polls, from 1959 through 1982, measuring the most frequently used news source for the American public. The wording of the question was: "I'd like to ask you where you usually get most of your news about what's going on in the world today—from the newspapers or television or magazines or talking to people or where?" The percentages in this table reveal an increasing reliance on television and a decreasing tendency to mention newspapers or radio as the most frequently consulted news source.

Table 500-B, also from a Roper Organization survey, addresses the subject of media credibility for the years 1939 through 1982. The question in 1939 was worded: "If you heard conflicting versions of the same story from these sources (radio, magazines, newspapers, an authority), which would you be most likely to believe?" For the other years, the question was very similar: "If you got conflicting or different reports of the same news story from radio, television, the magazines, and the newspapers, which of the four versions would you be most inclined to believe—the one on radio or television or magazines or newspapers?"

The trend shown here is similar to that in Table 500-A. Television was judged the most credible news medium in 1961, and the percentage of people who agree with this judgment has grown considerably over the past 15 years. Meanwhile, the relative credibility of newspapers and radio has declined slightly.

Table 500-C, the results of the Gallup Survey sponsored by the ANPA, asks a different question about the public's exposure to the news media and finds that more people mention newspapers, rather than television, as their news source. However, it should be noted that the percentage of people mentioning television rose from 1957 to 1973, while the percentage naming newspapers remained relatively constant. The wording of the Gallup Poll question was: "Did you read a newspaper yesterday, look at television news yesterday, or listen to radio news yesterday?"

A survey taken in March of 1977 by another polling organization, and quoted in a publication of the American Newspaper Publishers Association (Bogart, 1977, p. 3), presents similar figures concerning people's "daily exposure to the news" that year: 69 percent for newspapers, 62 percent for television news, and 49 percent for radio news.

Taking a different approach, Table 500-D measures the American public's confidence in the people who run television and the people who run "the press." The question for this survey: "I am going to name some institutions in this country. As far as the people running these institutions are concerned, would you say you have a great deal of confidence, only some confidence, or hardly any confidence at all in them?"

Apparently, there is some growth in the percentage of survey respondents who have "hardly any" confidence in the people running television, while there is a slight increase in the percentage of respondents who say they have "hardly any" confidence in the people running the press. However, these trends are for a very short period of time (1973–1982), and the shifts of opinion are not large, especially if the possibility of sampling error is considered. Moreover, the wording of the question does not make it clear whether the respondents are being asked to distinguish between newspapers and television news, or between newspapers and television in general (that is, as both an entertainment and a news medium), or between television in general and "the press," which could include both print and broadcast journalism.

In reviewing all of these survey results, one is reminded of an *I Ching* metaphor: "The footprints run criss-cross." All of the survey research organizations involved have good reputations. The choice of which results one accepts will usually depend on one's purposes. The most reasonable and objective approach to survey data of this kind is to supplement the material with other relevant information, such as audience characteristics, circulation, and news content.

The type of question asked by the Roper Organization in Table 500–A has come under particular criticism in recent years. The critics maintain that human behavior cannot be accurately measured by asking people what they "usually" do with their time. Instead, more specific questions, such as what the respondents actually did *yesterday*, are far more reliable measures of behavior (Welles, 1978). Greenberg and Roloff (1974) point out that individual respondent characteristics should be measured as well, since these characteristics (sex, age, socioeconomic status) inevitably affect the patterns of media use. Welles (1978, p. 14) also mentions that people "probably get different kinds of news from different media"—a factor that should be measured in this type of survey. In most cases, the survey organizations have attempted to respond to such criticisms by wording their questions more specifically and by broadening their surveys to include breakdowns by individual characteristics of the respondents.

Sources

The Roper Organization, the source of Tables 500–A and 500–B, described its sample and sampling procedure as follows:

A multi-staged, stratified, area probability sample is used for *Roper Reports* . . . It is a nationwide cross-section of the noninstitutionalized population, 18 years and older, living in the continental United States. It is representative of all ages 18 and over, all sizes of community, geographic areas, and economic levels. In each study–November and December–2,000 personal interviews were conducted by experienced, trained interviewers.

The samples since 1971 have included 18 to 20 year olds because of the lowering of age limits for voting. It was determined, through weighting procedures and retabulating, that inclusion of this younger group did not affect results in total. This means that trend differences found in the

Table 500–A Surveys Measuring Most Frequent Source of News for the Public, 1959–1982

Year	Radio	Television	Magazines	Newspapers	Other People	All Sources Mentioned	Don't Know/ No Answer
			"The most frequent source of news" (Percentage of those asked)				
1959	34	51	8	57	4	154	1
1961	34	52	9	57	5	157	3
1963	29	55	6	53	4	147	3
1964	26	58	8	56	5	153	3
1967	28	64	7	55	4	158	2
1968	25	59	7	49	5	145	3
1971	23	60	5	48	4	140	1
1972	21	64	6	50	4	145	1
1974	21	65	4	47	4	141	—[a]
1976	19	64	7	49	5	144	—[a]
1978	20	67	5	49	5	146	—[a]
1980	18	64	5	44	4	135	—[a]
1982	18	65	6	44	4	137	—[a]

Source: 1959–1982. The Roper Organization (1982). Note: [a] Less than 1 percent.

Table 500-B Surveys Measuring Public Trust in Credibility of News Media, 1939–1982

| Year | Radio | "The most believable news medium" (Percentage of those asked) | | | Don't Know/ No Answer |
		Television	Magazines	Newspapers	
1939[a]	40	N/A	N/A	27	20
1959	12	29	10	32	17
1961	12	39	10	24	17
1963	12	36	10	24	18
1964	8	41	10	23	18
1967	7	41	8	24	20
1968	8	44	11	21	16
1971	10	49	9	20	12
1972	8	48	10	21	13
1974	8	51	8	20	13
1976	7	51	9	22	11
1978	9	47	9	23	12
1980	8	51	9	22	10
1982	6	53	8	22	11

Sources: 1939 data is from Peter (1941). All remaining information is from Television Information Office, citing The Roper Organization. Note: [a] the 1939 survey included a fifth "medium"—"an authority you heard speak" which received 13 percent of the responses as the most believable news source.

Table 500–C   Surveys Measuring the Public's Daily Use of News Media, 1957–1977

Year	*Newspaper*	*Television Newscast*	*Radio Newscast*
"The news source used yesterday" (Percentage of those asked)			
1957	71	38	54
1965	71	55	58
1970	73	60	65
1973	70	62	59
1977	69	62	49

Sources: Data through 1973 is based on a Gallup Poll as reported by the American Newspaper Publishers Association (1973), p. 41. 1977 data is from Audits and Surveys Inc. data for a report designed and analysed by the Newspaper Advertising Bureau in a joint project with ANPA.

studies are meaningful and *are* due to changes in attitude of the population as a whole. (Television Information Office, 1977, p. 24)

The reader should note that a national probability sample of 2,000 usually has a sampling error of not more than plus or minus 2 percent.

Table 500–C data through 1973 was taken from a report by the American Newspaper Publishers Association of a survey done by the Gallup Poll organization. While that ANPA report did not discuss the particular sampling methods used by the Gallup Poll, Gallup's procedures are generally quite similar to those of the Roper Organization. However, the Gallup sample in the earlier years included only those persons 21 years and older. The Gallup Poll now measures 18– to 20 year olds as well, but the responses of this age group were deleted from the later years of this series in order to make the figures historically comparable. It may be, then, that the differences in the responses to these surveys and those of the Roper Organization are due in part to the media preferences of 18 to 20 year olds. However, the differences in the wording of the questions by the two organizations may well be the most significant factor in the responses. The 1977 information is from an Audits and Surveys Inc. study done for the Newspaper Advertising Bureau in a joint project with ANPA. It included two choices not shown here: "all 3 sources," with a 25 percent response, and "only one source" with a 28 percent response. Obviously, multiple responses were allowed.

The source of the information in Table 500–D is the National Opinion Research Center (NORC), an independent nonprofit research organization affiliated with the University of Chicago. In addition to conducting research, the NORC provides graduate training in survey research techniques. The data reproduced in Table 500–D are from the NORC's national data program for the social sciences, which it began in 1972 under the sponsorship of

Table 500–D Surveys Measuring Public Confidence in the Leadership of Television and the Press, 1974–1982.

	1974		1976		1978		1980		1982	
	Number	Percent	Number	Percent	Number	Percent	Number	Percent	Number	Percent
"Confidence in the people running television"										
Total Sample Size	1,484	—	1,499	—	1,532	—	1,468	—	1,506	—
Total Number Responding	1,464	100.0	1,464	100.0	1,498	100.0	1,442	100.0	1,483	100.0
"A great deal"	347	23.7	279	19.1	210	13.7	235	16.2	214	14.4
"Only some"	861	58.8	779	53.2	815	53.2	801	55.5	862	58.1
"Hardly any"	256	17.5	406	27.7	473	30.9	406	28.1	407	27.4
"Confidence in the people running the press"										
Total Sample Size	1,484	—	1,499	—	1,532	—	1,468	—	1,506	—
Total Number Responding	1,463	100.0	1,463	100.0	1,501	100.0	1,424	100.0	1,469	100.0
"A great deal"	383	26.2	424	29.0	307	20.0	322	22.6	272	18.5
"Only some"	821	56.1	776	53.0	893	58.3	849	59.6	887	60.3
"Hardly any"	259	17.7	263	18.0	301	19.6	253	17.2	310	21.1

Source: National Opinion Research Center (1974–1982), direct to author. Note: Responses of "don't know" and "no answer" are not shown separately here.

the National Science Foundation. The results here are based on a national representative cross-section of the total population, aged 18 or older, with quotas at the block level. NORC estimates the sampling error for this design at about what it would be for a random sample of 1,000 respondents— around plus or minus 2 to 4 percent. The work of the National Opinion Research Center is considered of high quality and reliability.

Further Information

The organizations cited in this unit are the main sources of information regarding media uses and credibility. Numerous surveys have been done with similar questions and issues. The best way to track them down is to contact the person in charge of machine-readable data bases at a large, research-oriented, university library. In addition, the reader may wish to know that the data presented in Table 500–D were also reprinted in *Social Indicators 1976* (U.S. Bureau of the Census, 1977). Updated versions of this compendium, including *Social Indicators III* (1981), contain similar information.

501
MEDIA COSTS AND COVERAGE OF POLITICAL CAMPAIGNS

Interpretation of the Tables

Table 501–A lists those media which various adult samples identified as their primary sources of information about local, state, and national election campaigns in the United States. The figures clearly demonstrate the increasing importance of television as an information source at all political campaign levels. Newspapers are the only other medium to show an increase, but only in the case of local election coverage. Even in 1952, when television was barely established nationwide, it had already become the highest ranking medium for political information.

Table 501-B details the costs of political party advertising on radio and television during U.S. general elections. This information covers general elections at all levels—local, state, and national. Some interesting trends are evident here: the slowly increasing uses of radio and television by third parties; the greater use of both media by Republicans (although the two major parties spent equal amounts in 1972); and the fluctuating proportions of total campaign expenditures for airtime, with steady increases until 1964, then a leveling off, and, finally, a decline in overall spending levels in 1972.

Table 501-C lists the broadcast advertising and other media advertising costs of the presidential and vice-presidential campaigns of the two major parties in 1968, 1972, and 1976. With the exception of the lavishly financed 1972 Nixon campaign, media advertising has accounted for 35 to 60 percent of the total expenditures for each campaign. The 1976 general election was the first to include a federal ceiling on presidential campaign expenditures, accompanied by federal matching funds to help finance the campaigns.

Table 501-D compares the total minutes of political advertising on network television during general election years versus the average per-household viewing time for this advertising. These figures reveal the small percentage of political advertising which is seen in the average household—typically about 10 percent of the total amount of advertising airtime.

Table 501-E demonstrates that the average U.S. household views between 20 and 30 percent of the total hours of network television airtime devoted to the party conventions and to election night coverage. Levels of viewing are higher on election nights, but this apparently has no correlation with voting patterns. Note that the viewing levels for the closely contested 1968 and 1976 elections are not much different from those for the 1964 and 1972 landslide elections.

Finally, Table 501-F provides what limited information is available on the hours of free broadcast time provided by the radio and television networks to presidential and vice-presidential candidates (and/or their supporters) from 1956 through 1972. Fairly substantial amounts of free radio time were still made available to candidates in both the primary and general election periods in 1972. But the amount of free network television time in general elections had dwindled from 39 hours in 1960 to a mere 1 hour in 1972.

This dramatic drop is mainly due to the politically turbulent 1960s, when strong third-party candidates and vocal political dissenters of all stripes demanded rigid enforcement of the equal-time provisions and the Fairness Doctrine (Section 315) of the Communication Act, as amended in 1959. Network television management insisted that television airtime had become far too costly to give it away to all of the candidates who would seek equal exposure; hence, the networks simply stopped providing such time. In 1975, the FCC determined that live debates between candidates are news events and, therefore, exempt from equal-time obligations to minor candidates, so long as the debates are produced and controlled by an independent, nonpartisan organization. Broadcasters are barred from involvement in the event other than covering the debate live with cameras and microphones. This FCC ruling opened the way for the Ford–Carter debates in 1976, and the single Carter–Reagan debate of 1980.

Sources

In Table 501–A, the 1952 information was taken from Kraus and Davis (1976), citing Campbell et al., in *Scientific American* (May 1953). The data were gathered by means of a survey questionnaire which was sent to over 1,700 voting-age citizens throughout the continental United States. Data for 1964 through 1982 were provided by the Roper Organization for the Television Information Office (TIO) (1982), which excluded national and state elections in 1980.

The TIO is the NAB's television public relations group, and the Roper surveys were clearly carried out with a persuasive purpose in mind—that is, in showing television as improving its already high position among the other media. During the two most recent election years, however, Roper asked a parallel question about which medium was most useful in learning about *issues,* and television did not do quite so well in that area.

Table 501–B data for 1952 are from Alexander (1970), citing Heard's *The Costs of Democracy* (1960). Data for 1956–1972 are from the FCC's *Annual Report* (1973) and are based on all reporting stations for all election-year political campaign broadcasting. Alexander and others note that although the FCC surveys are the only consistent information available for the elections covered, they still did not include *all* stations and elections. Consequently, these data are best viewed as close estimates. (The reader should know that these FCC surveys were discontinued on creation of the Federal Election Committee, which gathers somewhat similar information, but does not attempt to collate or publish it.) The estimated total campaign costs which appear at the bottom of Table 501–B are from Alexander (1972).

Table 501–C data for 1968 are from Alexander (1970); the 1972 data are from Alexander (1976). Information for 1976 for the Democrats was reported by the Carter campaign directly to Herbert Alexander, who made it available to the author. Republican information for 1976 was supplied to the

Table 501-A   Surveys Measuring Media as Sources of Information on Local, State, and National Elections, 1952–1982 (In Percent)

	1952[a]	1964	1968	1972	1976	1978	1980[b]	1982
				National Elections				
Newspapers	22	36	24	26	20	38	N/A	31
Television	31	64	65	66	75	48	N/A	46
Radio	27	9	4	6	4	8	N/A	5
Other People	—	4	4	5	3	10	N/A	9
Magazines	5	6	5	5	5	2	N/A	2
Other	—	3	2	2	1	6	N/A	7
Total Response		122	104	110	108	112	N/A	100
				State Elections				
Newspapers	N/A	41	37	39	35	39	N/A	29
Television	N/A	43	42	49	53	55	N/A	53
Radio	N/A	10	6	7	5	8	N/A	6
Other People	—	8	9	9	6	8	N/A	7
Magazines	N/A	1	1	1	1	2	N/A	1
Other	—	4	4	3	3	5	N/A	5
Total Response		107	99	108	103	117	N/A	101
				Local Elections				
Newspapers	N/A	42	40	41	44	45	36	39
Television	N/A	27	26	31	34	39	44	37
Radio	N/A	10	6	7	7	10	6	6
Other People	—	18	23	23	12	15	11	15
Magazines	N/A	1	1	2	1	1	2	1
Other	—	7	4	5	6	7	5	7
Total Response		105	100	109	104	117	104	105

Sources: 1952 from Kraus and Davis (1976), p. 82 citing Campbell et al. (May 1953). All other data from Television Information Office citing The Roper Organization. Notes: [a]1952 was for all elections and included only the four media categories plus more than one (9 percent) or none of the four (6 percent). [b]State and national elections were not included in the 1980 survey.

author by both Alexander and the GOP National Committee. While 1968 and 1972 data can be compared to official FCC reports, the 1976 information given here must be considered preliminary. 1980 Republican data was reported to the author by Alexander.

The reader should also keep in mind that the figures shown in Table 501-C were originally supplied by the respective campaigns. The details vary from year to year, and losing campaigns are often ended with limited details released. In view of the laxity of campaign reporting, the data for 1968 and 1972 should be considered approximations.

Table 501–B Broadcast Political Advertising Costs for General Elections, 1952–1972

Note: All Advertising Costs are in Thousands of Dollars.						
	1952	1956	1960	1964	1968	1972
Television Advertising Costs						
Network Time	N/A	2,931	2,927	3,807	7,362	4,911
Local Station Time	N/A	3,755	7,125	13,689	19,725	19,655
Total Costs	3,000	6,686	10,052	17,496	27,807	24,566
Percentage of Costs Paid by:						
Republican Party	N/A	56	54	54	56	47
Democratic Party	N/A	42	44	44	38	47
Third Parties	N/A	2	1	1	5	6
Radio Advertising Costs						
Network Time	N/A	321	79	119	663	489
Local Station Time	N/A	2,900	4,064	6,988	12,654	13,021
Total Costs	3,100	3,221	4,143	7,107	13,317	13,510
Percentage of Costs Paid by:						
Republican Party	N/A	52	51	51	55	44
Democratic Party	N/A	43	43	46	38	45
Third Parties	N/A	5	6	3	7	11
Total Advertising Costs	6,100	9,907	14,195	24,604	40,403	38,127
Percentage Change from Previous Election	—	62	45	73	64	− 6
Total Costs of Election (In Millions)	140	155	175	200	300	425
Percent Spent on Broadcasting	4	6	8	13	13	9

Sources: Advertising costs: Alexander (1976), p. 324, citing Heard (1960) for 1952 data and the Federal Communications Commission's *Annual Report* (1973), p. 207, for 1956–1972 data. Total costs of election: Alexander (1976), p. 78.

Two sources contributed to Table 501–D: the 1960 and 1964 campaign data were gathered from Lichty et al. (1965); the 1968 and 1972 campaign figures were taken from A. C. Nielsen's *Network Television Audiences to Primaries, Conventions, Elections* (1976). Table 501–E information through 1972 comes from the same A. C. Nielsen publication. The information for 1976 was gathered from the *Nielsen Newscast* No. 2 (1976), on the Democratic Convention; *Nielsen Newscast* No. 3 (1976), on the GOP Convention; and *Nielsen Newscast* No. 4 (1976), on the election night coverage.

Table 501–F was constructed from the information issued after each general election, from 1956 through 1972, by the FCC. General election and 1968 primary data come from Alexander (1976); the 1972 primary data are

Table 501-C Presidential Campaign Advertising Expenditures, 1968–1980

	1968		1972		1976		1980	
Note: All Dollar Figures are in Millions.								
	Nixon	*Humphrey*	*Nixon*	*McGovern*	*Ford*	*Carter*	*Carter*	*Reagan*
Broadcast Media Advertising Costs	8.1	4.0	3.9	4.9	7.9	8.6	N/A	14.5
Television Advertising								
Network Time		2.2	2.2	2.3	2.5	3.3	N/A	7.6
Spot Time	6.3	1.4	3.9	1.8	3.9	4.2	N/A	5.1
Radio Advertising	1.8	.4	.6	.8	1.5	1.1	N/A	1.7
Print Media Advertising Costs	.9	.4	.7	1.0	1.3	.6	N/A	2.6
Broadcast/Print Media								
Production Costs	2.0	1.1	1.5	.8	1.7	.5	N/A	2.2
Costs of Campaign Materials	1.3	N/A	1.3	.4	.7	N/A	N/A	N/A
Total Media Costs	12.3	6.3[a]	8.2[a]	7.2[a]	11.6	9.7	N/A	17.1
Total Campaign Expenditures	24.9	10.3	61.4	21.2	23.1	23.4	N/A	34.0
Percent of Expenditures								
for Media	49.4	61.2	13.4	34.0	50.2	41.5	N/A	52.3

Sources: 1968 data: Alexander (1970), pp. 81, 84, 92. 1972 data: Alexander (1976), pp. 272, 290, 339. 1976 data: Provided directly to the author by Herbert Alexander, who cited information from the Carter campaign and the GOP National Committee. 1980 data supplied directly to the author by Alexander. Note: [a]Includes other unspecified expenditures.

taken from *Broadcasting*. The 1960 television figures for the general election period include the airtime for the Kennedy–Nixon debates.

Further Information

The reader seeking an overview of the media's role in political campaigns should consult Chester (1969) for the historical context, Kraus and Davis (1976) for research findings and a bibliography, and Chaffee (1975) for research directions and methods. Although the FCC has issued reports on political broadcasting, covering the 1956–1972 elections, opinions differ on just how accurate and complete its data are.

The best sources for statistics and analyses of media advertising expenditures for election campaigns after 1960 are Alexander's quadrennial reviews (1972, 1976, and 1980). These reviews are based on both journalistic reports and data obtained directly from the major and independent party campaigns. The Citizen's Research Foundation, which Alexander directs (University of Southern California, Research Annex, 3716 S. Hope Street, Los Angeles, California 90007), is the collection point and the respository for much of the data reported here.

Table 501-D   Air Time and Viewing Time of Paid Network Television Political Advertising, 1960-1980

Election Year and Political Party	Total Minutes of Aired Advertising	Average Minutes Viewed per Household	Viewed Minutes as Percent of Aired Minutes
1960			
Republican (Nixon)	830.0	71	8.5
Democratic (Kennedy)	510.0	52	10.2
Total	1,340.0	123	9.2
1964			
Republican (Goldwater)	760.0	56	7.4
Democratic (Johnson)	375.0	35	9.3
Total	1,135.0	91	8.0
1968			
Republican (Nixon)	710.0	74	10.4
Democratic (Humphrey)	830.0	89	10.7
Independent (Wallace)	250.0	29	11.6
Total	1,790.0	129	10.7
1972[a]			
Republican (Nixon)	615.0	60	9.8
Democratic (McGovern)	540.0	59	10.9
Others	95.0	6	6.3
Total	1,250.0	125	10.0
1976[a]			
Republican (Ford)	448.5	49	11.0
Democratic (Carter)	503.0	60	11.9
Others	251.0	30	12.1
Total	1,202.5	139	11.6
1980			
Republican (Reagan)	583.0	47	8.1
Democratic (Carter)	358.0	33	9.2
Others	496.0	46	9.2
Total	1,437.0	126	8.8

Sources: 1960, 1964 data: Lichty et al. (1965), pp. 219, 223, tables 1, 2. 1968, 1972 data: A. C. Nielsen, *Network Television Audiences to Primaries, Conventions, Elections* (1976), p. 20; 1976 data: A. C. Nielsen Co. 1980 data supplied directly to the author from A. C. Nielsen Co. Note: [a]Candidates representing other than major parties are listed under "Others."

Table 501-E Air Time and Viewing Time of National Convention and Election Night Coverage, 1952–1980

	Network Hours Telecast	Average Hours Viewed per Household	Viewed Hours as Percent of Aired Hours
1952			
Republican Convention	57:30	10:30	18
Democratic Convention	61:06	13:06	21
Election Night	N/A	N/A	N/A
1956			
Republican Convention	22:48	6:24	28
Democratic Convention	37:36	8:24	22
Election Night	N/A	2:42	N/A
1960			
Republican Convention	25:30	6:12	24
Democratic Convention	29:20	8:20	28
Election Night	N/A	4:30	N/A
1964			
Republican Convention	36:30	7:00	19
Democratic Convention	23:30	6:24	27
Election Night	7:36	2:35	34
1968			
Republican Convention	34:00	6:30	19
Democratic Convention	39:06	8:30	22
Election Night	13:18	3:38	27
1972			
Republican Convention	19:48	3:30	18
Democratic Convention	36:42	5:48	16
Election Night	6:20	2:10	30
1976			
Republican Convention	27:21	7:09	26
Democratic Convention	30:48	5:53	18
Election Night	9:00	3:02	34
1980			
Republican Convention	22:00	4:25	19
Democratic Convention	24:00	5:02	21
Election Night	7:42	5:47	74

Sources: 1952–1972 data: Nielsen Television Index, A. C. Nielsen, *Network Television Audiences to Primaries, Conventions, Elections* (1976), pp. 8, 9, 21. 1976 data: Democratic convention: Nielsen Television Index, A. C. Nielsen, *Nielsen Newscast* No. 2 (1976), pp. 10–11; Republican convention: *Nielsen Newscast* No. 3 (1976), pp. 8–9; election night: *Nielsen Newscast* No. 4 (1976), pp. 2–3. 1980 data supplied directly to the author from A. C. Nielsen Co.

Costs and Coverage of Campaigns   169

Table 501-F   Free Network Time Given to Presidential Campaigns, 1956–1972

	Primaries Election Period		General Election Period	
Year	Television Networks	Radio Networks	Television Networks	Radio Networks
1956	N/A	N/A	29:38	32:23
1960	N/A	N/A	39:22	43:14
1964	N/A	N/A	4:28	21:14
1968	13:16	31:29	3:01	24:17
1972	20:00	31:00	1:00	19:00

Sources: All general election and 1968 primaries data: FCC figures cited in Alexander (1976), p. 329. 1972 primaries data: FCC figures cited in *Broadcasting* (May 14, 1973), p. 25.

560
BROADCAST NEWS PROGRAMMING

Interpretation of the Tables

The tables in this section provide a quantitative measure of the growth of broadcast journalism. Table 560–A lists the total weekly hours of *regularly scheduled* network radio and television news programs, with a breakdown by type of news program. While the data indicate a definite and steady growth in the number of radio newscasts, the trend in network television news is less consistent.

Table 560–B provides a census of the documentaries shown during the first 35 years of network television. These figures were taken from a dissertation on the topic, and they closely match each network's share of the total network billings over the period: ABC broadcast 10 percent of the documentaries and shared 26 percent of the billings; CBS broadcast 43 percent of the documentaries and had 39 percent of the combined billings; and NBC had 37 percent of the documentaries and received 35 percent of the billings. During the 1970s, CBS has most consistently broadcast documentaries of the "magazine" format—primarily telecasts of "60 Minutes." The reader should note the overall trend toward fewer documentary broadcasts since the 1960s, when many dealt with Vietnam. Also, the reader should note that figures for all years and all categories reflect the number of programs shown in a season, and do not take into account the varied lengths of programs, the hours when they were shown (prime-time or other time periods), or the seasons during which they were shown (the important season versus the summer and other months).

Table 560-C focuses on network television news programming from 1970 to 1976, showing the total average hours of regularly scheduled news for all three networks. About 80 percent of these figures are the standard evening news programs; the remaining 20 percent are sponsored news specials and network-sustained news specials which are usually scheduled on short notice in response to news events. A news-programming peak in the 1972–1973 season is probably due to the end of U.S. involvement in Vietnam and to coverage of the presidential election year.

Table 560-D provides averaged national figures for a sample week of nonentertainment programming by commercial television stations. The figures indicate the essentially static proportions of news, public affairs, and other nonentertainment programming between 1973 and 1979. Note that about half the news content comes from other than local sources—in most cases, from the networks.

Table 560-E offers comparative figures on the uses of television by recent presidents—an issue of interest to the networks (for financial reasons) and to observers and scholars of national politics. One striking trend in this table is the increasing concentrations of *prime-time* presidential appearances early in a new administration. Another interesting revelation, for which there is no clear explanation, is the substantially higher amounts of television appearances by President Kennedy during the daytime hours.

Table 560-F lists the percentage of radio and television stations which broadcast editorials on a daily, weekly, or "only occasional" basis. The information in this table is not particularly reliable (see "Sources" section below), but it seems to indicate a trend of increasing station uses of the editorial after the mid-1960s. The pattern is erratic, but this is due more to survey limitations than to documented changes in the field.

Sources

The information in Table 560-A on radio news programming up to 1955 is from Summers (1958), as interpreted and arranged by L. W. Lichty and C. H. Sterling. The 1969 radio figures were provided to the author by Lichty. The 1974 *total* radio data, from Lichty and Topping (1975), includes

Table 560-A Total Weekly Hours of Regularly Scheduled Network Radio and Television News Programs, 1930–1978

	Number of Hours per Week										
Programming Content	1930	1935	1940	1945	1950	1955	1960	1965	1969/70[a]	1973/74[b]	1977/78[f]
News Reporting											
Radio	2	7	18	34	30	39	N/A	N/A	133[c]	129[d]	N/A
Television	—	—	—	—	4	6	6	14	16	16	26
Forum-Interview and News Analysis/Commentary											
Radio	1	4	5	5	7	8	N/A	N/A	N/A	N/A	N/A
Television	—	—	—	—	5	6	4	2	2	2	2
Documentary and Information											
Radio	1	5	7	9	4	4	N/A	N/A	N/A	N/A	N/A
Television	—	—	—	—	1	4	3	8	3	6	4
Total											
Radio	4	16	30	48	41	51	N/A	N/A	133[e]	129[e]	N/A
Television	—	—	—	—	10	16	13	24	21	24	31
Radio and Television Combined	4	16	30	48	51	67	N/A	N/A	154[e]	153[e]	N/A

Sources: Radio data through 1955 based on Summers (1958) and calculated by C.H. Sterling and L. W. Lichty. Radio data for 1969 provided directly to the author by L. W. Lichty. Radio data for 1974 is from Lichty and Topping (1975), p. 434, table 31. All television data from Unit 582, except for weekend daytime data, which is from L. W. Lichty. Data for the 1977–1978 television season was supplied by A. C. Nielson Co. Notes: The figures in the original sources were all expressed in quarter hours. The author converted these figures to the nearest full hour. [a]Radio data are for 1969, television for 1970. [b]Radio data are for 1974, television for 1973. [c]Includes daytime and evening news programs on all national networks (including the four separate ABC-operated networks—hence, a few programs were duplicated, and those duplications are included in the total figure). [d]Includes all regularly scheduled day and night news analysis/commentary programming, but does not include forum-interview programs. [e]These totals exclude the very limited amount of radio programming in the forum-interview and documentary and information categories. [f]Television data only. Figures are rounded and thus do not total exactly.

Table 560–B Number and Type of Documentary News Programs Produced by Network Television, 1948–1982

	ABC				CBS				NBC				All Three			
Season	Regular Documentaries[a]	Magazine Documentaries[b]	Instant Special[c]	Total	Regular Documentaries[a]	Magazine Documentaries[b]	Instant Special[c]	Total	Regular Documentaries[a]	Magazine Documentaries[b]	Instant Special[c]	Total	Regular Documentaries[a]	Magazine Documentaries[b]	Instant Special[c]	Total
1948	—	—	—	—	6	—	—	6	8	—	—	8	14	—	—	14
1948–1949	7	—	—	7	33	—	—	33	2	—	—	2	42	—	—	42
1949–1950	2	—	1	3	8	—	2	10	33	16	1	50	43	16	4	63
1950–1951	11	—	—	11	13	—	4	17	16	32	2	50	40	32	6	78
1951–1952	3	—	1	4	52	2	1	55	30	—	4	34	85	2	6	93
1952–1953	1	—	8	9	61	—	3	64	41	—	3	44	103	—	14	117
1953–1954	15	—	1	16	78	—	34	112	16	—	33	49	109	—	68	177
1954–1955	4	—	1	5	107	—	2	109	31	—	2	33	142	—	5	147
1955–1956	36	—	—	36	64	—	3	67	56	—	—	56	156	—	3	159
1956–1957	40	—	8	48	98	—	3	101	72	—	2	74	210	—	13	223
1957–1958	23	—	3	26	75	—	11	86	62	—	4	66	160	—	18	178
1958–1959	16	—	14	30	95	—	25	120	57	—	16	73	168	—	55	223
1959–1960	29	—	23	52	99	—	24	123	88	—	34	122	216	—	81	297
1960–1961	43	—	31	74	129	—	14	143	84	—	35	119	256	—	80	336
1961–1962	69	—	11	80	134	—	11	145	184	18	20	222	387	18	42	447
1962–1963	75	—	12	87	98	—	24	122	142	14	31	187	315	14	67	396
1963–1964	65	—	8	73	104	—	7	111	123	—	14	137	292	—	29	321
1964–1965	51	—	8	59	125	—	10	135	81	—	21	102	257	—	39	296
1965–1966	55	—	3	58	88	—	19	107	97	—	28	125	240	—	50	290
1966–1967	85	—	5	90	76	—	12	88	78	—	14	92	239	—	31	270

Table 560–B Number and Type of Documentary News Programs Produced by Network Television, 1948–1982 (cont.)

Season	ABC				CBS				NBC				All Three			
	Regular Documentaries[a]	Magazine Documentaries[b]	Instant Special[c]	Total	Regular Documentaries[a]	Magazine Documentaries[b]	Instant Special[c]	Total	Regular Documentaries[a]	Magazine Documentaries[b]	Instant Special[c]	Total	Regular Documentaries[a]	Magazine Documentaries[b]	Instant Special[c]	Total
1967–1968	39	—	4	43	88	1	12	101	87	—	20	107	214	1	36	251
1968–1969	30	—	7	37	58	21	17	96	39	9	9	57	127	30	33	190
1969–1970	35	—	2	37	26	22	10	58	35	11	11	57	96	33	23	152
1970–1971	16	—	3	19	35	18	13	66	21	12	8	41	72	30	24	126
1971–1972	24	—	9	33	28	29	20	77	23	10	19	52	75	39	48	162
1972–1973	23	29	9	61	27	32	24	83	27	10	12	49	77	71	45	193
1973–1974	20	37	7	64	40	29	20	89	15	8	11	34	75	74	38	187
1974–1975	19	26	4	49	22	38	12	72	18	13	9	40	59	77	25	161
1975–1976	8	1	21	30	19	34	24	77	16	12	26	54	43	47	71	161
1976–1977	15	2	13	30	14	68	14	96	13	13	16	42	42	83	43	168
1977–1978	10	14	10	34	15	56	17	88	8	10	11	29	33	80	38	151
1978–1979	10	21	15	46	16	54	15	85	11	31	14	56	37	106	44	187
1979–1980	12	86	41	139	14	50	41	105	8	27	26	61	34	163	108	305
1980–1981	11	40	4	55	25	62	22	109	10	41	15	66	46	143	41	230
1981–1982	10	42	1	53	18	56	10	84	14	30	10	54	42	128	21	191
Total	912	298	288	1498	1988	572	480	3040	1646	317	481	2444	4546	1187	1249	6982

Source: Compiled by Raymond L. Carroll, University of Alabama. Figures include only the news division-produced documentary programs broadcast during the late afternoon, evening, and late evening time periods. Notes: Each year-pair given is for the years in which the television season occurs. For example, the numbers of documentaries listed as having been broadcast in 1950–1951 were actually aired during the season which extended from the fall of 1950 through the summer of 1951. [a]"Regular documentaries," nearly all of which deal with single subjects. [b]"Magazine documentaries," each of which covers a variety of subjects. [c]"Instant specials," each of which deals with a recent event and is broadcast from within hours to within a week of that event.

Table 560-C Amount of Television Network News Programming, 1970–1976

Season[a]	Regularly Scheduled News Programs	Sponsored News Specials	Network-Sponsored News Specials	Total News Hours
1970–1971	289	72	25	386
1971–1972	310	62	13	385
1972–1973	326	72	25	423
1973–1974	318	62	33	413
1974–1975	313	43	44	400
1975–1976	318	73	20	411

Source: Nielsen Television Index, A. C. Nielsen Company, *Television Audience* (1976), pp. 56, 62. Note: [a]Seasons run from September thru April of years given.

55 hours per week of public affairs and documentary-information programming. Not included on this table are such programs as NBC's *Monitor,* which ran on weekends for many years, and the weekend interview program *Face the Nation,* which is also carried on television. The cumulative totals for 1969–1970 and 1973–1974 are therefore not directly comparable to the radio-TV figures shown for 1950 and 1955. Directly comparable figures would be higher.

The television data for Table 560-A were taken from the tables in Unit 582, with the addition of weekend daytime figures which were supplied by Lichty. The 1969–1970 and 1973–1974 columns on the table represent a combination of materials: the radio data are for 1969 and 1974; the television data for 1970 and 1973. The Mutual and DuMont networks are included in these figures where applicable.

Table 560-B is directly from Raymond Carroll who first gathered much of this data for his dissertation. The method used to determine these figures was not reported, and the chief limitation of this table is that it gives only the numbers of programs and not the broadcast hours involved. For definitions of the three types of documentaries—"Regular documentaries," "Magazine documentaries," and "Instant specials"—which were counted here, the reader should see Table 560-B notes.

The Table 560-C data are all from A. C. Nielsen Company's *Television Audience* (1976). Since the information for sponsored news programs was multiplied from monthly averages, the "total news hours" column is a close estimate.

The figures in Table 560-D are from the FCC's annual *Television Broadcast Programming Data*, which is no longer gathered. These data are based on station reports of their schedules on random days throughout the year. The material is then collected into a composite sample week for all stations. Nearly all U.S. commercial television stations are included in the sur-

Table 560-D Prime-Time and Total Hours of Non-Entertainment Programming by Commercial Television Stations, 1973-1979 (In Percent)

	Total Programming				Locally-Produced Only			
	News	Public Affairs	Other	Total	News	Public Affairs	Other	Total
1973 (N = 694)								
prime-time	12	5	2	19	6	1	1	8
total time	9	4	9	22	5	2	2	9
1974 (N = 699)								
prime-time	12	3	2	17	6	1	1	8
total time	9	4	9	22	5	2	2	9
1975 (N = 686)								
prime-time	12	5	5	22	5	1	1	7
total time	10	5	10	25	6	2	2	10
1976 (N = 702)								
prime-time	12	3	5	20	6	1	1	8
total time	9	4	11	24	5	2	2	9
1977 (N = 707)								
prime-time	12	3	5	20	6	1	1	8
total time	10	5	11	25	5	2	2	8
1978 (N = 711)								
prime-time	12	3	4	20	6	1	1	8
total time	9	4	11	25	5	2	2	8
1979 (N = 726)								
prime-time	12	4	6	21	6	1	1	9
total time	9	5	12	26	5	2	2	9

Source: FCC, *Television Broadcast Programming Data,* annual issues. Total broadcast time is 6 AM to midnight; prime-time is 6-11 PM in the Eastern and Pacific time zones, and 5-10 PM in the Central and Mountain zones.

vey (compare the numbers of stations reporting for this table with the station totals listed in Unit 180).

Table 560-E, from Minow, Martin, and Mitchell (1975), is based on figures reported to the *New York Times* by the White House Press Office. Information on the Ford Administration comes from the A. C. Nielsen Company, *Nielsen Newscast* No. 3 (1975). The Nielsen material was converted by the author into information comparable with the rest of the table. The Carter data were drawn from *Nielsen Newscast* No. 1 (1978) and similarly converted by the author. Reagan data is directly from the White House.

Table 560-F is from issues of *Broadcasting Yearbook,* usually for the year after the date shown on the table. The data were gathered by mail survey and they are based in some cases on less than half of the broadcasting sta-

Table 560-E   Presidential Appearances on Network Television, 1960–1982

	Kennedy[a]	Johnson[a]	Nixon[a]	Ford[b]	Carter[c]	Reagan[c]
Number of Appearances, Prime-Time Only	4	7	14	12	13	19
Hours of Air Time, Prime-Time Only	1:54	3:20	7:03	7:00	6:59	N/A
Total Number of Appearances	50	33	37	19	48	26
Total Hours of Air Time	30:15	12:30	13:30	12:55	32:15	N/A

Sources: Kennedy, Johnson, and Nixon data: Minow et al. (1975), p. 171, table 1, which is based on figures reported to the *New York Times* by the White House Press Office. Ford data: Nielsen Television Index, *Nielsen Newscast* No. 3 (1975), pp. 6–7. Carter data: A. C. Nielsen Co. Reagan number of appearances data supplied from the White House to the author. Notes: [a]First 19 months in office. [b]First 15 months in office. [c]First 25 months in office.

Table 560-F   Broadcast Station Editorials, 1959–1975

	1959	1965	1969	1975
AM Radio Stations				
Number of Stations Reporting	N/A	3,225	3,465	2,612
Percent Which Broadcast Editorials				
On a daily basis	3	10	7	17
On a weekly basis	4	6	5	13
Only occasionally	23	45	37	70
Percent of Total Editorializing	30	61	49	N/A
FM Radio Stations				
Number of Stations Reporting	N/A	309	1,986	1,792
Percent Which Broadcast Editorials				
On a daily basis	3	2	3	15
On a weekly basis	2	4	4	13
Only occasionally	15	26	29	72
Percent of Total Editorializing	19	31	36	N/A
Television Stations				
Number of Stations Reporting	N/A	383	449	463
Percent Which Broadcast Editorials				
On a daily basis	4	13	12	23
On a weekly basis	3	10	10	20
Only occasionally	25	31	27	58
Percent of Total Editorializing	32	54	49	N/A

Source: Broadcasting Yearbook, appropriate issues.

tions in the United States (compare the totals in Units 170 and 180). The proportion of stations which do *not* broadcast editorials is not listed separately, because that information was not supplied in most cases. Thus, these figures in Table 560–F are at best only very approximate and must be used with caution. The surveys are no longer published.

Further Information

The literature on broadcast journalism is immense and expanding, though much of it is merely anecdotal. The best regular review of developments in radio and television news programming is Barrett (1968 to date, biennial). Useful quantitative studies include Wolf (1972), Epstein (1974), Johnstone et al (1976), Batscha (1975), Braestrup's 1977 in-depth case study of Vietnam coverage, and Lang and Lang's 1983 analysis of the Watergate crisis of a decade before. For television coverage of foreign news, see Unit 700.

570
COMMERCIAL RADIO
STATION PROGRAMMING

Interpretation of the Tables

From its beginning, radio was primarily a medium providing music to the home. Even in the heyday of network radio, local program hours were dominated by "musical clock" programs. With the decline of the radio networks in the 1950s, "formula" or format radio dominated the airways, with either MOR (middle-of-the-road) musical programming, or a combination of music and talk geared to the average listener, or a repetitive and tightly structured format of "top 40" records and frequent commercials aimed at youthful listeners. Most FM stations either broadcast the same programs as their AM owners, or provided classical or background music.

About 1965, radio programming began to change. In a ruling that called for separation of AM-FM station programming, the FCC provided the impetus for the diversification of FM programming into popular and even "talk" formats previously limited to AM stations. At first, the FCC ruling affected only markets of 100,000 or more and about half of the total broadcasting time of each station, but a decade later, the ruling was extended to more airtime and smaller markets.

Table 570-A provides limited documentation of the trend to greater diversification in both AM and FM radio between 1964 and 1982. The numbers are not strictly comparable, since many different surveys, with varied definitions of programming content, are summarized here. Nonetheless, the trend to more diversification is evident by the mid-1970s.

The rise in use of a Country/Western musical format, which became increasingly popular in the Northeast in the 1960s, is of special interest. In the larger cities, black "soul" music and other types of minority programming gained popularity in the early 1970s. Thus far, only the largest markets are able to economically support "all-news" stations and "talk" formats. With increasing diversification, however, there is also duplication—one can now drive across the country and hear the same three or four basic radio formats with very few regional differences.

Table 570-B provides measures of ethnic and foreign language programming on commercial radio stations for a recent year. But note the table footnotes carefully, as the definitions of what constitutes a "format" vary greatly. The table is really only an indication of the rise of Black and Spanish or Chicano programming in major enclaves of those minorities, plus the rise, of much more limited amounts, of other ethnic programming.

Sources

The data in Table 570-A for 1964 to 1973 were compiled and recategorized by Lichty and Topping (1975) from several different surveys. The 1964 figures are for musical formats only. The data for 1975 come from Cox (1976). The information for 1976 comes from "The Many Worlds of Radio, 1976" in *Broadcasting* (September 27, 1976). This article covered only the top 10 stations (in ratings) in the top 50 markets; thus, some data on minority-interest programming are excluded. Data for 1978 through 1982 comes from the reports issued each year by Duncan (1978, 1980, 1982) summarizing spring Arbitron ratings research data on formats. While data for 1980 and 1982 uses different format titles, the 1978–1982 material is directly comparable, coming from the same source consistently. See table footnotes for details on format definitions and limitations.

Table 570-A   Program Formats of AM and FM Radio Stations, 1964–1982

Year and Size of Market	Number of Stations	In Percent of Total								
		Middle of the Road	Top 40/ Contemporary	Beautiful and Background	Country/ Western	Black/ Soul	Progressive Rock	News and Talk	Classical	Other[c]
1964 (AM and FM)[a]										
Large, Multiple Station Markets	1,400	12	10	22	6	5	—[b]	—	—	45
Single Station Markets		22	9	21	12	1	—	—	—	35
1966 (FM only)										
Top 50 Markets	244	49	15	30	—	—	—	—	—	6
Other Markets	564	64	4	23	5	—	—	—	—	4
1968 (AM and FM)										
Top 50 Markets	1,076	40	15	13	11	7	—	—	—	14
1970 (AM and FM)										
All Markets	1,365	35	17	22	11	1	4	1	—	9
1971 (AM and FM)										
Top 100 Markets										
AM Stations	955	21	27	17	18	—	—	—	—	17
FM Stations	643	18	25	39	10	—	—	—	—	8
1973 (AM and FM)										
All Markets	4,193	22	26	8	21	14	3	3	3	—
1975 (AM and FM)										
Top 40 Markets										
AM Stations	600	26	17	5	16	10	2	9	2	13
FM Stations	475	13	21	24	9	5	10	2	6	10
1976 (AM and FM)										
Top 50 Markets[c]	500	14	27	18	6	5	—	8	1	22

Year and Size of Market	Number of Stations	Middle of the Road	Rock/Contemporary	Beautiful Music	Country	Black/Urban[d]	News and Talk	Religion	Classical	Other
1978										
AM Stations	1,479	26	24	3	21	6	5	6	1	11
FM Stations	1,174	6	41	26	11	4	0	4	3	5
AM/FM Combined	2,653	17	32	13	17	5	3	5	2	6
1980										
AM Stations	1,474	29	19	3	21	7	6	7	1	7
FM Stations	1,293	5	45	23	12	6	0	5	2	2
AM/FM Combined	2,767	18	32	12	17	6	3	6	1	5
1982										
AM Stations	1,530	29	8	2	21	11	6	9	1	13
FM Stations	1,374	11	39	18	17	6	0	4	2	3
AM/FM Combined	2,904	19	23	9	19	8	3	7	1	9

Sources: 1964–1973 data: Lichty and Topping (1975), p. 435, table 32. 1975 data: Cox Broadcasting Corp. (1976), p. 55, exhibit 16. 1976 data: *Broadcasting* (September 27, 1976), "The Many Worlds of Radio, 1976," p. 46. 1978, 1980, and 1982 data all from Duncan (1978, 1980, 1982 Spring Reports), using Arbitron ratings. Notes: [a]The percentages here refer only to musical content and therefore, are not strictly applicable to later figures. [b]Blank spaces generally indicate that the programming category has been included under "other." In some cases, however, the particular programming format was not broadcast that year. [c]This listing is based on the top 10 stations in the top 50 markets. Thus, while it encompasses the top 50 markets, the listing also excludes many stations in these markets which feature minority-taste programming. [d]Represents Black and disco combination. [e]Represents a variety of formats, including jazz, religious, Spanish and other ethnic (except Black) categories.

Table 570–B   Ethnic and Foreign Language Radio Programming, 1979

Type of Programming	Number of Stations Providing Programming According to SRDS[a]	Number of Stations Providing Programming According to Broadcasting Yearbook[b]
Native American	12	55
Black	416	793
French	27	105
German	43	121
Greek	27	58
Italian	55	120
Japanese	5	11
Polish	63	183
Portuguese	29	33
Spanish	270	570
Ukrainian	7	14

Source: FCC, *Inquiry and Proposed Rulemaking in Docket 79-219, Deregulation of Radio* 44 *Federal Register* 57683 (October 5, 1979), Table 8. Reprints data from [a]Standard Rate and Data Service Inc., *Spot Radio Rates and Data,* Vol. 61, No. 3 (March 1, 1979), pp. 19, 22–23; and [b]*Broadcasting Yearbook 1979,* pp. D–74 through D–104, as figured by FCC staff. A station using a combination of formats may appear under several classifications—a partial reason for the far larger number of stations in the *Yearbook* column.

Table 570–B is taken from a table prepared by (and counted up for) the FCC in its radio deregulation proceeding. FCC staffers compared two standard industry directory listings of station programming and formats. But amount of time devoted to any of these formats varies widely—some are on for only a few hours per week rather than full or even most of the time. In the Standard Rate and Data Service column, radio stations not maintaining full monthly listings in SRDS are unreported since it is not possible to maintain current information. For the *Yearbook* data column, stations with more than one format are listed under all that apply. So the data are merely very approximate as an indication of the many minority types of programming on radio.

Further Information

For pre-television statistics on "old" radio network programming trends, see Lichty and Topping (1975), and Sterling and Kittross (1978), especially Appendix C, Table 6. For historical data on selected stations in the period to 1939, see Albig (1956). Duncan as cited, plus his *Radio in the*

United States (1982) is essential to tracing recent format and other trends. Current formats are noted in the *Broadcast Yearbook* directory, and the regular issues of Standard Rate and Data Service's radio directory. For an update to the SRDS data shown in Table 570–B, see *Spot Radio Rates and Data*, Vol 65, No. 7 (July 1, 1983), pp. A26, A29, and A32.

580
COMMERCIAL TELEVISION STATION PROGRAMMING

Interpretation of the Tables

While information on network television programming trends is extensive and readily available (see Unit 582), data showing the "typical" weekly schedule of individual television stations are nowhere near so common or so easy to come by. Most such data tend to be limited by serious discontinuities.

Table 580–A reveals some of the trends developed over two decades of commercial television programming, from 1951 until 1970. Among the trends indicated by the figures: the limited amount of musical programming on television; the decline of variety shows; the expansion and then limited decline of drama, including comedy drama; the sharp drop in televised sports; the relatively low and fairly steady amounts of news, public affairs, and religious programming; and the fluctuating schedules of children's programming. The percentages shown here include both network and local programs, since they are based on *complete* station schedules for approximately one week.

Table 580–B compares the programming formats and sources of network-affiliate and independent television stations from 1954 to 1972. For affiliates, the reader will note two trends: (1) the increase in network programming (from one-half to two-thirds of total program time), and (2) the decline of local-live and syndicated-film programs, and the rise of syndicated and local videotaped programming after 1960. Among independent stations, both "made-for-TV," syndicated films and theatrical films have declined somewhat; but as of 1972, they still dominated nearly half of the programming hours. Syndicated and local videotaped programming moved into second place with 28 percent of all programming. The table also indicates that local-live programming is far more common on independent than on network-affiliate stations. The small percentage of network programming on the independent stations in 1972 usually occurred when a local affiliate refused the network offering.

Table 580-C provides a 25-year survey of the number of syndicated programs or program series (*not* individual episodes) available in a given month each year. All syndicated material up to 1960, and much of it after that date, was on film. However, by the 1970s, videotape was more commonly used for certain types of programming—especially news, quiz, sports, and some variety shows. The reader should take special note of the high percentage of available syndicated material which was *"first-run"*—that is, it had not previously been aired on one of the national television networks. (The "off-network" programs are those that were first broadcast by a network and then released into syndication, for sale to stations as "reruns.")

Table 580-D traces content trends in syndicated programs over a shorter period, from 1965 through 1974. Certain types of programming (variety, situation comedy, documentary, quiz shows, religion, and sports) have increased sharply over this period, while other genres, such as drama and cartoons, have either remained consistent or have declined somewhat. Taken together, Tables 580-A through 580-D reflect the growing demand for syndicated material as the number of independent stations (chiefly UHF) have increased (see Units 180 and 181).

Table 580-E provides a 1981 "snapshot" of the top-rated syndicated series, most of them first-run series. Programs 1, 8, 9, 10, 12, and 13 are "soft news" or documentary programs, the rest are pure entertainment series. Note that only three series (3, 7 and 9) approach a quarter of all commercial stations on the air.

Sources

Table 580-A is reprinted from Lichty and Topping (1975). The data through 1954 were gathered from surveys by the National Association of Educational Broadcasters (NAEB), which was attempting to persuade the FCC of the need for public (then educational) television allocations to offset the lack of public affairs and news programs on commercial stations. Data for 1958 through 1970 were taken by Lichty and Topping from student term papers. In all cases, these data represent a full week of programming on all stations in each of the cities. The selected week and the time of the year differ

Table 580-A Program Content of Selected Major Market Television Stations for Selected Years, 1951-1970 (In Percent)

Programming Content	1951 New York	1951 Los Angeles	1951 Chicago	1952 New York	1954 New York	1958 Washington, D.C.	1960 Los Angeles	1970 Washington, D.C.
Variety	24	26	16	17	11	5	5	14
Music	4	6	3	3	7	7	3	3
Drama	25	25	26	36	46	46	54	38
Quiz/Personality	11	8	14	9	10	9	6	8
News	6	13	6	6	6	4	5	9
Information/Talk	7	5	5	8	8	8	9	6
Religious	1	1	—	1	2	2	2	3
Children's	12	10	8	11	3	13	7	13
Sports	10	5	21	8	3	5	4	4
Miscellaneous	—	—	—	—	4	1	5	2

Source: Lichty and Topping (1975), p. 442, table 38, utilizing (for 1951-1954) data from National Association of Educational Broadcasters, and (for 1958-1970) data from student term papers.

Table 580-B Sources of Television Station Programming, 1954-1972

Year	Made-for-TV Films	Theatrical Films	Syndicated Videotaped Programs	Local Live Programs	Local Videotaped Programs	Network Programs
Network-Affiliate Stations						
1954	12	17	—	21	—	50
1956	14	15	—	14	—	56
1958	13	16	—	13	—	58
1960	13	13	0.3	11	1	63
1962	12	11	1.0	12	2	63
1964	11	10	2.0	11	3	64
1966	9	11	3.0	10	3	64
1968	7	8	7.0	10	2	63
1970	7	9	2.0	10	3	66
1972	7	8	7.0	10	2	63
Independent Stations						
1954	21	31	—	47	—	—
1956	20	48	—	23	—	—
1958	24	47	—	29	—	—
1960	36	28	4.0	31	2	—
1962	36	26	5.0	28	9	—
1964	43	26	5.0	23	4	—
1966	25	33	8.0	28	9	—
1968	27	29	11.0	20	8	—
1970	31	35	15.0	14	5	—
1972	23	24	20.0	18	8	4

Source: Broadcasting Yearbook, annual surveys.

Commercial T.V. Station Programming   185

Table 580-C   Number of Available Syndicated Television Series, 1951–1975

Year	Total Number of Syndicated Series	Number of "Off-Network" Series	Number of "First-Run" Series	Percentage of First-Run Series
1951	20	14	6	30
1952	26	12	14	54
1953	26	7	19	73
1954	37	0	37	100
1955	52	10	42	81
1956	36	17	19	53
1957	29	9	20	69
1958	47	17	30	64
1959	43	N/A	N/A	N/A
1960	58	N/A	N/A	N/A
1965	137	60	77	56
1967	196	63	133	68
1968	244	98	146	60
1970	213	94	169	64[a]
1971	262	110	152	58
1972	181	80	111	58[b]
1973	198	65	133	67
1974	313	110	203	65
1975	312	102	210	67

Sources: Hatcher (1976), utilizing data from *Telefilm* (February 1959), p. 14, for the 1951–1958 figures, and *Films for Television* for the 1959–1960 figures. 1965–1971 data figured by Hatcher from Arbitron's *Syndicated Programming Analysis* (November 1965, February–March 1967, November 1968, 1970, 1971). 1972–1975 data from Nielsen Television Index, A. C. Nielsen Company, *Report on Syndicated Programs* (November of each year). Notes: "Off-network" syndicated programs are those that were first broadcast by a network and then released into syndication for sale to television stations as "reruns." "First-run" syndications are original programming which has never appeared on a network. [a]Figure should be 79 percent, given the data here, but the source reports it as 64 percent. [b]Figure should be 61 percent, but the source reports it as 58 percent.

for each survey. Because of the differing survey methods, the variations in content categorization, and the varied numbers of stations in the surveyed cities, the reliability of this table is limited.

Table 580–B reprints figures for the even-numbered years from 20 years of surveys conducted by *Broadcasting Yearbook*. The data for these surveys were self-reported by the stations, and the number of respondent stations was never noted. These surveys were discontinued after 1973.

Table 580–C was derived by Hatcher (1976) from several different sources, and thus the data are not strictly comparable. The figures up to 1958

Table 580-D   Number of Available Syndicated Television Series, by Content Type, 1965-1982

	1965	1970	1974	1980	1982
Total Number of Syndicated Programs	146	263	313	305	277
Number of Programs Which are:					
Variety	22	36	39	10	7
Music	5	3	13	22	18
Drama	56	79	68	53	68
Situation Comedy	10	33	47	48	49
Cartoons	18	19	17	45[a]	47[a]
Documentary	8	14	16	11	16
Human Interest/Quiz/Panel	4	12	16	18	8
News/Public Affairs/Talk	3	12	11	26	30
Religion	18	33	60	56	N/A
Sports Play-by-Play	1	11	18	18[b]	19[b]
Other/Miscellaneous	1	11	8	11	15

Sources: Hatcher (1976), pp. 71-72, 109-110, citing 1965-1970 data from Arbitron, *Syndicated Programming Analysis*, appropriate issues; and 1974 data from A. C. Nielsen Company, *Report on Syndicated Programs*, appropriate issues. 1980-1982 data was supplied direct to author from A. C. Nielsen Co. Notes: [a]Category is actually "children," [b]includes sports comment.

Table 580-E   Top 15 Syndicated Television Series, 1981

Show	Number of Stations	"USA Rating"
1. PM Magazine	95	10.300
2. Family Feud PM	116	10.200
3. Hee Haw	188	8.700
4. Lawrence Welk	175	7.000
5. Muppet Show	140	6.900
6. Dance Fever	122	6.700
7. Solid Gold	189	6.700
8. Entertainment Tonight	110	6.300
9. Donahue	186	5.800
10. The New You Asked For It	98	5.600
11. Tic Tac Dough	113	5.500
12. In Search Of	60	3.800
13. Wild Kingdom	170	3.800
14. Jokers Wild	64	3.400
15. Hour Magazine	104	3.300

Source: Nielsen Syndicated Program Analysis as of October 1981, cited in ICF, Inc. "Analysis of the Impacts of Repeal of the Financial Interest and Syndication Rule," (January 26, 1983). Note: "First-run" actually includes some rerun episodes. See text for discussion of "USA Rating."

came from *Telefilm* (February 1959); the 1959–1960 figures came from *Films for Television*, which did not break down the total figures. (Although not shown here, Hatcher also presents totals reported in *Films for Television* for 1951–1958. These figures differ only slightly from the totals given in Table 580–C.)

The Table 580–C data for 1965–1971 data were calculated by Hatcher from Arbitron's *Syndicated Programming Analysis*, and the figures for 1972–1975 came from A. C. Nielsen Company's *Report on Syndicated Programs*. Because this table does not take program length into account, it is difficult to estimate the amount of syndicated material which is actually available. Most syndicated material runs 30 minutes, although some 15-minute material appeared prior to 1960, and some longer material has been available since that date.

Table 580–D was based on the same sources noted above for Table 580–C, with the categorization done by Hatcher (1976). Data for 1980–1982 was supplied to the author by the A.C. Nielsen Co., based on the Nielsen Syndication Index rankings. Note table footnotes for slight category variation in two cases. Why the large religion category is missing from the 1982 figures is not explained.

Table 580–E, based on A.C. Nielsen information from *Syndicated Program Analysis* as of October 1981, was provided in ICF, Inc. pleadings filed with the FCC on behalf of independent producers seeking to prevent the FCC dropping of several rules limiting network ownership of programming after network runs. Several series listed, notably "Muppet Show," "Lawrence Welk," and "Wild Kingdom" are actually reruns of former first-run material (though "Welk" and "Kingdom" were once network run). The "USA Rating" indicates the average percent of TV households watching the program, multiplied by the coverage ratio (percent of TV households in markets where program was broadcast). As the programs vary in length and frequency, ratings are not an indicator of net audience delivered.

Further Information

Data on syndicated television programs are currently reported by the A.C. Nielsen Company in its *Report on Syndicated Programs*. The history of syndication is best summarized by Hatcher (1976) and the earlier sources he cites. In addition, *Variety* and *Broadcasting* often contain television programming information. Historical descriptive material on major syndicated shows is included in such directories as McNeil (1981) and Gianakos (1978, 1980, and 1981).

581
PUBLIC TELEVISION
PROGRAMMING

Interpretation of the Tables

Over the two decades covered in Table 581–A, the figures illustrate the transformation of public television—referred to as *educational* television prior to 1967—from a strictly local-station medium, with some exchanged ("bicycled") film materials among the stations, to a national network with a full schedule of weekly programming. Program format information does not include network interconnection programming until after 1970, although some interconnected feeds began in 1967 through the Ford Foundation-supported Public Broadcasting Laboratory.

The program sources data show how much less self-reliant public stations have become since the early 1960s. They now get the majority of their programming from national sources (mainly the Public Broadcasting Service interconnection), and even state and regional exchanges and networks have given way to the national and syndicated materials. The format and sources structure of public television now bears a growing resemblance to that of the network-affiliated commercial stations.

Table 581–B reviews the content of public television's general programming and the age levels to which the PBS instructional programs are directed. (Most instructional programming is broadcast during school hours.) Note the increases in instructional programming during the mid-1960s—increases which, to some extent, paralleled the massive school and other educational funding available from the "Great Society" programs of that era. Decreased funding, combined with inflation and disillusionment with television instruction as the panacea for education's ills, brought levels of instructional programming down by a significant amount in the mid-1970s. After 1970, most of the children's programming shown on public television came from the Children's Television Workshop (CTW), which created such programs as *Sesame Street*.

In distinct contrast, the PBS programming for the general public has steadily increased in the 1970s, after a moderate decline in the mid-1960s. In

Table 581-A Hours, Format, and Sources of Public Television Station Programming, 1954–1980

Year	Hours per Week		Program Format (Percent of Total Hours)			Program Sources (Percent of Total Hours)			
	Total, All Stations	Average per Station	Live	Film or Tape	Network Interconnect	Local	National	State/Regional	Syndication
1954	197	N/A	58	42	—	N/A	N/A	N/A	N/A
1956	468	N/A	60	40	—	N/A	25	N/A	N/A
1958	1,027	38	52	48	—	N/A	28	N/A	N/A
1962	2,596	42	N/A	N/A	—	52	29	N/A	19
1964	3,715	42	13	87	—	37	31	15	18
1966	5,688	50	8	92	—	15	50	14	21
1968	8,534	56	9	91	—	13	51	21	15
1970	12,217	65	N/A	N/A	N/A	11	62	11	16
1972	15,587	71	3	63	34	16	54	10	20
1974	18,321	81	3	52	46	11	62	10	17
1976	22,096	91	2	52	46	10	70	6	14
1978	26,064	96	2	50	45	7	72	5	16
1980	28,036	100	2	51	44	7	70	8	15

Sources: 1954–1958 data: Educational Television and Radio Center (1958). All other years: Corporation for Public Broadcasting: 1962–1972 data: *One Week of Educational Television* (series); 1974 data: *Public Television Program Content: 1974*, pp. 24, 28, and inside front cover; 1976 data: *Public Television Programming by Category: 1976* (1977), pp. 19, 22, and inside front cover; 1978 data: *Public Television Programming Content by Category Fiscal Year 1978*; and 1980 data: *Status Report* (1980).

Table 581-B Content Trends in Public Television Station Programming, 1956-1982 (In Percent)

	1956	1958	1962	1964	1966	1968	1970	1972	1974	1976	1978	1980	1982
General Programming Categories:													
Public Affairs	11	13	N/A	13	13	14	18	19	13	13	11	12	12
Children's	10	10	N/A	10	10	10	20	21	32	25	25	24	22
Cultural and Arts	17	16	N/A	10	14	9	11	7	9	10	22	22	23
Entertainment	N/A	N/A	N/A	2	3	8	7	5	9	10	}		
Other[a]	47	24	N/A	19	18	10	8	20	20	21	29	28	29
Total	85	63	54	54	58	51	63	72	83	79	87	86	87
Instructional Programming Categories:													
Primary (Grades K–3)	N/A	11	N/A	23	6	8	9	7	N/A	N/A	N/A	N/A	N/A
Intermediate (Grades 4–6)	}	}	N/A	}	13	14	11	10	N/A	N/A	N/A	N/A	N/A
Junior High (Grades 7–9)	N/A	16	N/A	7	7	8	6	4	N/A	N/A	N/A	N/A	N/A
Senior High (Grades 10–12)	}	}	N/A	11	8	10	6	4	N/A	N/A	N/A	N/A	N/A
College	N/A	N/A	N/A	5	8	6	6	1	N/A	N/A	N/A	N/A	N/A
Adult	N/A	N/A	N/A	}	9	8	5	3	N/A	N/A	N/A	N/A	N/A
Total	15	27	46	46	42	49	37	28	17	21	13	14	14

Sources: 1956–1958 data: Educational Television and Radio Center (1958). All other data: Corporation for Public Broadcasting: 1962–1972 data: *One Week of Educational Television* (series); 1974 data: *Public Television Program Content: 1974*, pp. 24, 28 and inside front cover; 1976 data: *Public Television Programming by Category: 1976* (1977), pp. 19, 22 and inside front cover; 1978 data: *Status Report of Public Broadcasting 1980* (1980), p. 24; 1980 and 1982 data, direct to author from CPB. Note: [a]For 1974–82 includes "information/skills" category not separately shown.

Table 581-C Content of Public Broadcasting Service (PBS) Programming, 1973-1979

Year	Total Hours of Programming	Percentage of Total Hours Devoted to:		
		Cultural	Education/Children	Public Affairs
1973	1,102	34	26	40
1974	1,219	33	26	41
1975	1,367	26	32	41
1976	1,854	34	27	40
1977	1,819	27	32	41
1978	1,785	28	22	41
1979	1,995	30	15	48

Sources: Data from 1973 through 1976 CPB *Status Report* (1977), p. 19; data from 1977 through 1979 CPB *Status Report* (1980), p. 28.

specific categories of programming, a decline in art and culture and in public affairs is matched by a small but rising percentage of entertainment programs—often motion pictures—as public stations have worked to broaden their appeal.

Table 581-C provides a trend study of the content of television programs distributed by the Public Broadcasting Service, the major national programming agency for the industry. Beginning with the second season listed here (1974), PBS programming was largely determined by the Station Program Cooperative (SPC), a complicated system of bidding and voting by individual public television stations for the selection of the PBS offerings each season. It is not yet possible to discern any content trends resulting from the operation of the SPC. The total hours figures in the table do not include repeat feeds of programs by PBS.

Sources

The 1954-1958 data in Table 581-A and the 1956-1958 data in Table 581-B were taken from the Educational Television and Radio Center (1958). All other figures in both tables come from various reports and publications of the Corporation for Public Broadcasting (CPB). The source of Table 581-C is the *Status Report* (1977 and 1980) of the CPB.

A major drawback in describing public television programming trends is the lack of consistent information on which to base conclusions. Each of the tables in this unit is somewhat misleading, in that the author has had to combine different surveys, with different data-gathering approaches, in order to assemble figures which provide some comparability over time. Even since 1970, when the CPB took over the data-gathering and reporting process for the public television industry, there have been frequent and strange information discontinuities.

Another problem, which especially affects the Table 581–A figures, is that the data (particularly data reported up to the mid-1960s) have often included both general and instructional programs, and these two categories now tend to be reported separately. The editors have taken the general figures whenever they were available; but the reader is advised to keep this discontinuity in mind, since it unavoidably reduces the direct comparability of these figures.

Further Information

The only available, continuing statistical reports on public television programming are those issued by the CPB at approximately two-year intervals. They contain extensively detailed information on both general and instructional programming. The CPB's annual statistical surveys also contain limited information on programming.

For background and related information on public television, see Katzman (1976), Cater and Nyhan (1976), and Blakely (1971). The initial operation of the Station Program Cooperative is described and criticized in Reeves and Hoffer (1976). In addition, the reader may wish to check the bimonthly issue of *Public Telecommunications Review* (1967–1980) for background and occasional statistical reports.

582
NETWORK TELEVISION PROGRAMMING

Interpretation of the Tables

Table 582–A traces the first 25 years—from 1949 through 1973—of prime-time network television programming. The table lists the number of quarter-hours per week devoted by the networks to each program category. All of the networks are included—even DuMont up to 1955—and programs are listed whether or not they were sponsored. The reader will note interesting cycles of invention, imitation, and decline in such subject areas as westerns, sports, quiz shows, and documentaries. The network westerns, for example, emerged between 1958 and 1962, then experienced a lasting plateau until 1969. But just five years later, there were no prime-time westerns at all. Situation comedy programs have maintained their popularity throughout this period.

Table 582–B traces daytime programming trends for the same 25-year period. The reader should note that not until 1958 did the networks collectively offer approximately as many daytime programmed hours as they do today.

Table 582–C provides prime-time and daytime programming data for 1973 through 1982. However, the information here was drawn from a different source and should not be considered simply a continuation of Tables 582–A and 582–B.

Table 582–D categorizes the number of prime-time network specials in the even-numbered years since 1950. Two peaks—the first in 1960 and the second in the mid-1970s—indicate renewed popularity for this "one-shot" form of programming. The national elections of 1960, 1968, and 1972 are reflected by the increases in news/political/documentary specials for those years.

Table 582–E reveals some of the changes which have taken place (1) in programming formats (the decline of live programming and its replacement by film and tape), (2) in the sources of network-broadcast programs (the decline of network- and advertiser-produced programs in favor of programs produced by a "packaging" agency), and (3) in the length of programs (in general, they are getting longer). Most of the figures on this table are percentages of prime-time hours. The only exceptions are the format data, which cover *all* hours of network broadcasting.

Sources

Tables 582–A and 582–B were constructed from the copyrighted data of L. W. Lichty of the University of Maryland. These data are reprinted in Sterling and Kittross (1978). Lichty gathered this information from various printed sources, then categorized and analyzed it with the assistance of Sterling. The data may be considered accurate for the third week of January of each year. However, with the advent of network "second seasons" in the early 1970s, these annual listings become less representative of the overall network programming for the year.

Table 582–C is an attempt by the author to update Lichty's information, using different sources: A. C. Nielsen Company's *Television Audience 1976* and *1980*, for prime-time data, and *Television Audience 1975* and *1980* for daytime programming. Unlike Tables 582–A and 582–B, Table 582–C lists only sponsored shows. Moreover, whereas Table 582–C defines "prime-

Table 582-A Content of Prime-Time Network Television Programming, 1949-1973

	1949	1950	1951	1952	1953	1954	1955	1956	1957	1958	1959	1960	1961	1962	1963	1964	1965	1966	1967	1968	1969	1970	1971	1972	1973
Variety																									
Special/Varied	—	—	—	2	—	—	22	32	22	10	10	22	4	8	8	4	4	4	4	4	4	4	4	8	19
Comedy	42	40	86	65	50	43	44	42	39	20	14	22	14	14	28	40	40	24	28	33	34	35	34	20	20
Amateur/Talent	8	10	18	14	10	10	6	8	10	6	4	4	—	—	—	—	4	4	—	—	—	—	—	—	—
Country and Western	6	—	—	—	—	—	4	8	4	4	4	4	—	—	—	4	4	4	—	—	—	8	8	—	—
General/Talk	—	—	34	—	—	—	30	30	20	35	45	35	35	39	40	39	81	42	42	66	66	96	96	96	51
Music																									
Musical Variety	15	22	27	26	8	12	8	15	26	40	36	22	18	20	30	28	28	26	16	22	28	24	20	8	12
Light Music	15	12	25	13	12	12	14	6	4	—	—	—	—	—	—	—	—	—	—	—	—	—	—	—	—
Drama																									
General	24	42	64	54	44	58	80	70	76	30	35	32	28	34	54	60	34	18	8	3	10	34	34	20	24
Motion Pictures	34	8	12	—	—	—	—	12	10	—	—	—	—	8	16	16	24	32	48	52	56	72	64	72	101
Women's Serials	3	2	2	2	—	—	—	—	—	—	—	—	—	—	—	—	4	6	4	4	4	—	—	—	—
Action/Adventure	—	8	6	11	10	4	6	16	22	16	16	24	32	22	26	18	32	54	70	65	28	18	6	8	16
Crime/Detective	2	12	16	28	22	18	12	8	6	18	32	48	40	48	20	18	8	12	10	24	40	24	46	48	44
Suspense	—	8	16	18	8	10	4	2	6	6	4	6	—	8	8	14	12	—	4	4	4	—	—	4	4
Westerns	4	2	10	6	7	6	6	16	16	40	64	70	54	46	36	34	24	34	38	34	38	22	22	16	12
Comedy/Situation	—	15	16	24	36	50	60	38	36	40	26	32	52	50	48	38	62	72	52	38	42	56	50	40	42
Animated Cartoons	—	2	—	—	—	—	—	—	—	—	—	—	6	12	6	2	6	2	—	—	2	—	—	—	—
Quiz and Panel																									
Audience Participation	10	18	22	18	18	24	18	24	26	22	8	6	4	8	4	6	2	—	4	6	6	6	4	—	—
Human Interest	10	14	13	16	12	15	10	8	6	10	8	6	6	2	2	4	2	2	2	—	—	—	—	—	—
Panel Shows	13	10	20	26	24	22	16	10	6	6	10	12	8	6	8	6	6	6	6	—	—	—	—	—	—

Table 582–A Content of Prime-Time Network Television Programming, 1949–1973 (cont.)

	1949	1950	1951	1952	1953	1954	1955	1956	1957	1958	1959	1960	1961	1962	1963	1964	1965	1966	1967	1968	1969	1970	1971	1972	1973
News Information																									
Newscasts	27	14	13	13	19	18	22	16	16	21	21	16	16	23	23	32	29	30	40	35	27	39	41	39	39
Forums/Interviews	14	12	8	14	19	11	5	2	2	—	2	2	10	2	2	2	2	—	—	—	—	—	—	—	—
Documentary/Information	4	4	4	2	4	8	10	10	12	12	10	8	28	26	22	16	20	12	12	12	16	8	8	6	8
Other Types																									
Religion	—	2	4	4	7	3	2	2	2	—	—	—	—	—	—	—	—	—	—	—	—	—	—	—	—
Talk	30	6	3	10	11	10	5	5	1	—	—	—	—	—	—	—	—	—	—	—	—	—	—	—	—
Children's Shows	29	63	40	21	10	5	10	5	5	4	4	—	6	4	4	6	—	—	—	—	—	—	—	—	—
Sports	62	52	82	33	31	34	29	13	6	6	7	8	—	—	—	—	—	—	—	—	—	—	—	—	—
Miscellaneous	10	8	5	7	11	11	—	—	—	—	—	—	—	—	—	—	—	—	—	—	—	—	—	—	—
Total Quarter Hours	362	386	546	427	373	373	423	398	379	346	360	375	361	380	385	387	428	384	388	402	405	446	437	385	392

Source: Sterling and Kittross (1978), citing copyrighted data from L. W. Lichty.

Table 582-B Content of Daytime Network Television Programming, 1949–1973

	1949	1950	1951	1952	1953	1954	1955	1956	1957	1958	1959	1960	1961	1962	1963	1964	1965	1966	1967	1968	1969	1970	1971	1972	1973
Variety																									
Special/Varied	—	—	—	—	—	—	—	—	—	—	—	—	—	—	—	—	—	—	—	—	—	—	—	—	—
Comedy	—	—	—	35	—	—	—	—	—	—	—	—	—	—	—	—	—	—	—	—	—	—	—	—	—
Amateur/Talent	—	—	—	—	—	—	—	—	—	—	—	—	—	—	—	—	—	—	—	—	—	—	—	—	—
Country and Western	—	—	—	—	—	—	—	—	—	—	—	—	—	—	—	—	—	—	—	—	—	—	—	—	—
General/Talk	10	10	13	129	79	86	166	166	114	76	70	60	40	50	70	45	40	40	40	40	40	50	50	50	60
Music																									
Musical Variety	5	—	20	20	40	50	30	10	10	55	50	30	30	20	20	10	10	10	20	20	—	—	—	—	—
Light Music	10	5	5	5	—	—	—	—	—	—	—	—	—	—	—	—	—	—	—	—	—	—	—	—	—
Drama																									
General	—	—	—	—	—	—	—	20	20	30	20	50	50	50	40	20	—	20	20	20	—	—	—	—	—
Motion Pictures	—	—	—	—	—	—	—	40	30	—	—	50	—	—	—	—	—	—	—	—	—	—	—	—	—
Women's Serials	—	—	5	30	20	45	84	40	55	65	70	80	100	70	60	70	120	150	110	108	138	158	180	160	160
Action/Adventure	20	—	—	—	—	—	—	—	—	10	—	20	20	—	—	—	—	—	—	—	—	—	—	—	—
Crime/Detective	—	—	—	—	—	—	—	—	—	—	—	—	—	—	—	—	20	—	—	—	—	—	—	—	—
Suspense	—	—	—	—	—	—	—	—	—	—	—	50	10	10	—	—	—	—	—	—	—	—	—	—	—
Westerns	—	—	—	—	—	—	—	—	30	10	—	—	—	10	—	—	—	—	—	—	—	—	—	—	—
Comedy/Situation	—	—	15	—	—	10	—	—	—	—	10	40	50	20	40	50	60	60	50	50	50	60	60	70	20
Animated Cartoons	—	—	—	—	—	—	—	—	—	—	—	10	—	—	—	—	—	—	—	—	—	—	—	—	—
Quiz and Panel																									
Audience Participation	20	30	24	28	42	44	40	40	50	80	140	80	100	140	110	120	100	100	128	128	117	68	70	90	130
Human Interest	15	5	8	1	25	25	20	30	35	45	40	40	50	30	20	20	10	10	20	—	8	—	—	—	10
Panel Shows	—	—	10	—	—	—	—	—	5	—	—	—	—	—	—	—	—	—	—	—	—	—	—	—	—
News Information																									
Newscasts	—	—	—	10	5	5	—	—	5	5	5	5	9	22	16	24	24	24	22	18	18	26	24	25	25
Forums/Interviews	—	—	—	—	—	20	—	—	—	—	—	—	—	—	—	—	—	—	—	—	—	—	—	—	—
Documentary/Information	—	—	—	—	—	—	—	—	—	—	—	—	—	—	—	20	10	10	10	18	10	28	20	10	—
Other Types																									
Religion	15	5	—	—	—	—	—	—	—	—	—	20	20	30	40	10	10	10	—	—	—	—	—	—	—
Talk	10	90	28	11	—	—	27	—	—	—	50	15	15	40	20	20	20	—	—	—	—	—	—	—	—
Children's Shows	—	40	30	15	21	35	32	—	—	25	25	—	—	—	20	20	—	—	10	12	12	10	10	10	10
Sports	—	—	—	—	—	—	—	70	40	—	—	—	—	—	—	—	—	—	20	20	20	20	20	20	20
Miscellaneous	—	—	—	—	—	—	—	—	—	—	—	—	—	—	—	—	—	—	—	—	—	—	—	—	—
Total Quarter Hours	105	185	158	284	232	320	399	416	394	401	480	550	494	492	456	429	424	454	450	434	413	420	434	435	435

Source: Sterling and Kittross (1978), citing copyrighted data from L. W. Lichty.

Table 582-C Content of Prime-Time and Daytime Network Television Programming, 1973–1982

	Number of Quarter Hours per Week									
	1973	*1974*	*1975*	*1976*	*1977*	*1978*	*1979*	*1980*	*1981*	*1982*
Prime-Time Programs (7–11 PM)										
Type of Program:										
Variety	20	8	16	28	16	12	—	18	16	12
Drama/Adventure	40	68	68	52	60	72	48	60	76	76
Feature Film	64	58	40	46	48	48	56	56	40	40
Suspense/Mystery	68	76	84	66	48	48	56	28	48	48
Situation Comedy	48	30	44	50	64	58	68	70	60	64
Other	12	12	12	22	28	26	36	32	24	24
Total	252	252	264	264	264	264	264	264	264	264
Daytime Programs (10 AM–4:30 PM)										
Type of Program:										
Daytime Drama	148	138	158	180	180	200	210	220	220	220
Situation Comedy	20	10	10	30	50	30	20	40	30	20
Quiz/Audience Participation	158	188	168	130	120	100	120	60	80	80
News/Other	13	3	3	20	10	20	10	20	10	—
Total[a]	340	340	340	360	360	350	360	340	340	320

Source: All data from A. C. Nielsen, *Television Audience*, various annual issues. Hours are averages for the Fall of each indicated television season. *Some daytime data for 1977–1982 are estimated from Nielsen by the author; totals do not add up due to rounding. See text for further detail.
Note: [a]Some daytime data for 1977–1982 are estimated from Nielsen by the author; totals do not add up due to rounding. See text for further detail.

Table 582–D Content Trends in Prime-Time Network Television Specials, 1950–1981

Year[a]	Variety	Drama	Docu-mentary	Political	News	Sports	Other	Total Number of: Specials	Total Number of: Hours
1950	2	—	3	1	1	3	19	29	18
1952	3	—	2	2	2	1	20	30	19
1954	7	1	3	—	—	1	28	40	24
1956	10	3	11	4	1	2	12	43	32
1958	26	28	14	5	5	5	24	107	101
1960	43	50	19	—	69	9	15	205	185
1962	55	29	58	1	18	4	20	185	163
1964	33	11	30	8	10	10	28	130	160
1966	47	21	37	1	15	2	25	148	157
1968	48	54	43	8	22	19	34	228	256
1970	35	39	N/A	72	N/A	18	34	198	N/A
1972	51	41	59	27	36	10	44	268	330
1974	60	83	79	12	34	17	62	347	449
1976	77	46	22	10	54	137	211	557	779
1978	83	70	17	2	49	34	198	453	N/A
1980	88	59	15	11	46	35	202	456	N/A
1981	85	66	13	N/A	42	41	207	454	N/A

Sources: Data through 1968 from Bailey, *Journal of Broadcasting* (Summer 1970), p. 325ff; 1970 from Nielsen *Television Audience 1971*, p. 131; 1972–1974 from *Nielsen Newscast No. 3* (1974), pp. 12–14; remaining data was supplied direct to the author from A. C. Nielsen Co. Note: [a]Data is for the complete season, 1950 indicating the 1949–1950 season, etc.

time" as 7–11 PM, Table 582–A begins the prime-time category at 6 PM. Similarly, the daytime hours covered in Table 582–C run from 10 AM to 4:30 PM, whereas Table 582–B covers all network daytime hours up to 6 PM. Table 582–C data were converted to quarter hours to increase their comparability with the other tables.

In constructing Table 582–D, the author consulted Bailey (1970) for information through 1968; A. C. Nielsen Company's *Television Audience 1971*, for the 1970 figures; and "Evening Network TV Specials," *Nielsen Newscast* No. 3 (1974) for the 1972 and 1974 figures. Information through 1968 is for mid-September through mid-June of each season; the 1970 data are for September through April; and the 1972 and 1974 figures represent the entire network programming season (October–September). Because of the multiplicity of sources and the variety of categorizations involved in this table, the data should be considered more of a refined estimate than an actual census.

In Table 582–E, the format data were taken from *Broadcasting Yearbook*; the source information came from the A.D. Little Co. (1969) (based on survey returns from the networks); and the information on program

Table 582-E   Format, Source, and Length of Network Television Programs, 1956–1972 (In Percent)

	Program Format[a]			Program Source[b]				Program Length[b]				
Year	Film	Videotape	Live	Network	Sponsor	Packager	Combination	15 Minutes	30 Minutes	60 Minutes	90 Minutes	120 Minutes
1956	27	—	73	N/A	N/A	N/A	N/A	N/A	N/A	N/A	N/A	N/A
1958	24	6	70	30	28	42	1	0.4	63	33	2	—
1960	32	32	36	20	14	63	3	0.7	47	51	N/A	N/A
1962	35	37	28	18	9	70	3	0.3	30	62	2	6
1964	37	37	26	19	7	74	1	—	33	54	4	8
1966	39	38	23	15	4	79	2	—	29	55	2	14
1968	37	48	16	16	3	81	1	—	23	53	4	19
1970	36	49	14	N/A	N/A	N/A	N/A	—	23	52	6	19
1972	44	40	16	N/A	N/A	N/A	N/A	—	17	52	12	19

Sources: Format data: *Broadcasting Yearbook*, appropriate issues. Source data: A. D. Little Company (1969), p. 1, based on survey returns from the networks. Length data: 1958–1968: A. D. Little Company (1969), p. 10; 1970–1972: Columbia Broadcasting System, as printed in Office of Telecommunications Policy (1973), appendix table 4. Notes: [a]As a percentage of total network broadcast hours; [b]As a percentage of total prime-time hours only.

length came from the A. D. Little Co. (1969) (for data through 1968) and from the Columbia Broadcasting Service (CBS), as printed in a report of the Office of Telecommunications Policy (1973). All figures on Table 582–E are rounded percentages. Excluded from the data on programming length was a 45 minute category that never accounted for more than one percent of network hours.

Further Information

As noted before, information on network television programming abounds. Regular seasonal information on program content and costs appears in *Broadcasting*, *TV/Radio Age*, and *Variety*. Historical directories of programming include those by Gianakos (1978, 1980, and 1981) which provides specific episode data; Brooks and Marsh (1981) on prime-time and syndicated programming, Terrace (1979 and 1981), and McNeil (1981) which claim to cover all network and major syndicated programming. The broader reference books by Brown (1982), Norback and Norback (1980), Steinberg (1980), and Castleman and Podrazik (1982) are of use as well. All of these works cover several decades with either narrative or specific program information. Material on specific kinds of programs abounds, much of it popular in nature, though some scholarly histories and useful content analyses have appeared in recent years. For coverage of children's programs on the networks, including a good deal of statistical time series data, see Turow (1981). Most libraries stock a good deal of this material—some of it is listed in the bibliographies appearing toward the end of the annual *Broadcasting Yearbook*.

583
VIOLENCE IN NETWORK TELEVISION PROGRAMMING

Interpretation of the Table

Table 583–A summarizes the major findings of 13 years of analysis of network television content. A research team, working under the direction of Dean George Gerbner of the University of Pennsylvania, has been attempting to quantify violence in network television programming, according to the type of program and the hour it is presented. Each year, this group issues the *Violence Profile* (the *Violence Index* until 1973), a report which analyzes and summarizes a number of measures of television programming by the Gerbner team:

1. The percentage of programs containing any violence.
2. The rate of violent episodes per program.
3. The rate of violent episodes per hour.
4. The percentage of major characters involved in any violence.
5. The percentage of major characters involved in any killing.

The results in categories 2 and 3 are doubled by the researchers in order to raise their relatively low numerical value (because they are not percentages) to the significance that the factors of frequency and saturation deserve. Higher numbers on the table therefore indicate "more" violence in that category of programming or on that network.

The reader will note a general decline in levels of televised violence until 1976, when a sharp upward turn occurred in most categories. Early evening, for a time called "Family hour," programming (8 to 9 p.m.) has usually contained less violence than programming later in the evening. Comic-tone programs (other than cartoons) appear to have contained the least violence of all of the categories, while crime and action-adventure programs, along with cartoons, had high incidences of measured violence.

Sources

The data for Table 583–A come from Gerbner et al. (1976, 1977 and direct to the author). The reader should be aware that there is considerable controversy among researchers about the validity of this information. This controversy concerns both the methods of the study and Gerbner's definition of violence in any program context (which, for example, gives comedy equal consideration with serious drama). Gerbner's methods are too involved to describe here, but they are fully explained in each annual *Violence Profile*. Note that two categories are for prime-time *only*.

The seventh annual *Violence Profile*, which appeared in 1976, was the last edition to contain specific annual data for the series; the eighth edition resorted to aggregating data from earlier years because of space limitations. This practice was repeated in later editions.

Further Information

The reader should consult the complete series of the *Violence Profile* for details of the research. Gerbner and Gross (1976) also provide a layman's summary of the research, its findings, and some of the data not reported

Table 583–A Gerbner Violence Profile of Network Television Programming, 1967–1980

Note: Higher Numbers in Table Indicate a Higher Level of Violence Within Each Programming Category. See Text for Explanation of the Derivation of Figures.

Year	All Network Programs	Early Evening Programs[a]	Later-Evening Programs[b]	All Weekend Daytime Programs	Televised Feature Films[c]	Cartoon Programs	Crime/Western/ Action-Adventure Programs[c]	Comic Tone Programs[c]	All ABC Programs	All CBS Programs	All NBC Programs
							Prime-Time Only:				
1967	199	212	148	251	182	251	225	81	222	151	220
1968	181	161	179	232	236	239	225	84	193	167	187
1969	183	137	156	259	169	262	218	73	164	183	205
1970	173	113	165	250	250	250	220	77	161	162	203
1971	175	152	170	208	228	232	207	82	142	194	189
1972	173	149	165	207	225	217	244	59	175	150	203
1973	161	127	137	212	186	218	238	44	138	174	172
1974	182	146	210	192	273	196	219	67	197	174	177
1975	180	101	208	221	263	233	221	65	187	155	201
1976	204	145	209	247	220	273	234	132	207	182	224
1977	166	140	165	209	265	228	219	99	154	159	190
1978	183	116	180	249	248	252	185	119	186	183	179
1979	174	156	150	210	207	226	227	144	145	190	179
1980	187	153	150	249	214	256	228	146	150	188	196
Average Profile	179	141	174	224	228	234	225	92	173	172	192

Source: Data through 1976 from Gerbner et al. (1977) appendix tables; data for 1977–1980 plus average profile provided directly to the author by Gerbner and Nancy Signorelli, University of Pennsylvania. Notes: [a]Early evening is 8–9 PM Monday–Saturday, and 7–9 PM Sunday; [b]Later-evening is 9–11 PM all days (all of these times would be one hour earlier for Central and Mountain time zones); [c]Excludes cartoons.

here. For analysis of the data limitations, the reader should see the debate in "Violence Ratings: A Dialogue" (1972–1973), and in "The Violence Profile: An Exchange of Views" (1977).

590
CABLE TELEVISION PROGRAMMING

Interpretation of the Tables

In addition to the approaches shown in Unit 190, two useful ways of measuring the increasing significance of cable television are to: (1) trace the growing channel capacity of cable systems, especially in the 1980s, and (2) to detail the diversity of content origination. This unit explores both. Table 590–A shows that while systems with 6–12 channel capacity remain in the majority in the early 1980s, systems with more than 20 channels (and a few with upwards of 100 and more) increased sharply in the early 1980s. Systems with fewer than six are now an insignificant factor in the industry. Naturally, the availability of satellite-delivered pay network signals in the late 1970s drove much of this capacity expansion.

Cable system program origination is often considerably less than "programming." The most common form of "programming" has been time and weather dials which are continuously scanned by an automatic camera, thereby providing "content" for one cable channel at the least possible expense. Another type of automated origination is a news ticker which runs across the television screen.

As in the case of channel capacity, part of the impetus to originate both automated and studio programming came from FCC regulations. For several years, cable systems with more than 3,500 subscribers were required to provide some local origination in addition to simply feeding local and imported television channels into the homes. The expansion of cable into major cities also contributed to origination, as cable operators discovered that such services were often of as much interest to audiences—or to advertisers—as the "regular" television signals. The high costs of operation have discouraged any rapid growth of nonautomatic originations. However, 1972 FCC regulations requiring local public-access cable channels, though rescinded several years later, led to an increase in local-live (studio) capacity for cable systems.

Table 590–B provides a glimpse at the early development of initial satellite-delivered cable network services. Where possible, the table shows the month and year the service began (note only two began in the 1960s: AP Cable News—a "crawl" service, followed three years later by a similar offering from the British Reuters news agency). The oldest services especially designed with cable viewers in mind were the Spanish International Network, and Ted Turner's initial "superstation," WTBS in Atlanta, both beginning late in 1976. The variety of satellite offerings on cable by the early 1980s was more than most systems could carry (see previous table). And the services listed here were provided at little or no charge to cable system operators (for pay services, see Unit 195). There are a few attempts at broad national networks with a variety of programs—the USA Network is the prime example. But most listed here cater to specific audiences: religion (CBN and PTL), music (Nashville), news services (CNN, C–Span, the cable industry news actuality service), finance (Dow Jones and the Financial News Networks), ethnic (Black Entertainment TV, SIN) children (Nickelodeon) and education and culture (ACSN and ARTS). Not shown on the table are some services which folded prior to the Fall of 1983. And many observers were predicting a substantial shake-out of services remaining (the Health News Network ended separate operation, for example, in mid–1983).

Sources

The data presented in Table 590–A, based on a survey of the cable television industry, were taken from the annual *Television Factbook*. In the survey, systems were listed under as many self-reported categories as necessary. The categories varied from year to year, and the information was collected for various months. The figures should therefore be viewed as estimates of actual trends.

Table 590–B is taken from regularly published listings in *Cablevision*, the standard cable trade-weekly. Figures are often rounded estimates provided by the cable networks themselves.

Further Information

The National Cable Television Association (NCTA) has issued annual program directories under various titles which provide detailed regional and local information. Best weekly coverage of trends and developments in this area appear in *Cablevision*. See also Table 195–A for pay cable network development.

Table 590-A   Channel Capacity and Program Content of Cable Systems, 1966–1983

	1966	1969	1970	1971	1972	1973	1974	1975	1976	1977	1978	1979	1981	1983
Number of Reporting CATV Systems	1,440	2,300	2,490	2,578	2,839	3,032	3,190	3,405	3,715	3,911	3,997	4,180	4,637	5,748
Systems with Program Origination	N/A	883	1,089	1,190	1,514	1,764	1,982	2,159	2,404	2,571	2,650	2,785	5,045	3,407
Systems with No Program Origination	N/A	1,417	1,401	1,388	1,325	1,114	1,208	1,246	1,311	1,340	1,347	1,394	1,592	2,341
Systems Planning to Originate Programming	N/A	156	416	430	418	154	245	232	216	202	284	272	215	313
Number of CATV Systems, by Channel Capacities														
Over 20 channels	N/A	N/A	N/A	N/A	N/A	N/A	N/A	382	444	501	556	1,116	1,634	2,642
13 to 20 channels	N/A	29	86	157	361	469	590	354	424	465	482	103	132	263
6 to 12 channels	N/A	1,559	1,720	1,882	2,026	2,181	2,302	2,415	2,647	2,759	2,791	2,793	2,647	2,295
5 channels	N/A	511	459	371	332	287	328	195	170	157	139	129	109	72
Under 5 channels	N/A	61	61	50	55	49	39	32	10	19	17	22	15	11
Unspecified	N/A	140	164	118	65	46	31	27	11	10	12	17	100	465
Number of CATV Systems, by Content:														
Automated Origination:														
Time and Weather	N/A	825	1,019	1,477	1,514	1,664	1,887	2,074	2,311	1,474	1,615	1,598	1,672	1,803
News Ticker	430	797	984	1,206	1,309	1,597	1,812	1,989	2,224	2,359	2,412	2,547	2,762	2,897
Stock Ticker	52	88	116	159	211	288	337	410	513	603	650	739	889	916
Sports Ticker	1	15	18	35	63	124	163	191	237	274	302	347	442	484
Message Wheel	N/A	N/A	N/A	N/A	N/A	42	76	103	162	199	230	262	313	319
Music	40	61	74	77	87	189	271	321	390	394	370	421	447	432
Emergency Alert	N/A	13	10	N/A	70	62	49	46	N/A	N/A	90	134	207	330
Advertising	N/A	N/A	N/A	N/A	N/A	20	38	74	N/A	N/A	334	412	N/A	N/A
Other	N/A	N/A	N/A	N/A	59	322	444	454	475	451	276	568	1,112	1,159
Studio Originations:														
Local Live	97	282	399	524	594	768	912	949	1,030	1,035	1,035	1,187	1,373	1,604
Film	28	197	293	467	570	587	652	645	682	680	665	691	732	758
Videotape	3	35	54	—	—	181	224	224	228	197	170	178	171	148
CATV Network	N/A	39	66	—	—	288	401	403	421	389	394	432	486	520
School Channel	N/A	N/A	N/A	N/A	N/A	40	52	59	63	N/A	61	71	71	82
Public Access	N/A	N/A	15	N/A	N/A	N/A	81	103	181	243	252	331	497	730
Advertising	N/A	N/A	4	N/A	N/A	N/A	11	29	117	182	205	283	485	752
Pay Cable	N/A	N/A	N/A	57	151	233	295	298	306	284	87	44	524	701
Other	103	N/A	89	N/A	24	130	80	97	125	219	224	291	592	936

Sources: Television Factbook, appropriate issues. No 1980 or 1982 data available.

Table 590–B Basic Satellite Distributed Cable Television Programming Services, 1980–1983

Programming Service	Start-up date	July 1980		September 1981		September 1982		September 1983	
		Systems	Subscribers	Systems	Subscribers	Systems	Subscribers	Systems	Subscribers
AP Cable News	6/65	N/A	N/A	N/A	N/A	N/A	N/A	445	4,700,000
ACSN–The Learning Channel	10/79	35	251,000	218	1,130,000	262	1,843,352	461	3,600,000
ARTS	4/81	—	—	see Nickelodeon		1,725	8,000,000	1,936	12,300,000
Black Entertainment TV	1/79	372	3,710,000	742	8,132,112	122	2,000,000	246	5,370,000
Cable Health Network	6/82	—	—	—	—	N/A	N/A	1,315	13,278,000
Cable News Network	6/80	261	2,314,000	1,539	8,650,000	2,807	15,287,000	3,840	21,788,000
CNN Headline News	1/82	—	—	—	—	270	1,904,640	634	5,287,000
CBN Cable Network	4/77	2,500	7,500,000	2,900	13,300,000	3,245	18,200,000	3,868	22,500,000
C-Span	3/79	775	5,750,000	1,150	10,000,000	1,000	10,500,000	1,100	14,500,000
Country Music Television	3/83	—	—	—	—	—	—	45	1,200,000
Daytime	1/82	—	—	—	—	515	7,244,313	755	10,000,000
Dow Jones Cable News	4/81	—	—	—	—	60	640,000	138	1,700,000
ESPN	9/79	632	4,035,859	2,625	12,214,314	4,586	18,780,114	6,713	24,600,000
Electronic Program Guide	1/82	—	—	—	—	58	821,490	119	2,194,423
Eternal Word Television Network	8/81	—	—	13	285,900	33	600,000	100	1,625,000
Financial News Network	11/81	—	—	—	—	590	760,000	758	9,000,000
Modern Satellite Network	1/79	369	2,300,000	538	4,100,000	427	5,731,910	500	8,293,000
Music Television	8/81	—	—	300	2,500,000	825	6,750,000	1,900	15,000,000
Nashville Network	3/83	—	—	—	—	—	—	1,200	9,600,000

Table 590–B   Basic Satellite Distributed Cable Television Programming Services, 1980–1983 (cont.)

Programming Service	Start-up date	July 1980		September 1981		September 1982		September 1983	
		Systems	Subscribers	Systems	Subscribers	Systems	Subscribers	Systems	Subscribers
National Christian Network	6/80	—	—	N/A	N/A	72	1,690,377	108	1,439,153
National Jewish Television	5/81	—	—	57	1,433,850	98	2,146,100	147	2,823,916
Nickelodeon	4/79	489	2,518,360	1,300[a]	5,200,000	1,860	9,000,000	2,925	13,950,000
PTL Satellite Network	4/78	235	3,000,000	370	3,940,000	600	6,500,000	766	8,000,000
Reuters News Views	1969	N/A	N/A	N/A	N/A	375	3,500,000	350	3,500,000
Satellite News Channel[b]	6/82	—	—	—	—	342	3,292,130	760	7,700,000
Satellite Program Network	1/79	468	2,839,639	317	3,146,177	410	4,757,126	450	8,600,000
SIN Spanish International Network	9/76	N/A	N/A	134	2,756,800	199	3,750,900	241	3,237,200
Trinity Broadcast Network	5/78	300	3,500,000	140	1,160,000	231	2,267,000	272	3,218,400
USA Network	9/80	1,028	4,779,826	1,550	8,500,000	2,300	13,000,000	4,000	20,000,000
Weather Channel	5/82	—	—	—	—	550	6,000,000	1,000	10,000,000
WGN-TV	11/78	986	3,864,644	1,961	6,877,041	3,359	9,448,079	4,625	10,937,035
WOR-TV	4/79	385	2,753,000	1,028	4,188,685	655	4,337,824	807	4,172,224
WTBS	12/76	2,216	8,929,278	3,472	15,779,000	4,699	23,324,000	5,588	27,654,000

Source: CableVision Magazine/Titsch Communications Inc., 1980 data, Cablevision, 1/12/81, p. 28; 1981 data, Cablevision, 10/19/81, p. 79; 1981 data, Cablevision, 11/1/82, p. 119; 1983 data direct to author from Cablevision. Notes: [a]Figure combines Nickelodeon and ARTS. [b]Satellite News Channel off air October 27, 1983.

SECTION SIX
THE AUDIENCE
FOR
ELECTRONIC MEDIA

660
PRODUCTION AND SALES
OF BROADCAST RECEIVERS

Interpretation of the Tables

Tables 660-A and 660-B indicate that the changing patterns of the broadcast-receiver manufacturing industry generally conform to U.S. economic trends. The initial spurt of radio production in the 1920s was followed by a decline in the Depression, a prewar rise of radios in cars, and a postwar explosion in the demand for both home and car radios. Comparison of the unit production data (Table 660-A) with the factory price information (Table 660-B) shows that while radio unit production continues to increase, the cost per receiver has declined significantly—in spite of inflation. A similar trend is evident with television (see average set prices cited in Units 670 and 680).

According to the July 28, 1975, *Electrical Merchandising Week* (now called *Merchandising*), most radios are purchased at discount stores (35 percent), with 25 percent from catalog and mail order, 15 percent from appliance and radio-TV stores, 10 percent from department stores, 3 percent from furniture outlets, and 12 percent from "other" places. The television pattern is quite different. Most television sets come from appliance and radio-TV stores (30 percent), 19 percent from department stores, 27 percent from discount outlets, only 4 percent from mail-order outlets, 15 percent from furniture stores, and 5 percent from "other" outlets.

Table 660-C combines the information in the preceding tables to arrive at the cumulative number of radio and television receivers in use in the United States. The figures take into account new sets purchased and older sets scrapped.

Table 660-D provides a count of radio-TV stores and repair services. The larger number of repair services is mainly due to their smaller size. The

Table 660-A   Number of Radio and Television Receivers Produced in the U.S., 1922–1982

	Radio Receivers			Television Receivers			
				Note: All Figures are in Thousands.			Grand
Year	Home	Auto	Total	B & W	Color	Total	Total
1922	100	—	100	—	—	—	100
1923	550	—	550	—	—	—	550
1924	1,500	—	1,500	—	—	—	1,500
1925	2,000	—	2,000	—	—	—	2,000
1926	1,750	—	1,750	—	—	—	1,750
1927	1,350	—	1,350	—	—	—	1,350
1928	3,281	—	3,281	—	—	—	3,281
1929	4,428	—	4,428	—	—	—	4,428
1930	3,793	34	3,827	—	—	—	3,827
1931	3,412	108	3,420	—	—	—	3,420
1932	2,857	143	3,000	—	—	—	3,000
1933	3,082	724	3,806	—	—	—	3,806
1934	3,304	780	4,084	—	—	—	4,084
1935	4,901	1,125	6,026	—	—	—	6,026
1936	6,836	1,412	8,248	—	—	—	8,248
1937	6,315	1,150	8,065	—	—	—	8,065
1938	5,200	800	6,000	—	—	—	6,000
1939	9,300	1,200	10,500	—	—	—	10,500
1940	10,100	1,700	11,800	—	—	—	11,800
1941	11,000	2,000	13,000	—	—	—	13,000
1942	4,050	350	4,400	—	—	—	4,400
1945	500	—	500	—	—	—	500
1946	12,800	1,200	14,000	6	—	6	14,006
1947	13,800	3,200	17,000	179	—	179	17,179
1948	9,900	4,100	14,000	970	—	970	14,970
1949	6,500	3,500	10,000	2,970	—	2,970	12,970
1950	9,218	4,740	13,958	7,355	—	7,355	21,313
1951	6,445	4,544	10,989	5,312	—	5,312	16,301
1952	7,232	3,243	10,475	6,194	—	6,194	16,669
1953	7,283	5,183	12,466	6,870	—	6,870	19,336
1954	6,119	4,124	10,243	7,405	5	7,410	17,653
1955	7,327	6,863	14,190	7,738	20	7,758	21,948
1956	8,951	5,057	14,008	7,351	100	7,451	21,459
1957	9,952	5,496	15,448	6,388	85	6,473	21,921
1958	10,797	3,715	14,512	5,051	80	5,131	19,643
1959	15,772	5,501	21,273	6,278	90	6,368	27,641
1960	18,031	6,432	24,463	5,709	120	5,829	30,292
1961	23,654	5,568	29,222	6,168	147	6,315	35,537
1962	24,781	7,249	32,030	6,696	438	7,134	39,164
1963	23,602	7,946	31,548	7,236	747	7,983	39,531
1964	23,558	8,313	31,871	8,360	1,404	9,764	41,635
1965	31,689	10,037	41,726	8,753	2,694	11,447	53,173

Table 660–A   Number of Radio and Television Receivers Produced in the U.S., 1922–1982 (cont.)

	Radio Receivers			Television Receivers			Grand Total
Year	Home	Auto	Total	B & W	Color	Total	
1966	34,779	9,394	44,173	7,702	5,012	12,714	56,887
1967	31,684	9,527	41,211	6,001	5,563	11,564	52,775
1968	34,322	12,510	46,832	6,996	6,215	13,211	60,043
1969	39,414	11,939	51,353	7,117	6,191	13,308	64,661
1970	34,049	10,378	44,427	6,900	5,320	12,220	56,647
1971	34,105	13,505	47,610	7,647	7,274	14,921	62,531
1972	42,149	13,162	55,311	8,239	8,845	17,084	72,395
1973	37,652	12,546	50,198	7,296	10,071	17,367	67,565
1974	33,231	10,762	43,993	6,868	8,411	15,279	59,272
1975	25,276	9,239	34,515	4,418	6,219	10,637	45,152
1976	31,656	12,445	44,101	5,937	8,194	14,131	58,232
1977	40,036	12,890	52,926	6,090	9,341	15,431	68,357
1978	35,367	12,668	48,035	6,733	10,674	17,407	65,442
1979	27,648	12,381	40,029	6,575	10,042	16,617	56,646
1980	28,104	11,470	39,574	6,729	11,803	18,532	58,106
1981	31,476	12,883	44,359	6,056	12,423	18,479	62,838
1982	31,782	12,306	44,088	4,922	11,484	16,406	60,494

Note: All Figures are in Thousands.

Sources: Data through 1976 from *Broadcasting Yearbook 1977*, pp. B–175 (television) and C–310–11 (radio). 1922–1949 data for radio receivers originally supplied by Marketing World, Ltd. All other information provided to *Broadcasting Yearbook* by Electronic Industries Association. 1977–1982 data from EIA, *Consumer Electronics Annual Review, 1983*, p. 8 (television) and p. 31 (radio).

abrupt decline in radio stores from 1929 to 1939 seems extreme and probably results from a change in the classification or data-collection procedures.

Sources

Tables 660–A and 660–B have serious reliability limitations. All data to 1976 (660–A) or 1974 (660–B) are taken from *Broadcasting Yearbook 1977*. The radio information to 1949, from Marketing World, Ltd., appears to be estimated. Due to the wartime freeze in construction of consumer items, no radio sets were made in 1943–1944—hence, the omission of those years from the table.

Radio data after 1949 are from the Electronic Industries Association (EIA), which does not supply financial information from 1950 through 1957. Radio financial totals from 1958–1963 are low, and the sudden rise in 1964 is mainly due to the inclusion of the value of imports. The post-1963

Table 660-B   Factory Value of Radio and Television Receivers Produced in the U.S., 1922–1982

| | Radio Receivers | | | Television Receivers | | | Grand |
Year	Home	Auto	Total	B & W	Color	Total	Total
1922	5,000	—	5,000	—	—	—	5,000
1923	30,000	—	30,000	—	—	—	30,000
1924	100,000	—	100,000	—	—	—	100,000
1925	165,000	—	165,000	—	—	—	165,000
1926	200,000	—	200,000	—	—	—	200,000
1927	168,000	—	168,000	—	—	—	168,000
1928	400,000	—	400,000	—	—	—	400,000
1929	600,000	—	600,000	—	—	—	600,000
1930	297,000	3,000	300,000	—	—	—	300,000
1931	219,060	5,940	225,000	—	—	—	225,000
1932	132,850	7,150	140,000	—	—	—	140,000
1933	151,902	28,598	180,500	—	—	—	180,500
1934	186,500	28,000	214,500	—	—	—	214,500
1935	275,630	54,563	330,193	—	—	—	330,193
1936	380,812	69,188	450,000	—	—	—	450,000
1937	362,500	87,500	450,000	—	—	—	450,000
1938	178,000	32,000	210,000	—	—	—	210,000
1939	306,000	48,000	354,000	—	—	—	354,000
1940	390,000	60,000	450,000	—	—	—	450,000
1941	390,000	70,000	460,000	—	—	—	460,000
1942	141,750	12,250	154,000	—	—	—	154,000
1945	N/A	N/A	20,000	—	—	—	20,000
1946	628,000	72,000	700,000	1,000	—	1,000	701,000
1947	606,000	194,000	800,000	50,000	—	50,000	850,000
1948	307,000	293,000	600,000	226,000	—	226,000	826,000
1949	260,000	240,000	500,000	574,000	—	574,000	1,074,000
1950	N/A	N/A	N/A	1,397,000	—	1,397,000	N/A
1951	N/A	N/A	N/A	944,000	—	944,000	N/A
1952	N/A	N/A	N/A	1,064,000	—	1,064,000	N/A
1953	N/A	N/A	N/A	1,170,000	—	1,170,000	N/A
1954	N/A	N/A	N/A	1,040,000	2,000	1,042,000	N/A
1955	N/A	N/A	N/A	1,068,000	10,000	1,078,000	N/A
1956	N/A	N/A	N/A	934,000	46,000	980,000	N/A
1957	N/A	N/A	N/A	831,000	37,000	868,000	N/A
1958	159,000[a]	96,000	255,000	686,000	34,000	720,000	975,000
1959	192,000[a]	130,000	322,000	806,000	37,000	843,000	1,165,000
1960	190,000[a]	154,000	344,000	750,091	47,000	797,091	1,141,091
1961	190,000[a]	134,000	324,000	757,500	56,000	813,500	1,137,500
1962	207,000[a]	181,000	388,000	851,000	154,000	1,005,000	1,393,000
1963	179,000[a]	206,000	385,000	841,000	258,000	1,099,000	1,484,000
1964	267,000	205,000	472,000	896,000	488,000	1,384,000	1,856,000
1965	328,000	248,000	576,000	910,000	959,000	1,869,000	2,445,000

Note: All Figures are in Thousands of Dollars.

Table 660–B Factory Value of Radio and Television Receivers Produced in the U.S., 1922–1982 (cont.)

Note: All Figures are in Thousands of Dollars.

	Radio Receivers			Television Receivers			
Year	Home	Auto	Total	B & W	Color	Total	Grand Total
1966	346,000	267,000	613,000	756,000	1,861,000	2,617,000	3,230,000
1967	333,000	259,000	592,000	555,000	2,015,000	2,570,000	3,162,000
1968	371,000	330,000	701,000	591,000	2,086,000	2,677,000	3,378,000
1969	422,000	316,000	738,000	554,000	2,031,000	2,585,000	3,323,000
1970	380,000	271,000	651,000	518,000	1,684,000	2,202,000	2,853,000
1971	487,000	315,000	802,000	621,000	2,355,000	2,976,000	3,778,000
1972	606,000	377,000	983,000	649,000	2,825,000	3,474,000	4,457,000
1973	572,000	391,000	963,000	560,000	3,097,000	3,657,000	4,620,000
1974	559,000	370,000	929,000	543,000	2,658,000	3,201,000	4,130,000
1975	369,000	355,000	724,000	371,000	2,121,000	2,492,000	3,216,000
1976	398,000	497,000	895,000	528,000	2,860,000	3,388,000	4,283,000
1977	509,000	534,000	1,043,000	542,000	3,269,000	3,811,000	4,854,000
1978	485,000	582,000	1,067,000	572,000	3,736,000	4,308,000	5,375,000
1979	440,000	623,000	1,063,000	565,000	3,615,000	4,180,000	5,243,000
1980	468,000	961,000	1,429,000	599,000	4,339,000	4,938,000	6,367,000
1981	536,000	1,083,000	1,619,000	539,000	4,683,000	5,222,000	6,841,000
1982	516,000	1,049,000	1,565,000	437,000	4,288,000	4,725,000	6,290,000

Sources: Data through 1974 from *Broadcasting Yearbook* 1977, pp. B–175 (television) and C–310–11 (radio). 1922–1949 data for radio receivers originally supplied by Marketing World Ltd. All other information provided to *Broadcasting Yearbook* by Electronics Industries Association. 1977–1982 data from EIA, *Consumer Electronics Annual Review, 1983,* p. 8 (television) and p. 31 (radio). Note: ªimports are not included for these years.

figures can only be approximately compared to earlier totals. All the television information is also from the EIA.

For both radio and television, the data prior to 1971 reflect *factory sales* by U.S. manufacturers, plus products imported directly by U.S. distributors or dealers for resale. The post-1970 data differ, in that the figures showing factory sales are replaced by figures showing products produced or imports purchased by U.S. manufacturers. Complete financial data on imports are incorporated only after 1964—and the figures include import duties and freight. See Units 760 for details on radio-television imports and exports.

The final column in both tables is misleading in one important respect: It does *not* control for the overlap of radio-television console combinations. While it is difficult to estimate this overlap consistently, it appears to be two to three million units or more per year from the late 1950s to the present. All of the data are rounded estimates and, as suggested above, are not in reality as comparable as these tables make them appear.

Table 660–C   Number of Radio and Television Receivers in Use, 1922–1982

Year[a]	Note: All Figures are in Thousands. Radio Receivers	Television Sets	Total Receivers
1922	400	—	400
1923	1,100	—	1,100
1924	3,000	—	3,000
1925	4,000	—	4,000
1926	5,700	—	5,700
1927	7,000	—	7,000
1928	8,500	—	8,500
1929	10,500	—	10,500
1930	13,000	—	13,000
1931	15,000	—	15,000
1932	18,000	—	18,000
1933	22,000	—	22,000
1934	26,000	—	26,000
1935	30,500	—	30,500
1936	33,000	—	33,000
1937	37,600	—	37,600
1938	40,800	—	40,800
1939	45,300	—	45,300
1940	51,000	—	51,000
1941	56,600	—	56,600
1942	59,300	—	59,300
1943	57,850	—	57,850
1944	55,000	—	55,000
1945	56,000	—	56,000
1946	60,000	10	60,010
1947	66,000	16	66,016
1948	74,000	190	74,190
1949	81,000	1,000	82,000
1950	85,200	4,000	89,200
1951	96,000	10,600	106,600
1952	105,300	15,800	121,100
1953	110,500	21,200	131,700
1954	117,500	27,300	144,800
1955	121,000	32,500	153,500
1956	123,900	37,600	161,500
1957	135,000	42,700	177,700
1958	139,500	47,000	186,500
1959	146,200	50,000	196,200

Table 660–C   Number of Radio and Television Receivers in Use, 1922–1982 (cont.)

Year[a]	*Note: All Figures are in Thousands.* Radio Receivers	Television Sets	Total Receivers
1960	156,400	53,300	209,700
1961	168,300	55,600	223,900
1962	183,800	58,175	241,975
1963	200,300	61,200	261,500
1964	214,100	64,175	278,275
1965	228,300	67,210	295,510
1966	242,000	70,560	312,560
1967	262,700	74,800	337,500
1968	281,800	79,000	360,800
1969	303,400	83,600	387,000
1970	320,700	88,300	409,000
1971	336,000	93,200	429,200
1972	354,000	100,000	455,054
1973	369,000	109,800	478,800
1974	383,000	117,100	500,100
1975	401,000	121,000	522,000
1976	412,000	125,300	537,300
1977	425,000	131,500	556,500
1978	444,000	138,200	582,200
1979	450,000	145,700	595,700
1980	453,000	155,800	608,800
1981	460,000	162,500	622,500
1982	470,000	171,900	641,900

Sources: Radio data from Radio Advertising Bureau and television data from NBC Corporate Planning, as reprinted in *Television Factbook*, for data through 1971. 1972–1982 data from EIA, *Consumer Electronics Annual Review 1983*, p. 28. Note: [a]Data as of December 31 for each year.

One indication of the multiple data sources, and problems in tabulation, is that data is fairly continually revised. Readers comparing data for the 1970s in this book with its predecessor (Sterling and Haight, *The Mass Media*, 1978) will find several of the figures change as EIA continually updates and reevaluates its information. Indeed, a tabulating error was discovered by EIA for the 1970s' data shown in Table 670–B and is shown in correct form here for information from 1972 on.

The information in Table 660–C was printed in various editions of *Television Factbook*, with television data from the NBC Corporate Planning of-

Table 660–D Number of Radio-Television Stores and Repair Services, 1929–1977

Year	Radio-TV Stores	Repair Services	Total Number of Establishments
1929	16,037	N/A	N/A
1939	2,911	N/A	N/A
1948	7,231	12,558	19,789
1954	6,790	22,824	29,614
1958	16,761	37,884	54,645
1963	10,365	43,208	53,573
1967	9,701[a]	33,063[a]	42,764[a]
1972	12,711	34,810	47,521
1977	24,752	31,800	56,552

Sources: Radio-TV stores data: *Census of Business*. Repair services data: *Census of Selected Service Industries*. Note: [a]Includes establishments with payrolls only.

fice and radio data from the Radio Advertising Bureau. No information seems to be available on how these estimates were derived. As with Tables 660–A and 660–B, the total column is a bit misleading, since a small proportion of radio and television sets are combined in consoles—and, therefore, would be double-counted in the last column.

Table 660–D is from the Census Bureau's *Census of Business* (for radio-TV stores) later called *Census of Retail Trade*, while the *Census of Selected Service Industries* provided the data on repair services. The 1967 drop in numbers of both is due partially to the exclusion of establishments without paid employees, thus cutting out many small operations. Due to budget cuts at the Census Bureau, data for 1982 was gathered and analyzed much later than before and was thus not available as this book went to press.

Further Information

The standard information source for broadcast receivers is the major industry trade group—the Consumer Products Division of the Electronic Industries Association, which annually issues the *Electronic Market Data Book* and *Consumer Electronics*. Both volumes are based on regular, confidential sales reports to the EIA from several hundred companies in the field. Summary information from the EIA and other sources appears regularly in *Broadcasting Yearbook* and *Television Factbook*. Specific data on FM radio are in Table 670–B.

Another source for some of this information is the *Census of Manufactures* and the *Annual Survey of Manufactures*. However, the data aggregation in these volumes makes it difficult to "pull out" information specifically relating to broadcasting (see, for example, Unit 460).

Essential to a current understanding of trends in consumer electronics is that portion of the weekly *Television Digest* trade periodical. It provides regular analyses of sales trends, including updates of all data in this unit. See also Table 760–C.

661
HOURS OF BROADCAST
LISTENING/VIEWING

Interpretation of the Table

Table 661–A provides estimates of the average daily per-household hours of use of radio and television by the U.S. population. The data were taken from many different sources and are not strictly comparable. Also, the "total radio/television hours" column is misleading, in that it does not allow for the possibility that a typical household may have both a radio and a television playing at the same time in different rooms to different people. In that event, fewer actual clock hours would be consumed.

Despite these limitations, the table figures clearly indicate that radio use has declined since the advent of television, and that television use has reached higher levels than radio ever attained. The abrupt declines in average radio use in 1955 and 1960 are unlikely and are probably due to testing and sampling problems in *television* households.

Sources

All of this information comes from diverse sources, not readily comparable, but useful for overall trends. Specifically: 1931: Lumley (1934), p. 196; reporting on a survey of some 14,000 listeners in ten cities. 1935: Columbia Broadcasting System (1937), p. 30; reporting CBS research in communities of 2,500 population and over. 1943: Sandage (1945), p. 140; reporting Nielsen Radio Index research for January citing "total hours of radio

Table 661-A   Average Daily Hours of Radio and Television Use, 1931-1981

| Year | Daily Hours Per Household | | |
	Radio	Television	Total Hours
1931	4:04	—	4:04
1935	4:48	—	4:48
1943	4:48	—	4:48
1946	4:13	—	4:13
1950	4:06	4:35	8:41
1955	2:12	4:51	7:03
1960	1:53	5:59	7:52
1965	2:27	5:30	7:55
1971	2:52	5:56	8:48
1976	3:25[a]	6:18	9:43
1981	3:19[a]	6:45	9:64

Sources: See text. Note: [a]Refers to listening hours per person.

listening per home from midnight to midnight" in large cities (over 100,000 population). 1946: Lichty and Topping (1975), p. 523; citing A. C. Nielsen data, not further defined. 1950 and 1955: Data for both radio and television from A. C. Nielsen, *The Radio and Television Audience 1956*, p. 4; citing "average hours per U.S. radio home per day" for November–December. 1960: Radio from A. C. Nielsen, *Radio 60*, p. 8; citing winter listening per home, per day for all days of the week. Television from A. C. Nielsen, *Television 60*, p. 5; citing hours per home per day in January. 1965: Data for both from Lichty and Topping (1975), p. 523; citing A. C. Nielsen. 1971: Radio from *CBS Radio Network: Affiliate Research/Promotion Reference Guide* (1972), p. 4; citing RADAR® studies. Television from A. C. Nielsen, *Television Audience 1972*, p. 13; averaging the whole year. 1976: Radio from *Encyclomedia: Radio 1978*, p. 6; referring to total (all hours, all days for audience members 12 and older) audience average listening time per day. Television from *Broadcasting* (April 3, 1978), p. 48; citing Nielsen. 1981: Radio figure from Radio Advertising Bureau, citing RADAR® research; television from Nielsen.

Further Information

See the sources listed above for additional information on radio use. A. C. Nielsen Company publications provide the most comprehensive information on television use. See also Units 671 and 681.

670
DISTRIBUTION OF
RADIO RECEIVERS

Interpretation of the Tables

As Table 670–A indicates, radio penetrated half of all U.S. households within a decade of its introduction. The number of homes with radio receivers increased despite the Depression and the construction freeze of World War II (during the war, those homes with more than one radio often loaned or sold their extra receivers to others). Only the number of car radios declined during the war years, and it was not until 1951 that half of the cars on the road were equipped with a radio.

Average radio receiver costs dropped steadily as demand lowered the unit costs. In addition, such technological breakthroughs as plastic cases (just before and after World War II), transistors, and printed circuits (in the late 1960s) helped to lower the costs of receivers.

As Table 670–A concentrates on AM radio only, Table 670–B provides what statistical information is available on FM radio sales and penetration. Prior to 1960, FM sales were very limited, exceeding two million units only once in the 1949–1959 period (in 1950, when sales were at the 2.2 million mark), and generally running well under one million (in the 1950s, this figure was exceeded only in 1950, 1951, and 1959). From 1954–1958, sets sold per year were well under half-a-million units. More detailed information is available since 1960 and is summarized here, but readers are cautioned (see text below) that these figures are generally rough estimates. Still, one can see FM's climb to near parity with AM availability by the early 1970s—another indication, along with number of stations, audience ratings, and advertiser interest, of FM's slow but sure coming of age.

Sources

Table 670–A is reprinted from Sterling and Kittross (1978) updated with the assistance of the Radio Advertising Bureau. All figures are estimates drawn from various original sources, including NBC (for the number of radio homes up to 1950); the Radio Advertising Bureau (for the number

Table 670-A   Number and Percentage of U.S. Households and Automobiles with AM Receivers, 1922-1981

Year[a]	Households with Radio Receivers	Percent of All U.S. Households	Average Factory Cost of Home Receivers (In Dollars)	Automobiles with Radio Receivers	Percent of All U.S. Automobiles
1922	60,000	0.2	$50	—	—
1923	400,000	1.5	N/A	—	—
1924	1,250,000	4.7	N/A	—	—
1925	2,750,000	10.1	83	—	—
1926	4,500,000	16.0	N/A	—	—
1927	6,750,000	23.6	N/A	—	—
1928	8,000,000	27.5	N/A	—	—
1929	10,250,000	34.6	N/A	—	—
1930	13,750,000	45.8	78	80,000	0.1
1931	16,700,000	55.2	N/A	100,000	0.4
1932	18,450,000	60.6	N/A	250,000	1.2
1933	19,250,000	62.5	N/A	500,000	2.4
1934	20,400,000	65.2	N/A	1,250,000	5.8
1935	21,456,000	67.3	55	2,000,000	8.9
1936	22,869,000	68.4	N/A	3,500,000	14.5
1937	24,500,000	74.0	N/A	5,000,000	19.7
1938	26,667,000	79.2	N/A	6,000,000	23.8
1939	27,500,000	79.9	N/A	6,500,000	24.9
1940	28,500,000	81.1	38	7,500,000	27.4
1941	29,300,000	81.5	N/A	8,750,000	29.6
1942	30,600,000	84.0	N/A	9,000,000	32.3
1943	30,800,000	83.6	N/A	8,000,000	30.9

1944	32,500,000	87.6	N/A	7,000,000	27.5
1945	33,100,000	88.0	40	6,000,000	23.4
1946	33,998,000	89.9	N/A	7,000,000	24.9
1947	35,900,000	93.1	N/A	9,000,000	29.3
1948	37,623,000	94.2	N/A	11,000,000	33.1
1949	39,300,000	94.8	N/A	14,000,000	38.6
1950	40,700,000	94.7	26	18,000,000	49.6
1951	41,900,000	95.5	N/A	21,000,000	52.3
1952	42,800,000	95.6	N/A	23,500,000	55.3
1953	44,800,000	98.2	N/A	25,000,000	57.3
1954	45,100,000	96.7	N/A	26,100,000	56.4
1955	45,900,000	96.4	20	29,000,000	60.0
1956	46,800,000	96.3	N/A	30,100,000	57.9
1957	47,600,000	96.2	N/A	35,000,000	64.6
1958	48,500,000	96.3	N/A	36,500,000	65.5
1959	49,450,000	96.7	N/A	37,200,000	65.7
1960	50,193,000	95.6	20	40,387,000	68.1
1961	50,695,000	95.3	N/A	42,616,000	69.5
1962	51,305,000	94.5	N/A	46,900,000	74.4
1963	52,300,000	94.9	N/A	49,948,000	75.9
1964	54,000,000	96.6	N/A	58,308,000	77.7
1965	55,200,000	98.6	10	56,871,000	79.1
1966	57,000,000	98.6	N/A	60,000,000	79.9
1967	57,500,000	98.6	N/A	64,500,000	83.0
1968	58,500,000	98.6	N/A	69,000,000	85.8
1969	60,600,000	98.6	N/A	73,500,000	89.3

Table 670-A Number and Percentage of U.S. Households and Automobiles with AM Receivers, 1922–1981 (cont.)

Year[a]	Households with Radio Receivers	Percent of All U.S. Households	Average Factory Cost of Home Receivers (In Dollars)	Automobiles with Radio Receivers	Percent of All U.S. Automobiles
1970	62,000,000	98.6	11	80,500,000	92.5
1971	62,600,000	98.6	N/A	85,400,000	94.8
1972	64,100,000	98.6	N/A	91,700,000	95.0
1973	67,400,000	98.6	N/A	92,700,000	95.0
1974	68,500,000	98.6	N/A	94,500,000	95.0
1975	70,400,000	98.6	N/A	100,400,000	95.0
1976	71,400,000	98.6	N/A	101,000,000	95.0
1977	72,900,000	98.6	N/A	104,000,000	95.0
1978	74,650,000	98.6	N/A	106,000,000	95.0
1979	76,478,000	98.6	N/A	110,000,000	95.0
1980	78,600,000	98.6	17	113,200,000	95.0
1981	80,500,000	98.6	N/A	115,000,000	95.0

Sources: See text. [a]Data as of January 1 of each year.

Table 670–B Factory Production of Household and Automobile FM Receivers, 1960–1982

Year	All FM Receivers[a]				Automobile FM Receivers	
	Sold (In Thousands)	Percent of Radios Sold	In Use (In Thousands)	Percent of FM Households	Sold (In Thousands)	Percent of Auto Radios Sold
1960	1,994	8	6,500	N/A	N/A	N/A
1961	2,598	9	9,000	N/A	N/A	N/A
1962	3,583	11	12,000	N/A	75	1
1963	4,780	N/A	17,000	N/A	200	3
1964	4,323	14	23,000	N/A	310	4
1965	6,337	15	30,000	N/A	636	6
1966	11,320	26	38,000	48	653	7
1967	12,592	31	50,000	57	941	10
1968	17,316	37	65,000	65	1,369	11
1969	22,582	44	80,000	70	1,677	14
1970	21,332	48	93,000	74	1,437	14
1971	22,807	48	108,000	80	2,614	19
1972	27,230	49	125,000	85	3,119	24
1973	24,024	48	145,000	89	3,545	28
1974	26,130	59	166,000	92	3,424	32

Table 670–B Factory Production of Household and Automobile FM Receivers, 1960–1982 (cont.)

Year	All FM Receivers[a]				Automobile FM Receivers	
	Sold (In Thousands)	Percent of Radios Sold	In Use (In Thousands)	Percent of FM Households	Sold (In Thousands)	Percent of Auto Radios Sold
1975	22,420	65	180,000	93	3,482	38
1976	26,273	60	190,000	94	6,182	50
1977	34,878	66	205,000	95	7,214	56
1978	32,047	67	N/A[b]	95	7,308	58
1979	27,446	69	N/A	95	6,943	56
1980	30,822	78	353,000[c]	95	8,892	78
1981	34,953	79	367,000	95	10,285	80
1982	36,874	84	N/A	N/A	10,424	85

Sources: All data except those for household penetration originated with the Electronic Industries Association, *Electronic Market Data Book 1983*, p. 26. Household-penetration figures through 1976 are from Pulse, Inc., and 1977–1982 estimate is from the Radio Advertising Bureau. Automobile receivers sold for 1962–1969 inclusive as reported in Sterling (1969), p. 788, using data from EIA. Second column (FM as a percent of all radios sold) figured by the author based on total radios sold, as reported in Table 660–A. Last column figured by the author using total auto radios sold, as reported in Table 660–A. Notes: [a]Includes automobile receivers. [b]No data available as RAB does not like giving estimates based on unverified data. [c]Data for 1980 and 1981 was supplied directly to the author by Kenneth Costa of RAB, based on a special survey done by RADAR®.

of radio homes since 1950, and for number and percent of cars with radios); and Lichty and Topping (1975) (for the average-cost data).

The percentages of U.S. automobiles with radios are based on U.S. Department of Transportation estimates for the number of cars in the United States compared with figures for car radio sales and scrappage. The Radio Advertising Bureau reports that 95 percent has been used as an arbitrary cut-off point for these percentages, since "there is no indication of ever reaching 100 percent."

Table 670–B is based almost totally on information from the Electronic Industries Association which provided estimates based on number of sets sold in the United States. By the 1970s, these were mostly imports (see Unit 760). As the rounded figures indicate, especially in the columns on FM receivers in use, these are very approximate figures. They should be taken only as indications of the facts. The column on the percent of FM households is based primarily on audience research information from Pulse, Inc., the only national source for this data. It is probably biased on the high side because it is an average of Pulse's research in urban areas. Adding in rural regions would probably bring down FM penetration in the late 1970s to the 80 percent area (at best). In all, FM data is simply not as consistent or reliable as the longer runs of AM data in the previous table.

Further Information

The standard source of information on broadcast receivers is the Electronic Industries Association and its annual volumes—*Electronic Market Data Book* and *Consumer Electronics*. Summary information from the EIA and other sources appears regularly in *Broadcasting Yearbook*, *Television Factbook*, and the weekly *Television Digest* section on consumer electronics.

671
CHARACTERISTICS/ PREFERENCES OF RADIO AUDIENCES

Interpretation of the Tables

The several tables of this Unit seek to describe the present day radio audience, based on data gathered from both special and regular ratings surveys. Table 671–A and 671–B analyze the characteristics and programming

Table 671-A Characteristics of the Radio Audience, by Hours of Daily Listening, 1947, 1968, and 1982 (In Percent)

Characteristics of Audience	Light Use of Radio			Moderate Use of Radio			Heavy Use of Radio		
	1947: Less than 1 hour	1968: Less than 2 hours	1982: Less than 1 hour	1947: 1 to 3 hours	1968: 2 to 4 hours	1982: 1 to 4 hours	1947: 3 or more hours	1968: 4 or more hours	1982: More than 4 hours
Sex									
Male	30	40	35	50	29	35	20	30	30
Female	20	28	36	49	31	34	31	40	30
Age									
18 to 24 years	—	—	21	—	—	34	—	—	45
21 to 29 years	20	—	—	48	—	—	32	—	—
Under 34 years	—	31	—	—	29	—	—	38	—
25 to 34 years	—	—	33	—	—	36	—	—	31
30 to 49 years	24	—	—	49	—	—	27	—	—
34 to 49 years	—	32	—	—	29	—	—	38	—
35 to 54 years	—	—	41	—	—	35	—	—	24
Over 50 years	27	39	—	45	30	—	28	31	—
Over 54 years	—	—	46	—	—	34	—	—	20
Community Population									
1,000,000 and more	24	33	N/A	48	31	N/A	28	35	N/A
50,000 to 1,000,000	22	30	N/A	48	33	N/A	30	37	N/A
2,500 to 50,000	26	40	N/A	52	27	N/A	22	33	N/A
Under 2,500	28	37	N/A	51	25	N/A	21	36	N/A
Education Level									
Grade School	N/A	41	40	N/A	27	32	N/A	32	28
High School	N/A	29	33	N/A	28	32	N/A	42	35
College	31	39	36	31	36	39	18	24	25
Race									
White	N/A	34	36	N/A	30	35	N/A	35	29
Black	N/A	30	40	N/A	24	32	N/A	46	28
Hispanic	N/A	N/A	13	N/A	N/A	38	N/A	N/A	49

Sources: 1947 data: Lazarsfeld and Kendall (1948), pp. 132–134. 1968 data: National Association of Broadcasters (1970), pp. 24–27. 1982 data: Browne, Bortz, and Coddington study for National Association of Broadcasters, September 1982.

**Table 671-B Radio Audience Attitudes and Preferences, 1947 and 1968
(In Percent)**

	1947	1968
Listeners' Attitudes/Complaints		
Have some complaints about radio commercials[a]	25	29
Responses to local news coverage		
Too much time	2	2
About right amount	67	63
Not enough	24	25
Don't know/Not sure	7	10
Responses to national news coverage:		
Too much time	3	4[b]
About right amount	65	67
Not enough	26	21
Don't know/Not sure	6	8
Responses to international news coverage:		
Too much time	16	—[b]
About right amount	59	—
Not enough	16	—
Don't know/Not sure	9	—
Listeners' Program Preferences		
Public Affairs		
News	74	87
Talks or Discussion on Public Issues	44	31
Interviews with Interesting People	—	30
Telephone Interviews	—	19
Entertainment		
Comedy	59	—
Popular and Dance Music	49	77
Classical Music	30	—
Country/Western Music	26	—
Religion	21	26
Quiz and Audience Participation	56	—
Drama	46	—
Mystery	41	—
Sports	33	33
Programs that give advice	—	21
Miscellaneous (farm/weather/drama)	—	5

Sources: 1947 data: Lazarsfeld and Kendall (1948), pp. 119, 123. 1968 data: National Association of Broadcasters (1970), pp. 10, 35, 49–50. Notes: The total sample in 1947 was 3,225; in 1968, 3,148. [a]These are aggregate figures which combine several specific categories of complaints about commercials. [b]The 1968 survey combined the categories of national and international news coverage.

Table 671-C Format Preferences of Radio Audiences, 1972–1980

Program Category	Average Audience Share Percentage (6 AM-Midnight, All Days)								
	1972	1973	1974	1975	1976	1977	1978	1979	1980
Contemporary:	19.2	19.0	19.5	19.3	19.5	22.8	18.1	—	—
Top 40	(19.2)	(19.0)	(19.5)	(19.3)	(19.5)	(19.9)	(14.1)	7.9	9.2
Disco	—	—	—	—	—	(1.5)	(2.6)	3.4	1.1
Mellow	—	—	—	—	—	(1.4)	(1.4)	1.5	1.4
Urban	—	—	—	—	—	—	—	—	3.5
Rock:	4.8	5.4	5.8	7.2	7.7	10.3	9.6	—	—
Progressive	(4.8)	(5.4)	(5.8)	(7.2)	(7.7)	(4.2)	(1.4)	0.5	0.1
Album-Oriented	—	—	—	—	—	(6.1)	(8.2)	9.9	12.5
Good Music	15.1	15.3	15.1	15.7	15.5	14.9	13.6	14.5	14.8
Big Band	—	—	—	—	—	—	—	—	0.6
Middle-of-the-Road	19.7	18.8	18.2	17.0	17.4	13.9	9.7	7.1	4.5
Adult Contemporary	—	—	—	—	—	—	12.0	19.3	20.4
Country	4.4	4.7	6.1	6.9	6.7	7.3	7.6	7.7	8.7
News	3.2	3.5	4.3	4.8	5.2	5.2	5.8	6.5	6.4
Black	4.8	5.0	5.2	5.6	5.0	4.4	4.5	5.3	2.7
Talk	5.6	4.7	4.2	3.5	3.3	2.9	3.0	2.5	4.0
Classical	1.8	1.5	1.5	1.6	1.4	1.3	1.3	1.3	1.7
Oldies	1.4	1.5	1.3	1.1	1.2	0.4	0.2	0.7	1.3
Spanish	—	—	—	—	—	1.6	1.6	1.7	2.0
Jazz	—	—	—	—	—	—	—	0.6	0.7
Other	20.0	20.6	18.8	17.3	17.1	15.0	13.0	9.6	4.4

Source: McGavren-Guild data as reported in *Broadcasting* (May 2, 1977), p. 51 for 1972–1973 data; *Broadcasting* (April 23, 1979), p. 56 for 1974–1978 data; and McGavren-Guild Radio, "Trends in Radio Format Study, (1976–1980). Top 25 Markets," for 1979–80. See text for details. For this table, figures in parentheses merely indicate sub-totals.

Table 671–D Format Preference of Male, Female, and Teenaged Radio Listeners, 1972, 1976, and 1980

Average Audience Share Percentage, 3–7 PM, Monday–Fridays only:

Program Category	Males			Females			Teens		
	1972	1976	1980	1972	1976	1980	1972	1976	1980
Top 40	14.1	14.8	6.2	13.8	16.4	6.8	44.3	45.0	21.6
Disco	—	—	.7	—	—	.8	—	—	2.5
Mellow/Soft	—	—	1.8	—	—	2.0	—	—	.7
Urban Contemporary	—	—	3.9	—	—	4.4	—	—	13.2
Progressive Rock	6.3	9.5	0.6	3.7	5.9	0.2	12.9	18.2	0.2
Album Oriented Rock	—	—	11.9	—	—	5.8	—	—	24.3
Good Music	15.5	15.9	13.1	19.6	19.4	17.0	3.5	1.8	1.8
Big Band	—	—	1.3	—	—	1.1	—	—	—
Middle-of-the-Road	17.7	14.4	4.2	17.5	13.9	4.2	5.7	4.8	.7
Adult Contemporary	—	—	17.3	—	—	21.8	—	—	18.3
Country	3.3	6.6	7.8	3.1	5.3	6.5	.7	1.8	2.6
News	7.6	9.8	11.1	5.6	7.6	8.3	.7	.7	.9
Black	3.8	4.2	2.1	4.6	5.2	2.5	10.8	10.5	5.4
Talk	6.7	4.3	3.9	6.4	4.0	4.0	1.6	.5	.6
Classical	2.2	1.6	2.1	2.1	1.7	1.8	.2	.2	.2
Oldies	1.9	2.7	.9	1.9	3.1	.8	1.7	2.7	.4
Spanish	—	—	.8	—	—	1.1	—	—	.5
Jazz	—	—	1.5	—	—	1.0	—	—	1.4
Other	20.9	16.2	8.6	21.7	17.8	9.9	17.8	13.8	4.7

Sources: Data drawn from same sources as Table 671–C (all McGavren Guild Radio information).

Table 671-E   Format Preference of Radio Listeners, by Age and Sex, 1977 and 1982 (In Percent)

Type of Programming	Age Groups								Sex Groups			
	Teens		18–49		(18–34 only)		50+		Males		Females	
	1977	1982	1977	1982	1977	1982	1977	1982	1977	1982	1977	1982
Rock/Contemporary	28	24	66	71	54	58	6	5	45	43	55	58
Album-oriented Rock	21	26	78	72	74	69	1	1	65	64	35	36
Adult Contemporary/Soft Rock	6	5	87	84	74	60	7	12	43	42	57	58
Middle-of-the-Road	3	2	50	42	23	16	47	57	45	43	55	57
Beautiful Music	1	1	46	40	19	15	53	59	42	40	58	60
Country	4	4	63	64	30	32	34	31	47	48	53	52
News/Talk	1	1	36	32	15	12	63	68	51	47	49	53
Black/Urban	28	19	66	72	50	56	6	9	42	44	58	56
Nostalgia	N/A	0.3	N/A	26	N/A	6	N/A	74	N/A	44	N/A	56
Religion	4	2	43	43	21	23	53	55	35	33	65	67
Spanish	4	3	66	60	35	33	29	37	32	39	68	61
Classical	2	1	59	59	26	26	40	40	53	48	47	52

Source: James Duncan, *American Radio* (Fall 1978), pp. 24 and 27; and (Spring 1982), p. A45, citing Arbitron data in both cases.

232   Electronic Media

Table 671-F Ranking and Average Weekly Cumulative Audience of Radio Networks, 1978 and 1982

Network	Average Quarter-Hour Audience		Rank		Average Weekly Cumulative Audience		Affiliates	
	1978	1982	1978	1982	1978	1982	1978	1982
ABC Information	1,747,000	1,929,000	2	1	25,211,000	28,631,000	491	567
NBC	1,729,000	1,625,000	3	2	30,068,000	30,731,000	268	370
ABC Entertainment	1,438,000	1,615,000	5	3	22,744,000	22,755,000	477	491
ABC Contemporary	2,089,000	1,603,000	1	4	31,452,000	25,826,000	397	377
The Source	N/A	1,510,000	N/A	5	N/A	20,197,000	N/A	N/A
CBS	1,410,000	1,509,000	6	6	27,227,000	29,729,000	278	425
Mutual	1,612,000	1,377,000	4	7	22,215,000	19,784,000	950	876
ABC–FM	1,322,000	1,254,000	7	8	17,177,000	14,879,000	196	196

Sources: Statistical Research, Inc. (Westfield, N.J.), 1978 figures, Fall 1978 RADAR® reports, as summarized in Broadcasting (March 5, 1979), p. 128; 1982 figures RADAR® 25 Spring 1982 Network Audiences to All Commercials. Notes: Number of affiliates shown is merely a guide (taken from Unit 171), as many stations will not "clear" all network broadcasts. Sample size for 1978 was 5,000; for 1982, 6,000. Incorporating Monday–Sunday, 6AM–Midnight, Persons 12+.

preferences of radio audiences in 1947, when network radio had reached its pre-television peak, in 1968, when radio had been transformed by the competition of television into a very different medium, and (for 671–A only) in 1982, when radio's diversity of formats had matured in both AM and FM radio. Table 671–A provides a profile of the radio audience at three widely-separated periods of time, comparing light, moderate, and heavy listeners by sex, age, population of home community, educational level, and race. Not all questions were asked in all surveys, and the surveys were conducted differently, with different questions and with different numbers of respondents—and so should be used carefully, more as indicators of overall trends than as specific final figures. Table 671–B compares listener attitudes toward programs, and finds similar patterns of preference despite the changes made in radio in that 20 year period. Unfortunately, the 1982 survey did not include comparable questions. Table 671–C demonstrates trends in audience preference for the most popular radio formats in the 1970s, in the largest markets. As radio formats have changed, so have the surveys, so some format names appear only toward the end of the decade. Note the steady appeal of "good music" formats, the steady if slow increase in country music preference, the many developing "rock" formats, and the decline of the once standard middle-of-the-road, or variety, format. Table 671–D takes the same information as 671–C, but provides, for three selected years, some trends in format preference by sex and for the teen-aged audience. As many of us as parents have suspected, the differences in preference are due far more to age than gender! Compare, for example, the rock formats, middle-of-the-road, and "good music" all of which break sharply on age lines. Table 671–E takes similar data one step further, and focuses more sharply on the age factor for two selected years, 1977 and 1982. The source, and thus the format terms, vary here, but the patterns are similar—age is the prime determinant of specific format preference. Finally, Table 671–F provides summary data for a five year period on the weekly cumulative audiences of the several radio networks. Radio network specialization was begun in 1968 when ABC created four format-specific services (see Unit 171).

Sources

The data in Table 671–A were drawn from Lazarsfeld and Kendall (1948), the second such special national survey done by academics rather than ratings firms, the National Association of Broadcasters (1970) in a survey prepared to fill in the hole left when A. C. Nielsen Co. stopped reporting national radio audience data, and Browne, Bortz, and Coddington (1982) in a study done for the NAB. Thus all results are based on national surveys, including interviews with 3,225 (1947), 3,148 (1968), and 1,500 (1982) individuals. The three studies involved many parallel questions. Given that the data for 1968 and 1982 were gathered for and reported by the NAB, an industry trade association, they should be used with caution. Table 671–B reports data from the same 1948 and 1970 sources as just discussed. Tables 671–C and 671–D are drawn from a series of annual format survey reports conducted by the McGavren Guild radio station representative firm. Based on questionnaires to some 500 stations in the top 25 markets, and drawing data from Arbitron ratings findings, the surveys achieved a 60% response rate. They should be considered accurate in showing broad trends, though doubtless there is a likely "swing" of several percentage points either way (not made clear in the source). Only commercial stations are included (thus, for example, talk and classical music formats are under-represented).

Table 671–E is based on Arbitron ratings information, as compiled and summarized by James Duncan in his twice-yearly compilation, *American Radio*. The percentage columns are of the total national mean audience, aged 12 and over, in metropolitan areas. Data is included for some 500 stations in 1978, and 600 in 1982. Table 671–F provides several types of data, most of it based on information from special ratings surveys of network listenership as cited in the Table footnote. RADAR® is a broadcasting and advertising industry cooperative venture to research the radio audience, which has conducted surveys since the late 1960s. In all of the tables of this Unit, save for information in the 1940s, AM and FM stations are considered together.

Further Information

For historical information on the development of radio research, see Lumley (1934), Lichty and Topping (1975), and Sterling and Kittross (1978). Current information is regularly reported in trade periodicals and in such special reports as the cited Browne, Bortz, and Coddington (1982). An excellent regular source of data are the reports on Arbitron data, the earliest of which are summarized in Duncan (1982).

680
DISTRIBUTION OF
TELEVISION RECEIVERS

Interpretation of the Tables

The rapid growth of television is particularly remarkable when one considers that television sets in the early years were no small investment for a household, especially with the extra charges for antennas and installation.

Table 680–A Households with Television Receivers, and Average Receiver Cost, 1946–1982

Year	Homes with Television Receivers	Percent of All U.S. Homes	Television Homes			Average Factory Cost of Receivers	
			Percent with Two or More Receivers	Percent with UHF Receivers	Percent with Color Receivers	Black and White	Color
1946	8,000	.02	—	—	—		
1947	14,000	.04	—	—	—	279	—
1948	172,000	.40	1	—	—		
1949	940,000	2.30	1	—	—		
1950	3,875,000	9.00	1	—	—	190	—
1951	10,320,000	23.50	2	—	—		
1952	15,300,000	34.20	2	—	—		
1953	20,400,000	44.70	3	—	—		
1954	26,000,000	55.70	3	—	—		
1955	30,700,000	64.50	3	—	.02	138	500[a]
1956	34,900,000	71.80	5	—	.05		
1957	38,900,000	78.60	6	9.2	.20		
1958	41,925,000	83.20	8	8.1	.40		
1959	43,950,000	85.90	10	8.0	.60		
1960	45,750,000	87.10	13	7.0	.70	132	392
1961	47,200,000	88.80	13	7.1	.90	125	381
1962	48,855,000	90.00	14	7.3	1.20	128	352

Year							
1963	50,300,000	91.30	16	9.6	1.90	118	346
1964	51,600,000	92.30	19	15.8	3.10	109	348
1965	52,700,000	92.60	22	27.5	5.30	106	356
1966	53,850,000	93.00	25	38.0	9.70	98	371
1967	55,130,000	93.60	28	47.5	16.30	92	362
1968	56,670,000	94.60	29	57.0	24.20	74	336
1969	58,250,000	95.00	33	66.0	32.00	78	328
1970	59,700,000	95.20	34	73.0	39.20	75	317
1971	61,600,000	95.50	36	80.0	45.10	81	324
1972	63,500,000	95.80	38	81.0	52.80	79	319
1973	65,600,000	96.00	41	86.0	60.10	77	308
1974	66,800,000	96.10	42	89.0	67.30	79	316
1975	68,500,000	97.10	43	91.0	70.80	84	341
1976	70,500,000	97.30	45	N/A	73.30	89	349
1977	71,500,000	97.90	47	92.0	76.00	89	350
1978	74,500,000	98.00	48	N/A	81.00	85	350
1979	76,300,000	98.00	50	N/A	83.00	84	360
1980	77,300,000	98.00	50	95.0	87.00	89	373
1981	82,500,000	98.00	50	96.0	89.00	83	377
1982	83,200,000	98.00	N/A	N/A	N/A	N/A	N/A

Sources: Sterling and Kittross (1978), p. 535 for data through 1977. See text for original sources. 1978 data from Nielsen Television Index, *Television Audience 1978*, p. 3 which reports data as of September. 1979–80 data supplied direct to the author from TV Digest, Inc. 1981 data from Arbitron *Fall '81 Census Book* (homes with television) and National Retail Merchants Association (average cost of receivers). 1982 data from Arbitron supplied direct to the author. Note: [a]estimate.

Yet, as Table 680–A reveals, more than half of all American households had at least one television set by 1954; and by 1969, the figure had risen to 95 percent. By 1970, one-third of the American households had two or more sets. Penetration by color television, with its far more expensive receivers, has been nearly as rapid.

Table 680–A also reveals that UHF made significant progress in reaching the American consumer only after Congress passed an all-channel receiver bill in 1962, with provisions for its enforcement after 1964. Not until the early 1970s did UHF penetration begin to approach national VHF levels—though in UHF markets, the penetration naturally took place at higher levels more rapidly. (The effect of these developments on the growth of UHF stations can be seen in Unit 180.)

In Table 680–B, the household penetration of television is broken down by region and size of county. Early television penetration levels were highest in the Northeast and in urban communities. Regional penetration levels evened out only after 1970, when the South and rural communities throughout the country began to approach the national averages.

Sources

The data in Table 680–A are estimates gathered by the author from a variety of sources. Data through 1977 are as reported in Sterling and Kittross (1978), p. 535. Original sources for the information, as reported there: "NBC Corporate Planning data as reprinted annually in *Television Factbook*, except for UHF penetration data which are from NBC Research, based, in turn, on studies by the Advertising Research Foundation (to 1968) and U.S. Census reports. Average set prices [factory cost] taken from *Television Digest* (17:27:9, 1977) for 1960–1976, inclusive, using Electronic Industries Association data. Estimates for earlier years from Lichty and Topping (1975), page 522, table 42, and from the author. Column on multiple sets is a compromise by the author due to extensive disagreement on this statistic between various original sources (which is why figures are rounded to nearest whole number). Through 1963, the figures are those of NBC Research as published in *Television Factbook*—data closely paralleled by other sources. After 1963, the figures are a compromise most closely following data supplied by the A. C. Nielsen Co. 1976 television household and color penetration data derived from estimates in Blair's 1977 *Statistical Trends in Broadcasting*. 1977 data supplied by *Television Factbook* staff. Color and UHF data generally from Nielsen fall survey of the previous year." Data since 1977

Table 680–B   Percentage of Homes with Television Receivers, by Region and County Size, 1950–1980

	1950	1955	1960	1965	1970	1975	1980
Region							
Northeast	24	80	92	96	96	98	98
East Central	8	72	90	96	97	98	99
West Central	7	60	87	95	96	98	98
South	2	46	79	90	94	97	98
Pacific	9	64	88	93	95	97	97
County Size[a]							
"A" counties	21	82	93	96	97	98	98
"B" counties	6	72	90	95	97	98	98
"C" and "D" counties	2	44	78	91	93	97	98

Sources: 1950–1970 data: Nielsen Television Index, A. C. Nielsen Company data, in Lichty and Topping (1975), p. 523, table 43. 1975 data: Nielsen Television Index, A. C. Nielsen Company (1976a), p. 8. 1980 data: direct from A. C. Nielsen, reporting data as of January 1, 1981. Note: [a]County-size categories from Nielsen Television Index, A. C. Nielsen Company (1976), p. 53: "A" counties: All counties in the 25 largest metropolitan areas. "B" counties: All counties not in "A" category with populations of over 150,000 or in metropolitan areas over 150,000. "C" counties: All counties not in "A" category with populations of over 35,000 or in metropolitan areas over 35,000. "D" counties: All other counties.

is from Nielsen and Arbitron, primarily, as noted in table footnote. But again, all of these figures are estimates based mainly on factory output, import, and sales data and related projections.

Table 680–B is all A. C. Nielsen Co. data as reprinted in a variety of sources (see table footnote). It is derived from regular ratings research. See table footnote for county size definitions.

Further Information

The Consumer Products Division of the Electronics Industry Association (EIA) is the primary source of information on the manufacture of television receivers. Two annual publications of the EIA, *Electronic Market Data Book* and *Consumer Electronics*, are useful sources. *Broadcasting Yearbook* and *Television Yearbook* are also useful general references, providing summary tables of data similar to those here. Regular updates on receiver manufacture, penetration, and price are found in *Television Digest*, and other trade weeklies.

681
CHARACTERISTICS/ PREFERENCES OF TELEVISION AUDIENCES

Interpretation of the Tables

Table 681–A presents various characteristics of television-owning households—household size, number of children under the age of 18, income and educational level, and urban or rural location—in relation to the average number of television-viewing hours per household per week. Throughout the 20-year period, from 1960 to 1980, the reader will note the generally increasing amounts of television viewing, especially in households with more children and with medium income and educational levels.

Table 681–B examines household uses of television, by the sex and age of viewers. Perhaps the most striking change which has taken place during the 25 year period (1955 through 1980) is the steady decline of children watching television. The general levels of television use have increased, however, and a much greater percentage of men are watching television prior to 8 PM. Prime-time patterns of television use have not varied significantly during these two decades.

Table 681–C reports findings on viewer attitudes from three national surveys done a decade apart (1960, 1970, and 1980), all with very similar questions and research design. The data suggest that television has lost some of its initial attraction for viewers. The proportion of TV viewers describing themselves as "super-fans" has declined in all age groups over the two decades with the single exception of a rise in 1980 for the oldest group of viewers. Likewise, 1980 shows small increases in viewing by women and grade-school educated viewers from the levels of 1970. Reaction to television advertising shows a consistent decline in acceptance—the 1980 data due in small part to the rapid dissemination of pay television (no advertising) alternatives in many markets. Note that concern about violence is about the same through the period, while concern over sex and bad language is sharply up. Audiences clearly perceive television as having an educational potential, though there is less perception of its baby-sitting role—and surprisingly little agreement with entertainment as a major advantage of television!

Table 681-A Average Weekly Hours of Television Use, by Household Size, and other Characteristics, 1960-1980

Characteristics of Audience	Average Viewing Hours per Week				
	1960	1965	1970	1975	1980
Household Size[c]					
1 to 2 members	33:01	32:50	36:31	37:26	39:25
3 to 4 members	39:20	45:13	49:03	50:36	54:30
5 or more members	49:49	52:09	59:03	56:46	63:59
Children under 18 years					
None	N/A	34:05	39:00	38:41	41:57
1 or more	N/A	49:08	55:46	53:12	60:04
Income Level					
$5,000 or less[a]	42:42	38:26	42:55	42:17	43:43
$5,000 to $15,000	44:36	44:27	45:35	48:03	50:28
$15,000 or more	41:12	40:44	43:20	46:52	51:40
Education Level[d]					
Grade School	N/A	41:14	48:14	46:53	52:13
High School	N/A	43:03	49:50	48:21	51:37
1 or more years of College	N/A	39:33	40:22	40:27	44:24
County Size[b]					
Urban ("A" and "B" counties)	41:14	42:17	46:54	45:41	48:37
Rural ("C" and "D" counties)	37:31	40:53	42:58	43:56	50:24
National Average Viewing Hours	40:02	41:52	45:41	45:07	49:14

Source: Data supplied to the author by A. C. Nielsen Co. All data is as of November of each year. Notes: [a]income levels changed in 1975 to $10,000 or less, $10,000-15,000, and $15,000 or more; [b]County-size categories are the same as given in footnote to Table 680–B; [c]Household size categories changed in 1980 to 1-2 members, 3 members, and 4 or more members; [d]Education level categories changed in 1980 to less than 4 years of high school, high school graduate, and 1 or more years of college.

Sources

Of all mass media audiences, the television audience—especially at the national network level (see Unit 682)—has probably received the most attention from researchers. But because most audience data are gathered in an effort either to sell advertising time to more advertisers at higher prices or to convince funding sources of the worth of public television (see Unit 683), such data are necessarily somewhat suspect.

The most reliable source for national data on the television audience is the A. C. Nielsen Company, which provided the information for Tables 681–A and 681–B, and which has been conducting national television program ratings since network television's beginnings in 1948. The precise figures in Table 681–A would suggest complete refinement, but all of the data in

Table 681–B Average Daily Television Use, by Sex and Age of Viewers, and Time of Day, 1955–1980 (In Percent)

Time of Day and Viewer Characteristics	1955	1960	1965	1970	1975	1980
Early Day (10 AM to 1 PM), Monday through Friday						
Households Using Television	16	21	19	22	21	22
Men	12	14	15	16	19	22
Women	53	59	55	59	60	59
Teenagers	4	4	5	4	6	5
Children	31	23	25	21	15	14
Afternoon (1 to 4 PM), Monday through Friday						
Households Using Television	17	21	25	28	27	29[b]
Men	14	18	16	16	17	20
Women	52	62	64	66	63	58
Teenagers	6	5	5	5	7	8
Children	28	15	15	13	13	14
Early Fringe (5 to 8 PM), Monday through Friday						
Households Using Television	42	48	42	52	52	47[c]
Men	19	23	26	28	30	31
Women	27	34	36	38	39	42
Teenagers	13	12	10	10	10	9
Children	41	31	28	24	21	18
Prime (8 to 11 PM), Monday through Sunday						
Households Using Television	62	61	59	62	61	64
Men	32	32	32	32	34	36
Women	39	42	42	42	42	44
Teenagers	11	10	10	11	11	9
Children	18	16	16	15	13	11
Late Fringe (11 PM to 1 AM), Monday through Sunday						
Households Using Television	N/A	30[a]	31[a]	28	29	32
Men	N/A	37	39	39	41	43
Women	N/A	49	50	49	45	47
Teenagers	N/A	6	7	8	9	8
Children	N/A	8	4	4	5	2
Average Hours of Use per Day	4:51	5:06	5:29	6:32	6:26	7:02

Source: Data supplied to the authors by Nielsen Television Index, A. C. Nielsen Company. Note: Data are as of November of each year. [a]11 PM to midnight only; [b]1:00 to 4:30 PM; [c]4:30 to 7:30 PM.

Table 681–C Surveys Measuring Selected Viewer Attitudes on Television, 1960, 1970, and 1980 (In Percent)

Viewer Attitudes	Steiner Study— 1960	Bower Study— 1970	Bower Study— 1980
Television Programming—			
Viewers who described themselves			
as "super-fans" of television:			
Sex			
Male	40	24	21
Female	41	31	35
Age			
18 to 19 years	44	25	17
20 to 29 years	33	29	22
30 to 39 years	39	24	21
40 to 49 years	38	23	14
50 to 59 years	44	27	21
60 years and older	50	33	38
Education Level			
Grade School	54	43	47
High School	42	28	26
College	20	15	11
Television Advertising:			
"Fair price to pay for entertainment"	75	70	62
"Most are too long"	63	65	67
"Some are very helpful"	58	54	48
"Some are more entertaining than program"	43	54	48
"Would prefer TV without ads"	43	48	57
"Ads are generally in poor taste and annoying"	40	43	49
"Would rather pay small amount to have TV			
without ads"	24	30	42
Television's Role with Children:			
Major Advantages:			
Education	65	80	76
Baby-sitting	28	16	12
Entertainment	19	22	18
Major Disadvantages:			
Violence/Horror	30	30	28
Crime/Gangsters	10	8	9
Sex/Bad Language	5	11	16
Smoking/Drinking	2	5	3
Adult Themes	2	9	3

Sources: Bower (1973), pp. 25, 84, 157, 161 which also cites data from Steiner (1963). 1980 data from Bower (1984).

this unit (and all data on media audiences gathered by the sample process) are actually merely estimates. Nielsen Company ratings are usually given a three percent (plus or minus) margin of error.

Table 681-C data are estimates based on three nationwide, personal-interview surveys of large stratified sample populations. Both the Steiner (1963) and the Bower (1973) studies were financially supported by the CBS network, and the Bower study was also published by a CBS subsidiary. However, the researchers, and CBS as well, emphasize that the network did not enter into the process or results of the surveys in any way. The 1980 Bower study, unpublished as this volume went to press, was supplied to the author by Bower, allowing a 20 year comparison. All three studies were designed to build on predecessors—so the two Bower studies contained many of the same questions and audience sub-group break-outs as Steiner specifically to allow direct comparison. All three were based on special national surveys, unconnected with ratings or other industry-related research.

Further Information

Madow et al. (1961) remains the most exhaustive analysis and bibliography on the methods of television program ratings systems. The major ratings firms also regularly revise their booklets describing their methodologies. Readers interested in this field should consult A. C. Nielsen Company's *Reference Supplement* and Arbitron's *Description of Methodology*. Both publications are available from the companies. The best textual summary of research into television's various impacts on its audience is Comstock et al. (1978).

682
PREFERENCES OF NETWORK TELEVISION AUDIENCES

Interpretation of the Tables

If there is one topic of information on which an overabundance of data exists, it is certainly network television audience ratings and related information. This Unit provides several measures of that long-running audience appeal—but readers should remember that on this subject, a whole book the size of this one could readily be assembled from the data held by A. C. Nielsen Co., since 1948 the prime (and for many years, only) tabulator of national television ratings.

Table 682-A provides one measure of assessing network program popularity by ranking the top 20 entertainment telecasts over a 23 year period (1960–early 1983). The order is determined by the average audience percentage—a measure of the television audience which both shows the "pulling power" of the program in question while controlling for the fact that television audiences have gotten larger in this period of time as more sets are purchased and the population increases. Thus, while many other programs in recent years have had larger actual audiences in terms of millions of viewers, the programs listed have pulled a higher percentage of the available audience. News, unsponsored, shorter than five minutes, and combined network presentations are excluded from the list. The final episode of the comedy series *M*A*S*H* early in 1983 pulled the largest audience to that point for any entertainment episode. The record, given the pace of change in television, would likely not stand for long. Note that most programs on the list were special presentations of extra length (number three-ranked *Dallas* is the highest-ranked exception—and that episode had been ballyhooed for months).

Table 682-B lists those network series which were major audience draws in the period 1960–1976. Each series episode included had achieved an audience "share" (proportion of all viewing households tuned to that program) of 30 percent or better, which is generally considered a very good showing, indeed. Since in recent years most programs produce 20–23 episodes per season, it is evident that some of the programs on this listing sustained high viewing levels for a number of years. Programs ranked one, five and six were westerns, all others were comedies of one sort or another. No program aired in the years since has maintained a 30 percent share for anything close to 24 episodes, according to A. C. Nielsen researchers in correspondence with the author.

Table 682-C lists the top 50 or so feature films shown on network television, some of them features and some made especially for television. Note that *The Wizard of Oz*, the 1939 classic, shows up seven times on this list, from its initial showing in 1956 up to 1965 (it is still shown at least annually). Several of the made-for-TV films became series, the movie being, in effect, the pilot program.

Finally, Table 682-D is a highly selective listing of audience information on major news events over the past two decades. Unlike the average audience percentages in previous tables of this Unit, however, this shows the percentage of *all* U.S. households viewing at least some of the event. Audience data combines all three networks—which typically provide pool coverage of this kind of event.

Preferences of Network T.V. Audiences   245

Table 682–A   Ranking of the Top-20 Network Television Entertainment Episodes, 1960–1983

Rank	Program Name	Telecast Date	Network	Duration Minutes	Average Audience (Percent)
1.	M*A*S*H Special (Last Episode)	Feb. 28, 1983	CBS	150	60.2
2.	Dallas ("Who Shot J.R.?")	Nov. 21, 1980	CBS	60	53.3
3.	Roots Part VIII	Jan. 30, 1977	ABC	115	51.1
4.	Super Bowl XVI Game	Jan. 24, 1982	CBS	213	49.1
5.	Super Bowl XVII Game	Jan. 30, 1983	NBC	204	48.6
6.	Gone With The Wind-Part 1 (Big Event-Part 1)	Nov. 7, 1976	NBC	179	47.7
7.	Gone With The Wind-Part 2 (NBC Mon. Mov.)	Nov. 8, 1976	NBC	119	47.4
8.	Super Bowl XII Game	Jan. 15, 1978	CBS	218	47.2
9.	Super Bowl XIII Game	Jan. 21, 1979	NBC	230	47.1
10.	Bob Hope Christmas Show	Jan. 15, 1970	NBC	90	46.6
11.	Super Bowl XIV Game	Jan. 20, 1980	CBS	178	46.3
12.	Roots Part VI	Jan. 28, 1977	ABC	120	45.9
12.	The Fugitive (Last Episode)	Aug. 29, 1967	ABC	60	45.9
14.	Roots Part V	Jan. 27, 1977	ABC	60	45.7
15.	Ed Sullivan (Beatles)	Feb. 9, 1964	CBS	60	45.3
16.	Bob Hope Christmas Show	Jan. 14, 1971	NBC	90	45.0
17.	Roots Part III	Jan. 25, 1977	ABC	60	44.8
18.	Super Bowl XI Game	Jan. 9, 1977	NBC	204	44.4
19.	Super Bowl XV Game	Jan. 25, 1981	NBC	220	44.4
20.	Super Bowl VI Game	Jan. 16, 1972	CBS	170	44.2

Source: A. C. Nielsen Co., *Nielsen Newscast*, No. 1, 1973.

Table 682–B   Ranking of the Top-12 Network Television Entertainment Series, 1960–1976

Ranking	Series	Number of Episodes with 30 Percent or More of Viewing Households	Number of Seasons Aired
1	Bonanza	143	13
2	All in the Family	108	7[a]
3	Beverly Hillbillies	75	9
4	Andy Griffith Show	53	8
5	Gunsmoke	52	15
6	Wagon Train	52	5
7	Candid Camera	34	7
8	Dick Van Dyke Show	33	5
9	Red Skelton Hour	31	11
10	The Lucy Show and Here's Lucy	30	12
11	Sanford and Son	25	5
12[b]	Bewitched	24	8

Source: Nielsen Television Index, A. C. Nielsen Company, *Television Audience 1976*, p. 71. Note: [a]Still on the air as of the 1978–1979 season. [b]Nielsen reports that no program has achieved a 30 percent share 24 times since 1976 (like the number 12-ranked show above)—see text.

Table 682–C Ranking of the Top 50 Motion Pictures Shown on Network Television, 1956–1982

Rank	Title	Network	Day	Date	Rating	Share
1.	Gone With The Wind-Part 1	NBC	Sun	11/ 7/76	47.7	65
2.	Gone With The Wind-Part 2	NBC	Mon	11/ 8/76	47.4	64
3.	Airport	ABC	Sun	11/11/73	42.3	63
	Love Story	ABC	Sun	10/ 1/72	42.3	62
5.	The Godfather-Part 2	NBC	Mon	11/18/74	39.4	57
6.	Jaws	ABC	Sun	11/ 4/79	39.1	57
7.	Poseidon Adventure	ABC	Sun	10/27/74	39.0	62
8.	True Grit	ABC	Sun	11/12/72	38.9	63
	The Birds	NBC	Sat	1/ 6/68	38.9	59
10.	Patton	ABC	Sun	11/19/72	38.5	65
11.	Bridge on the River Kwai	ABC	Sun	9/25/66	38.3	61
12.	Helter-Skelter-Part 2[a]	CBS	Fri	4/ 2/76	37.5	60
	Jeremiah Johnson	ABC	Sun	1/18/76	37.5	56
14.	Ben-Hur	CBS	Sun	2/14/71	37.1	56
	Rocky	CBS	Sun	2/ 4/79	37.1	53
16.	The Godfather-Part 1.	NBC	Sat	11/16/74	37.0	61
17.	Little Ladies Of The Night[a]	ABC	Sun	1/16/77	36.9	53
18.	Wizard of Oz (R)	CBS	Sun	12/13/59	36.5	58
19.	Wizard of Oz (R)	CBS	Sun	1/26/64	35.9	59
20.	Planet Of The Apes	CBS	Fri	9/14/73	35.2	60
	Helter Skelter-Part 1[a]	CBS	Thu	4/ 1/76	35.2	57
22.	Wizard Of Oz (R)	CBS	Sun	1/17/65	34.7	49
23.	Born Free	CBS	Sun	2/22/70	34.2	53
24.	Wizard Of Oz	CBS	Sat	11/ 3/56	33.9	53
25.	Sound Of Music	ABC	Sun	2/29/76	33.6	49
26.	The Waltons' Thanksgiving Story[a]	CBS	Thu	11/15/73	33.5	51
27.	Bonnie and Clyde	CBS	Thu	9/20/73	33.4	38
28.	Ten Commandments	ABC	Sun	2/18/73	33.2	54
	Night Stalker[a]	ABC	Tue	1/11/72	33.2	48
30.	The Longest Yard	ABC	Sun	9/25/77	33.1	53
	A Case Of Rape[a]	NBC	Wed	2/20/74	33.1	49
32.	Wizard of Oz (R)	CBS	Sun	12/ 9/62	33.0	55
	Dallas Cowboys Cheerleaders[a]	ABC	Sun	1/14/79	33.0	48
34.	Brian's Song[a]	ABC	Tue	11/30/71	32.9	48
35.	Wizard of Oz (R)	CBS	Sun	12/11/60	32.7	52
36.	Beneath The Planet Of The Apes	CBS	Fri	10/26/73	32.6	54
37.	Wizard Of Oz (R)	CBS	Sun	12/10/61	32.5	53
38.	Women In Chains[a]	ABC	Tue	1/24/72	32.3	48
	Cat On A Hot Tin Roof	CBS	Thu	9/28/67	32.3	50
40.	Jesus Of Nazareth-Part 1[a]	NBC	Sun	4/ 3/77	32.2	50
41.	Sky Terror	ABC	Sun	9/19 76	32.0	51
	Apple Dumpling Gang	NBC	Sun	11/14/76	32.0	47
43.	Butch Cassidy and The Sundance Kid	ABC	Sun	9/26/76	31.9	51
	The Sting	ABC	Sun	11/ 5/78	31.9	48
45.	Heidi[a]	NBC	Sun	11/17/68	31.8	47
	Smokey and the Bandit	NBC	Sun	11/25/79	31.8	44
47.	Oh, God!	CBS	Sun	11/25/79	31.7	45

Table 682–C   Ranking of the Top 50 Motion Pictures Shown on Network Television, 1956–1982 (cont.)

Rank	Title	Network	Day	Date	Rating	Share
	Guyana Tragedy: The Story Of Jim					
	Jones-Part 2[a]	CBS	Wed	4/16/80	31.7	50
	My Sweet Charlie[a]	NBC	Tue	1/20/70	31.7	48
50.	Airport 1975	NBC	Mon	9/20/76	31.6	46
	Feminist And The Fuzz[a]	ABC	Tue	1/26/71	31.6	46

Source: Variety, (September 29, 1982), p. 82. Notes: (R) indicates repeat; [a] Indicates made-for-TV movie.

Table 682–D   Selected Major Televised News Event Audiences, 1960–1980

Year	Selected News Event	Percent of All U.S. Households Viewing Event[a]	Average Hours of Viewing per Household
1960	Kennedy-Nixon Debates	89.8	4:00
1960	Kennedy-Nixon Election Returns	91.8	4:30
1961	Kennedy Inaugural	59.5	—
1962	John Glenn Orbital Mercury Flight	81.4	5:15
1963	Assassination of Kennedy	96.1	31:38
1964	Goldwater-Johnson Election Returns	90.6	2:51
1965	Gemini IV "Space Walk" Mission	92.1	4:47
1966	Congressional Election Returns	84.4	6:10
1967	Johnson State of the Union Address	59.6	—
1968	Democratic Convention	90.1	9:28
1969	Apollo 11 Moon-Landing Mission	93.9	15:35
1970	Abortive Apollo 13 Mission	90.2	—
1972	Democratic Convention	86.1	36:42
1974	Nixon Resignation Speech	60.3	0:09
1975	Apollo-Soyuz Orbital Flight	71.3	—
1976	Democratic Convention	88.5	27:16
1976	Ford-Carter Debates	90.0	5:45
1977	First Carter Fireside Chat	59.5	0:17
1980	Election Night	82.5	5:47

Sources: Lichty and Topping (1975), p. 524, table 46, citing Nielsen Television Index, A. C. Nielsen Company data. Data on Kennedy-Nixon debates in 1960 and the special news events in 1970, 1972, and 1975–1978 were added by the author from other Nielsen publications. 1980 data supplied direct to the author from A. C. Nielsen. Note: [a] Figures represent percentage of *all* U.S. households, rather than TV-households only.

Sources

All of this information was derived from A. C. Nielsen reports. Table 682–C came from *Variety*, and 682–D includes information from Lichty and Topping (1975), p. 524, with updating past 1970 from A. C. Nielsen to the author.

Further Information

The A. C. Nielsen Company is the chief source of network television audience information. Its annual publications, *Nielsen Television* and *Television Audience*, are the most readily available sources of data. Furthermore, anyone may write to the Nielsen Company and ask to be placed on its mailing list for the quarterly *Nielsen Newscast* bulletins. The substantial *Television Audience*, issued each September since 1960, is a summation of special reports and data from regular ratings "sweeps." For general ratings data, see Unit 681. Data on the audience for crisis news events and political coverage appear in Greenberg and Parker (1965) and Kraus and Davis (1976). For further data on political program viewing, see Unit 501. For general background, see Comstock et al. (1978).

683
CHARACTERISTICS/ PREFERENCES OF PUBLIC TELEVISION AUDIENCES

Interpretation of the Tables

Table 683–A traces the percentage and number of U.S. television households viewing public television programming during the 14-year period beginning in 1970, when consistent information on the national public television audience first became available through the Corporation for Public Broadcasting (CPB). The figures suggest a slowly growing audience for public television. In 1973, public television stations reached an estimated audience of about 78 percent of the nation's television households. By 1977, that estimate had grown to 87 percent.

Yet the number of public television telecasts seen per household, either during prime-time or total hours, still represents only a fraction of commercial television viewing. The cumulative ratings by program type reveal the greater popularity of children's and arts/humanities programming over science/medicine and public affairs programming (though it is worth noting the peaks which occurred in the viewing of public affairs programs during the presidential election years of 1972 and 1976).

Table 683-B provides the scattered information available on the characteristics of public television viewers—annual income, educational level, and occupational status—from 1973 through 1981. The data here suggest that the average public television viewer has a higher income, is better educated, ar⁻¹ belongs to a higher socioeconomic status group than the average commercial television viewer.

The author has not reported data on public *radio* audiences because: (1) the CPB has only recently begun to gather and analyze such information, and (2) the available data are currently restricted to CPB-qualified stations (representing only about 25 percent of all noncommercial AM/FM stations in operation).

Sources

Although data on public television are becoming more detailed and sophisticated, they still are limited in a number of ways: (1) They have been gathered for only a few years; (2) they are affected by ever-changing research approaches and definitions; and (3) they involve such small numbers of viewers. The average public television viewer would not even be counted in most commercial ratings. Indeed, in a single typical evening, commercial television viewers will watch the same number of shows as public television viewers watch during an entire week.

A. C. Nielsen Company research for the Public Broadcasting Service (PBS) and the Corporation for Public Broadcasting provided the information in Table 683-A. The information in Table 683-B comes from two different sources: A. C. Nielsen Company developed the 1973 and 1977–81 data, while the CPB Office of Communication Research provided the 1975 and 1976 data. The author does not know what differences in research methods may have been involved, though the data is again over four weeks.

Further Information

An early, classic study of the public (formerly, educational) television audience is Schramm, Lyle, and Pool (1963). More recent discussions of public (and instructional) television audience research appear in Chu and Schramm (1968, 1974), and Lyle (1975), both of which reprint statistical information from a variety of surveys, and Frank and Greenberg (1982). CPB is the consistent source for data done by either CPB itself or by other organizations, such as the A. C. Nielsen Company. The reader will find the CPB's *Status Report* (1973, 1977 and 1980) most useful. Carnegie Commission (1979) includes much audience data for both public radio and television in the late 1970s.

Table 683-A Households Viewing Public Television, and Cumulative Ratings by Program Type, 1970–1983

Year	Prime-Time Hours Only			Total Hours			Cumulative Ratings by Type (In Percent)			
	Percent PTV-Viewing Households	Number PTV-Viewing Households	Average Programs Per Household	Percent PTV-Viewing Households	Number PTV-Viewing Households	Average Programs Per Household	Children Programs	Arts/ Humanities	Science/ Medicine	Public Affairs
8 Weeks[a]										
1970	27.4	16,470	3.7	N/A	N/A	N/A	N/A	18.1	N/A	13.9
1971	30.2	18,750	4.9	N/A	N/A	N/A	N/A	24.5	N/A	12.7
1972	36.1	23,390	4.6	N/A	N/A	N/A	N/A	25.4	N/A	19.1
4 Weeks[b]										
1973	32.8	21,710	3.0	48.9	32,370	7.0	N/A	28.6	N/A	14.1
1974	30.2	20,820	3.2	48.7	33,360	7.5	N/A	22.4	N/A	12.8
1975	32.6	22,330	3.6	49.2	33,700	8.0	26.9	22.3	17.9	12.8
1976	35.5	24,710	4.1	55.2	38,420	9.9	26.1	26.1	10.8	19.2
1977	39.4	28,050	3.5	60.1	42,790	8.8	N/A	N/A	N/A	N/A
1978	44.0	32,080	3.4	63.2	46,070	9.2	N/A	N/A	N/A	N/A
1979	48.0	35,760	2.5	65.9	49,100	9.7	N/A	N/A	N/A	N/A
1980	50.5	38,530	2.2	68.2	52,040	9.4	N/A	N/A	N/A	N/A
1981	55.2	42,950	2.5	72.7	56,560	9.1	N/A	N/A	N/A	N/A
1982	54.1	44,090	N/A	73.2	59,660	N/A	N/A	N/A	N/A	N/A
1983	57.5	47,900	N/A	74.7	62,230	N/A	N/A	N/A	N/A	N/A

Source: Corporation for Public Broadcasting, reporting data of A. C. Nielsen. Note: Data periods covered: October–December 1970, October–November for 1971 and 1972, November for 1973 and 1974, with all later years as of March. [a]Data covers 8 weeks; [b]Data covers 4 weeks.

Table 683–B Households Viewing Public Television by Income, Education, and Occupation by Head of Household, 1973–1981 (In Percent)

Head of Household Characteristics	1973	1975	1976	1977	1978	1979	1980	1981
Income								
Under $10,000	33.5[a]	41.0	43.8	48.7	53:4	54.7	52.5	54.1
$10,000 to $15,000	43.9	54.7	51.4	62.2	63.8	65.2	68.8	69.1
Over $15,000	47.5	55.7	69.7	68.3	70.6	73.5	74.8	81.6
Education Level								
Less than High School	30.4	40.3	45.5	45.3	50.8	56.1	54.3	61.8
High School Graduate	36.1	49.3	53.8	62.5	63.3	65.2	68.6	72.4
One Year of College or more	48.3	56.4	64.0	68.3	72.1	72.4	76.6	78.5
Occupation								
Professional/Managerial	45.0	N/A	67.7	68.7	71.6	72.6	78.7	80.9
Clerical/Sales	N/A	N/A	53.8	57.7	69.2	69.2	65.9	77.0
Blue Collar (skilled or semi-skilled)	31.6	N/A	51.0	57.7	60.8	63.7	65.9	69.8
Other (not in labor force)	38.1	N/A	N/A	56.4	56.5	61.0	61.2	64.4

Source: Corporation for Public Broadcasting. All data is as of March except 1973 which is as of November. Note: [a]According to S. Young Lee of CPB, this figure could be as low as 30.4%.

684
DEVELOPMENT OF THE HOME VIDEO MARKET

Interpretation of the Table

A phenomenon of the past half decade has been the proliferation of consumer electronic products built around the home television receiver. Most important and having an increasing impact on over-the-air viewing patterns, is the home video cassette recorder (VCR), and its newer and less versatile relation, the home video disc recorder. Introduced in 1975, and touted as the first new home video product since the inception of cable television, VCR's were in nearly five million American homes by the start of 1983. Virtually all VCR's are imported.

Table 684–A provides the few time-series statistics available thus far on these products. Sony introduced the "Beta" standard of VCR and it initially dominated the market. The newer VHS system (they are mutually incompatible—tapes for one system can't be played on machines for the other), however, has moved in the 1980s to a commanding position in both the United States and Europe, where approximately 70% of all blank cassette sales are for VHS-system material. Initial expansion of the VCR market, it has been noted (see *Television Digest*, January 31, 1983), closely parallels the expansion years of color television. The year-to-year sales of VCRs in the 1978–82 period are quite closer to color set sales in 1961–65. From this fact, afficionados of VCRs suggest a massive boom is on the horizon, while other observers feel growth will be steady, but not massive. Projected developments include quarter-inch portables by the mid-1980s, compared to the half-inch standard of VCRs to date.

Videodiscs are newer and have grown at a rate far below expectations of their chief backers—mainly due to their inability to record in the home environment (one buys pre-recorded material for them). Likewise, large-screen projection television equipment (an idea dating at least to the 1920s, but a consumer product of importance only in the 1980s)—limited in consumer eyes by substantial prices, often ranging to $3,000 and more per unit.

Sources

All of the material in Table 684–A is from the Electronic Industries Association, and is based on manufacturer and importer reports to the association, as published in their *Electronic Market Data Book* annually. The

Table 684-A   Sales and Use of Home Video Equipment, 1978-1982

Year	Sales to Dealers (thousands of units)				
	Home Video Cassette Recorders	Home Video Disc Players	Home Color Video Cameras	Projection Television Receivers	VCRs in use
1978	402	N/A	N/A	N/A	200
1979	475	N/A	61	26	600
1980	805	N/A	114	57	1,200
1981	1,361	157	190	122	1,900
1982	2,035	223	296	117	4,500

Source: Electronic Industries Association, *Electronic Market Data Book 1983*, pp. 18-20, for data in first four columns; and EIA, *Consumer Electronics Annual Review 1983*, p. 6, for data in final column, citing information from *Television Factbook*.

data on VCRs in use is from EIA's *Consumer Electronics* citing estimates from *Television Factbook*. All of the figures should be taken to be estimates. Figures show unit sales to dealers, not retail sales.

Further Information

In addition to the Electronics Industries Association sources cited above, see *The Home Video and Cable Yearbook*, and weekly issues of *Television Digest* which includes detailed reporting of the consumer electronics scene, including regularly updated statistics.

695
PAY TELEVISION
SYSTEM AUDIENCES

Interpretation of the Table

A phenomenon of the past decade has been the development and rapid expansion of pay television systems (see Unit 195) audiences. While most pay programming by far is delivered by cable, other systems, chiefly MDS and subscription television (STV), have actively developed as well. Table 695-A summarizes the audience growth of these three services, providing the esti-

Table 695–A Growth of the Pay Television System Audience, 1973–1982

Year	Pay Cable Number (In Thousands)	Pay Cable Percent of Homes	STV Number (In Thousands)	STV Percent of Homes	MDS Number (In Thousands)	MDS Percent of Homes	Total Pay Subscribers Number (In Thousands)	Total Pay Subscribers Percent of TV Homes
1973	18	N/A	N/A	N/A	N/A	N/A	18	N/A
1974	67	N/A	N/A	N/A	N/A	N/A	67	N/A
1975	265	N/A	N/A	N/A	N/A	N/A	265	N/A
1976	766	11	N/A	N/A	28	21	794	1
1977	1,174	11	5	4	65	21	1,244	2
1978	2,352	15	59	4	91	20	2,502	3
1979	4,334	20	260	4	207	9	4,801	6
1980	7,231	25	520	4	352	4	8,103	10
1981	11,320	30	1,082	5	479	4	12,881	16
1982	17,605	39	1,747	6	570	3	19,922	24

Source: Paul Kagan Associates, "Census of Pay TV Population," *MDS Databook 1982*, p. 13. All data is as of June 30 except 1973 (March 30) and 1974 (May 15). Last column (far right) from Unit 680, with percentage calculated by the author. See text for details on "Percent of Homes" columns.

mated number of total subscribers to each, the percentage of homes reached by each, and the total pay subscriber number and penetration. As the figures suggest, the growth has been uneven, with pay cable growing far faster and larger than either of the over-the-air systems. By the early 1980s, about a quarter of all television homes received one or another kind of pay programming, usually pay cable (one or more tiers).

Sources

Paul Kagan Associates, a consulting and newsletter firm in California, is the chief repository of this information and the only consistent gatherer and reporter of such data. The figures are based on various national surveys taken by Kagan and reported in "Pay-TV Census" publications. Percent of homes data is based upon: number of cable homes for pay cable (thus, 39 percent of homes with cable also took pay cable in 1982, etc.); homes reached by STV, and homes reached by MDS. In other words, while the number of STV subscribers is up in the period shown, the number of stations on the air has increased, thus vastly increasing the potential homes "passed" by the STV signal. Thus the penetration goes up much more slowly than the raw number of STV subscribers would otherwise suggest. For MDS service, the number of subscribers is up and the percentage of homes has actually declined. This is because, as with STV, the number of operating MDS units has created a huge potential audience while the number of subscribers has gone up fairly slowly. Thus MDS, which reached a fifth of its possible audience (given the number of transmitters) in the mid-1970s, only reached 3 percent of a much larger audience by 1982.

Further Information

See Unit 195 for general sources.

SECTION SEVEN
INTERNATIONAL ASPECTS OF ELECTRONIC MEDIA

700
FOREIGN NEWS COVERAGE
BY NETWORK TELEVISION

Interpretation of the Tables

Although international news flow has only recently become of major interest to U.S. and foreign communications policymakers, communications scholars have been studying the subject for some time. The subject was clearly outlined as an international policy issue at least as early as 1953 (UNESCO, 1969), and its main issues were discussed by Schramm (1964). Over the past few years, policymakers, too, have begun to recognize international news flow as an important element in the general issue of North-South political and economic relations.

However, no organization has yet undertaken any comprehensive statistical measurement of the entire news flow situation. Instead, studies are being carried out on an ad hoc basis by individual researchers. The results of three such studies are presented in this Unit. For other useful studies in this field, the reader is referred to the "Further Information" section at the end of this Unit.

Table 700-A covers the distribution of international news stories on American television evening news programs. This table lists 50 nations and the number and percentage of television news stories that refer to each of the countries. The data were gathered in a random sample of network evening news broadcasts during the 1972–1981 period.

A thorough analysis of this information would require much time and attention, but several overall characteristics of this table can be noted. First, the countries receiving the most attention on U.S. television news shows are almost identical for all three networks. Second, while all of the news stories in this analysis are international in character—that is, the stories include the mention of at least one foreign country or international organization—the United States is also mentioned in nearly 60 percent of the stories. Third, it is clear that a few countries are mentioned much more often than the rest. In fact, only about 15 of the more than 200 countries and territories in the world are mentioned in more than 2 percent of all the international news stories sampled.

Tables 700–B and 700–C apply the same source material, over the same period of years, to provide some summary results on the actual amount of foreign news time on the networks (it's rising), and the subject matter of that foreign news, regardless of countries covered. Note the decline in military and defense stories with the end of American involvement in Vietnam, and the rise of a general foreign relations category.

Sources

The information in Table 700–A was initially collected by Larson (1978) as part of a doctoral dissertation completed at Stanford's Institute for Communication Research. The source of these data were the abstracts of evening network news shows contained in the *Television News Index and Abstracts*, published by the Vanderbilt Television News Archive. The researcher's method of coding began with a decision as to whether a story was "national" or "international." Stories that mentioned international organizations or countries and territories other than the United States were coded as "international" and are the only news stories counted for this table.

To determine the reliability of the *Television News Index and Abstracts*, the researcher compared audio tapes of a random sample of television newscasts with the abstracts of these newscasts. This test verified that the abstracts were a reliable measure of international news coverage. The author therefore regards the data presented in Table 700–A as valid and reliable, but he also urges the reader to consult the original source, since space does not permit a detailed explication of the coding methods involved in the Larson study.

The data in Tables 700–B and 700–C are taken from an unpublished conference paper by Weaver, Porter, and Evans (1982), citing for the 1972–1976 data, an earlier study by Hester (1978). These studies, and tables, are also based on the *Television News Index and Abstracts*, using a sampling technique of one day per month, randomly selected, resulting in a sample of about 180 newscasts for each period (1972–1976, and 1977–1981). Normal content analysis coding techniques were applied, the 1977–1981 study being a replication of the method applied by Hester for the 1972–1976 period.

Further Information

The standard history of world news gathering and reporting is the multi-volume work by Desmond (1978, 1980, 1982, and 1984). See also the works by Read (1976), Schiller (1971, 1976), and Tunstall (1977). Two useful

Table 700-A Network Television Evening News Coverage of Events in 50 Countries, 1972–1981

Rank Nation	1972 Percent	1973 Percent	1974 Percent	1975 Percent	1976 Percent	1977 Percent	1978 Percent	1979 Percent	1980 Percent	1981 Percent	Total Percent	N
ABC-TV News N=	268	207	156	247	209	229	235	238	287	301	—	2377
1. United States	63.8	62.8	51.9	61.9	52.2	60.3	64.7	60.5	53.3	41.2	57.0	1355
2. U.S.S.R.	13.4	8.7	21.8	16.2	18.7	16.2	23.0	13.9	21.3	15.3	16.7	398
3. Israel	9.0	17.9	18.0	15.4	7.7	17.5	21.7	16.0	9.4	13.6	14.3	340
4. Britain	7.5	7.7	7.7	7.7	10.5	13.5	14.5	9.7	5.9	13.3	9.8	234
5. South Vietnam	40.3	20.8	5.1	17.4	5.7	—	—	—	35.9	—	9.1	215
6. Iran	1.0	1.0	—	0.8	0.5	—	0.9	27.7	5.6	9.3	8.7	206
7. Egypt	1.1	7.7	9.0	10.1	1.4	9.6	14.0	12.2	1.7	7.6	7.7	184
8. North Vietnam[a]	30.2	15.5	0.6	3.2	0.5	6.1	4.3	8.0	3.5	2.3	7.5	178
9. France	11.2	7.3	5.1	3.6	6.2	9.6	6.4	4.6	4.5	4.7	6.2	147
10. China (P.R.C.)	11.6	4.4	3.2	4.5	8.6	2.2	3.4	8.4	1.1	2.3	5.3	127
11. Lebanon	1.9	2.4	3.9	5.3	12.9	4.4	6.4	0.8	4.2	4.3	4.2	99
12. West Germany	5.2	2.4	1.3	1.6	1.9	9.2	4.7	3.4	4.2	5.7	4.1	98
13. Japan	4.9	7.3	3.9	1.2	5.7	4.4	3.0	5.5	3.5	2.7	4.1	97
14. Syria	1.5	5.8	10.3	4.5	4.8	4.4	1.7	0.4	1.4	3.7	3.5	83
15. Cuba	0.8	1.0	1.3	1.2	6.7	4.8	3.8	5.5	3.1	3.3	3.2	75
16. Poland	1.5	0.5	—	—	0.5	—	1.7	0.8	6.6	14.0	3.1	73
17. Saudi Arabia	—	3.4	1.9	1.6	1.9	3.5	2.1	4.2	1.1	8.0	2.9	68
18. Italy	1.1	1.5	1.9	1.6	4.3	4.4	5.1	4.2	1.7	2.7	2.8	67
18. Cambodia (Kampuchea)	1.5	13.5	1.9	6.9	0.5	0.9	0.4	4.2	—	0.3	2.8	67
19. Afghanistan	—	—	—	—	0.5	—	—	2.1	15.3	1.3	2.3	54
20. Rhodesia (Zimbabwe)	—	—	—	—	4.8	3.9	6.0	4.2	2.4	1.0	2.2	53
21. South Africa	—	—	—	0.4	6.7	8.3	2.1	1.7	0.4	2.3	2.2	51

Table 700–A   Network Television Evening News Coverage of Events in 50 Countries, 1972–1981 (cont.)

		1972	1973	1974	1975	1976	1977	1978	1979	1980	1981	Total	
Rank	Nation	Percent	Percent	Percent	Percent	Percent	Percent	Percent	Percent	Percent	Percent	Percent	N
22.	Northern Ireland	4.1	2.4	3.2	1.2	2.9	—	—	2.1	0.7	4.0	2.1	49
23.	Canada	0.4	1.9	3.2	1.2	3.8	3.1	2.6	—	2.1	1.3	1.9	44
24.	Iraq	0.4	1.0	—	0.4	1.4	0.4	0.4	1.7	5.9	4.3	1.8	43
25.	Turkey	—	—	10.9	2.4	1.9	—	1.3	1.7	0.4	1.0	1.6	38
25.	Jordan	0.8	—	1.9	2.8	0.5	4.4	3.0	2.5	0.4	0.3	1.6	38
26.	Switzerland	0.4	0.5	1.3	1.2	1.4	4.8	1.3	2.5	0.7	0.7	1.4	34
26.	Libya	—	1.9	0.6	—	1.4	0.9	—	0.8	3.5	4.0	1.4	34
27.	Mexico	0.8	0.5	1.9	—	2.9	0.9	0.9	3.8	1.1	1.3	1.4	32
28.	South Korea	2.2	—	—	1.2	1.0	5.2	1.7	0.4	0.4	0.7	1.3	31
29.	India	1.9	1.0	1.3	1.6	—	3.5	0.9	0.4	1.7	0.3	1.3	30
30.	Spain	0.8	—	1.3	2.4	2.4	3.1	0.4	0.4	0.4	1.0	1.2	28
30.	Pakistan	1.9	0.5	0.6	—	0.5	0.9	—	1.3	2.4	2.7	1.2	28
30.	Panama	—	0.5	—	—	—	3.1	4.3	1.3	2.1	0.3	1.2	28
31.	Cyprus	—	0.5	10.3	1.6	0.5	—	1.7	—	—	—	1.1	26
31.	Greece	—	1.9	6.4	1.2	1.4	1.3	—	—	0.7	0.3	1.1	26
32.	The Philippines	2.6	1.5	1.3	1.6	1.4	—	—	1.3	0.4	0.3	1.0	24
33.	Thailand	0.8	0.5	—	2.4	2.4	0.4	—	3.4	—	—	1.0	23
33.	The Vatican	0.4	—	—	0.8	—	—	3.4	0.4	1.7	2.0	1.0	23
34.	The Netherlands	—	0.5	1.3	2.8	1.0	1.8	0.9	—	—	1.3	0.9	22
34.	Algeria	—	1.5	1.3	0.4	—	0.4	—	0.8	4.2	0.3	0.9	22
34.	Angola	—	—	—	0.8	6.7	0.9	0.9	—	—	0.7	0.9	22
34.	Laos	1.1	4.4	1.3	2.0	0.5	—	0.5	0.4	—	—	0.9	22
34.	Uganda	—	—	—	1.6	2.4	3.5	0.4	1.7	—	—	0.9	22
35.	Portugal	—	—	1.9	4.9	1.0	0.9	—	0.4	—	—	0.8	20
36.	Austria	0.4	—	0.6	1.6	0.5	0.9	1.3	1.3	1.4	—	0.8	19
37.	Argentina	—	1.0	1.3	2.4	2.4	0.4	0.9	—	—	—	0.8	18
38.	Nicaragua	0.4	0.5	—	—	—	—	2.6	1.7	0.7	0.7	0.7	16

38. Chile	0.4	1.0	1.3	0.9	1.0	0.4	1.3	0.4	0.4	0.3	0.7	16
38. Sweden	1.1	0.5	0.6	0.8	1.4	0.9	0.9	—	—	0.7	0.7	16
38. East Germany	0.4	1.0	0.6	—	0.5	0.4	0.4	0.8	1.7	0.7	0.7	16
CBS-TV News N =	240	195	195	263	240	238	239	278	276	227	—	2391
1. United States	72.5	65.6	54.9	61.6	52.9	63.5	67.0	60.8	56.2	49.8	60.5	1446
2. U.S.S.R.	17.5	11.3	19.0	15.6	14.6	13.9	26.8	13.3	20.3	18.1	17.1	408
3. Israel	4.2	16.9	14.9	10.3	10.0	18.5	16.3	15.8	14.5	13.2	13.4	320
4. Britain	7.5	7.7	15.9	9.9	12.9	8.8	8.8	7.9	9.1	11.5	9.9	236
5. South Vietnam	40.0	22.1	2.6	19.8	4.6	—	—	—	—	—	8.7	207
6. Iran	1.7	1.0	2.6	0.8	0.8	0.4	2.5	27.3	29.4	10.1	8.5	202
7. Egypt	1.7	8.7	5.6	4.6	4.6	9.7	13.8	14.0	6.2	7.1	7.7	183
8. France	12.9	9.7	8.2	5.3	7.5	11.3	4.6	4.7	2.2	7.5	7.2	172
9. North Vietnam[a]	28.8	15.4	—	2.7	0.4	5.9	5.4	9.0	1.5	3.1	7.1	170
10. China (P.R.C.)	8.8	2.6	3.6	4.2	7.1	1.7	4.6	7.2	3.6	2.2	4.6	111
11. West Germany	3.3	5.1	5.1	4.2	4.6	8.4	5.0	2.5	2.5	3.5	4.4	104
12. Lebanon	0.8	2.1	2.6	4.9	13.3	3.8	4.2	1.8	1.5	4.0	3.9	93
13. Saudi Arabia	—	2.1	2.6	1.9	3.3	3.4	3.8	4.7	2.5	10.6	3.5	83
13. Syria	—	6.2	7.7	2.3	7.1	5.0	3.4	1.4	1.1	2.6	3.5	83
14. Japan	3.8	5.1	4.1	2.7	3.3	2.5	2.5	4.3	4.0	2.2	3.4	82
15. Cuba	1.3	1.5	1.5	1.9	2.5	5.0	4.6	3.6	5.4	4.0	3.2	77
16. Cambodia (Kampuchea)	2.9	13.9	1.0	8.4	—	0.8	0.8	2.9	1.1	—	3.1	73
17. Poland	0.8	1.0	—	0.8	0.8	0.4	1.7	1.8	6.9	14.1	2.9	69
18. South Africa	—	—	1.0	1.5	7.9	7.1	3.4	2.9	1.1	1.8	2.7	65
19. Canada	1.7	1.0	2.1	1.1	3.3	3.8	3.8	2.5	2.5	3.5	2.6	61
19. Switzerland	1.7	1.0	3.1	1.9	2.9	8.0	2.5	2.9	1.1	0.4	2.6	61
20. Italy	0.8	1.0	2.6	3.0	2.5	4.2	4.6	1.8	1.5	1.3	2.3	56
21. Rhodesia (Zimbabwe)	0.4	—	—	—	5.4	4.2	5.9	3.6	1.8	—	2.2	53
22. South Korea	0.8	1.0	1.0	2.7	2.1	6.7	3.4	0.7	0.4	0.4	1.9	46

Table 700–A Network Television Evening News Coverage of Events in 50 Countries, 1972–1981 (cont.)

Rank	Nation	1972 Percent	1973 Percent	1974 Percent	1975 Percent	1976 Percent	1977 Percent	1978 Percent	1979 Percent	1980 Percent	1981 Percent	Total Percent	N
23.	Mexico	1.3	—	0.5	0.8	2.9	2.5	1.3	3.6	1.5	4.0	1.9	45
24.	Jordan	0.8	1.5	2.6	1.1	0.8	5.5	2.9	1.4	0.7	1.3	1.8	44
25.	Libya	—	2.6	0.5	0.4	1.3	0.8	0.4	1.8	3.6	5.7	1.7	41
26.	Northern Ireland	3.3	1.0	3.6	0.4	2.5	0.8	—	0.7	0.4	3.5	1.6	37
26.	Spain	1.7	0.5	0.5	2.3	3.8	2.9	0.4	1.8	0.7	0.4	1.6	37
27.	Turkey	—	—	6.2	1.9	2.5	0.4	2.1	1.1	0.7	0.4	1.5	35
28.	Panama	—	0.5	—	—	1.7	2.9	5.0	0.7	2.9	—	1.4	34
29.	Afghanistan	—	—	—	—	—	—	—	0.7	9.8	1.8	1.4	33
30.	Iraq	—	1.0	1.0	0.4	2.1	0.4	0.8	1.8	2.2	3.1	1.3	31
30.	Greece	—	1.0	4.6	1.9	1.3	1.3	2.1	0.4	0.8	0.4	1.3	31
31.	India	1.7	—	1.0	0.8	0.8	1.3	2.5	0.4	2.2	0.4	1.1	27
32.	Portugal	—	—	2.6	5.7	2.5	—	—	—	—	—	1.1	26
33.	Cyprus	—	—	7.7	0.8	—	—	2.5	0.4	—	—	1.0	24
33.	Sweden	1.3	1.0	2.1	0.4	1.3	—	0.8	0.7	1.8	0.9	1.0	24
34.	Thailand	1.7	1.0	0.5	2.3	—	0.4	0.4	2.9	—	—	1.0	23
34.	Chile	1.3	4.1	0.5	1.1	0.4	0.8	1.3	—	0.7	—	1.0	23
35.	Angola	—	—	—	1.5	5.0	0.4	1.7	—	—	—	0.9	21
35.	Algeria	0.4	1.5	0.5	1.1	1.3	0.4	—	1.1	2.2	—	0.9	21
35.	Pakistan	0.8	—	0.5	0.8	—	—	—	1.1	2.9	2.2	0.9	21
35.	Uganda	—	—	—	1.5	1.3	2.5	0.8	1.4	0.4	0.4	0.9	21
35.	The Vatican	—	—	0.5	0.4	—	—	2.9	1.1	1.1	2.6	0.9	21
35.	Yugoslavia	0.4	—	—	0.8	1.7	0.8	2.1	0.4	1.8	0.4	0.9	21
36.	The Philippines	1.3	3.1	—	1.9	0.8	0.8	—	0.7	—	—	0.8	20
37.	Argentina	—	1.5	1.5	2.3	0.8	0.8	0.4	—	0.7	—	0.8	19
37.	The Netherlands	—	1.0	1.0	0.8	2.1	1.7	—	0.7	0.7	—	0.8	19
38.	El Salvador	—	—	—	—	—	0.4	—	1.4	1.1	4.4	0.8	18
38.	East Germany	0.4	0.5	1.0	0.4	0.4	1.3	0.8	0.4	1.1	1.3	0.8	18

NBC-TV News	N = 259	209	202	239	179	199	257	261	234	247	—	2286
1. United States	65.6	64.6	49.5	59.4	53.1	68.8	56.0	59.0	58.6	52.2	58.8	1343
2. U.S.S.R.	13.9	10.1	20.3	13.4	13.4	15.1	19.5	14.6	23.5	17.8	16.2	371
3. Israel	4.3	17.2	17.8	11.7	7.3	16.1	20.2	16.1	13.3	11.7	13.6	310
4. South Vietnam	40.9	21.1	2.5	16.3	—	—	—	—	—	—	9.0	205
5. Britain	7.0	5.7	12.9	6.7	11.2	13.6	7.0	4.6	6.4	14.6	8.8	200
6. Egypt	2.7	9.1	6.9	10.0	3.9	5.0	13.2	13.0	5.1	8.9	8.0	183
7. North Vietnam[a]	31.3	14.4	—	5.4	—	6.0	3.9	8.8	2.1	1.6	7.8	178
8. Iran	1.2	1.4	0.5	0.4	2.2	1.5	1.6	23.8	30.3	6.9	7.4	169
9. France	13.9	8.6	6.9	4.6	6.7	6.5	5.8	3.8	2.6	3.6	6.3	144
10. China (P.R.C.)	8.1	3.4	4.0	3.4	7.8	1.0	3.9	9.2	3.0	2.0	4.6	106
11. West Germany	3.9	3.8	3.5	3.4	5.6	5.5	5.5	2.7	2.6	4.1	4.0	91
12. Saudi Arabia	—	3.4	4.0	1.7	0.6	3.5	4.3	4.6	1.7	8.5	3.3	75
13. Syria	1.2	5.3	10.4	3.4	5.0	2.5	2.3	0.8	1.3	2.4	3.2	74
14. Cuba	1.9	1.0	1.5	2.5	5.0	3.5	3.9	3.5	6.0	3.2	3.2	73
15. Japan	4.6	4.8	5.0	1.7	2.8	2.5	1.2	1.9	3.0	4.5	3.2	72
16. Italy	1.2	1.4	2.0	2.9	2.8	4.0	6.2	3.5	3.0	3.6	3.1	71
17. Poland	1.5	1.9	—	0.8	1.1	0.5	2.0	0.8	6.4	13.8	3.0	69
17. Lebanon	0.1	1.9	5.0	4.6	10.6	1.0	3.9	1.2	1.7	1.6	3.0	69
18. Cambodia (Kampuchea)	3.1	14.8	0.5	6.7	—	0.5	0.8	3.1	—	0.4	3.0	68
19. Canada	1.2	1.9	1.5	1.7	3.4	3.5	3.1	2.3	3.9	1.2	2.3	53
20. South Korea	1.5	1.0	0.5	2.5	1.7	5.5	3.5	2.3	1.3	0.8	2.1	47
21. Mexico	0.4	0.5	1.0	0.4	1.7	3.5	2.7	3.1	1.3	2.8	1.8	40
22. South Africa	0.4	—	—	—	6.7	6.0	2.0	2.3	0.4	0.8	1.7	39
23. Afghanistan	—	—	—	—	—	—	0.4	1.2	12.0	1.2	1.5	35
23. Northern Ireland	4.6	2.4	2.5	0.8	0.6	3.5	—	—	0.9	3.2	1.5	35
24. Switzerland	0.8	0.5	3.5	1.7	1.1	0.5	0.8	2.3	0.4	0.4	1.4	33
24. Thailand	1.5	1.9	0.5	4.2	1.7	—	—	3.8	—	—	1.4	33
25. Rhodesia (Zimbabwe)	—	—	—	—	4.5	1.5	3.5	3.1	0.9	—	1.3	30

Table 700-A   Network Television Evening News Coverage of Events in 50 Countries, 1972–1981 (cont.)

		1972	1973	1974	1975	1976	1977	1978	1979	1980	1981	Total	
Rank	Nation	Percent	Percent	Percent	Percent	Percent	Percent	Percent	Percent	Percent	Percent	Percent	N
25.	Greece	—	1.0	6.9	1.3	1.7	1.5	0.8	—	0.4	0.8	1.3	30
25.	Spain	—	0.5	1.5	2.9	3.9	3.0	—	1.5	—	0.8	1.3	30
26.	Libya	—	1.9	0.5	—	0.6	—	0.4	1.9	5.6	1.6	1.3	29
26.	Jordan	0.4	1.0	3.5	1.3	0.6	2.0	1.6	1.9	0.4	0.4	1.3	29
27.	Turkey	—	—	6.4	1.3	2.8	—	1.6	0.4	0.4	0.4	1.2	28
27.	Iraq	0.8	—	0.5	—	0.6	—	1.2	2.3	2.6	3.6	1.2	28
25.	India	2.7	0.5	0.5	1.3	—	2.0	1.6	0.4	1.3	0.4	1.1	25
26.	The Vatican	0.4	—	0.5	0.8	—	—	3.1	1.2	0.9	2.8	1.1	24
27.	Portugal	—	—	1.5	5.4	2.2	—	0.4	—	0.4	—	1.0	22
27.	Laos	1.9	3.8	0.5	1.7	—	—	0.4	1.2	—	—	1.0	22
28.	Cyprus	0.4	—	7.4	—	—	—	2.0	—	—	—	0.9	21
29.	Uganda	0.8	—	—	1.3	1.7	3.5	0.8	1.2	—	—	0.9	20
30.	Pakistan	2.3	—	0.5	—	—	—	0.4	1.2	1.3	2.0	0.8	19
30.	East Germany	—	0.5	0.5	—	0.6	1.0	0.8	1.2	1.7	2.0	0.8	19
30.	Belgium	1.5	—	1.0	1.7	1.1	1.0	0.8	—	0.9	0.4	0.8	19
31.	The Philippines	1.5	2.9	—	1.3	1.1	0.5	0.8	—	—	—	0.8	18
31.	Taiwan	2.7	—	—	0.4	—	—	1.6	1.5	0.9	—	0.8	18
31.	Angola	—	—	—	1.7	5.6	1.0	0.8	—	—	—	0.8	18
31.	Chile	2.3	1.0	2.5	0.4	0.6	0.5	0.4	—	0.4	—	0.8	18
32.	The Netherlands	0.8	1.4	1.5	1.3	0.6	2.5	—	—	—	—	0.7	17
32.	El Salvador	—	—	—	—	—	—	—	0.4	1.7	4.9	0.7	17
32.	Panama	—	—	—	—	1.1	2.0	3.1	—	0.9	0.4	0.7	17
33.	Algeria	0.4	1.0	1.0	—	0.6	0.5	—	1.2	2.1	0.4	0.7	16

Source: James Larson, University of Texas–Austin, unpublished manuscript data provided directly to the author. Note: [a] For 1977–1981, all references to Vietnam are coded as North Vietnam, and are entered as such on the table, even if stories originate in what was once South Vietnam.

Table 700–B   Foreign News as a Percentage of Total Evening Network Newscast Time, 1972–1981

Network	1972	1973	1974	1975	1976	1977	1978	1979	1980	1981	Ten-Year Average
ABC	21.5	19.2	16.5	24.3	22.9	28.4	23.8	25.4	23.2	37.7	24.3
CBS	22.2	21.7	19.0	29.3	20.9	24.4	31.2	34.9	25.5	30.5	25.9
NBC	22.8	19.6	19.4	27.1	19.2	30.2	27.9	28.7	23.0	29.4	24.7
Yearly Average	22.2	20.2	18.3	26.9	21.0	27.7	27.6	29.7	23.9	32.5	—

Source: Unpublished paper by Weaver, Porter, and Evans (1982).

Table 700-C   Subject Matter of Foreign News on Evening Network Newscasts, 1972–1981 (In Percent)

	1972–1976			1977–1981			Average	
	ABC	CBS	NBC	ABC	CBS	NBC	1972	1977
Military–Defense	45.4	37.8	34.4	9.4	14.7	17.0	39.2	13.7
Foreign Relations	16.2	16.0	17.9	30.2	29.5	28.5	16.7	29.4
Domestic Government–Politics	7.8	15.2	17.8	20.6	15.1	16.9	13.6	17.5
Crime–Justice–Terrorism	8.8	8.5	10.9	11.2	9.4	10.8	9.4	10.5
Economics–Business	2.1	3.9	6.0	3.1	8.8	4.6	4.0	5.5
Human Interest–Features	2.3	3.4	3.3	3.2	3.3	5.5	3.0	4.0
Disasters	3.1	2.3	1.9	2.8	1.9	1.6	2.4	2.1
Prominent Persons	1.8	1.9	2.9	2.4	3.4	3.4	2.2	3.0
Sports	2.6	1.5	1.4	0.6	0.9	0.2	1.9	0.5
Race Relations	3.0	0.3	0.5	1.6	0.6	0.1	1.3	0.8
Arts–Culture–Entertainment	0.1	2.4	0.2	2.3	0.4	0.8	0.9	1.2
Education	2.3	0.4	0.3	—	—	—	1.0	—
Labor	1.3	0.4	1.0	2.4	2.9	2.8	0.9	2.7
Miscellaneous	0.4	1.8	0.3	5.4	3.3	4.8	0.8	4.5
Agriculture–Fisheries	2.7	—	—	—	0.5	—	0.9	0.2
Accidents	0.1	0.9	1.1	1.8	1.7	1.2	0.7	1.6
Religion	—	1.7	0.1	0.4	2.2	0.7	0.6	1.1
Science–Health–Medicine	—	1.6	—	2.6	1.4	1.1	0.5	1.7
Total News in Seconds	16,860	18,510	17,900	22,430	23,220	22,040	53,270	67,690

Source: Unpublished paper by Weaver, Porter, and Evans (1982).

bibliographies are Richstad and Bowen (1976), and Gerbner and Marvanyi (1977) which are broader than merely television news. For other works on television news, see Unit 560. Invaluable monthly records of network newscasts are found in *Television News Index and Abstracts*, on which the tables here are based.

701
INTERNATIONAL
BROADCASTING ACTIVITIES

Interpretation of the Tables

Table 701-A provides data on international broadcasting and the role of U.S. broadcasting outlets in this field. The data for 1945 are approximations and are therefore not directly comparable to the information for later years. With the exception of Cuba, which was included because of its proximity to the United States, all of the nations listed on this table were responsible for at least 350 hours per week of international broadcasts. The overall trend in Table 701-A is unmistakable. Most of the 11 nations listed have increased their weekly international broadcast hours since the 1950s. Until 1970, the United States broadcast far more hours per week than any other nation, but this lead had been cut sharply by 1973, until, by the late 1970s, the U.S.S.R.'s total weekly hours exceeded that of the United States.

Table 701-B examines the language and the target regions of Voice of America broadcasts over a 25 year period. These figures represent *approximate* hours of broadcast time per week, but the trend remains valid: Throughout the 25 year period, the Voice of America has focused on the Soviet Union, Eastern Europe, and the Far East. Africa and Latin America have received far less attention.

Table 701-C reveals the U.S. government's long-secret role in supporting Radio Liberty and Radio Free Europe—a role which was acknowledged only in the early 1970s. Support from private donations has always been insignificant and had declined to almost nothing in 1975.

Table 701-D provides a summary view of Radio Liberty and Radio Free Europe programming content in 1982. Radio Liberty directs its broadcasts to the Soviet Union, while Radio Free Europe broadcasts to the Eastern European communist nations.

Sources

Most of the data in Tables 701-B through 701-D were reported by the United States Information Agency (USIA) and Board for International Broadcasting (BIB) (for Radio Liberty and Radio Free Europe) during their annual treks to Congress for funding. In that sense, these data were released in the interest of self-preservation. However, the data are also audited by various other governmental agencies and should, therefore, be considered reliable.

Except for the 1945 figures, the information on foreign broadcasting in Table 701-A was originally gathered by the British Broadcasting Corporation's External Broadcasting Audience Research division and reprinted in the *BBC Handbook 1982*. The 1945 figures were estimated by the author from a chart, "Growth and Competition in International Broadcasting," in the *Foreign Service Journal* (1967).

Further Information

The best up-to-date discussion of the USIA [from 1978-1981, called the International Communication Agency (ICA)] and the BIB appears in the annual congressional budget hearings. These hearings offer a wealth of statistical information on current and past fiscal years, as well as insights into the rationale for the policies of these agencies.

Table 701-A Weekly Broadcast Hours of U.S. and Other Government Radio Services, 1945-1980

	Number of Broadcast Hours Per Week							
Geographical Area	1945	1950	1955	1960	1965	1970	1975	1980
U.S.	1,175	497	1,285	1,495	1,877	1,907	2,029	1,901
Voice of America	1,175	497	N/A	640	830	863	789	877
Radio Free Europe	—	—	N/A	444	1,077	547	554	555
Radio Liberty	—	—	N/A	411	1,077	497	686	469
U.S.S.R.	550	533	656	1,015	1,417	1,908	2,001	2,094
People's Republic of China	—	66	159	687	1,027	1,591	1,423	1,350
Warsaw Pact Nations								
(Except USSR)	—	386	783	1,009	1,215	1,264	1,499	1,528
Cuba	—	—	—	—	325	320	311	424
BBC External Service	730	643	558	589	667	723	719	719
Federal Republic of Germany	—	—	105	315	671	779	767	804
Egypt	—	—	100	301	505	540	635	546
Albania	—	26	47	63	153	487	490	560
Spain	—	68	98	202	276	251	312	239
The Netherlands	—	127	120	178	235	335	400	289
11 Nation Total	N/A	2,346	3,911	5,854	8,368	10,105	10,536	12,365

Sources: 1945 data from *Foreign Service Journal* (1967), p. 21; all remaining data is from the *BBC Handbook*, 1983, p. 59. Note: The total counts the Warsaw Pact countries as an entity, though it includes six East European countries.

Table 701-B Weekly Broadcast Hours of Voice of America, by Language of Broadcast, 1950–1980

Language and Target Region	Hours Broadcast Per Week[a]						
	1950	1955	1960	1965	1970	1975	1980
English (both world-wide and specific regions/countries)	63:00	49:00	161:00	260:45	225:45	202:00	211:30
Vernacular Languages							
Eastern Europe and USSR	55:30	396:48	204:45	178:30	171:30	251:30	255:30
Middle East and North Africa	10:00 ⎫		66:30	52:30	49:00	56:00	87:30
South Asia	⎬ 87:30		24:30	21:00	21:00	28:00	28:00
Africa	26:15 ⎭		3:30	31:30	42:30	51:00	54:30
Far East		197:45	140:00	175:00	248:30	143:00	140:00
Latin America	19:15	—	14:00	85:30	71:30	49:00	52:30
Western Europe	26:15	—	—	—	—	—	17:30[a]
Total Weekly Broadcast Hours	200:15	731:03	614:15	804:45	829:45	780:30	847:00
Percent of English-Language Broadcasts	31	7	26	32	27	26	26

Sources: 1950 data: International Information Program (Department of State), p. 2. All other data from *USIA Reports to Congress* as follows: 1955: *4th Report*, pp. 28–29. 1960: *14th Report*, p. 25. 1965: *24th Report*, pp. 26–27. 1970: *34th Report*, p. 17. 1975: *43rd Report*, p. 94. 1980: supplied direct to the author from the Voice of America Public Information Office, as statistics are no longer regularly reported to Congress. Note: [a]Includes Portuguese, Greek, and Turkish.

The most detailed discussion of U.S. government broadcasting can be found in Abshire (1976) and Hale (1975), while the report of the Presidential Study Commission on International Radio Broadcasting (1973) provides interesting comparative statistics on Soviet broadcast efforts and the changes in U.S. policy. The reader should see the USIA/ICA annual reports for data on the Voice of America and other agency affairs, and the BIB annual reports for further information on Radio Liberty and Radio Free Europe. Two dated but still interesting books on the USIA are those by Elder (1968) and Henderson (1969). Critical analyses of USIA and BIB activities are available

Table 701-C Sources of Financial Support for Radio Liberty and Radio Free Europe, 1950–1980 (In Dollars)

Year	Government Funding	Private Donations	Total
1950	3,108,969	—	3,108,969
1956	16,937,731	1,864,775	18,802,506
1960	21,785,979	1,613,574	23,399,553
1965	27,418,824	1,364,274	28,783,098
1970	32,844,535	1,277,280	34,121,815
1975[a]	49,510,000	181,392	50,294,000
1980	90,343,509	—	90,343,509

Source: Board for International Broadcasting, *Third Annual Report, 1977*, p. 62. 1980 data from *Seventh Annual Report, 1981*, pp. 51, 53. Note: [a]Figures for 1975 do not include the operating expenses of the Board for International Broadcasting, which was formed in 1973.

Table 701–D Subject Matter of Broadcasts by Radio Free Europe and Radio Liberty, 1982 (In Percent)

Subject Matter	Radio Liberty/Radio Free Europe
Political (Including News)	62.0
Economics, Labor, Agriculture	5.0
Social	1.5
Cultural	4.0
Youth, Education	1.0
Music	15.0
Documents	10.0
Religion	3.0
Sports, Human Interest	4.5
Other	3.0

Source: Supplied direct to the author from the Board for International Broadcasting, Statistical Report of Programs, January–March 1982, Radio Liberty/Radio Free Europe. Note: Percentages are of top six languages, which are approximately 80 percent of all languages.

in the reports by the GAO (1981, 1982). An overview of international propaganda can be found in Martin (1971), while international broadcasting is best covered in Browne (1982).

750
U.S. TRADE IN CONSUMER ELECTRONICS

Interpretation of the Tables

Table 750–A outlines the import/export trade patterns of the U.S. electronics industry, from 1965 through 1980. The product categories in the table were established by the Electronic Industries Association (EIA). The figures indicate that the overall balance of trade in this industry remains favorable to the United States, even with a 25 percent decrease in export margins during the past decade. The consumer electronics segment of the industry has clearly been hurt by the predominance of imported products in the U.S. marketplace. However, the superiority of U.S.-made communications and industrial products—made up largely of computers and related equipment— has benefitted the United States balance of trade, since this nation still exports far more of these products than it imports.

Table 750–B provides a longer run of similar data for consumer electronics products only. The reader will note that the figures presented here do not match those given in Table 750–A. This is a common occurrence caused by differing definitions of "consumer electronics" (see "Sources" section below). Table 750–B indicates that American exports of consumer electronic products were showing strong growth during the 1970s, but then declined sharply in 1977 and 1978.

The difficulties of the American consumer electronics industry are due primarily to the worldwide competition from Japanese products (see Unit 760). However, the American manufacturers' increasing uses of foreign locations, especially Mexico, for the assembly of consumer electronic devices (using U.S.-made components) has also had a negative effect on the export levels of the U.S. consumer electronics industry, as well as on the overall balance of trade for the United States.

Table 750–B also indicates a sharp rise in U.S. *imports* of consumer electronics products after 1959. This rise was due initially to the U.S. exportation of transistor technology. This new technology—combined with (1) lower wage rates overseas, (2) lighter components and, therefore, lower shipping costs, and (3) increasing automation of component assembly both here and abroad—resulted in nearly overwhelming foreign competition for American manufacturers of consumer electronics products. (See Table 460–E for the impact of this technological revolution on employment levels in the U.S. consumer electronics industry.)

Table 750–C is taken from a special Department of Commerce investigation into the rise and fall of the domestic consumer electronics industry. Imports, demonstrated in the table, are merely the result of a variety of factors, many within this country, that led to the decline of domestic manufacture of such products, though much "offshore" production capacity is controlled by American firms. Within the 1966–1973 period traced in the table, the role of Japan as a source of imports actually declined (from 75 to 55 percent of total) while other nations, chiefly Taiwan (which rose from nothing to nearly 20 percent of total) appeared. Domestic markets for these Far East countries, plus rising quality standards, have helped to increase their market share—along with their prices.

The most important sources of electronics imports are the countries of the Far East. According to the EIA, in 1982 the U.S. import percentages for the *entire* electronics industry were divided among the following nations: Japan, 39 percent; Taiwan, 9 percent; Mexico, 7 percent; Canada, 7 percent; Singapore, 6 percent; Malaysia, 6 percent; and Korea and Hong Kong about 5 percent each (for a total of 84 percent of electronics imports).

The major destinations for U.S. electronics exports in 1982 were Canada, 12 percent; Britain, 10 percent; West Germany, 8 percent; Japan, 7 percent; France, 6 percent; and Mexico, 5 percent (for a total of 48 percent of all electronics exports). In many cases these export figures represent U.S.-made

Table 750–A Value of U.S. Imports/Exports of Electronics Industry Products, 1965–1980

Year	Consumer Electronics	Communications and Industrial Products	Electron Tubes	Solid State Products	Electronic Parts	Other Products	Totals
1965							
Import Value	319	164	35	24	N/A	77	619
Export Value	55	871	60	82	N/A	205	1,273
Balance of Trade	(264)	707	25	58	N/A	128	654
Exports as a Percentage of Imports	17	531	171	341	N/A	266	206
1970							
Import Value	1,152	514	38	157	N/A	328	2,189
Export Value	77	2,439	126	420	N/A	463	3,525
Balance of Trade	(1,075)	1,925	88	263	N/A	135	1,336
Exports as a Percentage of Imports	7	474	331	268	N/A	141	161
1975							
Import Value	1,851	1,096	69	803	974	85	4,878
Export Value	517	4,172	216	1,054	923	200	7,082
Balance of Trade	(1,334)	3,076	147	251	(51)	115	2,204
Exports as a Percentage of Imports	28	380	313	131	95	235	145
1980							
Import Value	4,501	2,971	258	2,971	2,355	258	13,314
Export Value	814	13,564	367	2,748	2,654	44	20,191
Balance of Trade	(3,687)	10,593	109	(223)	299	(214)	6,877
Exports as a Percentage of Imports	18	457	142	92	113	17	152

Source: Electronic Industries Association, *Electronic Market Data Book* for 1971, p. 83; 1976, p. 105; and 1981, p. 100. All figures are in millions of dollars except percentages. Figures in parentheses indicate losses.

Table 750-B Value of U.S. Imports/Exports of Consumer Electronics Products, 1958-1982

Note: All Dollar Figures are in Millions.

	Current Dollar Values		Constant (1972) Dollar Values		
Year	Imports	Exports	Imports	Exports	Exports as a Percent of Imports[a]
1958	21	74	32	112	350
1959	78	72	116	107	92
1960	87	71	127	103	81
1961	121	80	175	115	66
1962	165	54	234	76	32
1963	158	54	221	75	34
1964	184	70	253	96	38
1965	264	80	355	108	30
1966	380	76	495	99	20
1967	562	98	942	139	17
1968	778	115	942	139	15
1969	893	135	1,030	156	15
1970	1,274	144	1,394	158	11
1971	1,487	169	1,549	176	11
1972	1,949	231	1,949	231	12
1973	2,203	318	2,082	301	14
1974	2,253	383	1,918	329	17
1975	1,810	392	1,439	312	22
1976	2,981	498	2,253	376	17
1977	3,740	463	2,670	331	12
1978	5,039	723	3,350	481	14
1979	4,864	767	2,976	469	16
1980	4,919	1,107	2,757	620	22
1981[b]	5,900	1,110	3,023	569	19
1982[b]	6,500	1,175	3,142	568	ˎ18

Source: Bureau of Domestic Commerce, *U.S. Industrial Outlook*, appropriate annual issues. Constant dollar figures were calculated by the author. Notes: [a]Percentages are based on the constant dollar figures which in turn are based on the GNP deflator. [b]The figures for these years are estimates.

components that later appeared in completed equipment imported back into the United States.

Sources

All of the data in Table 750-A come from the U.S. Bureau of the Census. These data were arranged and presented by the Electronic Industries Association, the chief trade association of U.S. electronics manufacturers, in its annual *Electronic Market Data Book*. The author has avoided unit information here in favor of dollar values, since the actual number of components is often impossible to determine. The figures do not, however, control for inflation.

Table 750-C   Penetration of U.S. Consumer Electronic Products Market by Foreign Imports, 1966-1973 (As a Percent of Total Sales)

Product	1966	1967	1968	1969	1970	1971	1972	1973
Tape Recorders and Players	78	83	91	95	97	98	99	99
Home-Type Radios, Except Combination	64	72	80	86	88	92	94	96
Black and White Television Receivers	16	22	29	43	50	58	62	63
Color Television Receivers	5	6	11	15	17	19	16	17
Radio-Phonograph Combinations	33	43	46	48	49	47	55	43
Phonographs, Record Players, Changers	51	40	47	47	53	58	61	76
Auto Radios	6	13	16	16	22	25	23	30

Source: U.S. Department of Commerce, Domestic and International Business Administration (1975), p. 23.

The category of consumer electronics products in Table 750-A is defined by the EIA as including the following equipment: radio and television receivers, phonographs and other disc-recording equipment, audio tape equipment, home video systems, citizens' band radios, personal calculators, and electronic watches (the latter two products are included only for the last three to five years). The category of communications and industrial products includes equipment for broadcast transmission and studios, navigation and guidance equipment, telephone and telegraph equipment, computers and related equipment, control and processing equipment, and other industrial products. The electron tubes category includes television picture tubes, receiving tubes, and power and microwave tubes.

According to the International Trade Commission, all of the statistics in Table 750-A are limited by problems of aggregation and classification and by imprecise trade records. Thus, the figures might best be termed "refined estimates" of actual practice.

In Table 750-B, taken from annual issues of the *U.S. Industrial Outlook*, the consumer electronics figures include radio and television receivers, phonographs and high-fidelity equipment, home video equipment (systems and games), and various accessories and combinations of the above. The differences between this definition and the definition of "consumer electronics" used in Table 750-A largely explain the differences in the totals for the two tables.

Table 750-C was taken from a special Department of Commerce investigation on the status of the consumer electronics industry. It is based on official information gathered from several sources, not all clearly or specifically identified, but seemingly based heavily on records filed in accordance with Section 807 of the U.S. Tariff Laws.

Further Information

Increasing attention is being paid to the U.S. balance of trade generally, and therefore more publications are appearing on the subject. The handiest regular compilation of data on an annual basis, with comparative tables covering the past 5 to 20 years, is the Electronic Industry Association's *Electronic Market Data Book* which reports company, government, and other data. For more specific and official information on a country-by-country level, see the Census Bureau publications, *U.S. Exports, Commodity by Country*, and the matching import publication of similar title. The consumer electronics section of the annual U.S. Department of Commerce, *U.S. Industrial Outlook* is invaluable for its projections. A highly detailed case study of a specific country and product is found in the U.S. International Trade Commission, *Television Receiving Sets from Japan* (June 1981), which provides a wealth of tabular information. For a broader analysis of all telecommunications manufactures in the export-import market, see U.S. Department of Commerce, International Trade Administration, *High Technology Industries: Profiles and Outlooks—The Telecommunications Industry* (April 1983).

760
U.S. TRADE IN RADIO/
TELEVISION RECEIVERS

Interpretation of the Tables

Tables 760–A and 760–B show that, with the exception of color television sets, broadcast receivers are predominantly an import product in the United States. Exactly the opposite is generally the case with station and studio equipment and other broadcast-related electronic equipment (see Unit 750).

Table 760–A provides a 30 year time-series study on American imports and exports of radio receivers. The small number of radio imports into the United States in the early 1950s were primarily quality equipment from Europe, especially Germany. However, as transistor technology spread from the United States abroad in the late 1950s and into the 1960s, the import flow both expanded and shifted to the Far East—mainly Japan, Taiwan, and Hong Kong. By the mid-1970s, this import flow had nearly excluded all U.S.-made radios from the domestic market.

This situation has naturally had an effect on ownership concentrations in the U.S. radio manufacturing industry (see Table 260–C) and on domestic prices of radio receivers, which have not risen as rapidly as the prices for products in other media fields (see Sterling and Haight [1978], Table 301–A).

Table 760–A U.S Imports/Exports of Radio Receivers, by Units and Value, 1950–1982

Note: All Unit and Dollar Figures are in Thousands.

| Year | Units[a] | | | Dollar Value | | | Export Totals as a Percent of Imports | |
	U.S. Imports, Total Units	Imports as a Percent of Total U.S. Market	U.S. Exports, Total Units	Current Dollar Value of Imports	Current Dollar Value of Exports	Units	Value
1950	2	—	—	—	—	—	—
1951	5	—	—	—	—	—	—
1952	12	—	—	—	—	—	—
1953	25	—	—	—	—	—	—
1954	55	—	—	—	—	—	—
1955	141	.1	—	—	—	—	—
1956	604	4.3	—	—	—	—	—
1957	1,011	7.0	—	—	—	—	—
1958	2,593	17.9	—	—	—	—	—
1959	5,876	27.6	—	—	—	—	—
1960	7,621	31.2	—	—	—	—	—
1961	12,359	42.3	—	—	—	—	—
1962	13,328	41.7	195	88,463	4,975	1	6
1963	13,783	43.7	212	86,431	5,279	2	6
1964	13,739	43.1	329	91,999	6,355	2	7

Year						
1965	19,637	47.1	352	125,103	8,667	2	7
1966	25,128	56.9	352	144,107	8,001	1	6
1967	24,200	58.7	438	171,110	9,409	2	5
1968	30,160	64.4	643	254,768	11,597	2	5
1969	36,396	70.9	770	336,136	15,258	2	5
1970	33,382	75.1	677	343,762	13,406	2	4
1971	34,138	71.7	719	358,088	16,171	2	5
1972	43,083	77.9	814	457,857	19,288	2	4
1973	45,366	90.4	754	540,007	19,950	2	4
1974	39,281	89.3	738	585,710	20,258	2	3
1975	31,941	92.5	654	477,347	21,375	2	4
1976	41,364	93.8	800	646,653	29,255	2	5
1977	43,205	81.6	873	755,142	35,473	2	5
1978	43,374	90.2	1,632	812,220	77,718	4	10
1979	33,429	85.5	1,193	657,177	65,217	4	10
1980	33,268	84.0	1,104	605,290	68,034	3	11
1981	37,081	83.6	1,335	693,686	91,623	4	13
1982	37,347	84.7	1,171	710,558	83,227	3	12

Sources: Electronic Industries Association: import data: *Consumer Electronics* 1968, p.15, and *Consumer Electronics* 1977, p. 27; export data: *Consumer Electronics* 1972, p. 27, and *Consumer Electronics* 1977, p. 27. 1978–1982 import and export data: *Consumer Electronics* 1983, p. 39. Note: [a]Includes automobile radios.

U.S. Trade in Radio/T.V. Receivers   279

Table 760–B   U.S. Imports/Exports of Television Receivers, by Units and Value, 1960–1982

Note: All Unit and Dollar Figures are in Thousands.

	Black and White TV Receivers[a]			Color TV Receivers			Totals, U.S. TV Imports		Totals, U.S. TV Exports		Export Totals as a Percent of Imports	
Year	U.S. Imports, Total Units	Imports as a Percent of Total U.S. Market	U.S. Exports, Total Units	U.S. Imports, Total Units	Imports as a Percent of Total U.S. Market	U.S. Exports, Total Units	Black and White and Color Units	Current Dollar Value	Black and White and Color Units	Current Dollar Value	Units	Value
1960	2	—	—	—	—	—	2	N/A	—	—	—	—
1961	13	—	—	—	—	—	13	N/A	—	—	—	—
1962	128	1.9	140	—	—	—	128	7,258	140	18,099	109	249
1963	391	5.4	143	—	—	—	391	22,616	143	17,672	37	78
1964	661	7.9	202	—	—	—	661	39,261	202	23,293	31	59
1965	1,048	12.0	182	—	—	—	1,048	59,587	182	21,261	17	36
1966	1,519	19.7	168	—	—	—	1,519	114,520	168	26,291	11	23
1967	1,290	21.5	139	318	5.7	—	1,608	123,837	139	23,559	9	19
1968	2,043	29.2	144	666	10.7	—	2,709	203,051	144	27,772	5	14
1969	3,121	43.9	99	912	14.7	58	4,033	295,777	157	33,339	4	11

Year												
1970	3,596	52.1	75	914	17.2	51	4,510	315,525	126	26,166	3	8
1971	4,166	54.5	74	1,281	17.6	88	5,447	413,316	162	37,146	3	9
1972	5,056	61.4	75	1,318	14.9	149	6,374	496,829	224	58,864	4	12
1973	4,999	68.5	99	1,399	13.9	215	6,398	531,253	314	83,618	5	16
1974	4,659	67.8	117	1,282	15.2	202	5,941	520,195	319	79,406	5	15
1975	2,975	67.3	91	1,215	19.5	141	4,190	401,490	232	59,504	6	15
1976	4,327	72.9	156	2,834	34.6	160	7,161	776,252	316	81,082	4	10
1977	4,908	80.6	153	2,539	27.2	186	7,447	744,937	339	81,379	5	11
1978	5,931	88.1	223	2,775	26.0	410	8,706	927,947	633	168,227	7	18
1979	5,874	89.3	158	1,369	13.6	375	7,243	645,208	533	150,792	7	23
1980	6,172	91.7	169	1,293	12.0	788	7,465	699,643	957	297,823	13	43
1981	6,246	103.1[a]	260	1,984	16.0	646	8,230	905,849	906	266,025	11	29
1982	5,521	112.1[a]	138	2,228	19.4	381	7,749	889,232	519	155,571	7	17

Sources: Electronic Industries Association; import data: *Consumer Electronics* 1968, p. 15, and *Consumer Electronics* 1979, p. 27; export data: *Consumer Electronics* 1972, p. 27, and *Consumer Electronics* 1979, p. 27, 1979–1982 data, both import and export: *Consumer Electronics* 1983, p. 39. Note: [a]More receivers were shipped than sold in these years when no domestic manufacture of black and white TV sets took place. See Table 660-A.

Table 760–C   Producers of U.S. Television Receivers, 1968–1980

Firm	1968	1969	1970	1971	1972	1973	1974	1975	1976	1977	1978	1979	1980
U.S.-Owned													
Curtis Mathes Manufacturing Co.	X	X	X	X	X	X	X	X	X	X	X	X	X
General Electric Co.	X	X	X	X	X	X	X	X	X	X	X	X	X
GTE Sylvania Inc.	X	X	X	X	X	X	X	X	X	X	X	X	X
RCA Corp.	X	X	X	X	X	X	X	X	X	X	X	X	X
Wells-Gardner Electronics Corp.	X	X	X	X	X	X	X	X	X	X	X	X	X
Zenith Radio Corp.	X	X	X	X	X	X	X	X	X	X	X	X	X
Admiral Group[1]	X	X	X	X	X	X	X	X	X	X	X		
Andrea Radio Corp.	X	X	X	X	X	X	X	X	X	X			
Warwick Electronics Inc.[2]	X	X	X	X	X	X	X	X	X				
Magnavox Consumer Electronics Co.[3]	X	X	X	X	X	X	X	X					
Motorola, Inc.[4]	X	X	X	X	X	X	X						
Philco Consumer Electronics Co.[5]	X	X	X	X	X	X							
Teledyne Packard Bell Co.	X	X	X	X	X								
TMA Co.	X	X	X	X	X								
Setchel-Carlson	X	X	X	X									
Arvin	X	X	X										
Emerson	X	X											
Cortron[6]	X												

Foreign-Owned:

Sony Corp. of America

Quasar Electronics Corp.[4]

Magnavox Consumer Electronics Co.[3]

Sanyo Manufacturing Corp.[2]

Mitsubishi Electric Sales[7]

Toshiba America, Inc.

Sharp Electronics Corp.

Hitachi Consumer Products of America, Inc.

Tatung Co. of America, Inc.

Source: Television Digest, various issues, as summarized by U.S. International Trade Commission (1981), p. A–14. Notes: [1]Rockwell International Corp. purchased Admiral Corp. (now Admiral Group) in 1974. [2]Sanyo Electric, Inc. (Japan), purchased the television-manufacturing facilities of Warwick Electronics Inc., effective Dec. 31, 1976. [3]North American Philips Corp. (subsidiary of the Philips Trust) purchased the Magnavox Consumer Electronics Co. in 1974. [4]Matsushita Electric Industrial Co., Ltd. (Japan), purchased the television receiver business of Motorola, Inc., in 1974 and renamed the business Quasar Electronics Co. [5]GTE Sylvania purchased the "Philco" trademark in 1974; Philco discontinued television receiver production in 1974. [6]Admiral Corp. (now Admiral Group), purchased Cortron in 1969. [7]Wholly owned by Mitsubishi (Japan); markets under the label "MGA."

The reader will note that even with the inflation rate over the past several years, the export percentages of import dollar values has remained at a constant two to three times the level of import *units*.

Table 760–B provides parallel information for television receivers, both black and white and color units. The figures clearly demonstrate that as manufacturing companies in the United States became more involved in the production of color receivers during the mid-1960s, the black and white receiver market was left increasingly to the Far East manufacturers. Furthermore, although the majority of color receivers sold in this country are still made domestically, this state of affairs now appears to be changing as well— and rather rapidly. In 1977, the United States and Japan signed a new trade agreement in an attempt to limit the importation of several Japanese-built products, among them color television sets. U.S. manufacturers had accused the Japanese firms of "dumping" the television receivers (selling them at a price lower than the actual production-shipping costs) on the U.S. market.

Table 760–C examines the television market from a different perspective—the nationality of television receiver producers over a crucial 12 year period. While in 1968 virtually all domestic television production was in the hands of domestic firms, by 1980, the vast majority of firms were foreign owned. The table cannot, however, show the causes of the decline of one and rise of the other—nor does it show the full extent of imports, many of which came from overseas-owned—and located—facilities (see, for example, Table 750–C). It does help to clarify the rise of foreign ownership of "onshore" located production facilities—and the resultant confusion in defining what is and what is not a true "import."

Sources

All data in Tables 760–A and 760–B come from the U.S. Department of Commerce as reported by the Electronics Industries Association (EIA). The author calculated the "export as percentages of imports" and the "imports as percentages of total U.S. market" from the basic data in this Unit and in Unit 660.

Although product classification is less of a problem here than it is with recording equipment (see Unit 750) and nonconsumer electronics, there are often classification differences between import and export categories as reported by the Department of Commerce. As a rule, specific subcategories are identified by the author only when a particular subcategory amounts to a substantial proportion of its larger category. For example, color television receivers are included with black and white receivers through 1966 for imports and through 1967 for exports. The author separated color sets after these dates in order to point up the decline in black and white figures.

Table 760–C is summarized from 12 years of trade publication reports, as analyzed in a special report issued by the U.S. International Trade Commission, investigating the role and impact of Japanese television receiver imports. The total number of firms producing television receivers in the U.S. declined from 16 in 1968 to 12 in 1976, then increased (all foreign-owned firms) to 15 by 1980. U.S. production of black and white receivers stopped about 1980; color receiver production continues.

Further Information

See Unit 750 text. See also Unit 660.

SECTION EIGHT
REGULATION OF
ELECTRONIC MEDIA

860
GROWTH OF FEDERAL
TELECOMMUNICATION
REGULATION

Interpretation of the Tables

The three tables in this Unit provide some statistical measures of the personnel and budget of the Federal Communications Commission and some of its predecessor agencies. At best, such statistics offer only a partial picture of the FCC, but they do suggest the expansion which has taken place in its scope and operations.

Table 860–A traces the increasing budget and number of persons employed by those agencies which have been charged with the regulation of electronic communications. The data available through 1925 represent various bodies (mainly the Bureau of Navigation) within the Department of Commerce, the first federal regulatory agency concerned with wireless communications. Data for 1930 include two agencies: the Radio Division of the Department of Commerce and the Federal Radio Commission. Data for 1935 and all years since 1935 are for the FCC exclusively. Not included on this table are data for such important and long-lasting organizations as the Interdepartmental Radio Advisory Committee (IRAC) and other, variously named agencies which led, in 1978, to the creation of the National Telecommunication and Information Agency (NTIA). However, the FCC has always been, by far, the biggest of the agencies concerned with broadcast regulation (as opposed to use of broadcasting, since many federal agencies regularly apply media in their usual activities). Given the general tendency of federal agencies to bloat in size, the relatively stable overall numbers of FCC employees shown by Table 860–A is quite remarkable. Only in the 1970s did the FCC's number of employees substantially exceed earlier levels, and one factor pushing that growth was the CB radio craze which placed tremendous processing pressure on the commission; another was Cable TV's rise.

Table 860–B and Table 860–C provide background information regarding FCC commissioners. Those who fill the seven (five as of 1983) commissioner positions are appointed by the president and must be approved by the Senate. Each appointment lasts seven years, and terms are staggered so that only one commissioner's term ends during a given year. In actuality, many commissioners serve for briefer periods, and this is especially true for chairmen. The record for FCC service is held by Commissioner Robert E. Lee who was first appointed in 1953 and whose last term expired in 1981. The second-longest FCC service record is held by Rosel Hyde whose time with the commission, from 1946 through 1969, included two separate periods as chairman.

Table 860–B provides a statistical profile of all those commissioners who served between 1952 and 1983. It is apparent that most commissioners came to the FCC from other federal posts, had previous experience in some aspect of regulation, were lawyers, and were in their late 40s or early 50s.

Table 860–C focuses specifically on the affiliation of FCC commissioners and other, high-level, staff officials with the communications industry before and after their FCC service. A common criticism of agency employment is that such work often places the regulators too close to the regulated. The subsequent employment of former FCC personnel in the industry which they had regulated suggests there may be some truth in this statement. Of the 33 commissioners who served between 1945 and 1970, two-thirds later accepted positions in the communications industry. The majority of high-level, FCC staff officials followed the same course after they retired from FCC service. On the other hand, few commissioners have come from the regulated industries to FCC service. One major industry complaint is that there is a need for greater numbers of industry-trained and -backgrounded participants in FCC deliberations.

Sources

The data in Table 860–A were drawn from various official government agency reports. All budget figures are publicly available, though sometimes difficult to locate. Data for the period prior to 1935 should be considered approximate since exact and inclusive figures are sometimes hard to piece together correctly. Unfortunately, the early reports did not provide personnel levels. Table 860–B and Table 860–C are based on primary research efforts by the authors of the sources cited—essentially biographical information retained by the commission and information from trade periodicals or personal contact with the commissioners.

Table 860-B has been largely updated for this book, by the addition of a column for commissioners appointed since 1974. Note that three of the commissioners in the 1975–1983 column are holdovers from the 1952–1974 period.

**Table 860–A   Budget and Personnel of the Federal Telecommunication
Regulatory Agencies, 1915–1982**

Year	Current Dollars	Constant Dollars[d] (1972 = 100)	Percent of Real Change	Personnel at End of Fiscal Year
		Budget		
1915[a]	45,000	217,391	—	N/A
1920[a]	65,000	152,224	(30)	N/A
1925[a]	205,238	607,213	298	N/A
1930[b]	755,400	2,382,965	292	131
1935[c]	1,125,599	4,093,087	72	442
1940	1,838,175	6,382,552	56	625
1945	6,213,343	16,524,848	159	1,513
1950	6,729,345	12,554,748	(24)	1,285
1955	6,911,769	11,330,768	(10)	1,094
1960	10,550,000	15,356,622	36	1,396
1965	16,911,000	22,760,430	48	1,502
1970	24,561,000	26,873,085	18	1,553
1975	46,900,000	36,731,343	37	2,073
1980	76,047,000	42,622,463	16	2,094
1982	79,900,000	38,621,423	(10)	1,842

Source: Data through 1965 from Sterling and Kittross (1978), "key indicator" tables throughout, reporting information from Department of Commerce (1915–1930), and FRC and FCC *Annual Reports*. Data since 1965 is direct from the FCC *Annual Report*. Notes: [a]Department of Commerce, Commissioner of Navigation, [b]Financial data combines Department of Commerce Radio Division ($295,400) and Federal Radio Commission ($460,000). Personnel data is only for the FRC. [c]FCC data only from this point on. The growth of OTP (Office of Telecommunications Policy [Executive Office of the President], 1970–1978) and NTIA are illustrated in their budget and personnel figures:

Year	Current Dollar Budget	Personnel
1970	2,100,000	45
1975	8,450,000	60
1980	17,644,000	269
1982	14,600,000	278

These are supplied to the author by NTIA. The jump in 1980 illustrates the combination of OTP with the Department of Commerce's Office of Telecommunications operation, some of it in Boulder, Colorado. By 1982, the political cutting of NTIA's size and role was becoming evident. [d]Based on GNP deflator.

Further Information

The FCC's *Annual Report* (usually published about a year after the cover date) and the annual budget hearings before the House Appropriation Committee (as well as annual, "oversight", hearings before both the House

Table 860–B Statistical Profile of FCC Commissioners, 1952–1983

Factor	Number of Commissioners (Total = 31) 1952–1974	Number of Commissioners (Total = 12) 1975–1983
Position Immediately Preceding Appointment:		
Academic	2	—
Broadcaster	2	—
Engineer, Private	2	—
Federal Government (Total)	17	6
(a) Staff, Same Agency	5	1
(b) Congressional Staff	2	3
(c) Congressional Member	1	—
(d) Executive Branch	6	1
(e) Other Federal Regulatory Agencies	2	1
Law, Private	5	4
State Government	3	—
Other	—	—
Regulatory Background:[a]		
In Staff of Same Agency	8	—
In Regulated Industry, Same Agency	8	1
In Other Federal Regulation	6	4
In State Regulation	5	—
No Background in Regulation	11	4
Principal Occupation Prior to Appointment:		
Academic	2	—
Broadcaster	2	—
Engineer	5	—
Lawyer	15	7
Elected Officeholder	1	—
Other	6	2
Employment Subsequent to Agency Service:		
Academic	2	1
Federal Public Office	2	1
State Public Office	—	—
Private Employment in Agency-Related Work	14	6
Public Interest Employment Agency-Related Work	1	—
Retired	3	—
Other	2	1
Still in Office	7	4
Party Affiliations:		
Democratic	16	4
Republican	14	5
Independent	1	—

Table 860–B   Statistical Profile of FCC Commissioners, 1952–1983 (cont.)

Factor	Number of Commissioners (Total = 31) 1952–1974	Number of Commissioners (Total = 12) 1975–1983
Race:		
Caucasian	30	9
Black	1	1
Sex:		
Male	29	6
Female	2	3
Education (Highest Level):		
Advanced Degree in Law (LL. M.)	3	—
Law Degree	15	7
Bachelor's Degree	10	1
Some College	3	1
No College	—	—
Age:		
Median Age at Appointment	47.5	39.2
Median Age at Departure	55.0	42.1
Tenure:		
Appointed to an Unexpired Term (Less Than 7 Years)	13	5
Resigned Before Expiration of Term	10	3
Served 7 Years or More	9	1
Still Serving	7	4
Average Length of Service as Commissioner	6.7[b]	2.1
Average Length of Service as Chairman	2.8[b]	4.4
Reappointment:		
Number Reappointed	7	2
By Same Administration	4	—
By One or More Subsequent Administrations	4[c]	2

Source: U.S. Senate, Committee on Commerce (1976), p. 422 for data through 1974. Data since 1974 figured by Robin Berry. Notes: [a]Totals for the first 4 categories exceed the number of commissioners, since some regulators had backgrounds in several relevant areas. [b]Based on a seven year term. [c]Robert E. Lee was reappointed by the same and by subsequent administrations.

and Senate communications subcommittees) are the best continuing sources of information on official FCC developments and budget. The trade press, especially *Broadcasting* and *Television Digest*, report weekly highlights of FCC activities. Recent issues of the commission's *Annual Report* provided detailed lists of all commissioners and their dates of service. Useful information on the effect of the FCC commissioners' backgrounds on FCC policy

Table 860–C Communications Industry Affiliations of FCC Commissioners and Other High-Level Staff Officials, 1945–1970

Status of Affiliation	Number of Commissioners[a]	Number of Other High-Level Staff Officials[b]
Total Number Holding Positions	33	32
Affiliation with Communications Businesses:[c]		
Before FCC Service	4	8
After FCC Service	21	13
Not at All[d]	11	11[e]

Source: Noll et al. (1973), table 4–5, p. 123. Notes: All officials whose date of departure from the FCC fell within the 1945–1970 period are included. [a]Three commissioners who were affiliated with the communications business both before *and* after FCC service are counted here in both groups. Therefore, the components of this column add up to three more than the total number of actual commissioners. [b]Includes the following positions: executive director, general counsel, chief engineer, chiefs of bureaus, chairman of the review board, chief hearing examiner (later called administrative law judges), chief of the office of opinions and review, and chief of reports and information. [c]"Affiliation" is defined as employment by a firm regulated by the FCC, either as a full-time employee or as an engineering or legal consultant. Former officials acting as lawyers representing communication firms before the FCC are considered to be affiliated with the industry. [d]Most with no affiliation after FCC service left the Commission to retire. [e]Includes three officials whose post-FCC service status is unknown, but who were not affiliated with the industry prior to FCC service.

can be found in Lichty (1962) and Williams (1976), while a comprehensive assessment of the appointment process for both FCC and Federal Trade Commission commissioners is available in the source for Table 860–B.

861
STATE REGULATION
OF BROADCASTING

Interpretation of the Table

It is commonly assumed that broadcasting is regulated only on the federal level. While that is substantially the case, virtually all state governments also have some statutes on their books which deal with some aspect of broadcasting.

Table 861–A provides a summarized listing of these state statutes as of 1972. Four major topic areas are covered by such statutes:

1. *Individual rights:* Only two states—Kansas and Vermont—have no statutes which outline the rights of individuals. The largest number of statutes in this area limit station liability from suits which might arise because of comments made over their facilities by political candidates. Statutes of this nature were enacted in the 1950s when the federal courts placed stations in jeopardy and the states reacted to protect "their own." These laws remain in force, though they were superseded two decades ago by a Supreme Court decision.
2. *Advertising:* State regulations regarding broadcast advertising tend to be included in statutes limiting advertiser practices in general. There are broad controls over fraudulent or deceptive advertising and specific limitations on particular products or services.
3. *Education:* Most of the regulations on education and broadcasting concern those specific state agencies or commissions which are allowed to operate noncommercial stations in each state.

Table 861–A State Regulation of Broadcasting, by Subjects of Statues, 1972

Statute Subject	Number of States with Statutes in Force
Individual Rights	48
Limitation of Station Liability from Comments Made by Political Candidates	31
Limitation of Station Liability from Comments by Non-Candidates, Non-Licensees	26
Monetary Damages	15
Private Sources of Information	14
Advertising	43
Fraudulent Advertising	21
Consumer Fraud	16
Specific Controls on Foods, Drugs, and Cosmetics	17
Loans	14
Insurance (Domestic)	10
Education	35
State Agencies or Commissions	23
Business Aspects	31
Taxes	10
Gambling Information Limits	11

Source: Sadowski (1974), pp. 433–452. Subcolumns will not add up to semi-totals as many states have regulations in duplicate areas. Not shown here are figures for "other aspects" (minor law areas in which only a few states have statutes).

4. *Business aspects:* Of the 31 states which regulate the business aspects of broadcasting, most of their statutes are concerned with limits on broadcasting of information regarding lotteries or with taxation of broadcasting advertising receipts.

When all state statutes on broadcasting are taken together, it is apparent that, as of 1972, no less than 86 specific aspects of broadcasting were regulated by one or more states. The three states most actively legislating broadcasting were California (25 aspects regulated), New York (17 aspects), and Illinois (15 aspects).

Source

The information here was condensed from a more detailed table which can be found in Sadowski (1974). That table was based, in turn, on Professor Sadowski's Ph.D. dissertation, and research that included examination of statutes of each of the 50 U.S. states.

Further Information

Data on current state regulatory activity in broadcasting can be obtained from the legal department of the National Association of Broadcasters. For state regulation of cable television, see Unit 890.

862
FCC ADMINISTRATIVE/LEGAL SANCTIONS AGAINST BROADCAST LICENSEES

Interpretation of the Tables

The law limits the number of options open to the FCC for disciplining rule-breaking broadcast licensees. For years, the primary threat the commission could apply was the draconian measure of lifting a station's license and taking it off the air. Since many license infractions were not worthy of such an extreme response, the FCC persuaded Congress to widen the available options, and in the early 1960s, Congress finally allowed the use of short-term license renewal (renewal for a period of less than the then-standard three years) and/or the imposition of fines. The tables in this unit reveal trends in the application of these FCC disciplinary options.

Table 862–A provides a 47 year summary of license denials (including denials of both new applications and renewals), outright revocations of licenses at times other than application or renewal, and revocations of construction permits. The overriding conclusion to be drawn from examination of this table is that the number of denials and revocations is relatively low when compared to the thousands of stations on the air and applications processed each year. The proportion of broadcast licenses which are routinely renewed every three years is well above 95 percent, approaching 99 percent in some cases. It is also worth noting that the rate of denials increased sharply after 1960 and appears to be still increasing, judging from the 15 denials in two recent years (1975–1976). On the other hand, the number of outright revocations during a standard license term has dropped down from the peak reached in the early 1960s. Construction permit revocations are usually prompted by a lack of activity by the permit holder (since every construction permit is granted with specific limitations on the times by which construction must be started and completed).

Table 862–B provides a breakdown, up to 1978, of the FCC's reasons for taking actions against broadcast licensees. Clearly, the FCC is most concerned with misrepresentation in applications or forms. In fact, one type of misrepresentation is identified here as a separate category: unauthorized transfers of station control, which usually is carried out through some kind of stock transfer. Ownership of stations is a matter of public record; elaborate procedures must be followed whenever a station is sold or otherwise transferred, and by law, the FCC must approve any such transfer. "Technical violations," the fourth category listed on Table 862–B, includes such things as hours of operation, the power of a station's transmitter, coverage patterns of the station, and the training and licensing of key engineering personnel. However, it is interesting to note that the third-most common reason behind FCC revocations and denials is simple lack of activity on the part of the applicant—essentially, abandonment of the application or license. The category entitled "character of licensee" includes legal difficulties the licensee may have had outside of broadcasting matters which the commission feels reflect on the licensee's ability to operate in the public interest. The remaining categories are self-explanatory.

Table 862–C details the two decades (1961–1978) of fines assessed against broadcast licensees, while Table 862–D details the first 21 years

(1960–1981) of short-term license renewals. Both sanctions act essentially as warnings to a licensee that the FCC is displeased with one or more aspects of the station's operation, but that the issues are not serious enough to warrant license denial or revocation.

In Table 862–C, a few of the reasons for assessment of fines need clarification. "Logging violations" are errors or misrepresentations in a station's written records of programming and engineering matters. In most cases, "underlicensed" operation means that a station did not have an engineer with a First Class license on duty when required. In addition, the FCC may fine a broadcast station for violating specifically assigned broadcast hours and given amounts of power usage. (Because AM station broadcasts cover larger areas at night than during the day, some AM stations are allowed to broadcast only after local sunrise in order that the signals of other stations may be protected from interference.)

Table 862–D reveals that most short-term renewals cover a period of one year. This is a substantial sanction, given the costs of completing and filing a renewal application. "Primary" reasons are violations which in themselves require short-term renewal, while "contributory" reasons are

Table 862–A   Number of Broadcast License Denials and License/Permit Revocations by the FCC, 1934–1982

	Number of Licenses/Permits Involved:		
Five Year Period	*Broadcast License Denials*[a]	*Broadcast License Revocations*	*Construction Permit Revocations*
1934–1939 (5½ Years)	7	2	—
1940–1944	2	—	—
1945–1949	6	4	1
1950–1954	2	3	2
1955–1959	1	1	3
1960–1964	15	12	—
1965–1969	14	5	—
1970–1974	29	3	—
1975–1979	25	3	—
1980–1982	7	—	—
Totals	109	34	6

Source: FCC *Annual Report 1982*, pp. 112–113. Denials or revocations are listed here according to date of the Commission decision. Actual deletion or other final action often takes place months or years later. Notes: [a]These are license renewals or applications for licenses denied by the FCC—no distinction between the two is made by the source. See also Table 863–C.

Table 862–B Reasons Cited for FCC Deletion of Licenses, 1934–1978

Reasons Cited by the FCC	Frequency Cited	Reasons Cited by the FCC	Frequency Cited
Misrepresentations to the FCC	58	Fairness Doctrine Violations	
Unauthorized Transfer of Control,		(Including Personal Attacks)	5
Misrepresentation of Ownership	42	Slanted News	4
Abandonment, Failure to Prosecute		Log Falsification	4
Renewal	36	Overcommercialization	2
Technical Violations	32	Lottery Violations	2
Character Defects of Licensees	21	Failure to Control Programming	2
Fraudulence (Contests, Billing,		Equal Employment Opportunities	
Improper Business and Advertising		Violation	1
Practices)	20	Indecent Programs	1
Departure from Promises	12	Miscellaneous	20
Financial Qualification Defects	7		

Source: Head & Sterling (1982), p. 452. Note: Total deletions (including 15 pending in 1978) were 142, most for multiple reasons.

generally violations of a less severe nature, and two or more may be considered together before the FCC takes action against a licensee.

Sources

All the data reported here were based on FCC records, some of which are summarized in its *Annual Report* and all of which are available on either a per-station basis or in various degrees of cumulation at the FCC offices in Washington, D.C. The FCC publishes its individual license decisions, but these decisions are also reported by a number of legal services and in the trade press. The reasons for each FCC enforcement action are made clear in those published decisions.

The secondary sources cited for all but Table 862–A (figured directly by the author), are all based on this primary and public FCC material. Given the relatively limited number of stations involved in the various categories, and the degree of careful agency record keeping over the years, all of this material may be judged as quite accurate—subject only to errors in the secondary sources.

Further Information

For specific details on the background and application of the FCC sanctions summarized here, see the source cited with each table in this unit. For more general background, the reader should consult a broadcasting text, such as Head and Sterling (1982), or one of the several available books on the regulation of broadcasting.

Table 862–C   Number, Frequency, and Reasons for Broadcast License Forfeitures (Fines) by the FCC, 1961–1978

Factor	1961–1971		1971–1978	
	Number	Percentage	Number	Percentage
Number of Forfeiture Notices by Type of Station:[a]				
AM	672	76	869	78
FM	187	21	168	15
TV	31	4	78	7
Total	890	100	1115	100
Frequency of Forfeiture Notice by Market Size:				
Small	443	50	N/A	N/A
Medium	330	37	N/A	N/A
Large	117	13	N/A	N/A

Major Reasons for
Forfeiture Notices:

	1961–1971		1971–1978	
Late Filing Renewal	319	29	72	5
Logging Violations	157	14	349	25
Failure to Make Equipment Performance Measurements	150	14	106	6
Unlicensed or "Underlicensed" Operation	117	11	154	11
Violation of Broadcast Hours, Power, Pre-sunrise Authorizations	89	8	327	23
Technical Operation Violations	63	6	124	9
Failure to File Information with FCC as Required	32	3	31	2
Failure to Identify Sponsorship	31	3	51	4
Remote Control Violations	23	3	60	4
All Other (12 Reasons)—1961–1971	130	11.6	—	
All Other (14 Reasons)—1971–1978	—	—	155	11

Source: 1961–1971 data: Clift, Weiss, and Able, (Fall 1971); 1971–1978 data: Clift, Able and Garay (Summer 1980). Note: [a]Figures for 1971 are divided between the two studies at June 30th. Figures for 1978 end at March 1978.

Table 862–D   Number and Reasons for Broadcast License Short-Term Renewals by the FCC, 1960–1981

Factor	Number	Percentage
Number of Short-Term Renewals by Type of Station:		
AM	190	71
FM	63	21
TV	16	6
Major Reasons Cited by the FCC:		
Improper Control of Operations	54	20
Repeated Violation of Rules	47	17
Promise Inconsistent with Performance	31	12
Other "Primary" Reasons	91	34
"Contributory" Reasons	46	17
Period of Short-Term License[a]:		
One Year	171	64
Over One But Under Three Years	56	21
Less Than One Year	42	16
Application of Reasons:		
Multiple Violations	121	45
Single Violation	148	55

Source: FCC data as arranged and gathered by Shelby (1974), updated through 1981 by Shelby and supplied directly to the author. Note: [a] In this period, the standard license period was three years. In 1981, Congress lengthened licenses to run for five years for television, and seven years for radio.

863
PUBLIC PARTICIPATION IN THE BROADCAST REGULATORY PROCESS

Interpretation of the Tables

The tables in this Unit measure public participation in the regulation of broadcasting. Most interaction between broadcasters and the FCC has consisted of confrontations between stations' counsels and Commission staff with little or no public input. However, that situation appears to be changing.

Table 863-A reports the FCC's official count of letters which were received from the public and which deal with any aspect of broadcasting, including noncomplaint mail. Data shown for 1966 and 1968 are very approximate, as they were reconstructed from brief narrative descriptions in the *Annual Report*; figures for all other years represent detailed reports by the FCC. The first general trend to note is that of increasing letter-writing to the FCC—and this tabulation does not include the most massive input of several million letters which flooded the commission in the early 1970s from those who were concerned that the FCC was about to ban religious or even noncommercial broadcasting. (For details on that fascinating story, see "The Curse of the Phantom Petition," *TV Guide*, July 24, 1976.) In recent years especially, the high numbers of letters to the FCC are due to organized campaigns of opinion for or against a given program (refer to Table 863-A notes). Until 1974, the amount of complaint mail did not exceed that of noncomplaint mail (letters of praise, general requests for information, etc.). However, in 1974 and especially in 1976, there were sharp rises in complaints received about all aspects of radio and television.

Table 863-B provides a 21 year run of details of public letters to the FCC on questions of controversial issues and political broadcasting. The Fairness Doctrine holds that stations should: (1) provide time for discussion of issues of importance in their communities, and (2) within that time provided, allow all sides of a controversial issue to be heard. Even though there are more radio stations than television stations (see Tables 170-A and 180-A), Table 863-B shows that most people who write to the FCC about the Fairness Doctrine are concerned about television programs. "Equal time" refers to quite specific regulations (Section 315 of the Communications Act of 1934) which govern the use of broadcast facilities by candidates for public office.

Table 863-C offers those few available statistics which summarize the peak of citizen participation—actual petitions to deny license renewals or new station applications. In the late 1960s, a series of important court decisions gave the public legal standing in broadcast proceedings before the FCC, and as the first column of this table suggests, generally increasing numbers of petitions have been filed in recent years. Most public petitions are filed at the time that stations file for renewal of their licenses (every three years [until 1981; then five years for television and seven for radio] under normal circumstances, with all stations in a given state coming up for renewal at the same time). Some of these petitions genuinely seek to gain access to the frequency to place their own stations on the air, but many are filed as a means of gaining leverage against a licensee for some concern of the petitioners (employment matters, programming, etc.). As the incomplete data

Table 863–A Categorization of Public Correspondence with the FCC on Broadcast Matters, 1966–1980

Category	1966[a]	1968[b]	1970	1972	1974	1976	1978	1980
Complaints								
Advertising	2,700		1,839	1,954	1,731	3,545	3,018	1,879
Miscellaneous Programming	} 3,500	23,800	12,561	7,738	13,193	10,613	13,812	24,419
Violation of FCC Rules, Policy, etc.			2,833	2,370	24,646[c]	6,337	6,135	14,923
Section 315 and Fairness Doctrine	1,900	3,800	2,722	3,002	2,859	44,975[d]	8,350	20,340
Miscellaneous Non-Programming	4,900	5,400	5,975	7,019	7,985	9,291	15,588	8,627
Totals:								
Radio	N/A	N/A	8,896	9,759	8,744	11,667	16,460	19,338
Television	N/A	N/A	16,888	12,158	41,228	62,724	27,813	50,485
Total[e]	13,000	33,000	25,920	22,083	50,414	74,761	46,903	70,188
Non-Complaints	39,800	34,000	34,375	22,598	27,715	20,922	27,300	24,316
Total Communications	52,000+	67,000+	60,295	44,681	78,129	95,683	74,203	94,504

Sources: 1966–1976 data from the FCC *Annual Reports*. 1978–1980 data from the FCC Broadcast Bureau Fiscal Reports. Notes: [a]Data for 1966 figured by the author from a narrative paragraph with percentages from the 1966 *Report*, p. 112. Figures are rounded to the nearest one hundred. [b]Data for 1968 figured by the author from a narrative paragraph with percentages from the 1968 *Report*, p. 44, also rounded to the nearest one hundred. [c]Of these 24,646 letters, 23,800 were concerned with obscenity, profanity, and indecency on television. [d]According to Simmons (1978), p. 213, note 5, some 36,000 of these 44,975 letters were due to "Guns of Autumn" (an NBC documentary) and letters on sex, violence, decency, and morality on television. [e]Totals include complaints not classified as concerning either radio or television.

Table 863–B Public Complaints to the FCC Regarding the Fairness Doctrine and Equal-Time Provisions, 1960–1981

Year	Fairness Doctrine	Equal-Time	Total
1960	233	N/A	N/A
1961	409	N/A	N/A
1962	850	N/A	N/A
1963	N/A	N/A	N/A
1964–1965 (Two Years)	993	N/A	N/A
1966	N/A	N/A	1,950
1967	N/A	N/A	1,650
1968	N/A	N/A	3,800
1969	1,632	366	1,998
(TV)[a]	56	60	
1970	1,736	558	2,294
(TV)	64	62	

Table 863–B Public Complaints to the FCC Regarding the Fairness Doctrine and Equal-Time Provisions, 1960–1981 (cont.)

Year	Fairness Doctrine	Equal-Time	Total
1971	1,124	941	2,065
(TV)	64	62	
1972	1,617	1,383	3,000
(TV)	62	58	
1973	2,406	4,234	6,640
(TV)	76	59	
1974	1,874	984	2,858
(TV)	70	53	
1975	3,570	1,435	5,005
(TV)	84	64	
1976	41,861[b]	3,113	44,974
(TV)	98	74	
1977	2,000	1,601	3,601
(TV)	72	69	
1978	3,831	4,487	8,318
(TV)	49	43	
1979	4,437	4,417	8,854
(TV)	42	48	
1980	10,440	9,896	20,336
(TV)	35	52	
1981	4,797	5,932	10,726
(TV)	39	50	

Source: Data through 1976 supplied from the FCC as cited by Simmons (1978), pp. 212–215. Data since then supplied direct to the author from FCC Broadcast (after 1982, Mass Media) Bureau. Note that the totals do not quite match those found in Table 863–A because the few statistics in which there was no mention of class of station in the complaint are not counted here. Notes: [a]Percent of complaints against TV stations. [b]See footnote "d" on Table 863–A.

provided in the second column of Table 863–C attest, the number of stations affected by such petitions has increased sharply. But the real effect of these actions is limited, as shown in the final two columns. Given the number of petitions and the number of stations affected, relatively few renewal applications are even set for hearing—that important first step when the commission agrees that the issues need public airing in a Washington hearing. The process is a very expensive one for both the station and the petitioner, but it is necessary before any license can be denied. The final column of Table 863–C suggests just how rare those denials are. (It should be remembered that thousands of stations are routinely renewed each year.) In other words, the chance of a petition successfully denying renewal is very slight.

Table 863–C   Public Participation in the Broadcast License Renewal Process, 1967–1981

Year	Petitions Filed	Stations Affected	Renewals Set For Hearing	Renewals Denied
1967	2	2	4	—
1968	3	3	15	1
1969	2	2	13	5
1970	15	16	9	5
1971	38	84	23	8
1972	68	108	20	4
1973	48	140	13	7
1974	37	58	20	2
1975	94	145	11	14
1976	35	224	23	4
1976 (Transition Quarter)	14	36	7	4
1977	19	68	13	3
1978	97	130	23	3
1979	19	54	14	1
1980	17	41	8	5
1981	N/A	N/A	19	2

Source: All data supplied direct to the author from the FCC except the final column which was taken from the FCC *Annual Reports*. All data is for fiscal years (1 July—30 June through 1975; 1 July—30 September of following year for 1976 which is shown above as a "normal" year plus the transition quarter; and 1 October—30 September for 1977 forward.)

Sources

Virtually all of this information is supplied by the FCC as the agency creating the actions (or receiving the letters) in question. Given the limited number of stations, station data can be termed accurate. There is no way to assess the accuracy of FCC record keeping on correspondence received, or the categories to which it is assigned.

Further Information

For general background on public participation in the broadcast regulatory process, the reader should refer to the FCC's *Annual Report*. Important cases (virtually all of those which involve actions taken against major stations and/or those which get to the hearing stage) are discussed in the trade periodicals. For a citizens' group viewpoint on this process and specific cases, see issues of *Access*, and Haight (1979).

890
STATE REGULATION OF CABLE TELEVISION

Interpretation of the Table

As the medium has developed more recently, so has state regulation of cable television developed more recently than comparable statutes for broadcasting (see Unit 861). Table 890–A demonstrates the number of states with statutes in force for three periods of time: the years prior to 1972, the highly active period of the mid-1970s, and the more recent period of lesser activity since 1979. Generally speaking, states are of greater importance in the regulation of cable due to the local franchising role. Yet to date, only a few states (11) have adopted comprehensive state regulation either through a special commission, or as part of the pre-existing public utility commission. The most important cable regulation thus far has come from Alaska, Connecticut (the first to regulate cable), Delaware, Hawaii, Massachusetts, Minnesota, Nevada, New Jersey, New York, Rhode Island, and Vermont. Note that in the table, the two most important areas of activity (measured in terms of states having statutes) are franchising standards or matters of right-of-way for cable (36 states), and sanctions for theft of cable service (42 states), the latter enacted generally under considerable pressure from cable firms. No other single area of regulation comes close. For a five year period through 1982, each year saw more state legislation introduced than in the previous year, though much of it did not pass.

Source

Sharon Briley, of the Policy and Planning Division of the FCC's Mass Media Bureau, has for a number of years annually traced state-level developments in cable regulation. Considerably more detailed break-outs of individual state actions can be found in such publications as her article in Hollowell (1980), pp. 35–72, and the annual "Cable Television: State Legislation" issued by the FCC, though researched by Briley. Data for these are gathered from each state's legislature.

Table 890–A State Statutes on Cable Television, 1972–1982

Subject	*Number of States with Statutes in Force*		
	Adopted Pre–1972	*Adopted 1973–1978*	*Adopted 1979–1982*
Access	1	—	—
Antitrust	1	—	—
Company/Subscriber Practices	1	—	—
Complaints	—	1	—
Construction or Equipment	5	3	—
Definition	—	3	1
Earth Station Location	1	—	—
Educational Uses	—	1	—
Forfeitures	—	3	1
Franchising or Right-of-Way	9	17	10
Landlord-Tenant Relationships	5	4	—
Liability	1	2	—
Occupational Licensing– Exemption	1	1	—
Ownership	7	2	—
Pole Attachment	6	6	3
Privacy	3	—	—
Programming or Channel Use	4	—	—
Property Damage or Removal	1	4	—
Rates	7	3	7
Safety	1	3	—
Service–			
a) Abandonment	—	1	—
b) Disconnections	—	2	—
c) Extensions	1	3	—
d) Interconnections	—	2	—
e) Theft	10	28	4
State Regulation (Comprehensive)–			
a) Independent New Commission	—	1	2
b) Existing Utility Commission	—	1	6
c) Other Agency	—	—	1
d) Amendments	9	10	—
Study Committees	—	9	—
Taxation or Fees–			
a) Tax Imposition	4	5	2
b) Exemption	6	5	—
c) Assessment	3	3	—
d) State or Franchise Fee	1	4	—

Source: Information supplied to the author by Sharon Briley, with the assistance of Robin Berry (see text).

Further Information

In addition to the Briley publications noted above, see also Hochberg (1978), among other publications of the Harvard Program.

SOURCES AND REFERENCES

Bibliographic Note: U.S. Government Statistical Publications

A good deal of the material reported in this volume has been based upon or come directly from government-gathered and -disseminated statistical reports from a variety of agencies. As noted, many of these government statistical functions, however, are being closed down in the face of economic pressure and political change. This short discussion deals briefly with the more important government publications, noting their background, intent, terminology and definitions, and commenting upon the reliability and validity of their data. Year of publication is given only for those publications not annually or regularly issued. All titles are listed in the government documents list of references, which follows.

Background

Until 1982, federal statistical policy was largely administered by an office in the Office of Management and Budget (formerly Bureau of the Budget) in the Executive Office of the President. After nearly a half century of varying degrees of coordination, however, the activity ceased due to budget and personnel reductions. See House of Representatives (1982) for discussion of current federal role in gathering data.

Two publications from the Office of Management and Budget (Statistical Policy Division) are of basic and continuing reference value. *Statistical*

Services of the United States Government (1975), though in need of revision, provides capsule background on major government statistics-gathering programs and their methods and rationale. It backgrounds in considerably more detail nearly all of the documents listed here. It notes which agencies are responsible for which data.

The *Standard Industrial Classification Manual* (1972) describes the system of industrial classification developed over the years by experts in both government and private industry. In 1972, the system was extensively revised. This revision process seriously affected the historical comparability of some data, since the last major revision had been carried out in 1957. The *SIC Manual* divides all industries into several divisions: agriculture, mining, construction, manufacturing, transportation-communication-utilities, wholesale trade, retail trade, finance-insurance-real-estate, services, public administration (mainly government), and a miscellaneous category of nonclassifiable establishments. These divisions are subdivided into two-digit "major groups," and each major group is divided into three- or four-digit industries. Five- or seven-digit entries identify products or other outputs of the same industries.

The *SIC Manual* uses establishments, rather than companies, as the basis of its scheme: "For the purposes of this classification, an establishment is an economic unit, generally at a single physical location, where business is conducted or where services or industrial operations are performed" (p. 10). Distinct and separate economic activities performed at a single location are counted separately if the employment levels are significant in both, and if separate statistics can be compiled on important economic factors, such as employment, wages and salaries, and sales or receipts. A short *Supplement* appeared in 1977.

From the Bureau of the Census (Department of Commerce) come the following broad background statistical collections:

Historical Statistics (1975) provides some 12,500 time-series concerning all aspects of American life, with supplementary text and notes. This two-volume work is a revision and expansion of a work which was first issued in 1949 (with 3,000 time-series carried to 1945) and later revised in 1960 (with 8,000 time-series carried to 1957), with shorter interim updates between editions. The present edition provides time-series to 1970, drawing data from both commercial and government sources. Some data in the present book are updated from material here.

The text information on source limitations and definitions is concise and generally excellent. As a general rule, data are presented for the nation as a whole, with few regional, state, or local breakdowns. Only annual or census year data are shown, and usually for periods no shorter than 20 years. Data are arranged in broad subject chapters with more specific subject subsections. A detailed 22-page index provides access to the two volumes.

Social Indicators (1973, 1976, 1980) are analytic reports on the state of the nation as viewed from the individual or family level. The emphasis throughout the text, charts, tables, and graphs is on results or outcomes rather than on various kinds of inputs. The 1980 report is divided into 11 major areas of social concern, and each area includes a brief text and color charts, statistical tables (providing details regarding the charts), and technical notes and definitions in support of the other materials.

Statistical Abstract, produced annually, is the official compendium of government and privately derived statistics concerning most aspects of American life. Issues since 1973 also serve as updates to *Historical Statistics*. The emphasis here is on current information with a minimum of descriptive text and discussion of statistical limitations. Since its first appearance in 1878, *Statistical Abstract* has become the single most important statistical compendium and reference issued by the government. In each of its sections, information is provided for the past three years or so, with several selected earlier benchmark years also included. Appendixes detail major sources and provide a cross-reference table with *Historical Statistics*.

U.S. Industrial Outlook has been published since the early 1960s. It provides data on recent trends and the immediate outlook of some 200 industries with regard to changes in supply and demand, domestic and foreign markets, prices, employment and wages, and investment. The work is typically issued in January and contains hard data for the preceeding two years, as well as end-of-the-year estimates for the year prior to publication, and estimates for the cover-date year and the next several years to come. Industries are classified using the SIC system. A 50-page chapter in recent issues has dealt with communications—telecommunications, printing and publishing, and broadcasting—with a separate section on motion pictures.

For an invaluable, though unofficial guide to most of the publications noted in this discussion, see Hoel et al., eds. *Economics Sourcebook of Government Statistics* (Lexington Books, 1983).

Economic Censuses

The Bureau of the Census (Department of Commerce) is the major publisher of regular census and survey-based economic information. Complete information regarding its many publications may be found in the latest annual issue of its Catalog *of publications. This section treats only Census Bureau publications which were used extensively throughout* Electronic Media: *(1)* Annual Survey of Manufactures, *(2)* Census of Manufactures, *(3)* Census of Retail Trade, *(4)* Census of Selected Service Industries, *(5)* Current Industrial Reports.

The *Annual Survey of Manufactures* has appeared since 1949, except during years ending in "2" or "7" (the *Census of Manufactures* years). It provides general statistics of manufacturing activity for industry groups, for important individual industries, and for geographic divisions of the country, including large Standard Metropolitan Statistical Areas (SMSAs). Beginning with 1960, figures are also provided for large industrial counties. Data include value added by manufacture, value of shipments, cost of materials, fuels and electric energy consumed, employment, man-hours and payrolls, capital expenditures, gross book value of assets, rental payments, and supplemental labor costs. According to the 1976 *Statistical Abstract*: "The most recent annual survey is based on a sample of about 70,000 of an approximate total of 320,000 manufacturing establishments. It comprises all large plants, which account for approximately two-thirds of total manufacturing employment in the United States, and a representative selection of the more numerous small plants. Government-owned and -operated establishments are excluded."

The *Census of Manufactures* first appeared in 1899. The 1977 census is the 30th and most recent in this series. Current legislation calls for the census to be held every five years, during years ending with "2" or "7".

Like other censuses conducted since 1947, the 1972 *Census of Manufactures* was primarily a mail canvass. The diversity of manufacturing activities made it necessary to use more than 200 different forms to collect data from the approximately 450 industries covered in the census. The 120,000 firms in the United States with less than 10 employees were not required to file reports. Estimates for these small establishments were mainly constructed from industry averages, although payroll and sales data were supplied by the Social Security Administration and the Internal Revenue Service. In most industries, these small establishments accounted for less than 3 percent of the payroll and value-added figures.

The census is conducted on the basis of "establishments," and an "industry" is generally defined as a group of establishments producing either a single product or a number of closely related products. The SIC system of industry definition is employed, and definitions become progressively narrower with the additions of numerical digits. There are 20 very broad two-digit major industry groups, approximately 150 three-digit groups, and 450 four-digit industries, while some 10,000 products have seven-digit codes and are grouped into 1,300 classes of products with five-digit codes. The seven- and five-digit products are considered the primary products of the industry with the same first four digits. Consequently, an establishment is classified in a particular industry if its production of the primary products of that industry exceeds the value of its production of the products of any other single industry.

The following industry groups appear in the *Census of Manufactures* and are of importance in the *Electronic Media* data series. They are listed in ascending order of their SIC numbers. The reader should keep in mind that the definitions of various industries and products included in the censuses have often changed over time and that these changes have created difficulties in historical comparability.

Industry 3651: Radio and Television Receiving Sets (60, 70, and 80 Series). These establishments are engaged mainly in manufacturing electronic equipment for home entertainment. They also include those engaged in the manufacture of public address systems and music distribution apparatus, except records. Classification code and definitions were unchanged from 1967 through 1977.

Industry 3671: Electron Tubes, Receiving Type (60, 70, and 80 Series). These establishments are engaged primarily in the manufacture of radio and television receiving electron tubes, except cathode-ray tubes. No change in classification or definitions occurred between 1967 and 1972, but for 1977 the separate category was discontinued.

Industry 3672: Cathode-Ray Television Picture Tubes (60, 70, and 80 Series). These establishments are engaged primarily in the manufacture of receiving-type cathode-ray tubes. No changes in classification or definitions were made between 1967 and 1972, but for 1977, the category was collapsed into that above.

The *Census of Retail Trade* was classified as part of the *Census of Business* prior to 1972. The first economic census was conducted as a part of the 1810 population census; and prior to 1929, these censuses did not specifically cover wholesale and retail trade. After 1933, various services were also included. Business censuses were taken in 1935 and 1939, then resumed after the war in 1948 and continued in the same years as the manufacturing census: 1954, 1958, 1963, 1967, 1972 and 1977 (the tenth such census). Future censuses (divided in 1972 into separately titled sections on wholesale trade, retail trade, and selected service industries) will cover years ending in "2" and "7". The following industry group, important to *Electronic Media*, appear in the *Census of Retail Trade*.

Industry 5732: Radio and Television Stores (60, 70, and 80 Series). These establishments are engaged primarily in the retail sale and installation of radios, televisions, record players, high-fidelity and sound-reproducing equipment. Such establishments may also sell additional products such as household appliances, musical instruments, or records.

The *Census of Selected Service Industries* was part of the *Census of Business* prior to 1972, and its background is related to that of the retail trade census described above. A combination of Social Security and Internal Revenue Service information, along with a mail survey, produces the information it contains on location, kind of business, volume of receipts and payrolls, and number of employees. Firms with no paid employees during 1977, or firms with small payrolls below specific levels for various industries (generally one to three employees), were not included in the mail survey.

Historical comparability between this 1977 census and the 1972 or 1967 census (part of the *Census of Business*) is harmed by some changes in classification, by changes in SMSA composition, and by lack of information on proprietors of unincorporated businesses in 1972. All forms of payroll (including salaried officers and executives of corporations who were on payroll for the entire year) are counted. The census reports employment for the pay period beginning March 12th and for the first quarter of the census year. (*Electronic Media* uses only the full-year figures.)

Receipts include total receipts from customers for services rendered and merchandise sold during 1977, whether or not payment was received in 1977. Receipts are net after deductions for refunds and returns, and include both local and state sales taxes. Excise taxes paid by the establishment are also included. Non-operating income, such as investments and rental of real estate, are not included. While the count of establishments given is for the end of the year, receipts are for all firms operating during the census year. The following service industries, important to *Electronic Media*, appear in the *Census of Selected Service Industries*.

> Industry 7622: Radio and Television Repair Shops (50 and 60 Series). These establishments are engaged primarily in repairing radios, television sets, phonographs, high-fidelity or stereophonic equipment, and tape recorders. Also included are establishments which install and repair television sets, and amateur and citizens band antennas—or those which install and service radio transmitting and receiving equipment in homes, offices, small boats, automobiles or other vehicles.
>
> Industry 7814: Motion Picture and Tape Production for Television (80 Series). These establishments are engaged primarily in the production or distribution of theatrical and nontheatrical motion pictures and tape—including commercials—for television exhibition.

Current Industrial Reports is a series of over 100 monthly, quarterly, and annual reports containing detailed statistics on some 5,000 manufactured products. Each report generally includes between two and eight tables concerning production, shipments, stocks and inventories, and foreign trade. A related title is *Radio Receivers and Television Sets; Phonographs and Record Players, Speakers and Related Equipment* (MA-36M). *Current Industrial Reports* also uses SIC product designations, allowing easy comparison of the data given here with those given in the *Annual Survey of Manufactures* and the *Census of Manufacturers*. Each report typically provides data for the past three years or so (with revisions in earlier figures designated by notes), detailed definitions, and discussion of the limitations of the data. Prior to 1959, these reports were titled *Facts for Industry*.

Other Economic Data

Three works produced by the Bureau of Economic Analysis (Department of Commerce) are used throughout Electronic Media, *(1)* Survey of Current Business, *(2)* Business Statistics, *and (3)* The National Income and Product Accounts of the United States, 1929–76, Statistical Tables *(1981).*

The *Survey of Current Business* is the most important single current source of business and trade statistics. This monthly publication includes general business indicators and data on domestic and foreign trade, employment, and wages for specific industry groupings using the SIC scheme. The July issue provides cumulative data for the past three years on national income, with tables and supporting text on GNP, personal income and outlay, government receipts and expenditures, foreign transactions, savings and investment, production-income-employment by industry, implicit price deflators and indexes, and so forth. Several other special issues are produced, including the following two publications issued as supplements to the *Survey*.

Business Statistics (biennial) provides cumulative information from the *Survey of Current Business* from 1947 to date and is published in odd-numbered years. Explanatory notes and source references supplement the tables, which make up the bulk of *Business Statistics*. Some 2,500 series are included, with annual data in most cases and monthly figures for the most recent years.

The *National Income and Product Accounts of the United States, 1929–76, Statistical Tables* (1981) is issued irregularly—every 8 to 10 years—and cumulates the July sections of similar title from the monthly *Survey of Current Business*. It includes basically the same sections listed under the *Survey*'s July issue. The first four pages provide detailed definitions underlying the tables. The publication of this volume often coincides with benchmark revisions in the historical series presented.

Four publications originating with the Bureau of Labor Statistics (Department of Labor) were particularly useful to the author: (1) BLS Handbook of Methods for Surveys and Studies *(1976), (2)* Consumer Price Index

Detailed Report, *(3)* Employment and Earnings, United States, 1909–1975 *(1977), and (4)* Handbook of Labor Statistics.

BLS Handbook of Methods for Surveys and Studies (1976) is a compilation of technical notes on the major BLS survey publications. The *Handbook* details the statistical methods of these surveys and discusses their limitations. Various sections deal with statistical series on such topics as current employment analysis, manpower structure and trends, prices and living conditions, wages and industrial relations, and productivity and technology.

The *Consumer Price Index Detailed Report* is a monthly publication which reveals average changes in prices of goods and services usually bought by urban wage earners and clerical workers. The Consumer Price Index (CPI) is based on prices of about 400 items selected to represent the movement of prices of all consumer goods and services. Prices for these items are collected from about 18,000 establishments in urban portions of 39 major statistical areas and 17 smaller cities. Each year, the December issue of *CPI Detailed Report* contains the annual average figures for the various CPIs, compared to the previous year. Notes in each issue detail methods of calculating index changes and the problem of seasonally adjusted data. The CPI uses 1967 as a base year, while this volume generally employs a uniform base year of 1972. In January of 1978, the CPI was divided into two parts, separately reported: CPI-U, covering urban workers, and CPI-W covering more specifically urban wage earners and clerical workers, or about half the population covered by CPI-U. For more detail, see "The Consumer Price Index: Concepts and Content over the Years" (BLS Report 517, revised May 1978).

Employment and Earnings, United States, 1909–1978 (1979) is the 12th comprehensive data book on national statistics to be released by the Bureau of Labor Statistics since 1961. Summary tables and charts included in past editions of this publication have been omitted from this edition. Data usually summarized in the analytical tables appear in detail within this publication. Charts containing related information are published each month in *Employment and Earnings*.

Detailed industry statistics on the nation's nonagricultural work force are presented in this volume, which includes monthly and annual employment averages for all employees, women, production workers in manufacturing and mining, construction workers in contract construction, and nonsupervisory workers in the remaining private nonmanufacturing industries. Also shown are average weekly and hourly earnings, average weekly and overtime hours, and labor turnover rates—with seasonally adjusted data for a number of these series. Each industry title in this work is identified by the appropriate SIC code. Only national data are presented in this work. A companion volume, *Employment and Earnings, States and Area, 1939–74*, provides similar information for all states, the District of Columbia, and more than 220 areas.

The *Handbook of Labor Statistics* provides some 400 pages of historical series—generally for the past decade—on the labor force, employment, unemployment, hours, productivity and unit labor costs, compensation, prices and living conditions, unions and industrial relations, occupational injuries and illnesses, foreign labor statistics, and general economic data. The data, supplied by the BLS and other departments, are accompanied by brief statements of the method and limitations of each series. Some 20 pages of "Technical Notes" begin the *Handbook* and deal with derivation and limits to the data presented on each topic.

Special Note on Canadian Broadcasting

Statistics in this volume refer almost entirely to electronic media in or from the United States. Readers interested in statistics on radio, television, and cable in Canada are urged to consult the two-volume *Special Report on Broadcasting in Canada, 1968–1978* (Canadian Radio-television and Telecommunications Commission, Information Services, Ottawa, Ontario K1A ON2, Canada). The first volume of 120 pages provides text, tables, and charts comparing 1967 and 1977 data (with some intervening years' data offered on occasion) concerning coverage, penetration, audience patterns, program trends, ownership, and economic status for all three media. The second volume provides supplementary tables. Both volumes provide national data and provincial-level information, and cover most information categories discussed in this volume, plus a few more.

Government Documents

NOTE: all publications are issued by the United States Government Printing Office in Washington, D.C., unless otherwise noted.

Board for International Broadcasting. *Annual Report.* 1974–date.

Bureau of the Census (Department of Commerce):

> *Annual Survey of Manufactures.* 1948–date except in years when Census of Manufactures is taken.
>
> *Census of Business.* 1929, 1933, 1935, 1939, 1948, 1954, 1958, 1963, 1967.
>
> *Census of Manufactures.* 1899, 1914, 1919, 1921, 1923, 1925, 1927, 1929, 1931, 1933, 1935, 1937, 1939, 1947, 1954, 1958, 1963, 1967, 1972, 1977.
>
> *Census of Retail Trade.* (earlier data in Census of Business) 1972, 1977.
>
> *Census of Selected Service Industries.* (earlier data in Census of Business) 1972, 1977.

County Business Patterns (annual).

Current Industrial Reports (various dates and subtitles: see text above).

Current Population Reports. August 1977.

Foreign Commerce and Navigation of the United States. Annual, then irregular (final issue, for 1965 data, published in 1970).

Historical Statistics of the United States, Colonial Times to 1970: Bicentennial Edition. 1975.

Monthly Retail Trade: Sales and Accounts Receivable.

Social Indicators 1976. 1977.

Social Indicators III. 1980.

Statistical Abstract of the United States, The. 1878–date, annual.

U.S. Exports, Schedule B, Commodity and Country (FT 410, monthly).

U.S. General Imports, Schedule A, Commodity by Country (FT 135, monthly).

U.S. Imports for Consumption and General Imports, SIC-Based Products and Area (FT 210, annual).

1972 Survey of Minority-Owned Business Enterprises. 1975.

Bureau of Domestic Commerce (Department of Commerce). *U.S. Industrial Outlook* 1961–date, annual (formerly titled *Current Industrial Outlook*).

Bureau of Economic Analysis (Department of Commerce):

Business Statistics. 1947 to date (biennial).

National Income and Product Accounts of the United States, 1929–74. 1976 (periodically revised).

Survey of Current Business (monthly).

Bureau of Labor Statistics (Department of Labor):

BLS Handbook of Methods for Surveys and Studies (Bulletin 1910). 1976.

Consumer Price Index, Detailed Report (monthly).

Employment and Earnings, 1909–1975 (Bulletin 1312-10). 1976 (periodically revised).

Handbook of Labor Statistics (Bulletin 1966). (annual).

Bureau of Navigation (Department of Commerce). *Radio Service Bulletin No. 62.* (June 1, 1922).

Commission on Civil Rights. *Window Dressing on the Set: Women and Minorities in Television*, and *Update*. 1977 and 1979.

Domestic and International Business Administration (Department of Commerce). *The U.S. Consumer Electronics Industry* by Stuart A. Pettingill et al. 1975.

Federal Communications Commission: (note: "FCC" prior to publication date indicates material issued by the agency, not GPO):

Annual Report. 1935 to date (issues for 1935–55 reprinted by Arno Press, 1971).

AM and FM Broadcast Financial Data. FCC, 1938–80 annual (series discontinued).

An Economic Study of Standard Broadcasting. FCC, 1947 (reprinted by Arno Press, 1974).

Cable Industry EEO Study. FCC, 1975.

Cable Television Employment Statistics. FCC, 1977–82.

Cable TV Industry Revenues [title varied]. FCC, 1977–81, annual (series discontinued).

EEO Trend Report. FCC, 1981.

FCC Policy on Cable Ownership: A Staff Report by the Office of Plans and Policy. FCC, 1981.

Inquiry and Proposed Rulemaking in Docket 79-219, Deregulation of Radio as reprinted in *Federal Register* 44:57683 (October 5, 1979).

Network Broadcasting, Report of the Network Study Staff to the Network Study Committee. Issued by the U.S. House of Representatives as House Report 1297, 85th Cong., 2nd Sess., 1958.

New Television Networks: Entry, Jurisdiction, Ownership and Regulation, Final Report of the Network Inquiry Special Staff. 1980 (two volumes).

Report on Chain Broadcasting. 1941 (reprinted by Arno Press, 1974).

Television Broadcast Programming Data. FCC, 1973–79, annual (series discontinued).

Television Channel Utilization as of June 30, 1980. FCC, 1980 (semi-annual).

TV Broadcast Financial Data. FCC, 1948–80, annual (series discontinued).

Federal Radio Commission. *Annual Report.* 1927–33.

Federal Trade Commission. *Proceedings of the Symposium on Media Concentration, December 14 and 15, 1978.* 1979 (two volumes).

General Accounting Office, U.S. Congress:

Improvements Made, Some Still Needed in Management of Radio Free Europe/Radio Liberty GAO, Report ID-81-16, March 2, 1981.

U.S. International Communication Agency's Overseas Programs; Some More Useful than Others. GAO, Report ID-82-1, February 11, 1982.

The Voice of America Should Address Existing Problems to Ensure High Performance. GAO, Report ID-82-37, July 29, 1982.

International Information Program (Department of State). *The Voice of America: 1950–1951*. 1951.

International Trade Administration (Department of Commerce). *High Technology Industries: Profiles and Outlooks—The Telecommunications Industry.* 1983.

International Trade Commission. *Television Receiving Sets from Japan.* USITC, Publication 1153, June 1981.

Office of Management and Budget (Executive Office of the President):

Social Indicators 1973. 1973.

Standard Industrial Classification Manual, and *Supplement.* 1972, 1977.

Statistical Services of the United States Government. 1975.

Office of Telecommunications Policy (Executive Office of the President). *Analysis of the Causes and Effects of Increases in Same-Year Rerun Programming and Related Issues in Prime-Time Network Television.* OTP, 1973.

Presidential Study Commission on International Broadcasting. *The Right to Know.* 1973.

Temporary Commission on Alternative Financing for Public Telecommunications:

Alternative Financing Options for Public Broadcasting. Issued through Federal Communications Commission, July 1982.

Final Report. Issued through FCC, October 1983.

Surgeon General's Scientific Advisory Committee on Television and Social Behavior. *Television and Growing Up: The Impact of Televised Violence.* 1972.

U.S. House of Representatives. Committee on Energy and Commerce, Subcommittee on Telecommunications, Consumer Protection, and Finance. *Telecommunications in Transition: The Status of Competition in the Telecommunications Industry.* Majority Staff Report. 97th Cong., 1st Sess., November 1981.

U.S. House of Representatives. Committee on Government Operations. *Federal Government Statistics and Statistical Policy: Hearings.* 97th Cong., 1st Sess., June 1982.

U.S. Information Agency. *Report to Congress* [title varied]. 1953–81.

U.S. Senate, Committee on Commerce. *Appointments to the Regulatory Agencies: The Federal Communications Commission and the Federal Trade Commission (1949–1974).* Committee Print. 94th Cong., 2nd Sess., April 1976.

Other Publications

Abel, John D., Charles Clift III and Frederic A. Weiss. "Station License Revocations and Denials of Renewal, 1934–1969," *Journal of Broadcasting* 14:411–421 (Fall 1970).

Abshire, David M. *International Broadcasting: A New Dimension of Western Diplomacy.* Beverly Hills, Calif.: Sage Publications (Washington Papers No. 35), 1976.

Access (monthly).

Advertising Age (weekly).

Agee, Warren K. "Cross-Channel Ownership of Communication Media," *Journalism Quarterly* 26:410–416 (December 1949).

Albig, William. *Modern Public Opinion.* New York: McGraw-Hill, 1956.

Alexander, Herbert E. *Financing the 1968 Election.* Lexington, Mass.: Lexington Books, 1972.

——. *Financing the 1972 Election.* Lexington, Mass.: Lexington Books, 1976.

——. *Financing the 1976 Election.* Lexington, Mass.: Lexington Books, 1980.

——. *Financing the 1980 Election.* Lexington, Mass.: Lexington Books, 1983.

American Film Institute Guide to College Courses in Film and Television. Princeton, N.J., 1980 (7th ed.).

American Newspaper Publishers Association. *Comments of American Newspaper Publishers Association in Opposition (to FCC Docket No. 18110).* 3 vols. New York: ANPA, 1971.

——. *News and Editorial Content and Readership of the Daily Newspaper.* New York: ANPA, 1973.

Arbitron Television. *ADI Book.* Beltsville, Md.: (annual).

——. *Description of Methodology.* Beltsville, Md.: Arbitron (annual).

——. *Syndicated Programming Analysis.* Beltsville, Md.: Arbitron (annual).

——. *Population Book.* Beltsville, Md.: Arbitron (annual).

Aspen Handbook on the Media: 1977–79 Edition: A Selective Guide to Research, Organizations and Publications in Communications. New York: Praeger, 1977.

Baer, Walter S. et al. *Concentration of Mass Media Ownership: Assessing the State of Current Knowledge* (R-1584-NSF). Santa Monica, Calif.: The Rand Corporation (September 1974).

Bagdikian, Ben H. *The Information Machines.* New York: Harper and Row, 1971.

Bailey, Robert Lee. "The Content of Network Television Prime-Time Special Programming: 1948–1968," *Journal of Broadcasting* 14:325–336 (Summer 1970).

Baldwin, Thomas F., and McVoy, D. Stevens. *Cable Communication.* Englewood Cliffs, N.J.: Prentice-Hall, 1983.

Barnouw, Eric. *Tube of Plenty: The Evolution of American Television.* New York: Oxford University Press, 1975.

Barrett, Marvin, ed. *The Alfred I. Dupont–Columbia University Survey of Broadcast Journalism.* New York: Grosset & Dunlap, 1968 to 1971 (annual); New York: Crowell, 1973 to 1978 (biennial); and New York: Everest House, 1982.

Batscha, Robert M. *Foreign Affairs News and the Broadcast Journalist.* New York: Praeger Special Studies, 1975.

BBC Handbook. London: British Broadcasting Corporation, 1928–to date, annual.

Bergreen, Laurence. *Look Now, Pay Later: The Rise of Network Broadcasting.* New York: Doubleday, 1980.

Blair Television, Division of John Blair & Company. *Statistical Trends in Broadcasting.* New York: Blair, 1964–79 (annual).

Blakely, Robert J. *The People's Instrument: A Philosophy of Programming for Public Television.* Washington: Public Affairs Press, 1971.

Bogart, Leo. *The Age of Television.* 3rd ed. New York: Frederick Ungar, 1972.

———. "How the Public Gets its News," Washington, D.C.: American Newspaper Publishers Association, 1977.

Bolter, Walter G. *The Commercial Television Industry: Public Policy and Market Development. A Report on the Development and Growth of Commercial Television, New Competition, and the Policy Goals of Efficiency and Diversity.* Bethesda, Md.: Bolter & Nilsson Consultants, 1983.

Bower, Robert T. *Television and the Public.* New York: Holt, Rinehart & Winston, 1973.

———. "The Changing Television Audience, 1960–1980." NY: Columbia University Press, 1984.

Braestrup, Peter. *Big Story: How the American Press and Television Reported and Interpreted the Crisis of Tet 1968 in Vietnam and Washington.* 2 vols. Boulder, Colo.: Westview Press, 1977.

Branscomb, Anne W. *The First Amendment as a Shield or a Sword: An Integrated Look at Regulation of Multi-Media Ownership* (P-5418). Santa Monica, Calif.: The Rand Corporation (April 1975).

Braunstein, Yale M. *Recent Trends in Cable Television Related to the Prospects for New Television Networks.* Washington, D.C.: Federal Communications Commission Network Inquiry Special Staff, January 1980.

Briley, Sharon A. "State Regulation of Cable TV—Progress and Problems," in Hollowell (1977), pp. 31–53.

———. *Cable Television: State Legislation 1982.* Washington, D.C.: Federal Communications Commission, Cable Television Bureau, 1982.

Broadcast Advertisers Reports. New York: Broadcast Advertising Research.

Broadcasting (weekly).

Broadcasting Yearbook (annual).

Brooks, Tim, and Earle Marsh. *The Complete Directory of Prime-Time Network TV Shows, 1946–Present.* New York: Ballantine Books, 1981 (2nd ed.).

Brown, James W., *Educational Media Yearbook.* New York: Bowker, 1973 to 1978; Littleton, Colo.: Libraries Unlimited, 1980–date (annual).

Browne, Bortz & Coddington (Consultants). *Radio Today—And Tomorrow.* Washington, D.C.: National Association of Broadcasters, 1982.

Browne, Donald R. *International Broadcasting: The Limits of the Limitless Medium.* New York: Praeger, 1982.

Bunce, Richard. *Television in the Corporate Interest.* New York: Praeger, 1976.

Cablevision (weekly).

Campbell, Augus et al. "Television and the Election," *Scientific American* 188:5:46–48 (May 1953).

Carnegie Commission on Educational Television. *Public Television: A Program for Action.* New York: Harper and Row. 1967.

Carnegie Commission on the Future of Public Broadcasting. *A Public Trust.* New York: Bantam Books, 1979.

Castleman, Harry, and Walter J. Podrazik, *Watching TV: Four Decades of American Television.* New York: McGraw-Hill, 1982.

Cater, Douglass, and Michael J. Nyhan, eds. *The Future of Public Broadcasting.* New York: Praeger, 1976.

CATV and Station Coverage Atlas. Washington: *Television Digest* (annual).

Chaffee, Steven H., ed. *Political Communication: Issues and Strategies for Research.* Beverly Hills, Calif.: Sage Publications, 1975.

Chapin, Richard E. *Mass Communications: A Statistical Analysis.* East Lansing: Michigan State University Press, 1957.

Chappell, Matthew N., and C. E. Hooper. *Radio Audience Measurement.* New York: Stephen Daye Press, 1944.

Cherington, Paul W. et al. *Television Station Ownership: A Case Study of Federal Agency Regulation.* New York: Hastings House, 1971.

Chester, Edward W. *Radio, Television and American Politics.* New York: Sheed and Ward, 1969.

Chu, Godwin C., and Wilbur Schramm. *Learning from Television: What the Research Says.* Washington: National Association of Educational Broadcasters, 1968 (revised 1974).

Clift, Charles, and Archie Greer, eds. *Broadcast Programming: The Current Perspective.* Washington: University Press of America (annual).

———, Frederic A. Weiss and John D. Abel. "Ten Years of Forfeitures by the Federal Communications Commission," *Journal of Broadcasting* 15:379–385 (Fall 1971).

———, John D. Abel, and Frederic A. Weiss. "Forfeitures and the Federal Communications Commission: An Update," *Journal of Broadcasting* 24:301–310 (Summer 1980).

Columbia Broadcasting System, Inc. *Radio in 1937.* New York: CBS, 1937.

———. *Comments of CBS, Inc. in BC Docket No. 82-345 before the Federal Communications Commission.* New York: CBS, 1983.

Communications Daily.

Compaine, Benjamin et al. *Who Owns the Media? Concentration of Ownership in the Mass Communications Industry.* White Plains, N.Y.: Knowledge Industry Publications, 1982 (2nd ed.).

Comstock, George et al. *Television and Human Behavior.* New York: Columbia University Press, 1978.

Corporation for Public Broadcasting. *Annual Report.* Washington, D.C.: CPB, (1969 to date, Annual).

———. *Status Report of Public Broadcasting.* Washington, D.C.: CPB, 1973, 1977, and 1980.

———. *Public Broadcasting Income.* Washington, D.C.: CPB, annual.

———. *Public Television Licensees.* Washington, D.C.: CPB, annual (title varies).

———. *CPB-Qualified Public Radio Licensees.* Washington, D.C.: CPB, annual (title varies).

———. *Public Television Programming Content By Category.* Washington, D.C.: CPB, (biennial, even-numbered years; title varies).

———. *Public Radio Programming Content By Category.* Washington, D.C.: CPB, (biennial, even-numbered years; title varies).

Cox Looks at FM Radio. Atlanta: Cox Broadcasting Corp., 1976.

Desmond, Robert W. *World News Reporting.* Iowa City: University of Iowa Press, 1978, 1980, 1982 and 1984 (four volumes).

Duncan, James. *American Radio.* Kalamazoo, Mich.: the author, twice yearly.

———. *Radio in the United States: 1976–1982, A Statistical History.* Kalamazoo, Mich.: the author, 1983.

Eastman, Susan Tyler et al., eds. *Broadcast Programming: Strategies for Winning Television and Radio Audiences.* Belmont, Ca.: Wadsworth, 1981.

Educational Television and Radio Center. *Educational Television Program Survey.* Ann Arbor, Mich.: 1958.

Elder, Robert E. *The Information Machine: The United States Information Agency and American Foreign Policy.* Syracuse, N.Y.: Syracuse University Press, 1968.

Electronic Industries Association. *Electronic Market Data Book.* Washington, D.C.: EIA, annual.

————. *Consumer Electronics Annual Review.* Washington, D.C.: EIA, annual.

Encyclomedia, 1977 Newspaper Edition. New York: Decisions Publications, 1977.

Encyclomedia, 1978 Radio Edition. New York: Decisions Publications, 1978.

Epstein, Edward Jay. *News from Nowhere: Television and the News.* New York: Random House, 1973.

The Ford Foundation. *Ford Foundation Activities in Noncommercial Broadcasting, 1951–1976.* New York: The Ford Foundation, 1976.

Foreign Service Journal (monthly).

Fortune (monthly).

Frank, Ronald E., and Marshall G. Greenberg. *Audiences for Public Television.* Beverly Hills, Ca.: Sage Publications, 1982.

Gerbner, George et al. *Violence Profile No. 7* and *Violence Profile No. 10.* Philadelphia: Annenberg School of Communications (University of Pennsylvania), 1976 and 1978.

————, and Larry Gross. "Living with Television: The Violence Profile," *Journal of Communication* 26: 173–199 (Spring 1976).

————, and George Marvanyi. "The Many Worlds of the World's Press," *Journal of Communication* 27 (1):52–66 (Winter 1977).

Gianakos, Larry J. *Television Drama Series Programming.* Metuchen, N.J.: Scarecrow Press, 1978–83 (four volumes).

Gibson, George H. *Public Television: The Role of the Federal Government, 1972–76.* New York: Praeger, 1977.

Greenberg, Bradley S., and Edwin B. Parker, eds. *The Kennedy Assassination and the American Public: Social Communication in Crisis.* Stanford, Calif.: Stanford University Press, 1965.

Gross, Lynne Schafer. *The New Television Technologies.* Dubuque, Iowa: Wm. C. Brown, 1983.

Haight, Timothy R., ed. *Telecommunications Policy and the Citizen.* New York: Praeger, 1979.

Hale, Julian. *Radio Power: Propaganda and International Broadcasting.* Philadelphia: Temple University Press, 1975.

Hatcher, David M. *Syndication in American Television, 1950–1975* (unpublished MA thesis). Madison: University of Wisconsin, 1976.

Head, Sydney W., and Christopher H. Sterling. *Broadcasting in America: A Survey of Television, Radio, and New Technologies.* Boston: Houghton-Mifflin, 1982 (4th ed.).

Heard, Alexander. *The Costs of Democracy.* Chapel Hill: University of North Carolina Press, 1960.

Henderson, John W. *The United States Information Agency.* New York: Praeger, 1969.

Hester, A. "Five Years of Foreign News on U.S. Television Evening Newscasts," *Gazette* 24:88–95 (1978).

Hochberg, Philip R. *The States Regulate Cable: A Legislative Analysis of Substantive Provisions.* Cambridge, Mass.: Harvard University Program on Information Resources Policy, 1978.

Hoel, Arline Alchian. *Economics Sourcebook of Government Statistics.* Lexington, Mass.: Lexington Books, 1983.

Hollowell, Mary Louise, ed. *Cable Handbook 1975–1976: A Guide to Cable and New Communications Technologies.* Washington, D.C.: Communications Press, 1975.

———. *The Cable/Broadband Communications Book 1977–1978.* Washington, D.C.: Communications Press, 1977.

———. *The Cable/Broadband Communications Book, Volume 2, 1980–1981.* Washington, D.C.: Communications Press, 1980.

———. *The Cable/Broadband Communications Book, Volume 3, 1982–1983.* Washington, D.C.: Communications Press, 1983.

The Home Video & Cable Yearbook. White Plains, N.Y.: Knowledge Industry Publications, 1981–date (annual).

Hope Reports. Rochester, N.Y.: Hope Reports, Inc. (monthly surveys and biennial compilations).

Howard, Herbert H. "The Contemporary Status of Television Group Ownership," *Journalism Quarterly* 53:399–405 (Autumn 1976). (Howard, 1976b)

———. "Recent Trends in Broadcast Multiple Ownership," *Client* 4:1:6–14 (Fall 1976). (Howard, 1976a).

———. *Television Station Group Ownership: 1980.* Knoxville: University of Tennessee College of Communications, 1980.

———. *Television Station Group Ownership and Cross-Media Ownership: 1982.* Knoxville, University of Tennessee College of Communications, 1982.

———. *Television Station Group Ownership and Cross-Media Ownership: 1983.* Knoxville: University of Tennessee College of Communications, 1983.

———, and S. L. Carroll. *Subscription Television: History, Current Status and Economic Projections.* Knoxville: University of Tennessee College of Communications, 1980.

ICF Inc. *Analysis of the Impacts of Repeal of the Financial Interest and Syndication Rule.* Washington, D.C.: ICF Inc., 1983 (three volumes).

Johnstone, John W. C., et al. *The News People: A Sociological Portrait of American Journalists and Their Work.* Urbana: University of Illinois Press, 1976.

Joint Council on Educational Television. "The 1959 Educational Television Directory," *Educational Television Factsheet*. Washington: JCET (January 1959).

Paul Kagan Associates. *Pay TV Newsletter.* (weekly).

―――. *The Pay TV Census.* Carmel, Ca.: Kagan Associates, semi-annual, then annual.

―――. *MDS Databook.* Carmel, Ca.: Kagan Associates, annual.

Katzen, May. *Mass Communication: Teaching and Studies at Universities.* Paris: UNESCO (New York: Unipub), 1975.

Katzman, Natan. *Program Decisions in Public Television.* Washington: Corporation for Public Broadcasting, and National Association of Educational Broadcasters, 1976.

Kittross, John M., comp. *A Bibliography of Theses and Dissertations in Broadcasting, 1920–1973.* Washington: Broadcast Education Assoc., 1978.

The Knowledge Industry 200: 1983 Edition. White Plains, N.Y.: Knowledge Industry Publications, 1983.

Koenig, Allen E., ed. *Broadcasting and Bargaining: Labor Relations in Radio and Television.* Madison: University of Wisconsin Press, 1970.

Kraus, Sidney, and Dennis Davis. *The Effects of Mass Communication on Political Behavior.* University Park: Pennsylvania State University Press, 1976.

Kroeger, A. R. "How Things Stand with the Groups," *Television* (March 1966), pp. 30–31ff.

Lang, Gladys Engel, and Kurt Lang. *The Battle for Public Opinion: The President, The Press and the Polls During Watergate.* New York: Columbia University Press, 1983.

Larson, James F. *International Affairs Coverage on U.S. Network Television Evening News Broadcasts, 1972–1976.* Stanford, Calif.: Institute for Communication Research, Stanford University, 1978.

Larson, Timothy L. "Concentration in the U.S. Television Industry and the Question of Network Divestiture of Owned and Operated Television Stations." (Paper delivered before the 1977 Annual Meeting of the Broadcast Education Association, Washington, D.C., 1977.)

Lashner, Marilyn A. "The Role of Foundations in Public Broadcasting, I: Development and Trends," *Journal of Broadcasting* 20:529–547 (Fall 1976).

―――. "The Role of Foundations in Public Broadcasting, II," *Journal of Broadcasting* 21:235–254 (Spring 1977).

Lavey, Warren G. *Toward a Quantification of the Information/Communication Industries.* Cambridge, Mass.: Harvard University, Program on Information Technologies and Public Policy (May 1974).

Lazarsfeld, Paul F., and Patricia Kendall. *Radio Listening in America.* New York: Prentice-Hall, 1948.

Levin, Harvey J. *Broadcast Regulation and Joint Ownership of Media.* New York: New York University Press, 1960.

———. "The Policy on Joint Ownership of Newspapers and Television Stations: Some Assumptions, Objectives, and Effects." New York: Center for Policy Research (April 1971). (Statement on Docket No. 18110 before the Federal Communications Commission.)

———. *Fact and Fancy in Television Regulation: An Economic Study of Policy Alternatives.* New York: Russell Sage Foundation, 1980.

Lichty, Lawrence W. "A History of Network Television Programming, 1948–1973." Madison: University of Wisconsin, Department of Communication Arts (mimeograph), n.d. (work in progress for eventual publication).

———. "Members of the Federal Radio Commission and Federal Communications Commission, 1927–61" and "The Impact of FRC and FCC Commissioners' Background on the Regulation of Broadcasting." *Journal of Broadcasting* 6:23–34; 97–110 (1962).

———, and Malachi C. Topping, eds. *American Broadcasting: A Sourcebook on the History of Radio and Television.* New York: Hastings House, 1975.

——— et al. "Political Programs on National Television Networks: 1960 and 1964," *Journal of Broadcasting* 9:217–229 (Summer 1965).

A. D. Little Co. *Television Program Production, Procurement and Syndication.* 2 vols. Cambridge, Mass.: A. D. Little Co., 1966.

———. *Television Program Production, Procurement, Distribution and Scheduling.* Cambridge, Mass.: A. D. Little Co., 1969 (with subsequent corrections issued by publisher).

Lumley, Frederick H. *Measurement in Radio.* Columbus: Ohio State University Press, 1934 (reprinted by Arno Press, 1972).

Lyle, Jack. *The People Look at Public Television: 1974.* Washington: Corporation for Public Broadcasting, 1975.

Machlup, Fritz. *The Production and Distribution of Knowledge in the United States.* Princeton, N.J.: Princeton University Press, 1962.

Madow, William G. et al. *Evaluation of Statistical Methods Used in Obtaining Broadcast Ratings.* House Report 193, 87th Congress, 1st Session (1961).

Mahoney, Sheila et al. *Keeping PACE with the New Television.* New York: Carnegie Corporation, 1980.

Marketing and Media Decisions (monthly—see especially annual Fall forecast issue).

Martin, L. John, ed. "Propaganda in International Affairs," *The Annals No. 398.* Philadelphia: American Academy of Political and Social Science (November 1971), pp. 1–139.

McAlpine, Dennis B. *The Television Programming Industry.* New York: Tucker Anthony & R. L. Day (January 1975).

McCombs, Maxwell E. "Mass Media in the Marketplace," *Journalism Monographs* No. 24 (August 1972).

McGavren-Guild Radio. *Trends in Radio Formats Study (1976–1980) Top 25 Markets.* New York: McGavren-Guild Radio, 1981.

McNeil, Alex. *Total Television: A Comprehensive Guide to Programming from 1948 to 1980.* New York: Penguin Books, 1980.

Minow, Newton N. et al. *Presidential Television.* New York: Basic Books, 1973.

Moody's Industrial Manual. New York: Moody's Investor's Service.

Mosco, Vincent, and Janet Wasko, eds. *The Critical Communications Review: Volume I: Labor, the Working Class, and the Media.* Norwood, N.J.: Ablex, 1983.

National Association of Broadcasters. *Radio Financial Report.* Washington: NAB, 1955 to date (annual).

———. *Radio in 1985.* Washington: NAB, 1977.

———. *Radio Today.* Washington: NAB, 1970.

———. *Television Financial Report.* Washington: NAB (annual).

National Association of Educational Broadcasters. *Directory of Public Telecommunications.* Washington: NAEB (annual).

———. *The Financial Status of Public Broadcasting Stations in the United States, 1968–69.* Washington: NAEB, 1969.

———. *Four Years of New York Television, 1951–1954.* Urbana, Ill.: NAEB, 1954.

———. *Los Angeles Television: May 23–29, 1951.* Urbana, Ill.: NAEB, 1951.

National Association of FM Broadcasters, *National FM Programming Trends.* New York: NAFMB, 1967.

New York Times (daily).

Newspaper Advertising Bureau (see Bogart, 1977).

Nielsen Television Index, A. C. Nielsen Co. *Network Television Audiences to Primaries, Conventions, Elections.* Northbrook, Ill.: A. C. Nielsen Co., 1976. *Update Edition* (1979).

———. *Nielsen Newscast* (quarterly).

———. *Nielsen Television.* Northbrook, Ill.: A. C. Nielsen Co., 1955 to date (annual).

———. *Radio and Television Audience 1956.* Northbrook, Ill.: A. C. Nielsen Co.

———. *Radio 1960.* Northbrook, Ill.: A. C. Nielsen Co.

———. *Reference Supplement.* Northbrook, Ill.: A. C. Nielsen Co. (annual).

———. *Report on Syndicated Programs.* Northbrook, Ill.: A. C. Nielsen Co.

———. *Television Audience.* Northbrook, Ill.: A. C. Nielsen Co., 1959 to date (annual).

Niven, Harold. *Broadcast Education*, Second Report (1956); Fifth Report (1960); Ninth Report (1965); Twelfth Report (1970); Fourteenth Report (1975) and Fifteenth Report (1981). Washington: National Association of Broadcasters, 1956 to date (approx. biennial).

Noll, Roger et al. *Economic Aspects of Television Regulation*. Washington: Brookings Institution, 1973.

Norback, Craig T., and Peter G. Norback, eds. *TV Guide Almanac*. New York: Ballentine Books, 1980.

One Week of Educational Television No. 3, April 19-25, 1964. Waltham, Mass.: Morse Communication Research Center, Brandeis University, 1965.

———. *No. 4, April 17-23, 1966*. Bloomington, Ind.: National Center for School and College Television, 1966.

———. *No. 5, May 6-12, 1968*. 2 vols. Bloomington, Ind.: National Instructional Television Center, 1969.

———. *No. 6, March 9-15, 1970*. Bloomington, Ind.: National Instructional Television Center, 1971.

Owen, Bruce. *Economics and Freedom of Expression: Media Structure and the First Amendment*. Cambridge, Mass.: Ballinger Publishing, 1975.

——— et al. *Television Economics*. Lexington, Mass.: Lexington Books, 1974.

Perry, Martin. "Recent Trends in the Structure of the Cable Television Industry." Stanford, Calif.: Stanford University Department of Economics (May 1974, discussion paper).

Peter, Paul F. "The American Listener in 1940," *The Annals No. 213*. Philadelphia: American Academy of Political and Social Science (January 1941), pp. 1-8.

Phillips, Kevin. "Busting the Media Trusts." *Harper's* (July 1977), pp. 23-34.

Read, William H. *America's Mass Media Merchants*. Baltimore: The Johns Hopkins University Press, 1977.

Reeves, Michael G., and Tom W. Hoffer. "The Safe, Cheap and Known: A Content Analysis of the First (1974) PBS Program Cooperative," *Journal of Broadcasting* 20:549-565 (Fall 1976).

Richstad, Jim, ed. *New Perspectives in International Communication*. Honolulu: East-West Communication Institute, East-West Center, 1977.

———, and Jackie Bowen. *International Communication Policy and Flow: A Selected Annotated Bibliography*. Honolulu: East-West Communication Institute, East-West Center, 1976.

Roper Organization Inc. *Trends in Attitudes Toward Television and Other Media: A Twenty-Four Year Review*. New York: Television Information Office, 1983. (13th in a series dating back to 1959, most of the data reported in cumulative fashion over the years.)

Ross, Leonard. *Economic and Legal Foundations of Cable Television*. Beverly Hills, Calif.: Sage (Publications in the Social Sciences No. 90-012), 1974.

Routt, Edd. *Dimensions of Broadcast Editorializing*. Blue Ridge Summit, Penn.: TAB Books, 1974. Rucker, Bryce W. *The First Freedom*. Carbondale: Southern Illinois University Press, 1968.

Sadowski, Robert P. "Broadcasting and State Statutory Laws," *Journal of Broadcasting* 18:433–450 (Fall 1974).

Sandage, C. H. *Radio Advertising for Retailers*. Cambridge, Mass.: Harvard University Press, 1945.

Schiller, Herbert I. *Mass Communications and American Empire*. Boston: Beacon Press, 1971.

———. *Communication and Cultural Domination*. White Plains, N.Y.: International Arts and Sciences Press, 1976.

Schramm, Wilbur. *Mass Media and National Development: The Role of Information in the Developing Countries*. Stanford, Calif.: Stanford University Press, 1964.

———. *Big Media, Little Media: Tools and Technologies for Instruction*. Beverly Hills, Calif.: Sage Publications, 1977.

———, Jack Lyle, and Edwin B. Parker. *Television in the Lives of our Children*. Stanford, Calif.: Stanford University Press, 1961.

———, Jack Lyle, and Ithiel de Sola Pool. *The People Look at Educational Television*. Stanford, Calif.: Stanford University Press, 1963.

———, and Lyle Nelson. *The Financing of Public Television*. Palo Alto, Calif.: Aspen Program on Communications and Society, 1972.

Seiden, Martin H. *Who Controls the Mass Media? Popular Myths and Economics Realities*. New York: Basic Books, 1975.

Shelby, Maurice E., Jr. "Short-Term License Renewals: 1960–1972," *Journal of Broadcasting* 18:277–288 (Summer 1974).

Simmons, Steven J. *The Fairness Doctrine and the Media*. Berkeley: University of California Press, 1978.

Standard and Poor's Corporation. *Standard and Poor's Directory of Corporations*. New York: S & P (annual).

———. *Standard and Poor's Industry Surveys*. New York: S & P (quarterly and annual surveys of 36 industries). (Of special value here are the following annuals: *Amusements* to 1973, *Leisure Time* since 1973, and *Communication* since 1973.)

———. *Standard and Poor's Corporation Descriptions*. New York: S & P (weekly, with a daily news section).

Steinberg, Cobbett. *TV Facts*. New York: Facts on File, 1980.

Steiner, Gary A. *The People Look at Television.* New York: Knopf, 1963.

Sterling, Christopher H. "Newspaper Ownership of Broadcast Stations, 1920–68," *Journalism Quarterly* 46:227–236, 254 (Summer 1969).

———. "Trends in Daily Newspaper and Broadcast Ownership, 1922–1970," *Journalism Quarterly* 52:247–256, 320 (Summer 1975).

———. "Broadcast Education: Status and Trends," *Educational Media Yearbook 1977.* Edited by James W. Brown. New York: R. R. Bowker, 1977, pp. 56–63.

———, and Timothy R. Haight. *The Mass Media: Aspen Institute Guide to Communication Industry Trends.* New York: Praeger Special Studies, 1978.

———, and John M. Kittross. *Stay Tuned: A Concise History of American Broadcasting.* Belmont, Calif.: Wadsworth Publishing Co., 1978.

———. "Radio and Television Broadcasting," (Chapter 6), and "Cable and Pay Television," (Chapter 7) in Benjamin Compaine, et al. *Who Owns the Media: Concentration of Ownership in the Mass Communications Industry.* New York: Knowledge Industry Publications, 1982 (2nd ed.), pp. 299–450.

Summers, Harrison B. *A Thirty Year History of Programs Carried on National Radio Networks in the United States, 1926–1956.* Columbus: Ohio State University Department of Speech, 1958 (reprinted by Arno Press, 1972).

Television Digest (weekly).

Television Factbook. 2 vols. Washington: *Television Digest* (annual).

Television Information Office, The. See Roper Organization, Inc.

Television News Index and Abstracts. Nashville, Tenn.: Vanderbilt Television News Archives, Vanderbilt University, 1972–date (monthly).

Television/Radio Age (biweekly).

Terrace, Vincent. *The Complete Encyclopedia of Television Programs, 1947–1979.* South Brunswick, N.J.: A. S. Barnes, 1979 (2nd ed; two volumes).

———. *Television: 1970–1980.* San Diego, Ca.: A. S. Barnes, 1981.

Tunstall, Jeremy. *The Media Are American.* New York: Columbia University Press, 1977.

Turow, Joseph. *Entertainment, Education and the Hard Sell: Three Decades of Network Children's Television.* New York: Praeger, 1981.

UCLA Communications Law Symposium. *The Foreseeable Future of Television Networks: Legal Resource Manual.* Los Angeles: UCLA School of Law and UCLA Extension, 1979.

Udelson, Joseph H. *The Great Television Race: A History of the American Television Industry 1925–1941.* University of Alabama Press, 1982.

UNESCO. *News Agencies: Their Structure and Operation.* New York: Greenwood Press, 1969. (Reprint of 1953 UNESCO Publication.)

———. *Press Film Radio, Volume IV.* Paris: UNESCO, 1950 (includes United States)/(reprinted by Arno Press, 1972).

United Church of Christ, Office of Communication. *Television Station Employment Practices: The Status of Minorities and Women.* New York: United Church of Christ, Office of Communication, 1973 to 1977 (annual).

Variety (weekly).

"The Violence Profile: An Exchange of Views," *Journal of Broadcasting* 21:273–303 (Summer 1977).

"Violence Ratings: A Dialogue," *Journal of Broadcasting* 17:3–35 (Winter 1972–1973).

Wagner, Paul H. "The Evolution of Newspaper Interest in Radio," *Journalism Quarterly* 23:182–188 (June 1946).

Weaver, James B. III et al. "A Comparative Analysis of Ten Years of Foreign News on Network Evening Newscasts," Paper presented to Mass Communication Division of Speech Communication Association, Louisville, Ky., November 1982. (revision published in Summer 1984 issue of *Journalism Quarterly*).

Welles, Chris. "Do Most People Depend on TV for News?" *Columbia Journalism Review* 16 (5): 12–14 (January/February 1978).

Westinghouse Broadcasting Co. *Petition for Inquiry, Rule Making and Immediate Temporary Relief* before the Federal Communications Commission, September 3, 1966.

———. *Reply Comments* before the Federal Communications Commission, December 1, 1978 as reprinted in UCLA Communications Law Symposium (listed above).

Willey, Malcolm M., and Stuart A. Rice. *Communication Agencies and Social Life.* New York: McGraw-Hill, 1933.

Williams, Wenmouth, Jr. "Impact of Commissioner Background on FCC Decisions: 1962–1975," *Journal of Broadcasting* 20:239–260 (1976).

Wolf, Frank. *Television Programming for News and Public Affairs: A Quantitative Analysis of Networks and Stations.* New York: Praeger Special Studies, 1972.

Wood, Donald N., and Donald G. Wylie. *Educational Telecommunications.* Belmont, Calif.: Wadsworth, 1977.

ABOUT THE AUTHOR

Christopher H. Sterling is a Professor of Communications and Director of the Center for Telecommunications Studies at George Washington University in Washington D.C. His undergraduate degree in political science and Masters and Doctorate in communication were earned at the University of Wisconsin in Madison. After teaching at Temple University in Philadelphia for a decade, he joined the Federal Communications Commission as special assistant to Commissioner Anne P. Jones from 1980–82.

This volume is the latest expression of an interest in communication trends that dates back to Sterling's graduate work more than 15 years ago. Now in preparation is a comparable analysis of telecommunications common carriers in the United States over the past century. Sterling is coauthor or coeditor of six previous books on various aspects of the electronic media.